"This book is much more than just Alcatel-Lucent QoS [product] line as it takes the reader through a holistic QoS journey. [...] novice and expert alike because it ties QoS concepts to the 7x50 product functionality. The knowledge acquired from this book will enable the network professional to create a solid QoS architecture/design which is mandatory to prioritize services throughout the network. The book is a reference I will return to again and again."
 —BRENT CONRAD, B.Sc.(Chem), B.Sc.(CS),
  Bell Canada Technology Development

"A comprehensive book that describes QoS principles and datapath traffic management capabilities of Alcatel-Lucent Service Routers. QoS is made easy with well described examples on how to design, deploy and configure services in IP/MPLS networks. A must reference for network designers or for those aspiring to become architects of modern networks."
 —DR. SUDHKAR GANTI, Professor, University of Victoria

"The concept of a single IP/MPLS multiservice network provides huge economical benefits for service providers in reducing CAPEX and OPEX. With multiservice networks, the ability to assure Service Level Agreements for new service oriented application traffic has become the differentiating factor among competitors. This book educates readers on the detail operation of Quality of Service through IP/MPLS networks for converged services. I highly recommend it for network designers and test engineers."
 —DEAN LEE, Senior Product Manager, IXIA

"With the dual objectives of providing cost-effective high bandwidth services and meeting stringent customer service guarantees, hierarchical service-based QoS has become invaluable for today's service providers."
 —JONATHAN NEWTON, Senior Architect,
  Cable & Wireless Europe, Asia & US

Advanced QoS for Multi-Service IP/MPLS Networks

Advanced QoS for Multi-Service IP/MPLS Networks

Ram Balakrishnan

WILEY PUBLISHING, INC.

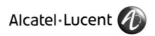

Advanced QoS for Multi-Service IP/MPLS Networks

Published by
Wiley Publishing, Inc.
10475 Crosspoint Boulevard
Indianapolis, IN 46256
www.wiley.com

Published by Wiley Publishing, Inc., Indianapolis, Indiana

Published simultaneously in Canada

ISBN: 978-0-470-29369-0

Manufactured in the United States of America

10 9 8 7 6 5 4 3 2 1

For general information on our other products and services or to obtain technical support, please contact our Customer Care Department within the U.S. at (800) 762-2974, outside the U.S. at (317) 572-3993 or fax (317) 572-4002.

Library of Congress Cataloging-in-Publication Data is available from the publisher.

To my late grandmother, Umayal,
and to my parents, Ramasamy and Alamelu:

It is your love and guidance that have made me who I am today.

—Ram Balakrishnan

About the Author

Ram Balakrishnan, a senior Network Design Architect with Alcatel-Lucent, is a renowned QoS and Triple-Play expert and educator. Leveraging his IP/MPLS knowledge in addition to his QoS expertise, Ram has led service provider and enterprise initiatives globally to design and implement converged multi-service networks. He holds patents related to intelligent routing algorithms. A frequent contributor to the *Alcatel-Lucent Telecommunications Review*, Ram has over 10 years experience in the telecommunications industry. He holds a BE degree in Electronics and Instrumentation from Annamalai University, India, and MS degrees in Engineering and Computer Science from the University of Saskatchewan, Canada. Ram is also a certified Alcatel-Lucent Service Routing Architect (Alcatel-Lucent SRA No. 10).

Credits

Executive Editor
CHRIS WEBB

Development Editor
SARA SHLAER

Production Editor
DEBRA BANNINGER

Copy Editor
FOXXE EDITORIAL SERVICES

Editorial Manager
MARY BETH WAKEFIELD

Production Manager
TIM TATE

Vice President and
Executive Group Publisher
RICHARD SWADLEY

Vice President and Executive Publisher
JOSEPH B. WIKERT

Project Coordinator, Cover
LYNSEY STANFORD

Compositor
HAPPENSTANCE TYPE-O-RAMA

Proofreader
NANCY CARRASCO

Indexer
TED LAUX

Service Routing: Making IP/MPLS the Bearer of Multi-Service Traffic

The evolution of quality of service (QoS) for IP is really synonymous with the evolution of IP platforms. If you are in the service provider business, you will know the challenge of IP—especially if you were around in 2000 when the Internet really started to heat up.

Prior to the dawn of the Internet, service providers had always offered services that required service level agreements. QoS was inherent in the underlying technologies such as Frame-Relay, ATM and SONET/SDH. But the Internet was different. Its new service definition was simple: "best-effort" delivery. Despite this anomaly, service growth was explosive and made IP part of any network discussion.

Back in 2000, the question we all pondered was whether IP would form the network for all services—not just Internet services. I can recall, in the early 2000s, how often I would read about or hear a carrier calling routers "these bloody IP platforms" and bemoaning the fact that they were not carrier-class.

The challenge was clear: Could IP platforms, when blended with MPLS technology, effectively become the bearer of multi-service traffic? It was a big question. Certainly major improvements would have to occur on a number of dimensions. For example, we needed a carrier-class router design that included scalable control planes, better Operation Administration and Maintenance (OAM) features, true high availability and quality of service. So I joined up with some other like-minded veterans of switching and routing development. We pulled together a small team and conceived of and delivered to market in 2003 the world's first true "Service Router." The Alcatel-Lucent 7×50 family quickly became the leading carrier-grade routing platform of its kind, and it has since helped the world's leading service providers realize their multi-service infrastructure goals. It was designed from the ground up to support multiple services with multiple levels of QoS over IP/MPLS.

No one questions now that IP/MPLS can manage multiple services on a common infrastructure. And that is why QoS is so critically important now. This book provides essential information for today's multi-service architects. In these pages, Ram Balakrishnan will explain QoS technology and how IP/MPLS network architectures are best designed for multi-service delivery.

Enjoy the book . . . and welcome to the new era of service routing.

Basil Alwan
President, IP Division
Alcatel-Lucent

Preface

In the face of relentless competition, service providers are turning to a new wave of next generation IP-based services to retain customers, increase average revenue per user and to attract new customers. These initiatives require the highest percentage of service reliability to ensure uninterrupted subscriber sessions, to meet stringent service level agreements (SLAs) and to ensure customer satisfaction. A key means by which to ensure service reliability is through service-aware hierarchical quality of service (HQoS). HQoS ensures that the service requirements of all types of traffic flow are satisfied and controlled across the network and that each service has the reliability and the required resources to meet customer performance expectations.

Ram Balakrishnan, has created a wonderful educational resource for you. With over a decade of experience in supporting service providers globally, Ram has written a publication that provides you with a solid theoretical and practical overview of how QoS can be implemented to reach the business objectives defined for an IP/MPLS network.

From our extensive engagements delivering and supporting global customers with our Network Design and OSS Engineering services, Alcatel-Lucent has captured its vast IP service-routing knowledge and expertise in this new publication and our industry-first Service-Routing based certification (SRC) program. The future holds many new telecommunication opportunities for all of us. Have fun with this wave of IP transformation!

Enjoy the knowledge adventure you are about to begin.

Ravi Parmasad
Vice President, Customer Support
IP Division
Alcatel-Lucent

Acknowledgments

To begin, I would like to express my appreciation to Basil Alwan, Ravi Parmasad, and Mac Virdy, members of the Alcatel-Lucent IP Division senior management team for their constant support. Mac: Your enthusiasm is infectious and it made my task of writing this book much easier.

I would like to extend special thanks to Karyn Lennon and George Carroll for getting me all the additional support that I needed during the course of writing this book and helping me to focus on the content development. Karyn: Thank you for your hard work in managing the various publishing tasks of this book. George: It was your continued words of encouragement that helped me to maintain the intensity of my focus throughout this project.

I extend my gratitude to the technical reviewers: Mustapha Aissaoui, Erica Poppe, Yanick Champoux, and Olivier Le Moigne. Thank you all for your detailed comments, and for those frequent and lengthy technical conversations, even in the late evenings. Special appreciation to John Coulter, Bashar Bou-Diab, Matthew Bocci, and Jim Guillet for reviewing different sections of the book and providing valuable inputs. Thanks to Phil Cole for the cover design and for providing input on the internal layout design.

The book also benefited enormously by the inputs provided by external reviewers: Many thanks to Brent Conrad of Bell Canada; Carey Williamson, Professor in the Department of Computer Science at the University of Calgary; Sudhakar Ganti, Professor in the Department of Computer Science at the University of Victoria; Jonathan Newton of Cable&Wireless; and Dean Lee of Ixia.

Special thanks to the staff members of Wiley Publishing for their excellent support. Sara Shlaer: Your involvement in the project made a big positive change to the outcome.

An application note that I wrote on the topic became the stepping-stone for writing this book and thanks to Stephen Rowlandson for encouraging me to write it. Special appreciation to Todd Craw and Miroslav Vrana, not only for providing me with the support documentation, but also for thoroughly reviewing the application note.

My thoughts on the subject were refined because of the lengthy discussions I had with some of Alcatel-Lucent's customers. It is my good fortune that I had the opportunity to work with these people. It is not possible to list all their names here, but my heartfelt thanks to all of them.

Finally, it is the understanding and love of my wife Meena that helped me to complete this book. I spent too many nights and weekends writing this book. She not only kept feeding me, but also brought her own additional work home to keep me company. Meena: I cannot thank you enough and I love you very much.

Ram Balakrishnan

Contents at a Glance

Contents

Introduction

Internet Protocol/Multi Protocol Label Switching (IP/MPLS) quality of service (QoS) is a rapidly evolving, and with the advent of service routers, maturing technology. The legacy "best-effort" service offered by IP networks is no longer adequate. The developments in the IP/MPLS QoS is enabling IP/MPLS networks, including the world's biggest network—the Internet, to offer multiple application services. With these changes, IP is becoming the preferred networking technology for end-to-end network convergence. Therefore, QoS design is becoming a major and inevitable aspect of modern IP/MPLS network design process.

One of the fundamental goals of the Alcatel-Lucent philosophy in designing a family of service routers and offering end-to-end network solutions is to let service providers expand their service infrastructure as they grow. Service routers provide significant customization options, which enable networks to expand seamlessly. In addition, they are deployable in a wide range of network scenarios. QoS features, as core service-related features of service routers, are also fully customizable.

The growing importance of QoS considerations while designing an IP network, and the flexibility provided by service routers in configuring QoS features, increases the responsibilities of the network design and maintenance personnel in gaining a thorough understanding of the subject. The intention behind this book is to help readers to gain such a thorough knowledge of the subject.

How This Book Is Organized

Many readers may entertain the notion that QoS is a complicated topic to understand. As someone who started exploring IP/MPLS networking from a QoS perspective, I beg to differ, and I hope you will find this book provides a simple and straightforward presentation of the subject. Wherever appropriate, I have used real-life analogies to aid readers' understanding of technical concepts.

The book is divided into three parts and presents the QoS discussion in three levels of abstraction to provide a complete view of the topic. Part 1 presents a high-level end-to-end perspective and fundamental details of QoS. Part 2 explains the theoretical and practical details of the QoS features. The chapters in Part 2 also explain in detail how to configure, apply, and validate the QoS features. Wherever possible, configuration samples and example analyses are also presented. Part 3 rounds off the discussion by providing QoS design principles, a step-by-step approach to designing QoS, and case studies that illustrate using QoS design to meet business objectives.

You will find the material in the Notes and Best Practices sidebars that appear throughout the chapters to be useful as quick reference reminders while designing QoS and during the design verification process in the lab.

In topics related to networking, it is not possible to avoid TLAs (Three-Letter Acronyms) or acronyms in general. The acronyms are so heavily used in the networking industry that some of the terms are more readily recognized by their acronyms, rather than through the expanded terms. For easy reference, most of the commonly used terms and acronyms in the book are listed along with their definitions in the Glossary at the end of the book.

Conventions Used in the Book

Alcatel-Lucent provides a modular approach for configuring the individual entities of Alcatel-Lucent Service Router Portfolio (ALSRP) nodes. In the approach, most of the QoS features and Access Control Lists (ACLs) are configured as policies and applied under appropriate entities. The modular approach and QoS policies make network and QoS designs simple and elegant. This makes node configurations easier to understand and maintain.

ALSRP nodes can be provisioned and managed either directly using the command line interface (CLI) of individual nodes or through a service-aware network management system (Alcatel-Lucent 5620 SAM). Alcatel-Lucent 5620 Service Aware Manager provides different types of interfaces, including a graphical user interface (GUI), for provisioning the nodes of a network. In this book, only the command line configuration option for configuring and managing ALSRP nodes is considered.

CLI commands are entered at the command line prompt. Entering a command makes navigation possible from one command context (or level) to another. When you initially enter a CLI session, you are in the root context. At the root context, the prompt indicates the active central processor module (CPM) slot and the name of the node. For more information on CPM, see Chapter 5. Navigate to another level by entering the name of successively lower contexts. As you change through the levels, the prompt also changes to indicate the context you are in. Listing 1 shows an example CLI navigation and prompt change according to the context.

Listing 1 Navigation and prompt change

```
A:Pod2#
A:Pod2# show
A:Pod2>show#
```

The root prompt of Listing 1 indicates that the active CPM slot of the node is A and the name of the node is configured as Pod2. In the listing, on entering the command show, the prompt changes to indicate the show context. As you can see in this paragraph, when CLI codes are used inline along with the main text, they are indicated by the use of monofont text.

To get contextual help at a given prompt, simply enter a question mark (?). In a given CLI context, you can enter commands at that context level by simply entering the text. It is also possible to enter a command in a lower context as long as the command is formatted in the proper command and parameter syntax. Listings 2 and 3 show the two methods to navigate to the show qos context.

Listing 2 Navigation by entering context level commands

```
A:Pod2# show
A:Pod2>show# qos
A:Pod2>show>qos#
```

Listing 3 Navigation by entering lower context level commands

```
A:Pod2# show qos
A:Pod2>show>qos#
```

Listing 4 shows the command options for the show qos sap-ingress command. The listing is presented here to explain the syntax of CLI command options. The purpose of the command in Listing 4 is explained in Chapter 6.

Listing 4 An example of CLI command options

```
A:Pod2>show>qos# sap-ingress
  - sap-ingress [<policy-id>] [association|match-criteria|detail]

<policy-id>          : [1.65535]
<association>        : keyword - display associations
<match-criteria>     : keyword - display match criteria
<detail>             : keyword - display detailed information
```

In the command syntax, square brackets indicate optional parameters of a command; angle brackets indicate that a substitution is required for the placeholder; and a pipe (|) indicates an either/or relationship between the parameters on either side of the pipe. To shorten some of the listings, later in the book, part of the listings' outputs are stripped and replaced with … to indicate the stripping.

For further information regarding the use of the command line interface, refer to the *System Basics Guide*, which is a part of the ALSRP product manuals. This book is the first in a series of technical books to be published related to Alcatel-Lucent service routers. This book provides references to the Alcatel-Lucent manuals that come with the Alcatel-Lucent 7750 Service Router, the Alcatel-Lucent 7450 Ethernet Service Switch, or the Alcatel-Lucent 7710 Service Router platforms. If you are an Alcatel-Lucent customer and you don't have access to the Alcatel-Lucent's Service Router product manuals, contact your Alcatel-Lucent account manager. If you are not a customer of Alcatel-Lucent, visit the Contact Us area at www.alcatel-lucent.com.

A standard set of icons are used throughout this book. A representation of these icons and their meanings are listed under the section "Standard Icons".

Audience

This book is targeted for a wide audience, including but not limited to network architects, engineers, administrators, and operators of all types of IP/MPLS based networks. The book is also an excellent resource for students interested in gaining a practical understanding of advancements in IP QoS. If you need to design, support, or just understand IP QoS from an applied perspective, you should find this book useful.

To gain maximum benefit from this book, a basic understanding of IP and MPLS networking is required. Some familiarity with configuring the Alcatel-Lucent 7750 Service Router, the Alcatel-Lucent 7450 Ethernet Service Switch, or the Alcatel-Lucent 7710 Service Router platforms will also be useful. This book also serves as a general technical reference guide to IP/MPLS QoS.

Feedback is Welcome

It would be our pleasure to hear back from you. Please forward your comments and suggestions for improvements to the following email address:

sr.publications@alcatel-lucent.com

With that, I would like to welcome you to the exciting world of quality of service.

Ram Balakrishnan

Standard Icons

Generic ALSRP node

Generic ALSRP node

Alcatel-Lucent 5620 SAM

IP/MPLS Tunnel

Scheduler

Virtual Scheduler

Traffic Policer

Rate-Limiter

Traffic Filter

Traffic Classifier

Queues

Datagrams

Scheduling loop

Network

Basic Router

Residential Customer

Business Organizational Entities

Advanced QoS for Multi-Service IP/MPLS Networks

Fundamentals of IP/MPLS QoS

1

Gaining the knowledge of the end-to-end quality of service model will give you an appreciation for roles played by the individual QoS features. The chapters in Part 1 walk you through the need for QoS, the enhancements offered by service routers from a QoS perspective, and the QoS models standardized by IETF. They describe the QoS support built into different Layer 2 and Layer 3 technologies, and the functions of fundamental QoS features.

The Need for Quality of Service

1

QoS is an integral set of features in a service router, which can help service providers exceed service level agreements for the different application traffic types carried over a multi-service network.

Chapter Objectives

- To explain the need for QoS

- To introduce the Alcatel-Lucent Service Router Portfolio

- To explain the differences between a service router and a traditional IP router

- To explain the restrictions in forwarding traffic within a network

- To discuss formalizing service commitments through service level agreements

When offering commercial airline services, there is a big difference between using an airplane designed specifically for carrying commercial passengers and using an airplane designed purely for transportation (say, a military transport plane). Although both types of aircrafts are meant for transportation, their purposes are very different. The architectural design of commercial aircraft is oriented towards satisfying the service needs of different classes of passengers, which result in increasing the profit of the airline. In contrast, military aircraft are not designed for servicing customers but are meant for transporting mainly a homogeneous class of passengers (or cargo).

Similarly, there is a big difference in using service routers and traditional IP routers to deliver carrier grade multiple application services and maximizing the profit of the service provider. In contrast to traditional IP routers, service-related capabilities were integrated into the product architecture of service routers at inception. Quality of service (QoS) is an integral set of features in a service router, essential for satisfying diverse service needs of different application traffic, while maximizing the resource utilization of the router within a multi-service network.

This book introduces you to the fundamentals of QoS for an Internet Protocol/ Multi Protocol Label Switching (IP/MPLS) network. It also addresses the theoretical and practical details of advanced QoS features offered by service routers, and concludes by teaching you how to design QoS in a multi-service network.

1.1 The Changing Service Delivery Landscape

The distinction among telephone companies, cable companies, and Internet service providers (ISP) is vanishing fast. All these players are facing increasing demands to offer personalized user-centric services involving voice, video, and data application traffic. To enhance the customer network experience with media-rich application content, the service providers are embracing service convergence and delivering all killer applications over a single infrastructure. A service provider offering voice, video, and data application services using a single network infrastructure is commonly referred to as a *triple-play* service provider.

Note: In this book, the term *service provider* is used in a broad sense and includes all commercial and noncommercial broadband network operators. For noncommercial network administrators, the clients are their own enterprise or organization.

In the residential market, the High Speed Internet (HSI) infrastructures built around business models that allowed significant oversubscription and service level leniency are no longer efficient with the advent of service convergence. The new service level agreement (SLA) standards for voice and video applications have stringent quality of service (QoS) requirements. These SLAs also impose rigorous constraints on availability, system characteristics, and multicast requirements.

In the enterprise space, customers are increasingly doing business electronically, using communication technology to drive sales, improve customer relationships, train staff, simplify procurement, and collaborate between different sites. This is taking place across metro, national, and international boundaries. Enterprises want convenience and simplicity along with strict QoS and control, both in their local area networks (LANs) and across wide area networks (WANs). QoS, flexible bandwidth, and availability are critical for business networking applications such as voice, video, and data.

1.2 What Is Quality of Service?

The increasing convergence of network services leads directly to the need for a QoS approach. *Quality of service* is defined as the ability of a network to recognize different service requirements of different application traffic flowing through it and to comply with SLAs negotiated for each of the application services, while attempting to maximize the network resource utilization. QoS is absolutely essential in a multi-service network, in order to meet SLAs of different services and to maximize the network utilization.

Without QoS, datagrams are serviced in a network on a first-in, first-out (FIFO) basis, also referred to as *best-effort service*. In such scenarios, datagrams are not assigned priority, based on the type of application that they support. As a result, differential treatment for different types of application traffic is not possible. Therefore, service level agreements for any service other than best-effort service cannot be met.

Note: Because service routers can support different media interfaces, including Ethernet, SONET, Asynchronous Transfer Mode (ATM), and Frame-Relay, the word *datagram* is used to refer to all types of traffic that can flow through a network using service routers. As such, in this book, the word *datagram* is used to collectively refer to packets, frames, and cells.

QoS allows the service provider to utilize a network infrastructure for offering multiple application services, thereby saving the capital and operating costs involved in maintaining multiple networks for each of the applications separately. Although network traffic flows are dynamic in nature, QoS allows the service provider to maximize network resource utilization, thereby increasing their profit. QoS maximizes network resource utilization and optimizes revenue generation by providing priority access to network bandwidth for high-priority traffic, and by allowing low-priority traffic to gain the bandwidth committed to high-priority traffic in the absence of high-priority traffic.

When *Don't* You Need QoS?

To play devil's advocate, you could argue that you don't need QoS if your network meets any of the following conditions:

*   There will not be any congestion in your network.
*   You will have only homogeneous traffic in your network.
*   You are beyond the worldly pleasure of making money out of your network.

1.3 Alcatel-Lucent Service Router Portfolio

Alcatel-Lucent has unveiled the industry's first service router portfolio that provides solutions to service providers to address the challenges of the rapidly changing service delivery landscape.

The Alcatel-Lucent Service Router Portfolio (ALSRP) considered in this book includes the Alcatel-Lucent 7750 Service Router, the Alcatel-Lucent 7450 Ethernet Service Switch, and the Alcatel-Lucent 7710 Service Router. These platforms come with different chassis options and with a wide variety of interfaces. These highly scalable platforms offer outstanding density and service performance. They provide solutions for a wide range of situations: from a small point of presence (PoP) to a pan-continental carrier class network, and from a simple vertical market network to a big enterprise network.

The Alcatel-Lucent 7750 Service Router, the Alcatel-Lucent 7450 Ethernet Service Switch, and the Alcatel-Lucent 7710 Service Router platforms differ in terms of their throughput, offered services, and available types of interfaces. These platforms also differ in terms of their applications, the:

- Alcatel-Lucent 7750 Service Router is a multi-service edge router, built for service providers to deliver media-rich residential, business, and mobile services on a single IP/MPLS network.

- Alcatel-Lucent 7450 Ethernet Service Switch is service switch router designed to deliver carrier grade SLA-based triple-play services for consumer markets and Ethernet VPN services for business markets.

- Alcatel-Lucent 7710 Service Router is a multi-service edge router, ideally suited for locations with lower throughput requirements (such as smaller point-of-presence, distributed hub sites and enterprise customer offices) to aggregate lower-speed subscribers over a wide variety of interfaces. The platform enables service providers to extend IP transformation to the furthest edge of their networks.

From a QoS perspective, these three platforms share some essential characteristics:

- They share a common operating system.

- They can all be managed using a common management system: the Alcatel-Lucent 5620 Service Aware Manager (SAM). The 5620 SAM is a single management platform that offers element, network, and Layer 2 and Layer 3 service management. This management system excels at streamlining network commissioning, service activation, maintenance, troubleshooting, and operations support systems (OSS) integration, thus allowing service providers to increase their level of competitiveness.

- The QoS features of each platform behave and are configured the same across ALSRP unless otherwise noted.

Using the Alcatel-Lucent 5620 SAM to Graphically Configure Your Platform

From a QoS perspective, the Alcatel-Lucent 5620 SAM presents an advanced multi-service management capability through which nodes can be configured and maintained, in addition to command line interface (CLI) of individual nodes. All the QoS command line configuration examples in this book can also be done easily through the Alcatel-Lucent 5620 SAM. While configuring some of the advanced ALSRP QoS features such as Random Early Detection (RED) and Hierarchical QoS, the Alcatel-Lucent 5620 SAM provides graphical representation of the configuration, and thus provides valuable insight into the design. For further details about the Alcatel-Lucent 5620 SAM, see the Alcatel-Lucent *5620 SAM User Guide*, *Statistics Management Guide*, and *Parameter Guide*, provided as part of the Alcatel-Lucent 5620 SAM product manuals.

The Evolution of Routers

Routers have evolved significantly since their inception. Legacy IP routers were designed to offer best-effort Internet service and basic enterprise routing. Whereas, *service routers* are designed to deliver carrier grade multiple application services over IP/MPLS. A service router based IP/MPLS network offers network convergence, by carrying all types of network traffic including ATM, Frame-Relay, Ethernet, and SONET traffic. In addition, a service router provides a scalable control plane, non-stop routing protocols, and true high availability. Service routers also offer enhanced service-based Operation and Maintenance (OAM) functions, in contrast to plain port-based OAM functions.

Some of the critical features that make ALSRP distinctly superior to traditional IP routers are its traffic forwarding performance characteristics, service-related capabilities, and the ability to customize QoS features according to specific service needs. As mentioned earlier, service-related capabilities were tightly integrated into the ALSRP architecture at inception. The traffic forwarding characteristics, including minimal jitter, minimal delay, and low loss, enable ALSRP to exceed the new high SLA standards associated with triple-play, business networking applications, and other multimedia services. The ALSRP system architecture is discussed in detail in Chapter 5.

Service Routers Are All about Services

From a networking perspective, the word *services* means a set of features or benefits offered to subscribers. In the case of residential subscribers, services might include carrying end customers' traffic, such as voice, video, or data, across a network. In the case of business customers, services could also include providing interconnections between different sites through a virtual private network (VPN) service.

An ALSRP node readily supports offering both VPN and public networking services by isolating traffic through its service configuration. The type of service configuration indicates to an ALSRP node whether the traffic has to be forwarded to one or more destinations, and also whether to handle traffic at the Layer 2 or Layer 3 level. Layers 2 and 3 refer respectively to the Data Link and Network layer of the Open Systems Interconnection (OSI) reference model. A node handling traffic at Layer 2 is expected to preserve the original Layer 2 encapsulation of the traffic. While handling traffic at Layer 3, a node is expected to extract packets from any Layer 2 encapsulation they arrive with, before forwarding them.

If a service is required to forward traffic to only one destination, it is referred to as *point-to-point* (or *unicast*) service, and the traffic is referred to as point-to-point (or unicast) traffic. If a service configuration allows forwarding traffic to multiple destinations, it is referred to as *multipoint* service. Within a multipoint service there can be both point-to-point and multipoint (destined for more than one destination) traffic. Multipoint forwarding can be further classified into the following three types:

- **Multicast**—Forwards datagrams to a group of selected destinations.
- **Broadcast**—Forwards datagrams to all the destinations of the service configuration.
- **Unknown-cast**—Forwards a datagram to all the destinations of the service configuration, because the specified destination address is yet unknown.

The Alcatel-Lucent 7750 Service Router and the Alcatel-Lucent 7710 Service Router offer the following four different types of service configuration:

- **Virtual private routed network (VPRN)**—A Layer 3 IP multipoint-to-multipoint VPN service as defined in RFC2547bis. RFC2547bis is an extension to RFC2547.
- **Internet-Enhanced Service (IES)**—A direct Internet access service where the subscriber is assigned an IP interface for Internet connectivity.
- **Virtual private LAN service (VPLS)**—A Layer 2 multipoint-to-multipoint VPN service.
- **Virtual leased line (VLL)**—A Layer 2 point-to-point service, also referred to as *virtual private wire service* (VPWS). A VLL service is a pseudo-wire-service used to carry traffic belonging to different network technologies over an IP/MPLS core. In the Alcatel-Lucent 7750 Service Router and the Alcatel-Lucent 7710 Service Router, the following VLL services can be configured:
  - **Epipe**—Ethernet VLL service
  - **Fpipe**—Frame-Relay VLL service
  - **Apipe**—ATM VLL service
  - **Ipipe**—IP interworking VLL service

In the Alcatel-Lucent 7450 Ethernet Service Switch all the above service configurations with the exceptions of VPRN, Apipe, and Fpipe are available. For further details about these ALSRP service configurations refer to the *Service Guide*, which is a part of the ALSRP product manuals.

Only VPLS supports all the four forwarding types that are discussed earlier in the section. VLL uses only unicast forwarding. VPRN and IES support unicast and multicast forwarding.

Depending on the service configuration type, different stacks of encapsulations are used to carry the traffic within the core of a network. Different types of encapsulation use different sets of QoS markings to indicate the service requirement of a datagram. Chapter 3 explains different QoS markings available for different types of encapsulation.

1.4 Network Service Restrictions and Service Level Agreements

Regardless, of the underlying technology or protocols, a network imposes certain restrictions over the traffic flowing through it. The notable restrictions that impact the performance of network applications are throughput, delay, jitter, and datagram loss. Different types of applications can tolerate each of these restrictions to a different extent. Therefore, in order to maintain a certain degree of quality in a network application, the network service restrictions imposed on the application traffic should be within the tolerable extent for the application.

In order to understand the impact of each type of restriction, consider the simple network shown in Figure 1.1. The network consists of three hosts (H1, H2, and H3) connected through a node (N1), respectively through three links (L1, L2, and L3). The node can be an IP/MPLS router, Ethernet switch, ATM switch, or Frame-Relay node. Specifically, the node is not a shared medium such as an Ethernet hub. Also assume that the node does not have any QoS features.

Figure 1.1 A Simple Network Diagram

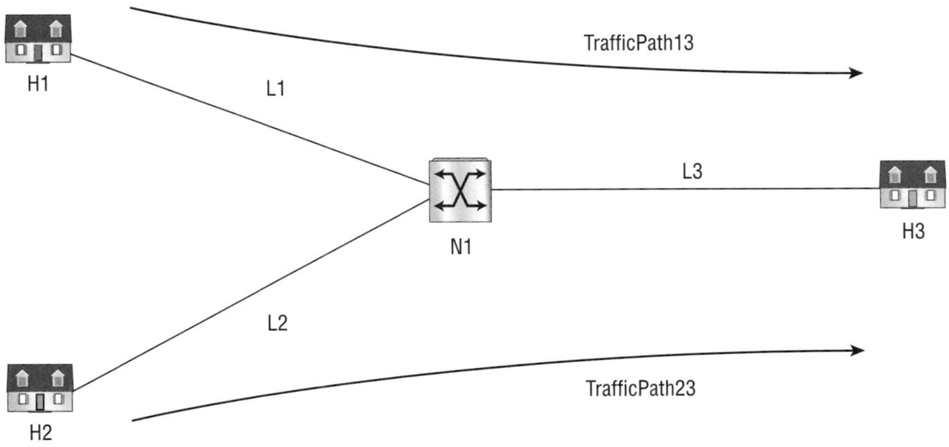

The following subsections address the impact of various restrictions on traffic flow using the example shown in Figure 1.1.

Throughput

Consider the traffic flow from H1 to H3 through TrafficPath13. Assuming that all the network resources in the path are available to the traffic flow, the traffic flow is restricted by the following resources:

- The rate at which H1 can transmit
- The bandwidth of L1
- The rate at which N1 can receive traffic arriving through L1
- The rate at which N1 can forward traffic in its core
- The rate at which N1 can transmit through L3
- The bandwidth of L3
- The rate at which H3 can receive traffic arriving through H3

The *throughput* of the traffic is the rate at which traffic can flow through the most constricted segment in its path. Given the dynamic nature of traffic flow across a network, different resources can become bottlenecks at different times.

An Analogy from Fluid Dynamics

Imagine this is a hydraulic flow, and the path is created by connecting different pipes with different diameters. Then the throughput of the water is determined by the pipe with the smallest diameter. In other words, the throughput of the water is the rate at which water can flow through the pipe with the smallest diameter.

Different segments within carrier networks are hidden from a customer. In the SLA, a network path is treated as a single end-to-end pipe provisioned for the customer and the throughput is defined as the bandwidth of the pipe.

The negotiated bandwidth in an SLA will not be entirely available for an application's traffic, because of the traffic datagram overheads. For example, for an Ethernet frame with a VLAN tag the following constitutes the frame overhead of 42 bytes:

- 12 bytes inter-frame gap
- 8 bytes preamble
- 18 bytes header
- 4 bytes trailer

The size of the frame payload can vary anywhere from 46 to 1500 bytes. Thus, the overhead for Ethernet traffic without the upper-layer overheads can consume anywhere from 2 percent to 47 percent of a path's bandwidth, depending on the frame size.

Delay

RFC 2679 defines a metric for measuring one-way delay as the difference in the time at which the datagram crosses two reference points. The *delay* of a datagram experienced within a service provider network is defined as the difference in the time at which the datagram enters the network and the time at which it leaves the network. Delay is also commonly referred to as *latency*.

Each element through which a datagram flows in a traffic path will increase the delay experienced by the datagram. For example, in TrafficPath13 within the network illustrated in Figure 1.1, links L1 and L3 will impose a propagation delay, and the node N1 will impose a processing delay to the traffic flowing through them.

From an SLA perspective, the delay is the average fixed delay that an application's traffic will experience within the service provider's network.

Jitter

RFC 3393 has defined a metric for measuring one-way jitter. *Jitter* is the variation in the network delay experienced by datagrams. More specifically, it is measured as the delay variation between two consecutive datagrams belonging to a traffic stream.

In the example shown in Figure 1.1, assume background traffic is flowing through TrafficPath23. The background traffic is bursty and saturates the L3 link capacity frequently. Under this scenario, when the L3 port is congested in N1, if datagrams arrive through TrafficPath13, the datagrams will be dropped. In order to avoid dropping datagrams when a resource is temporarily congested, buffer space is made available in network nodes and the datagrams are queued. Queuing within a network node introduces delay variation between different datagrams of a traffic stream.

Although queuing is the main cause of traffic jitter, lengthy reroute propagation delays and additional processing delays can also affect traffic jitter.

Datagram Loss

RFC2680 and RFC3357 have defined metrics for measuring one-way traffic loss. Traffic loss characterizes the datagram drops that occur in the path of a one-way traffic flow between two reference points: one at the beginning as the traffic enters a network and the other at the end as the traffic leaves the network.

Although having buffer space to temporarily queue datagrams in network nodes helps reduce datagram loss, it cannot be completely eliminated. Some of the factors that contribute to datagram loss are:

- **Congestion**—Bursty traffic can cause queue overflows resulting in datagram loss.
- **Traffic rate-limiting**—In order to ensure customer traffic is conforming to a negotiated SLA, service providers may rate-limit incoming traffic and drop nonconforming datagrams.
- **Physical layer errors**—Noise in physical layers (such as satellite links) can cause bit errors. As a result, upper-layer protocols may drop datagrams.
- **Network element failures**—Network element failures may cause datagrams to drop until the failure is detected and the connectivity is restored.

As specified in RFC3357, for some real-time applications (such as streaming video traffic), certain datagram loss characteristics are more important than the actual number of datagrams lost:

- **Loss distance**—The difference in the sequence number between two successively lost packets (which may or may not be separated by successfully received packets).
- **Loss period**—The duration of a loss or error event once it starts. In other words, *loss period* is defined as the frequency at which loss occurs and the number of consecutive packets dropped each time loss occurs.

Handling Restrictions with Quality of Service

Different types of application traffic can handle the different network service restrictions to different degrees. In order to formalize the tolerable extent of network service restrictions for different applications offered by a service provider to a customer, a service level agreement (SLA) is negotiated when contracting the service. The SLA also becomes an element of the process when formalizing a service-customer relationship between two service providers. Tolerable limits of an application for different network service restrictions are defined as the application's service requirements. Service requirements of common application traffic are explained in Chapter 14.

The ability of a network to recognize the diverse service requirements of different types of applications and to provide the service appropriately is the essence of quality of service. See Chapter 5 for an overview of how end-to-end traffic management is enforced over a traffic flow path within an ALSRP network in order to achieve the SLA associated with the traffic.

Summary

Quality of service refers to the ability of a network to recognize the differing service requirements of different application traffic flowing through it and to comply with service level agreements negotiated for each of the application services. In today's service delivery climate, all service providers are expected to offer personalized media-rich application services. In order to reduce operational costs and to enrich user experience, providers are migrating toward offering all killer applications over a single IP/MPLS core infrastructure. Quality of service features enable networks to handle traffic for efficient multi-service delivery.

Alcatel-Lucent Service Router Portfolio includes three different platforms: the Alcatel-Lucent 7750 Service Router, the Alcatel-Lucent 7710 Service Router, and the Alcatel-Lucent 7450 Ethernet Service Switch. These platforms share a common operating system and can be managed using a Service Aware Manager or via the command line interface. The platforms come in different chassis options, thus allowing service providers to build their infrastructure as they grow.

The chapter outlined the differences between a service router and a traditional IP router. From a QoS perspective, traditional IP routers have a static QoS implementation, which is not flexible for customization and inadequate for voice and video applications. ALSRP has a flexible QoS implementation, which allows customization of QoS features according to service needs in different networking application scenarios.

The chapter discussed the network service restrictions that impact network applications' throughput, delay, jitter, and loss. QoS helps service providers overcome these restrictions and comply with SLAs.

QoS Models And Network Convergence

Adhering to standard QoS models makes quality of service interoperable between multi-vendor nodes within a network. IETF has standardized two competing QoS models—IntServ and Diff-Serv—for IP/MPLS networks.

Chapter Objectives

- To provide an overview of the Integrated Services QoS model and the Differentiated Services QoS model

- To describe DiffServ Per-Hop Behavior and DiffServ Per-Domain Behavior

- To assess the suitability of MPLS to support the Integrated Services QoS model

- To explain the support offered by MPLS for the Differentiated Services QoS model

For many years, QoS was offered exclusively by Layer 2 technologies such as Asynchronous Transfer Mode (ATM) and Frame-Relay. Like "tax returns" and "cafeteria food," "IP QoS" was considered an oxymoron. The only QoS model offered in the IP architectures was the best-effort service model, which attempts to deliver the datagrams in the order in which they entered the node. This model might best be described as "first-in, first-out, if alive to serve."

So why the need for improved IP QoS now? Network convergence! As discussed in Chapter 1, maintaining a separate network for different applications such as voice, video, and data costs many times the price of a single network in which all these different types of applications are supported. IP has become the most common end-to-end network technology used around the world; the biggest network, of course, being the Internet. Most applications have converged or adapted to use IP networks. QoS is essential to support the service requirements of diverse application types within a converged single network. Because QoS is an end-to-end element of a network path, it is easier to maintain service commitments using the IP QoS, compared to stitching together QoS techniques of different Layer 2 technologies that may be used in isolated segments of a Layer 3 path.

In 1994 the Internet Engineering Task Force (IETF), realizing the importance of having IP QoS, created the Integrated Services working group. The recommendations of the working group are referred to as the *Integrated Services (IntServ) QoS model*. Further in 1998, the IETF created the Differentiated Services working group, which produced the *Differentiated Services (DiffServ) QoS model*.

The objective behind having standard QoS models is to make quality of service interoperable between multi-vendor nodes within a network. This chapter introduces you to the IntServ and DiffServ QoS models, and outlines the relative advantages of each model.

2.1 The Integrated Services QoS Model

In its effort to establish a set of standards for IP QoS, the Integrated Services working group made recommendations not only on overall Integrated Services QoS architecture but also on service models, flow specifications, and frameworks for related components of the QoS model. Some of the related components include connection admission control (CAC) and flow identification. The Integrated Services model is described in RFC 1633.

Many of the IntServ QoS model features evolved from the QoS model used in ATM networks. Some elements are derived from the efforts of other groups that work closely with the Integrated Services group. The Integrated Services over Specific Link Layers (ISSLL) working group has defined specifications and techniques needed to implement Integrated Services capabilities within specific link layer technologies such as ATM and Ethernet (`www.ietf.org/html.charters/OLD/issll-charter.html`). The Resource ReSerVation Protocol (RSVP) working group standardized the RSVP signaling protocol for the Integrated Services QoS model (`www.isi.edu/rsvp`). RSVP requests resource reservation for simplex flows (i.e., unidirectional). In a bidirectional traffic flow, RSVP signaling is done independently in each direction. RSVP is described in RFC 2205. RSVP is not a routing protocol by itself but is designed to operate over other routing protocols.

In the IntServ QoS model, hosts or routers using RSVP can specify the resource requirement or quality of service required for the end-to-end path for each individual flow or data stream. Each node in the path that receives the RSVP message checks to see if it has sufficient resources to accept the flow. If the check fails, an error notification is sent to the sender that originated the RSVP. If the RSVP signaling is successful, then each node in the path makes the requested reservation for the connection and the data transmission begins.

Two services, Guaranteed Service and Controlled Load Service, are defined for IntServ. Guaranteed Service is described in RFC 2212 and Controlled Load Service is described in RFC 2211. Guaranteed Service caters to the needs of real-time or delay-sensitive application traffic with deterministic delay guarantees. Guaranteed Service enforces a maximum delay for traffic flows but does not provide any guarantee on jitter, average, or minimum delay. Controlled Load Service emulates the behavior of best-effort service in a lightly loaded network. It provides the same QoS assurance for a flow when the network is congested as for an unloaded network. Controlled Load Service assurance is derived through admission control and the statistical multiplexing gain of network resources.

To make IntServ compatible with DiffServ, RFC 2997 defined a third type of service called Null Service. When an application requests Null Service in the RSVP signaling message, the network is duty bound to determine the appropriate service parameters for the data flow.

IntServ is well suited for meeting the dynamically changing network service needs of applications. However, because IntServ requires the network elements to keep track of the state information of individual flows to provide per-flow QoS guarantees, scalability is a big issue. In huge networks (like the Internet), several million flows may exist simultaneously. Maintaining state information for all these flows in the steady state can be overwhelming, let alone reestablishing these flows while rerouting them following a network segment failure. Thus, IntServ is ill suited for deployment in large networks.

Although IntServ and RSVP share a common history, each can function independently. IntServ can use other signaling mechanisms, and RSVP can function as a signaling protocol outside IntServ. The scalability issue persists when MPLS is adapted to support the IntServ QoS model. Although Multi Protocol Label Switching (MPLS) can make use of RSVP for label distribution, MPLS is not readily suitable for either per-flow resource reservation or connection admission control, because it faces the same scalability issue that IntServ does. Supporting IntServ over MPLS would require the label switched paths (LSPs) to be provisioned on a per-flow basis, which makes the approach unscalable over networks with a high volume of connections.

2.2 The Differentiated Services QoS Model

The Differentiated Services QoS model is a less fine-grained model than Integrated Services, in the sense that DiffServ does not keep track of individual flows. Instead, DiffServ maintains per-customer states and performs QoS functions on microflows from customers only at the edges of a DiffServ domain. At the edge, microflows with similar network service requirements are aggregated into forwarding classes. In the core, DiffServ maintains only the state of a limited number of forwarding classes. Therefore, DiffServ does not have the same kind of scalability issue that IntServ has. DiffServ is described in RFC 2475.

The same DiffServ QoS model is applicable to both IPv4 and IPv6. The DiffServ QoS model can also be implemented over MPLS. DiffServ is by far the most widely used QoS model in multiservice IP/MPLS networks.

The Differentiated Services Framework

An IP network that supports DiffServ is referred to as a *DS domain*. RFC 2475 defines a DiffServ domain as ". . . a contiguous set of DS nodes that operate with a common service provisioning policy and set of PHB groups implemented on each node." Figure 2.1 shows the conceptual diagram of the DiffServ architecture. Traffic entering a DiffServ domain is optionally conditioned (rate-limited) and classified into different Behavior Aggregates (BAs). Conditioning helps to ensure that a traffic flow conforms to the traffic profile agreed to between the service provider and the customer. Classification can be based on certain field values of the packet header. Each BA is identified using a unique value, called a Differentiated Service Code Point (DSCP), in the Type of Service (ToS) field of the packet header (Chapter 3 explains the various ToS markings). At the core of the DiffServ domain, the packets are forwarded according to the Per-Hop Behavior (PHB) associated with the packets' DSCP marking. PHBs are defined in terms of externally observable forwarding behaviors such as latency, jitter, packet loss, and throughput. The method to achieve a PHB is not specified by the DiffServ model and is left to the discretion of individual nodes. With the concatenation of independent PHBs, end-to-end QoS is achieved.

BA is more commonly referred to as class of service (CoS). Forwarding class (FC) is a configurable entity to which a CoS traffic can be mapped. Chapter 6 discusses forwarding classes in detail.

Figure 2.1 Conceptual Diagram of DiffServ Architecture

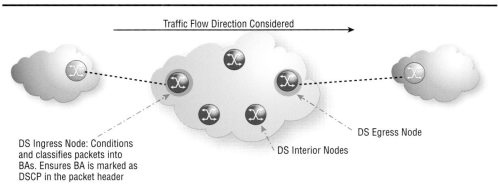

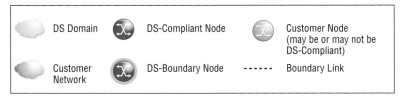

The following list details the steps of the DiffServ framework:

1. **Aggregation of microflows in forwarding classes**—When packets arrive at a DiffServ ingress node, they are mapped to different forwarding classes based on multi-field classification rules of the access ingress classifier. Based on the classification, packets may have to be re-marked with an appropriate DSCP value. For example, at a DiffServ ingress, Voice over IP (VoIP) traffic arriving from different customers is aggregated into one forwarding class (referred to in this example as the VoIP forwarding class).

2. **Traffic policing on the edge**—Metering and policing are required to prevent excessive traffic from congesting the network core and degrading the overall QoS. The policer brings microflows into compliance with their provisioned traffic contracts by discarding nonconforming traffic or assigning a lower priority to it. For example, if a network commits 64 Kbps in the service level agreement (SLA) to carry a high-priority VoIP traffic stream from a customer, then the VoIP traffic arriving from the customer can be policed at 64 Kbps.

3. **Resource allocation to aggregated traffic**—The performance assurance of individual flows within a forwarding class is guaranteed through resource allocation at each node for the forwarding class. However, unlike IntServ, no per-flow reservation or admission control is made. In our example, at the core of the network an aggregated amount of bandwidth is reserved for the VoIP forwarding class, instead of reserving 64 Kbps for every individual VoIP traffic flow.

4. **Class-based forwarding in the core**—Once the traffic is classified, the packets are serviced at all DiffServ nodes according to the PHB associated with the packets' DSCP marking. In our example, traffic belonging to the VoIP forwarding class gets scheduling priority over low-priority traffic. Also, certain buffer space can be exclusively reserved for the VoIP forwarding class.

5. **Achieving the SLA through concatenation of PHB**—The purpose of DiffServ is to ensure that the SLA associated with a traffic flow is achieved. DiffServ achieves the SLA associated with a traffic flow on the basis that all the DiffServ nodes, and in turn all of the DiffServ domain in the data path of the flow, honor the PHB associated with the DSCP marking of the packets in the flow. In the example, the stringent time requirements of the VoIP traffic are met on the basis that all the nodes in the traffic path prioritize the VoIP forwarding class in some manner relative to the other traffic.

Figure 2.2 summarizes the functional behavior of the DiffServ architecture discussed so far. In the illustrated example, a high-priority application (such as VoIP) microflow and a low-priority application (such as web browsing) microflow arriving from different customers are policed and aggregated into two classes of service. DSCP marking of Expedited Forwarding (EF) is used for the aggregated high-priority application traffic, and CS1 is used for aggregated low-priority application traffic (specific DSCP markings are discussed in Chapter 3). Within a class of service, more than one DSCP marking may be used to differentiate dropping precedence (queuing priority) of different packets. The oval insert in the figure shows that the network resources are reserved on per-aggregate traffic basis, and the EF traffic gets preferential forwarding treatment over the CS1 traffic.

Figure 2.2 Functional Behavior of DiffServ Architecture

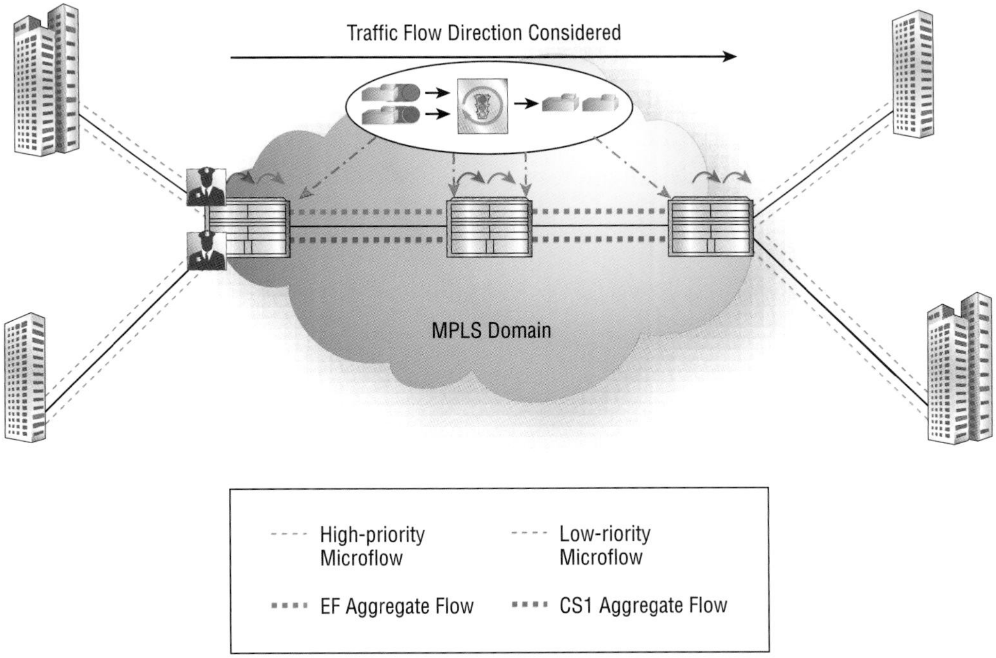

Per-Hop Behaviors

RFC 2475 defines PHBs as "the externally observable forwarding behavior applied at a DiffServ-compliant node to a DiffServ behavior aggregate." In other words, DiffServ defines PHB as the QoS traits that a class of traffic should achieve as it moves between nodes within a DS domain. DiffServ defines the PHBs in abstract form but does not provide the actual rules for the scheduling or buffering for a class of service.

DiffServ also recommends DSCP markings for different PHBs. A PHB can have more than one DSCP marking mapped to it but not vice versa. If more than one DSCP marking is mapped to a PHB, then all these markings are treated as if they are the same.

> **Note:** The DSCP markings suggested for different PHBs are only recommendations, and they are not mandatory. Therefore, if a nonrecommended DSCP marking is used along with a PHB, it does not make the QoS design noncompliant with DiffServ. The key to achieving the service requirement of an application's traffic is that there is consistency in the mapping between the associated DSCP marking and the PHB offered throughout the data path of the traffic.

The DiffServ working group has defined four PHBs so far: Expedited Forwarding (EF), Assured Forwarding (AF) group, Class Selector (CS), and the default PHB. We will look into these PHBs along with the ToS fields of Ethernet, IP, and MPLS headers in detail in Chapter 3.

Per-Domain Behavior

By extending the idea of PHB for an entire DS Domain, RFC 3086 defines Per-Domain Behavior (PDB). PDB can be defined as externally observable behavior experienced by packets belonging to a class of service as they transit through a DiffServ domain.

So far only one PDB, called *Lower Effort Per-Domain Behavior* (LE PDB) has been defined (see RFC 3662). The LE PDB can be defined as a class of service that gets lower priority than all other classes of service, including the default best-effort class of service. Traffic belonging to the LE PDB can help maximize the resource utilization of a DiffServ domain particularly when there are spare network resources left unused by other classes of service. However, when there are no spare network resources (specifically network bandwidth) available, traffic belonging to LE PDB is left to starve. Some example application traffic, suggested as suitable for LE PDB, includes Internet bulk mail and Internet search engine robot traffic.

Using Differentiated Services over Multi Protocol Label Switching

MPLS can readily support DiffServ with only minor modifications required to DSCP markings. MPLS forwarding is done using the outermost MPLS label. Besides IP traffic, MPLS can also carry other types of traffic such as ATM or Frame-Relay. Therefore, in order to carry the PHB selection the 3-bit EXP field on the MPLS label shim header is used for QoS marking. Chapter 3 describes the EXP field of the MPLS label shim header in detail. Readers not familiar with EXP field may find it useful to read this subsection after reading Chapter 3.

MPLS support for DiffServ is described in RFC 3270. RFC 3270 introduces two types of label switched paths for supporting DiffServ: EXP-inferred-class LSPs (E-LSP) and Label-inferred-class LSPs (L-LSP). The two types of LSPs differ essentially in terms of whether they carry multiple or single classes of service traffic.

With E-LSPs, traffic belonging to multiple classes of service can be carried over a single LSP. The EXP field of the MPLS shim header is used to determine the PHB associated with a datagram. One-to-one mapping between the 6-bit DSCP field of IP header and the 3-bit EXP field of MPLS shim header is not possible, because of the difference in the field lengths. The 6-bit DSCP field can represent 64 distinct values, whereas the 3-bit EXP field can represent only 8 distinct values. Because of the EXP field size restriction, multiple DSCP values have to be mapped to a single EXP value at the ingress label switch router. Figure 2.3 illustrates the E-LSP behavior.

With L-LSPs, only the traffic belonging to a single class of service can be carried over a single LSP. The class of service associated with an LSP is inferred from the label of the LSP itself. Therefore, while signaling an LSP setup the forwarding class associated with the LSP has to be specified. While using L-LSPs, the drop precedence (or buffer queuing priority) of a datagram can be specified by using the LSP's EXP field. The use of E-LSPs and L-LSPs on an MPLS network is not mutually exclusive. Figure 2.4 illustrates the L-LSP behavior.

Figure 2.3 E-LSP Behavior

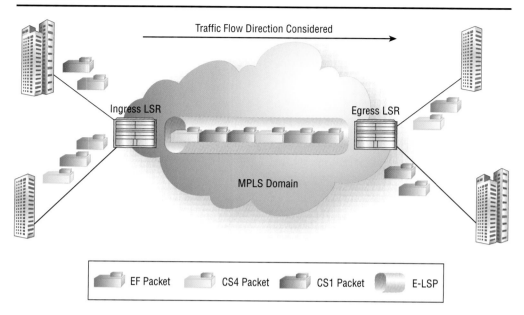

Traffic Flow Direction Considered

Ingress LSR

Egress LSR

MPLS Domain

EF Packet   CS4 Packet   CS1 Packet   E-LSP

Figure 2.4 L-LSP Behavior

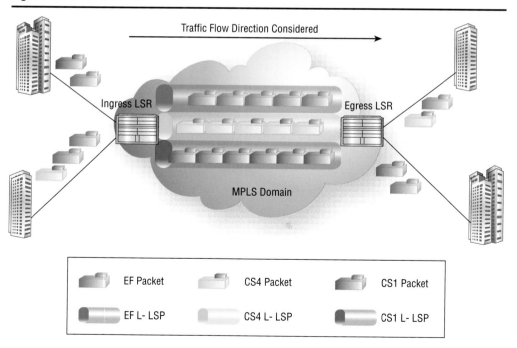

Traffic Flow Direction Considered

Ingress LSR

Egress LSR

MPLS Domain

EF Packet   CS4 Packet   CS1 Packet

EF L- LSP   CS4 L- LSP   CS1 L- LSP

For further information about IntServ and DiffServ QoS models as well as MPLS Traffic Engineering, see *Internet QoS-Architecture and Mechanisms for Quality of Service* by Zheng Wang (Morgan Kaufmann Publishers, 2001).

Summary

The chapter began by outlining the need for developing more sophisticated IP QoS models to address the growing need to handle network convergence.

The Integrated Services QoS model is well suited for meeting the dynamically changing network service needs of applications. However, because IntServ requires the network elements to keep track of state information of individual flows to provide per-flow QoS guarantees, scalability is a big issue. The scalability issue persists when MPLS is adapted to support the IntServ QoS model. Therefore, the Differentiated Services QoS model is more popular and more commonly used in IP/MPLS networks.

The Differentiated Services QoS model addresses the scalability issue by maintaining per-customer flow states only at the edge, and at the network core maintaining the state of a limited number of forwarding classes. MPLS can readily support the DiffServ QoS model, with only minor modifications required in terms of using EXP marking in the place of DSCP marking.

Understanding Type of Service Markings

3

Most of the Layer 2 and Layer 3 encapsulations include a specific field to indicate the service requirement of the associated payload. Depending on the technology, the field length and the maximum number of markings varies.

Chapter Objectives

- To explain the different fields of IPv4 and IPv6 headers

- To describe standardized Per-Hop Behaviors in DiffServ and the DSCP markings recommended for these PHBs

- To introduce different Ethernet frame formats

- To discuss the 802.1p ToS field in the Ethernet Q tag

- To outline the different fields of MPLS shim header and the use of the EXP field within the header for indicating QoS

A datagram arriving from a customer device or network may or may not have a standard marking indicating its service requirement. Therefore, ALSRP allows the classification of traffic at the ingress of a DiffServ domain based on the values of multiple fields belonging to layer 2–to–layer 4 headers/encapsulations in addition to standard Type of Service (ToS) markings. Chapter 6 addresses these multi-field traffic classifications in detail.

Once classified at the ingress, and in order to expedite traffic reclassification at the interior nodes, a datagram's classification is marked in the standard ToS field of its header.

ALSRP supports the transport of traffic belonging to different technologies over an IP/MPLS core. Protocols of different technologies have different header fields to indicate the ToS required for a datagram. In IPv4, it is the Type of Service field, in IPv6 it is Traffic Class, in Ethernet it is 802.1p, and in MPLS shim headers it is EXP field. In this book, all these fields are commonly referred to as the Type of Service (ToS) field.

Within an IP ToS field, ALSRP can recognize the DSCP markings and also the legacy IP precedence. This chapter discusses the ToS fields and the QoS markings of different header types. As a part of the IP header ToS field discussion, it also covers the different PHBs defined so far by the DiffServ working group.

3.1 The IP Header ToS Field

Before looking into the ToS field and its composition, you may want a refresher course on the header fields of both version 4 (IPv4) and version 6 (IPv6) of the Internet Protocol (IP), and where the ToS field is located in the two header formats.

IPv4 Header Fields

Figure 3.1 shows the IPv4 header format. The numbers on the top of the figure indicate the bit positions. Excluding the options and padding fields, the total length of the IPv4 header is 20 bytes.

The essential fields of the IPv4 header are:

- **Version**—The 4-bit Version field indicates the version (IPv4 or IPv6) of the packet. The field value helps in interpreting the rest of the header values and payload correctly, because IPv4 and IPv6 have different packet formats.
- **IHL**—The 4-bit Internet Header Length field gives the length of the header in terms of 32-bit word, which also indicates where the payload of the packet begins.

Figure 3.1 IPv4 Header Format

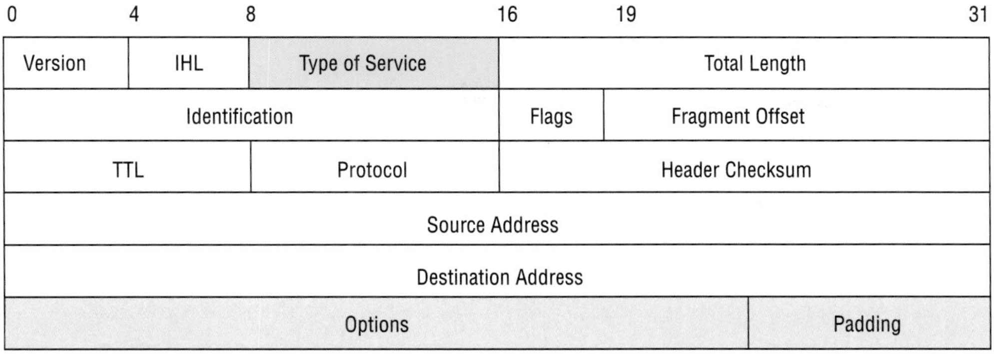

0	4	8	16	19	31
Version	IHL	Type of Service	Total Length		
Identification			Flags	Fragment Offset	
TTL		Protocol	Header Checksum		
Source Address					
Destination Address					
Options				Padding	

- **Type of Service**—The 8-bit Type of Service (ToS) field indicates the quality of service desired for the packet. The ToS field is the main focus of this section.

- **Total Length**—The 16-bit Total Length field indicates the length of the packet, including the header and the payload, in terms of number of octets.

- **Identification**—The 16-bit Identification field is used for identifying the fragments of an original data segment.

- **Flags**—The 3-bit Flags field indicates fragment related information. The first bit is reserved and must be zero. The second bit, Do not Fragment (DF), indicates whether the packet can be further fragmented (0) or not (1). The third bit, More Fragments (MF), indicates if the payload of the packet is the last fragment (0) or if more fragments are to follow (1).

- **Fragment Offset**—The 13-bit Fragment Offset field indicates the position of the payload to the beginning of the original unfragmented data segment. The fragment offset is expressed in terms of 64 bits or 8 octets. The offset of the first fragment is zero.

- **TTL**—The 8-bit time to live field indicates the upper bound of time the packet is allowed to exist.

- **Protocol**—The 8-bit Protocol field indicates the upper-layer protocol to which the packet belongs. The protocols are indicated by their Assigned Internet Protocol Numbers. For example, the assigned number for TCP is 6 and for UDP is 17.

- **Header Checksum**—The 16-bit Header Checksum field value is used to cross-verify the validity of the header. If any of the header values change at some point (e.g., TTL), the value is re-computed and re-marked.

- **Source Address**—The 32-bit Source Address field indicates the IPv4 address of the packet's source.
- **Destination Address**—The 32-bit Destination Address field indicates the IPv4 address of the packet's destination.

IPv6

Figure 3.2 shows the IPv6 header format. The numbers on the top of the figure indicate the bit positions. The total length of the IPv6 header is 40 bytes.

Figure 3.2 IPv6 Header Format

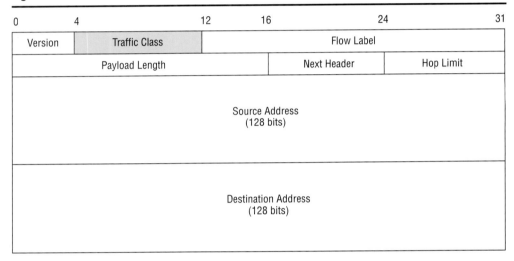

The IPv6 header fields are as follows:
- **Version**—The 4-bit Version field indicates the version of the packet.
- **Traffic Class**—The 8-bit Traffic Class field, although named differently, is identical to the IPv4 ToS field. In the rest of this book, the IPv4 ToS field and IPv6 Traffic Class field are collectively referred to as the *IP ToS field*.
- **Flow Label**—The 20-bit Flow Label field identifies the traffic flow to which the packet belongs. At the edge of a DS domain, the field value can also be used for traffic classification.
- **Payload Length**—The 16-bit Payload Length field indicates the length of the IPv6 payload.
- **Next Header**—The 8-bit Next Header field indicates the upper-layer protocol to which the packet belongs. The field is referred to as protocol field in IPv4.

- **Hop Limit**—The 8-bit hop limit field indicates the maximum number of hops that the packet can travel. The field is similar to the TTL field of IPv4, but the metrics are different.
- **Source Address**—The 128-bit Source Address field indicates the IPv6 address of the packet source.
- **Destination Address**—The 128-bit Destination Address field indicates the IPv6 address of the packet destination.

The IP ToS Field Format

Although IP ToS field is an 8-bit field, RFC 791, which originally specified the Internet Protocol in 1981, recommended class of service markings of 3 bits, called IP precedence markings. With 3-bit space, only eight different precedence markings are possible. As explained in Chapter 6, eight different PHB markings are inadequate for modern multi-service routers. Therefore, the DiffServ working group introduced new standards, which expanded the 3-bit IP precedence markings to 6-bit DSCP markings and later made use of the additional 2-bit space of the ToS field to indicate Explicit Congestion Notification (ECN).

Figure 3.3 summarizes the progressive standardization of the IP ToS field. In the figure, MSB refers to Most Significant Bit, and LSB to Least Significant Bit.

According to the RFC 791, the ToS field in the IP header consisted of the following subfields:

- **Precedence**—The 3-bit Precedence subfield indicates an independent measure of the importance of the packet. Alternatively, the subfield indicates the class of service to which the packet belongs.
- **Delay**—The 1-bit delay subfield indicates whether the packet is delay sensitive. A value of 0 indicates that a normal delay is acceptable, and a value of 1 indicates that a low delay is required.
- **Throughput**—The 1-bit throughput subfield indicates whether the packet has to be given priority access to bandwidth. A value of 0 indicates that normal throughput is acceptable, and a value of 1 indicates that high throughput is required.
- **Reliability**—The 1-bit reliability subfield indicates the drop probability of the packet. A value of 0 indicates that normal drop probability should be used, and a value of 1 indicates that a low drop probability should be used (for high reliability of packet delivery).

Bits 6 and 7 are reserved for future use, and those bits' values must be zero.

Figure 3.3 IP ToS Field Evolution Summary

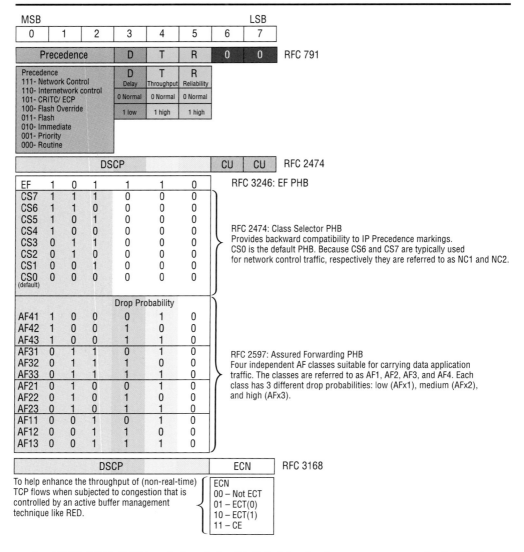

In 1998, RFC 2474 redefined the ToS field, which is common to both IPv4 and IPv6 headers. It amalgamated the precedence, delay, throughput, and reliability subfields (the first 6 bits) into one DSCP subfield. The last two bits of the ToS octet (bits 6 and 7) were defined as Currently Unused (CU) and left undefined without specifying any values. Although the DSCP field is unstructured and the values are defined as a whole, remembering the original structure of these bits will help you to understand the DSCP markings defined for different PHBs.

With 6 bits, the DSCP field can express 64 distinct Code Points (CPs). The 64 code points are classified into three different pools, as summarized in Table 3.1. (The common notion of using "x" to represent wildcard values of a bit position is adopted in RFC 2474 to define the pool values in a binary format.)

Table 3.1 Classification Summary of DSCP Space into Pools

Pool	CP Space	No. of CPs in the Pool	Purpose
1	xxxxx0	32	Standard Action
2	xxxx11	16	Exp/LU
3	xxxx01	16	Exp/LU

The 32 CPs within pool 1 are reserved for use by PHBs standardized through IETF. RFC 2474 itself recommended 8 of the CPs within pool 1 and so far a total of 21 CPs within pool 1 have been recommended for different PHBs.

The 16 CPs within pool 2 and the 16 CPs within pool 3 are reserved for experimental or local use. However, should the pool 1 CPs be exhausted in the future, then the purpose of pool 3 may be redefined, and CPs from pool 3 may be drawn for standardized assignments.

Table 3.2 lists the CPs belonging to the different pools. In the table, the pool 1 CPs assigned to standardized PHBs are also noted.

Table 3.2 DSCP Belonging to Different Pools

Pool 1: xxxxx0 (Standard Action)	Pool 2: xxxx11	Pool 3: xxxx01
CP0 (CS0/BE/Default)	CP3	CP1
CP2	CP7	CP5
CP4	CP11	CP9
CP6	CP15	CP13
CP8 (CS1)	CP19	CP17
CP10 (AF11)	CP23	CP21
CP12 (AF12)	CP27	CP25
CP14 (AF13)	CP31	CP29
CP16 (CS2)	CP35	CP33
CP18 (AF21)	CP39	CP37

(continued)

Table 3.2 DSCP DSCP Belonging to Different Pools (*continued*)

Pool 1: xxxxx0 (Standard Action)	Pool 2: xxxx11	Pool 3: xxxx01
CP20 (AF22)	CP43	CP41
CP22 (AF23)	CP47	CP45
CP24 (CS3)	CP51	CP49
CP26 (AF31)	CP55	CP53
CP28 (AF32)	CP59	CP57
CP30 (AF33)	CP63	CP61
CP32 (CS4)		
CP34 (AF41)		
CP36 (AF42)		
CP38 (AF43)		
CP40 (CS5)		
CP42		
CP44		
CP46 (EF)		
CP48 (CS6/NC1)		
CP50		
CP52		
CP54		
CP56 (CS7/NC2)		
CP58		
CP60		
CP62		

Note: www.iana.org/assignments/dscp-registry provides the centralized registry that keeps track of the DSCP recommended for different PHBs.

In 2001, RFC 3168 (which made RFC 2481 obsolete) redefined bits 6 and 7 of the IP ToS field, so they could be used for Explicit Congestion Notification (ECN). The objective of using ECN is to improve the throughput of TCP (and eventually the throughput of other transport layer protocols) flows when subjected to congestion that is managed by active buffer management techniques such as Random Early Detection (RED).

As discussed in Chapter 8, RED proactively drops some packets prior to buffer exhaustion to communicate the raising buffer occupancy to TCP sources and thereby request them to reduce their transmission rate. RFC 3168 suggests that ECN be used instead to request that the transport protocol at a source reduce its transmission rate, rather than dropping packets.

Table 3.3 shows the four possible markings of the ECN field and their meanings. With the 2-bit field, four distinct markings are possible. However, RFC 3168 does not distinguish between ECT(0) and ECT(1), and thus effectively uses the four markings to represent only three different states. The Not-ECT marking is used if the end systems are not using an ECN-capable transport (ECT) layer protocol. On the other hand, if both the end systems use an ECT protocol, it has to be communicated using the ECT markings. A router can use the CE marking to indicate Congestion Experienced.

Table 3.3 ECN Markings and Purpose

ECN Value	Purpose
0 0	Not-ECT
0 1	ECT(0)
1 0	ECT(1)
1 1	CE

The benefits of ECN can be reaped only if all the end systems of a network are ECT-capable.

3.2 DiffServ Per-Hop Behaviors

Four different types of DiffServ PHBs have been standardized so far. RFC 2474, which defined DSCP, itself has defined two types of PHBs: the default PHB and Class Selector (CS) PHBs. Later in 1999, RFC 2597 defined Assured Forwarding (AF) PHBs for forwarding data traffic. Also in 1999, RFC 2598 defined Expedited Forwarding (EF) PHB for forwarding real-time traffic.

The Default Per-Hop Behavior

According to RFC 2474, DS Domains must provide a default PHB. The default PHB should offer the traditional best-effort (BE) service specified in RFC 1812. Packets that are not explicitly mapped to other behavior aggregates or forwarding classes belong to the default PHB. Under the BE PHB, a DS domain will forward as many packets as possible and as soon as possible. No explicit delay, jitter, or loss characterization is associated with the PHB. However, the traffic belonging to the BE PHB should not be left to starve. Therefore, at least some minimum network resources—buffer and bandwidth—should be reserved for the default PHB. DSCP CP0 is recommended for the default PHB.

Class Selector PHBs

To provide backward compatibility with legacy nodes or hosts using IP precedence, RFC 2474 defined CS PHBs. The recommended DSCP values for CS PHBs are xxx000. According to CS PHBs, the higher a CS is numerically, the better the service precedence it gets. No explicit delay, jitter, or loss characterization is associated with the PHBs. The CS0 PHB is the same as the default PHB. Because precedence values 6 and 7 are meant for network control traffic, the corresponding CS PHBs are referred to as NC1 and NC2. Table 3.4 summarizes the mapping between IP precedence value and DiffServ CS PHBs.

Table 3.4 Mapping of IP Precedence to CS PHBs

Precedence Name			DSCP		
	Decimal	Binary	Binary	Decimal	Name
Network Control	7	111	111000	56	CS7/NC2
Internetwork Control	6	110	110000	48	CS6/NC1
CRITIC/ECP	5	101	101000	40	CS5
Flash Override	4	100	100000	32	CS4
Flash	3	011	011000	24	CS3
Immediate	2	010	010000	16	CS2
Priority	1	001	001000	8	CS1
Routine	0	000	000000	0	CS0/BE

Assured Forwarding PHBs

RFC 2597 defines four classes of Assured Forwarding (AF) PHBs. These classes are suitable for carrying data application traffic with some minimum assured bandwidth guarantees. Each of the four classes of AF PHBs supports three levels of drop probabilities. Under congestion, the higher the drop probability of a packet, the higher the chances that the packet will be dropped. A node offering AF PHBs must accept all three drop precedence code point markings and should provide at least two different levels of loss probability. No delay, jitter, or loss characterization is associated with the PHBs. The four classes of AF PHBs forward packets independently of one another. Packets belonging to a microflow going through an AF class should not be re-ordered.

The four classes of AF, with their three levels of drop probabilities and resulting 12 PHBs are summarized in Table 3.5.

Table 3.5 AF PHBs and Their Recommended DSCP Values

Drop Probability → Classes ↓	Low(1): 01 0	Medium(2): 10 0	High(3): 11 0
AF1: 001	AF11: 001 010	AF12: 001 100	AF13: 001 110
AF2: 010	AF21: 010 010	AF22: 010 100	AF23: 010 110
AF3: 011	AF31: 011 010	AF32: 011 100	AF33: 011 110
AF4: 100	AF41: 100 010	AF42: 100 100	AF43: 100 110

The suggested application traffic suitable for carrying over an AF class has the following characteristics: Traffic flow from a customer site that conforms to a committed information rate should be forwarded with a high probability, and packets that are sent in excess of the committed information rate have lower probabilities of forwarding. The packets that are sent in excess can be dropped under congestion.

Expedited Forwarding PHB

RFC 3246, supplemented by RFC 3247, replaced RFC 2598 in defining Expedited Forwarding (EF) PHB. EF PHB is suitable for carrying application traffic that requires low-loss, low-latency, and low-jitter network service. In other words, EF PHB is suitable for carrying time- and loss-sensitive application traffic at a certain configured rate.

To satisfy the EF PHB service requirements, a node should service packets belonging to EF PHB at a rate higher than their arrival rate and irrespective of the offered load of non-EF traffic at the servicing point. By servicing at a rate higher than the arrival rate, queues belonging to EF can be maintained at an empty or nearly empty state, and thereby queuing latency can be minimized. Low-queuing occupancy helps minimize jitter, latency, and packet loss.

Packets belonging to a microflow going through an EF class should not be reordered. DSCP 101110 is recommended for EF PHB. The standards suggest that packets marked as EF can be mapped to other forwarding classes that have the same forwarding behavior as EF PHB.

The standards also suggest that if EF PHB is implemented such that EF traffic has strict servicing priority over any other traffic, then the EF traffic should be policed at a committed rate in order to limit the impact of EF traffic over other traffic, and also to protect against denial of service (DoS) attacks. Any packets exceeding the limited rate must be dropped.

Using EF PHB for Different Application Traffic

If a network offers many real-time applications such as VoIP, broadcast TV, Video on Demand, online gaming, and so on, should they all be forwarded to the same EF behavior aggregate because they all need the same EF PHB service?

Not necessarily. In conformance to the RFC 3246 mutability policy, different application traffic that requires EF PHB can be mapped to different behavior aggregates (or forwarding classes) and mapped to queues corresponding to those behavior aggregates. The different types of application traffic can even use different DSCP markings, provided that all the different behavior aggregates used conform to the defined EF PHB.

3.3 Ethernet Frame Formats and the 802.1p ToS Field

Ethernet is the most prevalent family of frame-based Layer 2 networking technologies commonly used in local area networks (LANs) and in metropolitan area networks (MANs). ALSRP allows Ethernet based LANs and MANs to seamlessly extend over an IP/MPLS Network by offering Ethernet based Layer 2 services such as virtual private LAN service (VPLS) and Epipe. Besides offering customer facing connections over Ethernet, the technology can also be used in an ALSRP network to connect the internal nodes of the network.

The IEEE 802.1p field in the Ethernet header is the standard ToS field of the Layer 2 protocol. In an ALSRP network, traffic can be classified at all nodes (access or network core) using the 802.1p field marking. At an access ingress of an ALSRP network, as discussed in Chapter 6, frames can also be classified using the values of other Ethernet header fields. This section addresses different Ethernet header fields, including the 802.1p field.

There are four different types of Ethernet frames:

- Ethernet II
- IEEE 802.3 (without an LLC header)
- IEEE 802.2 LLC
- IEEE 802.2 SNAP

Ethernet II and IEEE 802.3 are the basic underlying frame types. Figure 3.4 shows the Ethernet II and IEEE 802.3 frame formats. All the fields are common for both the formats, except for the fourth header field. The Ethernet II frame format uses the field as a 2-byte EtherType field, and the IEEE 802.3 frame format uses it as a 2-byte length field instead.

Figure 3.4 Ethernet II and IEEE 802.3 Frame Formats

Ethernet II

Preamble 8 bytes	Dst. MAC 6 bytes	Src. MAC 6 bytes	EtherType 2 bytes	Payload 46-1500 bytes	FCS 4 bytes

IEEE802.3

Preamble 8 bytes	Dst. MAC 6 bytes	Src. MAC 6 bytes	Length 2 bytes	Payload 46-1500 bytes	FCS 4 bytes

The different fields of the two frame formats are:

- **Preamble**—The preamble is used to let the receiving device synchronize with the incoming bit stream. Start frame delimiter is a part of the preamble, and it indicates to the receiving device that the bits of an actual frame follow.
- **Destination MAC**—The 48-bit media access control (MAC) or hardware address hardcoded into the Ethernet Network Interface Card (NIC) of the receiving device.
- **Source MAC**—The MAC or hardware address hardcoded into the NIC of the source device.
- **EtherType**—The Ethernet II frame uses EtherType field to identify the Layer 3 (network) protocol.

- **Length**—The value indicates the length of the LLC field, including padding if any.
- **Payload**—The upper-layer protocol data unit.
- **FCS**—The Frame Check Sequence field contains a cyclic redundancy check value that helps identify the validity of the frame.

The raw IEEE 802.3 frames were used within a proprietary LAN (e.g., IPX); therefore, the need to identify the network layer protocol did not arise. However, in order to make the frame format suitable for generic use, the IEEE 802.2 Logical Link Control (LLC) sublayer specifications were introduced, and an LLC encapsulation is added to the data before inserting it into an IEEE 802.3 frame.

The IEEE 802.2 LLC fields are:

- **DSAP**—The Destination Service Access Point is a unique user-level address, which indentifies a higher-level protocol used on the destination device.
- **SSAP**—The Source Service Access Point is a unique user-level address, which indentifies a higher-level protocol used on the source device. For two nodes to communicate, the SSAP and the DSAP must be the same.
- **Ctrl**—The Control field identifies IEEE 802.2 PDU type.

The Subnetwork Access Protocol (SNAP) is an extension to the 802.2 LLC header. Figure 3.5 shows the IEEE 802.2 LLC fields and the SNAP Extension fields. An LLC encapsulation with a DSAP and a SSAP with a hexadecimal value of AA or AB indicates use of a SNAP extension. SNAP is used to indentify more protocols within IEEE 802.2 LLC frames than can be identified by DSAP and SSAP fields. SNAP uses the Type field to identify higher-level protocols. An Organizationally Unique Identifier (OUI) is a 24-bit number that can be purchased from the IEEE Registration Authority. The OUI field within a SNAP extension uniquely identifies a vendor, manufacturer, or organization globally.

Figure 3.5 IEEE 802.2 LLC and SNAP Extension Fields

802.2 LLC

DSAP 1 byte	SSAP 1 byte	Ctrl 1 or 2 bytes	Payload

802.2 LLC SNAP

DSAP (AA) 1 byte	SSAP (AA) 1 byte	CTRL 1 or 2 bytes	OUI D 3 bytes	Type 2 bytes	Payload

VLAN Tagging

IEEE 802.1Q tagging is commonly referred to as *virtual local area network (VLAN) tagging* or as *Q tagging*. VLAN tagging allows multiple LANs to use a common medium or network, without compromising the privacy of each individual LAN. Also, a VLAN tag has a ToS field that indicates its QoS requirement. VLAN tagging also supports the use of different Media Access Control methods within a single network.

Figure 3.6 shows the process of VLAN tagging. As a part of the VLAN tag, a type field and a 2-byte Tag Control Information (TCI) field are inserted (inserted fields are shaded green in the figure) in the original Ethernet header of the frame.

The value of the Type field inserted as part of the VLAN tag identifies the insertion of the VLAN tag. The different subfields of the TCI are:

- **802.1p**—The 3-bit 802.1p field indicates the QoS desired for the frame.
- **CFI**—The 1-bit Canonical Format Indicator is used for compatibility between Ethernet and Token Ring networks. The bit is set to zero for Ethernet switches.
- **VID**—The 12-bit field indicates the VLAN to which the frame belongs. VID 0 indicates that the frame does not belong to any particular VLAN and the VLAN tag is inserted only to indicate the QoS desired for the frame.

Figure 3.6 Tagging Ethernet Frames with 802.1Q Tags

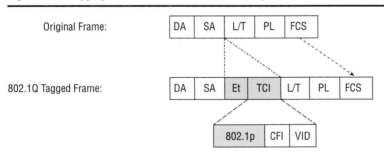

802.1p ToS Field

The 3-bit IEEE 802.1p ToS field can indicate up to eight different QoS markings. IEEE does not define how to handle frames with certain 802.1p markings; however, it makes some broad recommendations on providing the QoS using the field. An 802.1p-compliant switch should be able to segregate frames, based on their 802.1p marking, into different classes of service. The highest-priority value is 7, and lowest-priority value is 0. Table 3.6 lists the 802.1p markings suggested for different types of traffic.

Table 3.6 Suggested 802.1p Markings for Different Types of Traffic

802.1p Marking		Traffic Type
Decimal	Binary	
7	111	Network Control
6	110	Real-Time
5	101	Real-Time
4	100	Controlled Load/Critical Data
3	011	Excellent Effort
2	010	Spare
1	001	Background
0	000	Default: Best Effort

3.4 MPLS Shim Header and EXP Field

Figure 3.7 shows the different fields of a MPLS shim header. An MPLS header is 4 bytes long, and the numbers at the top in the figure indicate the bit positions.

Figure 3.7 MPLS Header Format

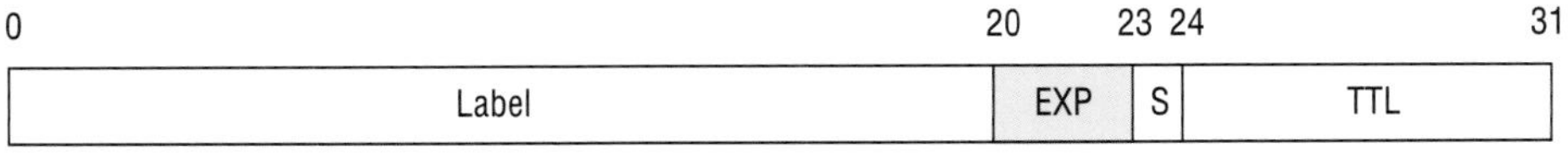

0	20	23 24	31
Label	EXP	S	TTL

The different fields of an MPLS header are:

- **Label**—The 20-bit value of the field indicates a label based on which the multi-protocol label switching occurs. When a labeled packet arrives at a label switch router (LSR), based on the label value, the next hop of the packet is decided, and it is forwarded accordingly. A label value is relevant only for a given hop. Before forwarding a packet, the LSR will either replace the label value or pop the top MPLS header out of the label stack.

- **EXP**—The 3-bit EXP field was originally reserved for experimental use, but it is used to indicate the QoS desired for the labeled packet.

- **S**—The 1-bit Stack field value indicates whether the header is the last entry within the label stack. A value of 1 indicates that the header is the last entry (i.e., bottom most entry) of the label stack, and a value of 0 indicates that there are more entries after this header.

- **TTL**—The value of the 8-bit field indicates the time to live for the frame.

As mentioned in the previous chapter, for supporting Differential Services over MPLS, the EXP field of the MPLS header is used to indicate the QoS desired for the labeled packet. As in the case of the 802.1p field of Ethernet Q tag, the EXP field can represent eight different QoS markings.

Using 802.1p Markings to Indicate PHB

As with MPLS EXP markings, can you also use 802.1p markings to indicate the PHB of a frame within a DS domain?

Ethernet standards do not specify how to satisfy QoS requirements of frames belonging to different applications. DiffServ provides the flexibility of using different field markings to indicate the desired PHB of a datagram. Therefore, either MPLS EXP or 802.1p of Ethernet encapsulation can be used, instead of the DSCP field of the IP header, to indicate the desired PHB of a datagram.

However, the 6-bit DSCP field can represent up to 64 code points, whereas the 3-bit EXP field and the 3-bit 802.1p field can represent only up to 8 different QoS markings. Therefore, using the EXP or 802.1p field in the place of the DSCP field would limit the number of PHBs provided within the domain.

Summary

ALSRP can recognize standard QoS markings of different network technologies. In addition, at the ingress of a DiffServ domain, ALSRP can classify traffic based on multiple header fields.

IPv4 and IPv6 have the same ToS field format. The IP ToS field format has evolved over the years. Originally, 3-bit-long IP precedence markings were used to indicate the class of service of a packet. Because modern routers offer more than eight PHBs, 6-bit-long DSCP QoS markings replaced IP precedence markings. ALSRP recognizes both IP precedence and DSCP markings.

So far, four Per-Hop Behaviors have been standardized for networks supporting DiffServ QoS architecture. These PHBs are the default, CS, AF, and EF. The default PHB provides the best-effort service traditionally provided by IP routers. According to the best-effort PHB, as many packets as possible should be forwarded as soon as possible, but the class of service should not starve. The CS PHBs are defined to provide backward compatibility for legacy devices using IP precedence markings. The AF family of PHBs with multiple drop priorities is suitable to carry data application traffic. EF PHB is suitable for real-time application traffic.

ALSRP also allows the seamless extension of LANs/MANs over IP/MPLS networks by offering Ethernet-based layer 2 services such as VPLS and Epipe. Besides offering customer facing connections over Ethernet, the technology can also be used in an ALSRP network to connect the internal nodes of the network. There are four different Ethernet frame formats: Ethernet II, IEEE 802.3, IEEE 802.2 LLC, and IEEE 802.2 SNAP. A ToS field, IEEE 802.1p, can be added to an Ethernet encapsulation by inserting an IEEE 802.1Q tag into the encapsulation.

The MPLS shim headers use their EXP field to indicate the QoS desired for the labeled datagram. Like an IEEE 802.1p field, the EXP field is also 3-bits long and can have up to eight different markings.

Fundamental
QoS Features

4

Real-life examples can make it easier to understand abstract concepts and they can also inspire innovations. In this chapter, fundamental QoS features essential for implementing the DiffServ QoS model are compared to different steps involved in flying on a commercial airline service.

Chapter Objectives

- To introduce the fundamental QoS features

- To illustrate the DiffServe QoS model using a commercial airline service model analogy

The QoS models discussed in Chapter 2 suggested frameworks for providing QoS in IP/MPLS networks, but left the implementation details to equipment vendors. To implement a QoS model, many QoS features are required. To achieve network QoS in general, and more particularly for DiffServ QoS, the following features are essential:

- Traffic classification
- Queuing and buffer management
- Scheduling
- Rate-limiting

Although filtering is predominantly a security feature, because it drops unauthorized traffic flowing through a network and thereby increases network resources available for authorized traffic, it can also be considered a QoS feature. This chapter provides highlights about these fundamental QoS features and also about some of the advanced QoS features that ALSRP offers.

Often real-life examples inspire technology advancements. Birds have influenced flight designs, and fluid dynamics have influenced traffic flow theory. One real-life analogy for network rate-limiting is dams constructed across rivers. There are many analogies for the DiffServ QoS model. One of the most notable is the commercial airline service model.

In this chapter, we will compare the essential QoS features against different aspects of differentiated service offered by commercial airline services.

4.1 Traffic Classification

In order to fly in a commercial airplane, a booking confirmation has to be presented at the airport check-in counter of the airline company. The confirmation comes in different forms, including e-tickets, vouchers issued by a travel agent, or cash paid directly at the counter. Irrespective of the mode of the confirmation presented, travel class—first, business, premium economy, or economy class—is determined, and the confirmation is replaced by a boarding pass. For connecting flights, all you need to do is present the boarding pass, and the check-in process is much simpler.

Depending on the travel class, the service treatment will differ throughout the trip. For example, if you are traveling in first class, the staff behind the check-in counter will greet you with a smile, make every effort to keep you from waiting in a long line, and address you by name. By contrast, if you are flying in economy class, the staff behind the counter may or may not smile at you, and you may wait in a long, slow-moving, roped-off line. The process described in this paragraph is passenger classification: The service offered to a passenger is based on his/her travel class.

DiffServ traffic classification is similar to airline passenger classification. As the traffic arrives at the access ingress, datagrams are classified into different forwarding classes, and within a forwarding class into high- or low-queuing priority (also referred to as *profiles*). Traffic classification can be based on multiple header fields. Similar to the way a boarding pass is issued, datagrams may be marked with standard ToS field markings. At the subsequent nodes, the traffic is classified according to the standard marking present in the ToS field.

Figure 4.1 shows a conceptual representation of the traffic classification. Datagrams entering a node are shown in gray. A datagram is represented with two rectangular boxes (cuboids): a bigger and a smaller cuboid. The color of the bigger rectangle indicates the forwarding class of the datagram, and the color of the smaller rectangle indicates its queuing priority. As the datagrams go through the traffic classifier, their forwarding class and queuing priority are determined.

Figure 4.1 A Conceptual Representation of Traffic Classification

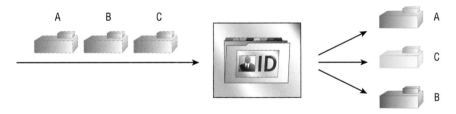

In Chapter 6, traffic classification and traffic-marking features of ALSRP are presented in detail. Besides the standard traffic classification features, ALSRP offers some advanced traffic classification features including color-aware profiling, marking based on the trust nature of the interface, traffic classification and marking of QinQ-encapsulated Ethernet frames, and tunnel termination QoS over-riding. These advanced traffic classification features are discussed at length in Chapter 7.

4.2 Queuing and Buffer Management

After you check in with a commercial airline, you have to wait in the terminal until it is time to board the flight. If you are flying in first class or in business class, you may be allowed to wait in a luxury lounge, where free drinks and snacks are provided, along with business services such as private rooms, Internet access, phone and fax services, and many other commodities. In between long-haul flights, relaxing in a lounge is more comfortable than sitting in the general waiting area, because of the spacious seating, quieter environment, and easy access to airline customer service representatives.

On the other hand, if you are flying in an economy class, you will have to wait in the seating area near the gate in the boarding area for your flight. The chairs here are less comfortable than those in the first class lounges, the environment is busier and noisier, and there are no free snacks. In the worst case, if the area is too crowded, you may not even be able to get a seat and will have to wait standing.

Datagrams flowing through a node may also have to wait before being serviced by a scheduler toward their respective destinations. The wait is inevitable, if the arrival rate of datagrams destined for a particular egress port is greater than the rate at which they leave. In networking terms, the waiting period is referred to as *queuing delay* or *latency*. Similar to the segregation of passengers belonging to different travel classes, datagrams belonging to different classes of service are queued in isolated queues. The datagram belonging to a high-priority traffic class is assured of buffering space. On the other hand, overflowing is common among the queues belonging to low-priority traffic classes. Figure 4.2 shows a conceptual representation of datagram queue isolation. The datagrams in the top row are the equivalent of first class passengers.

Figure 4.2 A Conceptual Representation of Datagram Queue Isolation

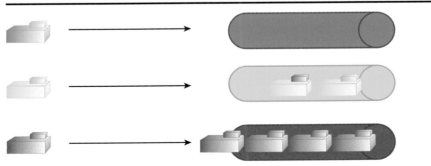

Queuing and buffer management topics are discussed in detail in Chapter 8. ALSRP also allows service providers to control the number of hardware queues created for a service at access ingress. The advanced queuing flexibility offered by ALSRP is presented in detail in Chapter 9.

4.3 Scheduling

When it is time to board a flight, the boarding staff at the terminal decides the order in which passengers belonging to different travel classes are allowed into the plane. Typically, the first class passengers are allowed to board first, followed by the business class passengers, and finally by the economy class passengers. There may not be any strict order for boarding among different economy classes, but passengers who are going to be seated in the back of the plane are asked to board prior to the economy class passengers with seat assignments in the middle or front portion of the flight. The same is the case when it is time to disembark from a flight. The first class passengers are allowed to leave first, followed by the business class passengers, and finally by the economy class passengers. Within a travel class, the passengers seated closer to the exit are allowed to exit first.

Similarly, a scheduling function within a node decides the order in which queues belonging to different forwarding classes are serviced. Typically queues belonging to high-priority forwarding classes are serviced before queues belonging to low-priority forwarding classes. Figure 4.3 shows a conceptual representation of traffic scheduling. The figure shows the arrival traffic directed into different queues, as the scheduler is servicing traffic in different queues.

Figure 4.3 A Conceptual Representation of Traffic Scheduling

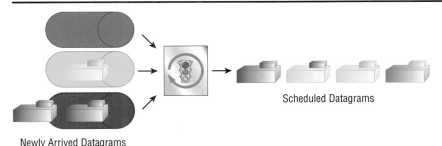

Scheduled Datagrams

Newly Arrived Datagrams

The scheduling behavior of ALSRP is presented in detail in Chapter 10. In addition to traditional scheduling, ALSRP offers Hierarchical QoS (HQoS), which allows a service provider to customize the priority and weight with which queues belonging to different forwarding classes are serviced. Using HQoS, a service provider can redistribute unused bandwidth of one application of a service connection to another application's traffic within the service connection, or can redistribute unused bandwidth of one site to another of a customer. HQoS is discussed in length in Chapter 11.

4.4 Rate-Limiting

A flight has a limitation on how much weight it can carry, and in addition the number of passengers is also limited by the number of seats available on the plane. Airlines attempt to maximize the occupancy of the plane in order to maximize revenue generation. However, all the seats of a flight will not necessarily be sold, and not all the passengers who have reserved a seat will show up in time to catch the flight. Discounted pricing, overbooking, and offering standby tickets are some of the means by which airlines try to maximize the capacity of a flight.

Typically, airlines do not overbook first class and business class. However, overbooking economy class is a common practice. If more passengers for a flight show up than the number of available seats, then the excess passengers with confirmed tickets are compensated and scheduled on alternate flights.

One of the cheapest ways to travel on a commercial flight is with standby tickets. When you use a standby ticket, you are not guaranteed a seat in any particular flight. However, you are allowed to travel on a flight if there are empty seats at the time of the flight's departure after all the passengers who showed up with confirmed tickets have boarded the flight. If it is a busy day and the flights are full, you may have to wait several hours to get a seat, or may not get a seat at all. Standby tickets are suitable provided that you need not be at the destination by the next day or within a specific time frame.

To address the weight limitation of a flight, airlines ensure that each and every passenger honors the number of bags and baggage weight limitations. Excess baggage is charged for significantly, and if the weight or space limitation is reached, excess baggage may be denied space on the flight.

A network path has limited bandwidth to carry traffic. Service providers attempt to maximize the bandwidth utilization of their network in order to maximize revenue generation. Similar to commercial airlines, network providers also overbook low-priority traffic classes, allow customers to utilize excess bandwidth whenever available, and offer best-effort PHB and lower-effort PDB services as different means to maximize network bandwidth utilization.

There are different approaches to rate-limiting, and each has its own specific applications. The most popular rate-limiting approaches are policing and shaping.

When traffic arriving from a customer consistently exceeds a certain rate negotiated through an SLA, the excess datagrams are dropped. This rate-limiting approach is referred to as *policing*. Figure 4.4 shows a conceptual representation of traffic policing.

Figure 4.4 A Conceptual Representation of Traffic Policing

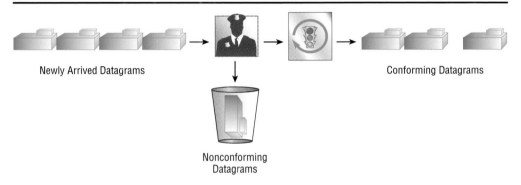

Newly Arrived Datagrams

Conforming Datagrams

Nonconforming
Datagrams

Due to variable latencies experienced by the datagrams of a traffic stream as they flow through a network, some of the datagrams can cluster together to make the flow temporarily nonconforming. The *shaping* function stores such nonconforming datagrams in a queue and de-queues them at the conforming rate. Thus, shaping can help a traffic stream experiencing temporary nonconformance pass through a downstream policer. Figure 4.5 shows a conceptual representation of traffic shaping.

Rate-limiting approaches offered by ALSRP are presented in detail in Chapter 12.

Figure 4.5 A Conceptual Representation of Traffic Shaping

Newly arrived datagrams in bursts (clusters)

Shaped and conforming datagrams

4.5 Filtering

International security requirements make it mandatory that all the flight passengers and their belongings undergo a security check before they board their flights. Although most passengers clear the security check, occasionally a few are prevented from boarding their flights. If a passenger fails or is delayed by the security check, nothing prevents the airline from reallocating the passenger's seat to another passenger. Thus, the process of the security check impacts the services offered to both the passenger held up by the security process and the passenger who was offered the seat.

Similarly, the traffic-filtering process is a network security measure. However, unlike airline service traffic, filtering is not mandatory for a network service. Traffic filtering, based on certain criteria, prevents some of the datagrams from flowing through the node. As a result, traffic filtering impacts the overall quality of service. Figure 4.6 shows a conceptual representation of traffic filtering. In ALSRP, configuring IP and MAC filter policies are similar to configuring IP and MAC criterion within a SAP-ingress policy. In an IP or MAC criteria, based on a matching clause, the action will be to map to a forwarding class and/or to a queuing priority. In the filter policy, based on a matching clause, the action will be either to forward or drop datagrams. Configuring SAP-ingress policy is discussed in Chapter 6.

Figure 4.6 A Conceptual Representation of Traffic Filtering

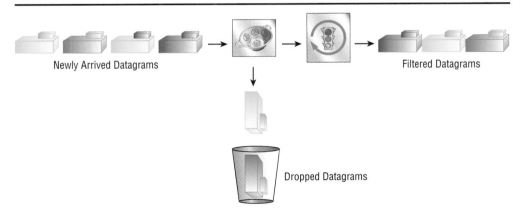

Newly Arrived Datagrams

Filtered Datagrams

Dropped Datagrams

Summary

This chapter presents a brief conceptual overview of essential QoS features. A network designer has to undergo the difficulty of visualizing abstract concepts. Having good real-life examples for technical concepts makes the visualization easier and helps one to make appropriate design choices.

The commercial airline service example is a good analogy for the DiffServ QoS model. Classifying traffic into forwarding classes at the ingress of a DiffServ domain is similar to classifying the passengers of a flight into different travel classes at a check-in counter in an airport. Airlines offer separate waiting areas for passengers belonging to different travel classes. The DiffServ QoS model also isolates traffic belonging to different forwarding classes in different queues until the traffic is serviced by a scheduler. First class passengers are given priority over economy class passengers to embark on and disembark from a flight. A network scheduler prioritizes servicing queues mapped to high-priority traffic over queues that are mapped to low-priority traffic. Airlines have to limit the maximum number of passengers and the weight of baggage loaded in an airplane according to the airplane's seating and weight restrictions. DiffServ domains also have to rate limit traffic to make it conform to negotiated SLAs. Traffic may be subjected to filtering within a network node similarly to the way that passengers are subjected to security checks at an airport.

ALSRP QoS Features

2

In addition to the essential QoS features, ALSRP also offers advanced features that enhance the Quality of Experience of the end users. In Part 2, you learn the theory behind different QoS features offered by ALSRP, how to configure and apply different features, related best practices, and ways to verify the configurations.

ALSRP Architecture and Quality of Service Implementation

5

ALSRP system architecture has three major modules: switch fabric and central processor module, input/output module, and media dependent adapter. Implementation of all the Layer 3 QoS functions is confined to the IOM module.

Chapter Objectives
- To understand ALSRP generic system architecture
- To investigate QoS implementation in ALSRP
- To learn the sequence in which different QoS features are enforced when a datagram flows through an ALSRP node
- To learn about network demarcation points
- To review end-to-end traffic management within a typical ALSRP network

This chapter explores the generic architecture of ALSRP. It shows you the high-level implementation details of QoS features and walks you through the sequence in which different QoS features are enforced when a datagram flows through an ALSRP node.

Gaining insights into the system architecture and implementation details of the features will help you understand the capabilities of the features, which will lead to better QoS design. Knowing the sequence in which different QoS features are enforced is vital to understanding how to optimize performance.

5.1 An Overview of ALSRP's Generic Architecture

ALSRP has an underlying generic and modularized system architecture. Its modularized nature allows network operators to initially build a small service infrastructure and add to it as it grows. In essence, the modularized system architecture of ALSRP allows network operators to build cost-optimized and highly resilient service delivery infrastructures that can scale, adapt to different network needs, and ensure profitability while minimizing the overall deployment risk in the long run.

Figure 5.1 shows the three major modules of the ALSRP generic architecture: the switch fabric and central processor module (SF/CPM), the input/output module (IOM), and the media-dependent adapter (MDA). Each module is covered in detail in the following sections.

Figure 5.1 Major Modules of an ALSRP System

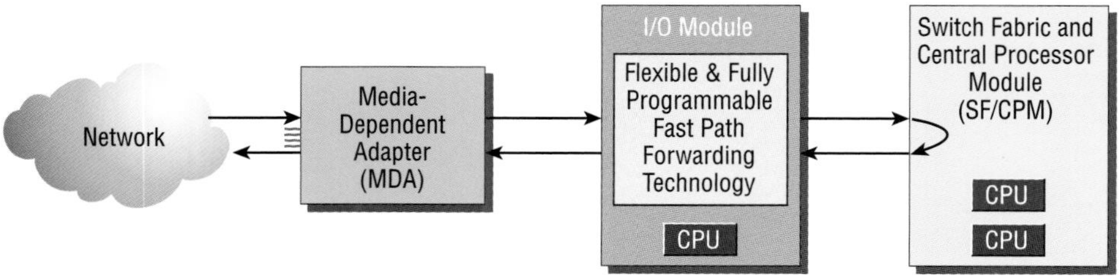

Switch Fabric and Central Processor Module

The switch fabric and control processor are built into one module to conserve chassis slots. This module provides the traffic switching and core control processing for the system. The switch fabric is also commonly referred to as the *fabric core*. The core control processing includes centralized chassis management and protocol stack implementations such as Border Gateway Protocol (BGP), Open Shortest Path First (OSPF), Intermediate System to Intermediate System (IS-IS), and MPLS.

All the QoS features are isolated from the SF/CPM module. The QoS features are process-intensive, and by isolating them from the SF/CPM module, the module can be made fast, robust, and lossless.

Input/Output Module

The IOM receives traffic and transmits from and to the MDAs mounted into it. In the ingress direction, it performs all required datagram manipulation, takes switching and routing decisions, and forwards the traffic to the switching fabric. In the egress direction, it receives traffic from the switching fabric, does all required datagram manipulation, performs egress-specific encapsulation, mirrors the traffic if configured to do so, and forwards the traffic to the appropriate MDA.

The datagram manipulation done by the IOM includes the implementation of most of the QoS features, filter policies, security aspects, and accounting policies for billing. All the Layer 3 QoS features are implemented in the IOM. For handling Asynchronous Transfer Mode (ATM) cells at the access of an IP/MPLS network, ATM-specific Layer 2 QoS features are required in addition to the Layer 3 QoS features. These ATM-specific QoS features are isolated from the Layer 3 QoS features and are implemented in ATM specific MDAs.

Each IOM:

- Contains two fast-path complexes (network processor arrays).
- Supports two pluggable MDAs.
- Contains a CPU section to manage the forwarding hardware in each fast-path complex as well as to participate in the distributed control plane used in the system.
- Connects into the SF/CPM by way of a fabric access device.

By incorporating all the generic datagram manipulation in the IOM and by isolating these manipulations from MDAs, consistency is maintained in configuring Layer 3 QoS features, filter policies, security aspects, and account policies irrespective of the underlying media.

Media-Dependent Adapter

There are different types of MDAs, and some of the ALSRP platforms (Alcatel-Lucent 7710 SR) also support different types of Compact MDAs (CMA). The different MDAs support different underlying media, different physical interfaces, and different framing functions.

Small form factor pluggable (SFP) optics provide greater flexibility by populating MDAs with the required optics on a per-port basis.

5.2 The IOM Layout and Fast-path Complexes

In order to get a better insight into Layer 3 QoS features implementation, you can take a closer look at an IOM layout and the design of a fast-path complex. Figure 5.2 shows the general layout of an IOM.

Figure 5.2 General Layout of an IOM

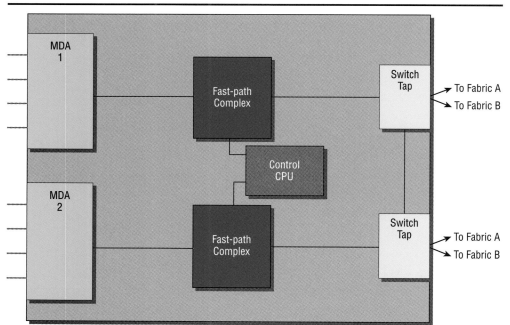

The main components of the IOM layout are two fast-path complexes, their common control CPU, associated memory, interfaces of the fast-path complexes to the active and standby SF/CPMs, and interfaces of the fast-path complexes to the MDAs.

As shown in Figure 5.2, for each MDA that can be plugged into an IOM there is a fast-path complex. In other words, for each MDA there is a separate set of hardware resources in the IOM. However, with the help of a common control CPU of the IOM, the state information of the two fast-path complexes is collectively maintained. As a result, the state of one fast-path complex can be controlled according to the state of the other complex. This flexibility is utilized in some advanced QoS features, such as in virtual hierarchical QoS (HQoS) schedulers. Using HQoS, the traffic of multisite customers that is flowing through different ports spread across the two different MDAs of an IOM can be scheduled at an aggregate level.

Both the fast-path complexes send and receive traffic through both active and standby SF/CPM units simultaneously, resulting in 1:1 hot-standby and hot-swappable SF/CPM redundant units.

Figure 5.3 shows the high-level architecture of the fast-path complex. Within the fast-path complex, the fast-path Network Processor Array (NPA) is a network processing and buffering subsystem that supports applications that require deep packet filtering and full flexibility.

Unless noted specifically, almost all the QoS features of the fast-path complex are designed to perform at wire-speed. In other words, enabling the QoS features, filter policies, security aspects, and/or accounting policies for billing does not impact the throughput of a fast-path complex and exceptions are noted.

The programmability of the fast-path complex means that any future enhancements are as simple as a microcode download. Comparatively, the routers built using Application-Specific Integrated Circuits (ASICs) require a costly and lengthy line card respin each time a new feature or extension is required. For service providers, this results in high cumulative capital expenditure, disruption of service, and slot exhaustion as each new feature and capability requires a new specialized line card or module. This approach to ASIC-based routers lengthens time-to-market for services and introduces significant support and turnaround time issues.

In the high-level architecture of the fast-path complex, shown in Figure 5.3, the yellow dotted horizontal line in the middle makes it obvious that all the components in the upper half of the complex are also present in the bottom half. The components in the upper half of the complex are reserved exclusively for ingress traffic use, while the components in the lower half of the complex address the egress traffic. In short, there are exclusive hardware resources for the ingress and egress traffic of an MDA.

Figure 5.3 Fast-path Complex Architecture

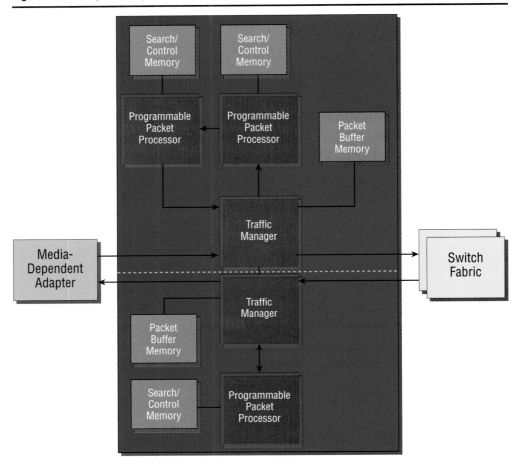

5.3 The QoS Features Enforcement Sequence

Figure 5.4 shows the sequence in which fundamental QoS features are implemented in ingress/egress traffic direction within a fast-path complex.

As shown in the figure, the traffic flowing through a fast-path complex is subject to the different QoS features in the following order:

- Traffic filter or Access Control List (ACL)
- Traffic classification/traffic marking

Figure 5.4 QoS Features Enforcement Sequence within a Fast-Path Complex

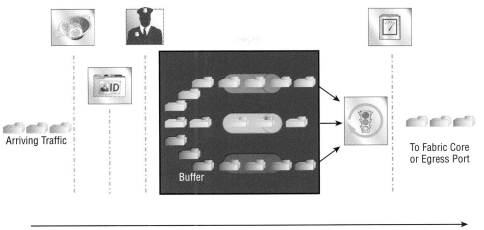

Arriving Traffic

Buffer

To Fabric Core
or Egress Port

Traffic Flow Direction Considered

- Buffering
- Scheduling
- Rate-limiting

By having the traffic flow through the traffic filter, network resources are conserved on the filtered datagram. The filtered traffic is then subject to traffic classification in the ingress direction. In the egress direction, they are subjected to traffic marking instead. Traffic classification maps traffic to different forwarding classes, which in turn can be mapped to different queues.

Figure 5.4 highlights the fact that in ALSRP the traffic belonging to different forwarding classes can be mapped to different queues and thus held in isolation from other forwarding class traffic.

In ALSRP, rate-limiting is achieved implicitly as a part of the queuing process. Therefore, in Figure 5.4 policing, which may result in dropping some of the datagrams, is shown as a part of adding datagrams to queues and metering as a part of taking datagrams out of the queues.

The schedulers determine the order in which different queues are serviced. Thus, they do the job of taking datagrams out of queues and forwarding them to their appropriate destinations within the node.

5.4 Network Demarcation Points

The first step in evaluating a QoS design for a network is to fix the demarcation points of the network. Figure 5.5 shows an example of how to fix the demarcation point in a service provider network. In the figure, the network infrastructures belonging to the service provider are shown in blue.

Figure 5.5 Network Demarcation Points

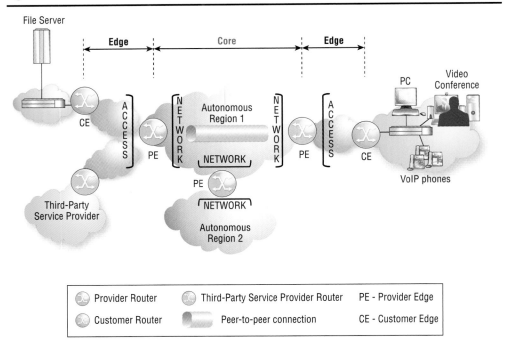

The *edge* of a network is the segment that connects the network to its subscribers, any third-party networks, or any other network to which the service provider under consideration does not have any control. The *core* of a network is the central segment of the network that carries aggregated traffic from different edge segments of the network. The core of a network is typically characterized by high-speed and redundant links.

Nodes can be divided into three categories:

- A *provider edge (PE) node* is part of the network core; however, it has some of its ports connected to edge segments. A PE node typically aggregates traffic from several subscribers and/or third-party networks.

- A node that is part of the network core and has all its ports connected to other nodes in the network core is referred to as a *provider-node* or more commonly as a P-node.
- A *customer edge (CE) node* is a node that aggregates traffic from a single customer or subscriber and is connected to a PE node.

ALSRP formalizes the natural network demarcation points by configuring the ports as `access` or `network`. All the ports of a P-node are typically configured as `network` ports. On a PE node, the ports facing the network core are configured as `network` ports, and typically the ports connected to CE nodes and to third-party networks are configured as `access` ports.

There are exceptions to this general rule in configuring a port as `access` or `network`. If a CE node is exclusively managed by the service provider, the port of the PE connected to the CE can be configured as either `access` or `network`, depending on the traffic rate-limiting and marking abilities of the managed CE node. Figure 5.6 shows an example service provider network where the network demarcation has been extended to managed CE nodes and where the ports of the PE-node-facing CE nodes are configured as `network`. Similarly, if the two autonomous regions of a network do not have a common QoS marking agreement, then the two regions have to be connected through PE routers, by using `access` ports.

Based on the DiffServ QoS model, the QoS requirement of an `access` port is different from that of a `network` port. Therefore in ALSRP, configuring a port as `access` or `network` makes different sets of QoS policies available for the traffic flowing through the port. Table 5.1 summarizes the QoS policies available for `access` and `network` ports. Slope policy is the only QoS policy commonly available for both `access` and `network` ports.

Table 5.1 Set of QoS Policies Available for Traffic Flowing through Access and Network Ports

Access Port	Network Port
SAP-ingress policy	Network policy
SAP-egress policy	Network-Queue policy
Slope policy	Slope policy
Shared-Queue policy	
Scheduler policy	

Figure 5.6 Alternative Network Demarcation in a Managed CE Network

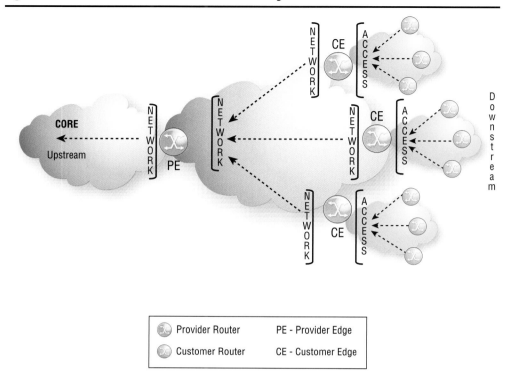

Provider Router	PE - Provider Edge
Customer Router	CE - Customer Edge

In SAP-ingress and SAP-egress policies, *SAP* stands for *service access point*. In ALSRP, a SAP identifies a customer interface point for a service. A SAP is specified using (IOM) slot, MDA, and port/channel information. An entire port configured as a single SAP, for example, is specified as 1/2/3, where 1 refers to the slot in which the customer interface exists, 2 refers to the second MDA mounted on the IOM, and 3 refers to the third port of the MDA.

A SAP is a local entity within an ALSRP node and is uniquely identified by:

- Its physical port/channel
- Its encapsulation type
- Its encapsulation identifier

Depending on the encapsulation, a physical port or channel can have more than one SAP associated with it. SAPs can only be created on access ports or channels, and cannot be created on network ports. For further information on configuring a SAP, refer to the *Service Guide*, provided as a part of the ALSRP product manuals.

Along with the configuration of a port as `access` or `network`, the direction of the traffic flowing through a port also plays a vital role in the QoS management that the traffic is subjected to. Depending on the port configuration as `access` or `network`, and based on the traffic flow direction, the four key networking points from a QoS perspective are:

- **Access/service ingress**—The data path (more specifically the fast-path complex) in the ingress direction of an access port is referred to as *access ingress* or *service ingress*.

- **Access/service egress**—The data path in the egress direction of an access port is referred to as *access egress* or *service egress*.

- **Network ingress**—The data path in the ingress direction of a network port is referred to as *network ingress*.

- **Network egress**—The data path in the egress direction of a network port is referred to as *network egress*.

5.5 End-to-End Traffic Management in an ALSRP Network

This chapter and those in Part I of the book have introduced you to all the main elements of the traffic management process. Now it's time to put them all together. This section provides an overview and an example of end-to-end traffic management within an ALSRP network.

If you are new to the subject or to ALSRP, you may find the information presented in the upcoming chapters difficult to absorb all at once. You may want to return to this section when necessary to put the material back into perspective.

The following list summarizes the management rules for traffic in an ALSRP network:

- Traffic that flows through an ALSRP network typically enters the network through an access ingress and exits through an access egress.

- Between the access ingress and the access egress, depending on the route, the traffic may flow through a number of network nodes, passing through a network egress and network ingress to reach each node.

- At the access ingress, traffic is managed according to the associated SAP-ingress QoS policy and datagrams are buffered according to forwarding classes in isolation from datagrams from other SAPs.

- At each network ingress and network egress, traffic is managed according to the associated Network and Network-Queue QoS policies.

- At each network ingress, all datagrams that enter through a common MDA are buffered together in the same pool, but not necessarily in the same queue.

- At each network egress, all datagrams that belong to an exit port are buffered according to their forwarding classes, in isolation from other port traffic.

- At the service egress, traffic is managed according to the associated SAP-egress QoS policy and datagrams are buffered according to forwarding classes in isolation from datagrams belonging to other SAPs.

- At all the queuing points (access ingress, network egress, network ingress, and access egress) the traffic is scheduled according to basic scheduling of ALSRP. Optionally, a Scheduler policy can be enabled to customize the scheduling at an access ingress or access egress.

- At all the queuing points, buffer space is managed using a Tail Drop buffer management technique. Optionally, a slope policy can be enabled to manage certain portions of the buffer space using the Random Early Detection (RED) buffer management technique.

Figure 5.7 shows a simple example for a traffic flow through an ALSRP network. The network consists of four ALSRP nodes (N1, N2, N3, and N4). There are three customers: Purple, Orange, and Blue. Each customer has two sites (A and B). Each customer subscribes to a point-to-point service from the network service provider to communicate between their sites. In the network, ports connected to customer sites are configured as `access` and ports connected to other ALSRP nodes within the network are configured as `network`. The main focus in the example is on the traffic flowing from Purple A to Purple B, in relation to the other traffic flowing in the same direction.

The first node the flow encounters is N1:

- **Access ingress**—At N1, purple and orange traffic arrive through two different SAPs of an MDA. As the traffic enters the ingress forwarding complex, incoming datagrams of purple and orange traffic are classified into one or more forwarding classes, as determined by SAP-ingress QoS policies for purple and orange traffic, respectively. The mapping of traffic to forwarding classes is based on multi-field classification rules in the SAP-ingress QoS policy. See Chapter 6 for more information about traffic classification using a SAP-ingress policy.

Figure 5.7 An End-to-End Traffic Flow Scenario

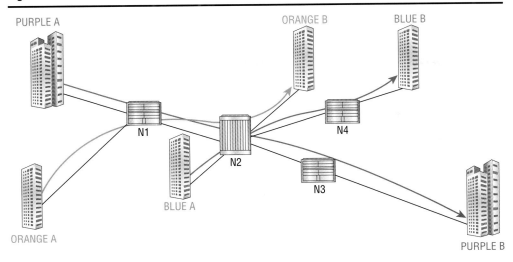

The classified datagrams are then queued according to the SAP that they enter and their forwarding classes. Therefore, the purple traffic is queued separately from the orange traffic on the ingress IOM. Within purple or orange traffic, datagrams can be queued according to their forwarding classes. Queue allocations for the forwarding classes are determined by the SAP-ingress QoS policy. The traffic flowing through a queue is rate-limited according to the configuration of the queue parameters. A flow cannot exceed its queue's peak information rate (PIR) and maximum buffer size (MBS) limit. In other words, the PIR is the maximum rate at which a queue can be serviced, and the MBS of a queue is its maximum buffering space. As a result, the queuing and scheduling processes implicitly perform policing and shaping. See Chapter 12 for information about policing and shaping functions. The queued traffic is serviced by the schedulers and sent toward the fabric core. See Chapter 10 for information about scheduling.

- **Network egress**—Because purple and orange datagrams belong to a point-to-point service and come from the access ingress, their forwarding classes and queuing priority are marked in a standard ToS field (EXP, DSCP, or 802.1p bits) in their tunnel encapsulation headers. Marking the forwarding class and queuing priority of a datagram in the ToS field of its tunnel header is done as specified by the associated Network QoS policy. Because both purple and orange traffic from N1 flows toward N2, all the datagrams (regardless of whether they are purple or orange) that belong to the same forwarding class are queued together at the N1 network egress. Network queue parameters are different from those of SAP-ingress queues and are configured through an associated Network-Queue QoS policy. The queued datagrams are serviced by the schedulers and sent toward the appropriate port.

The traffic then arrives at N2:

- **Network ingress**—At N2, purple and orange datagrams arrive through a network interface. Based on the tunnel headers, the datagrams are classified according to their forwarding classes. The mapping of the tunnel header to a forwarding class is specified by the associated Network QoS policy at N2. Because the same MDA-level buffer pool is used to queue all the network ingress traffic of an MDA in a node, purple and orange datagrams are queued together according to their forwarding classes. Because blue datagrams arrive at N2 through an access ingress, they are queued in isolation from purple and orange traffic.

- **Network egress**—Because purple datagrams come from the network ingress, their tunnel headers are re-marked only if the `remark` flag in the associated Network QoS policy is enabled. Because the egress port for the purple traffic differs from the egress ports of the orange and blue traffic, the purple traffic is queued independently according to the datagrams' forwarding classes.

Next the traffic arrives at N3:

- **Network ingress**—At the ingress of N3, purple datagrams go through the same processes as they do in the ingress of N2. However, at N3, obviously orange traffic does not share the ingress buffer space with the purple traffic.

- **Access egress**—The SAP-egress QoS policy specifies queuing and datagram marking based on the forwarding classes. Datagrams are queued according to their SAP and forwarding class. The queued packets are serviced by the schedulers and sent toward the egress port for delivery to the customers.

The traffic leaving the N3 Access egress exits the service provider network and arrives at its destination CE.

Summary

The three major modules of ALSRP are the switch fabric/control processor module, the input/output module, and the media-dependent adapter. The modularized architecture of these platforms allows service providers to build their infrastructure as they grow.

From a QoS perspective, all the Layer 3 QoS functions are achieved in the IOM. The IOM consists of two fast-path complexes; one for each of the two pluggable MDAs within an IOM. The fast-path complex is programmable, which means that future enhancements are as simple as a microcode download as opposed to a laborious, expensive hardware replacement required by most conventional routers and switches. In the fast-path complex, there are separate sets of hardware resources for ingress and egress traffic of an MDA.

The chapter outlined the sequence in which different QoS functions are enforced over the traffic flowing through a fast-path complex. The QoS function enforcement sequence is the same for both ingress and egress traffic flowing through a fast-path complex.

ALSRP formalizes the natural demarcation points of a network by configuring ports as **access** or **network**. Depending on whether a port is configured as **access** or **network**, different sets of QoS policies are available to manage the traffic flowing through the port.

The final section of this chapter provided an overview of end-to-end traffic management in a network. You may want to return to this information whenever you need a reminder of the complete process.

Network Traffic Classification

Isolating traffic with similar service requirements within a forwarding class is key to providing service differentiation in the DiffServ QoS model.

Chapter Objectives
- To identify and explain the purpose of the different forwarding classes available in ALSRP
- To describe how to maintain end-to-end service differentiation in an ALSRP network between different applications
- To recognize the different QoS mapping criteria available in ALSRP and their order of evaluation at access ingress and network ingress
- To introduce and describe traffic classification/marking features of SAP-ingress, SAP-egress, and Network QoS policies

Classifying traffic into different forwarding classes is one of the fundamental steps in providing service differentiation for different applications' traffic. This chapter explains how to map different classes of service traffic to different forwarding classes and how to further classify a forwarding class's traffic as high- and low-queuing priorities. Marking a datagram to facilitate traffic classification at downstream nodes is also addressed in detail.

Before proceeding, you may find it helpful to review the end-to-end traffic classification model of DiffServ QoS architecture, as discussed in Chapter 2. Traffic entering an edge node is classified into forwarding classes depending on a number of mapping criteria. Before exiting the edge node, the forwarding class and queuing priority of a datagram is marked in the ToS field of its header. The subsequent nodes in the network re-map the datagram to its associated forwarding class and recognize its queuing priority based on the ToS field marking. Thus, in a DiffServ network, the mapping of datagrams into different forwarding classes and marking the classes in datagram headers are essential for sustaining a uniform end-to-end traffic classification scheme.

This chapter focuses solely on traffic classification. This chapter does not address how the service differentiation is achieved; that topic is covered in the chapters related to buffer management and scheduling.

The chapter begins by providing an overview of how uniform traffic classification is achieved within an ALSRP network. It then describes the different forwarding classes and the queuing priorities available within an ALSRP node. Next, it explains the difference between profile states of datagrams and profile states of queues. Section 6.4 describes a SAP-ingress policy and explains using a SAP-ingress policy to classify traffic at an access ingress point. In the subsequent section, applying a SAP-ingress policy under the ingress configuration of a SAP is discussed. Then the chapter explains Network policy in detail and shows how to apply a Network policy under a network interface configuration. Respectively, in Sections 6.8 and 6.9, the chapter describes how to construct a SAP-egress policy and how to apply a SAP-egress policy under the egress configuration of a SAP. Finally, the chapter describes the traffic classification–related verification commands available in ALSRP.

6.1 End-to-End Traffic Mapping and Marking

To understand how uniform traffic classification is maintained within an ALSRP network, consider the example data path shown in Figure 6.1.

Figure 6.1 Traffic Flow Example

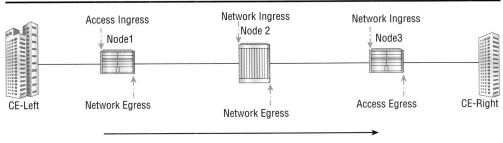

In the example, unidirectional traffic flows from customer edge (CE) on the left to the CE on the right. The traffic flows through three ALSRP nodes. The customer-facing ports of the nodes are configured as access ports, while the rest are configured as network ports.

The following sections explain how traffic is classified and marked as it travels through the data path shown in Figure 6.1. You will also see how the traffic is marked as it enters the network and how the traffic is classified as it enters each node in the network.

Traffic Mapping at Access Ingress

How does a network assess a datagram's status when it first arrives at the threshold? The standard ToS field marking of a datagram arriving at the access ingress port of Node 1 may be either trustworthy or not, depending on the configuration of the CE-left node and the service agreement between the customer and the carrier. For example, the CE-left node may be just a personal computer with no ability to mark different application traffic appropriately using different standard Type of Service (ToS) fields. Therefore at access ingress, the carrier node should have the ability to classify traffic not only based on standard ToS markings but also based on the values of other header parameters such as port numbers, or the IP or Ethernet address of the source or destination.

The SAP-ingress policy associated with the service access point through which the traffic comes, dictates the traffic mapping at access ingress. As a part of traffic mapping at access ingress, the forwarding class and the queuing priority of the datagrams are determined. The queuing priority assigned during the traffic classification is temporary and is used only during queuing at access ingress. When a datagram is scheduled out of the access ingress queue, its temporary queuing priority is typically overwritten with the one determined based on the scheduling rate of the queue. This overwriting of queuing priority is discussed in detail in the "Profile States of Datagrams and Queues" section of this chapter.

> **Note:** Unlike queuing priority, the forwarding class of a packet determined during traffic classification is not changed when the packet is scheduled out of an access ingress queue.

ToS Marking and Re-Marking at Network Egress

What happens to a datagram's status as it leaves the first and the subsequent network egress points in the network? A datagram's forwarding class and queuing priority determined at access ingress are local to the current node. Therefore, in order for the classification to be preserved for the subsequent nodes, it is usual to mark the datagram's status in one of the standard ToS fields at the network egress of the edge node. The ToS field used for marking is selected according to the datagram's encapsulation within its network path and in the following order of preference:

1. EXP (experimental bits) field for Multi Protocol Label Switching (MPLS) encapsulated traffic
2. DSCP (differentiated service code point) field in routed IP or Generic Routing Encapsulation (GRE) tunneled networks
3. 802.1p field for Ethernet encapsulated traffic

At subsequent network egress points, where traffic is forwarded from a network ingress point (such as the network egress of Node 2), QoS classifications would already be marked by the upstream edge node within a selected ToS field. Therefore, at the subsequent network egress points the QoS classifications are not re-marked by default.

The Network QoS policy associated with the network interface dictates how a datagram's forwarding class and its queuing priority are marked (or re-marked) into a ToS field in the datagram's header.

Traffic Mapping at Network Ingress

What happens to a datagram's status as it reaches each network ingress point in the path? Unlike their access ingress counterparts, network ingress nodes can only classify an incoming datagram based on a selected standard ToS field marking in the datagram's header.

The Network QoS policy associated with the network interface dictates how a datagram is classified in terms of its forwarding class and queuing priority based on a selected standard ToS field in the datagram's header.

ToS Marking at Access Egress

If tunnel encapsulations are used over a service provider network, they are removed before a datagram is delivered to its access egress. As a result, any QoS marking noted in the ToS field of the tunnel encapsulation is also removed.

Once a datagram leaves the access egress node, it is either handed over to its destination (in the example in Figure 6.1, CE-right) or to another carrier network. In most cases, the downstream network does not care about the forwarding class used to transport the datagram within the present carrier network, as long as the carrier has respected the service contract associated with the datagram. Therefore, by default, traffic is not marked at access egress.

However, for non-IP traffic and for IP packets for which DSCP marking is irrelevant, the downstream network may request the service provider to mark the 801.1p field of the Ethernet frames at access egress. ALSRP marks the 802.1p field at access egress depending on the forwarding class associated with the frame and as dictated by the associated SAP-egress policy.

Now that you understand the roles played at different networking points in terms of traffic classification, we will turn to the specifics of ALSRP's traffic classification abilities at different network points.

6.2 Forwarding Classes and Queuing Priorities in ALSRP

ALSRP supports eight forwarding classes. Within each forwarding class, ALSRP further classifies datagrams into two different queuing priorities: high and low.

Table 6.1 lists the eight forwarding classes and their default intended usage. The per-hop behavior of all the forwarding classes is configurable; thus, the intended usage of any of the forwarding classes can be modified as required.

Table 6.1 ALSRP Forwarding Classes

Forwarding Classes of ALSRP		Default	
Name	Abbreviation	Class Type	Intended Use
Network control	NC	High-priority	Network control traffic
High-1	H1	High-priority	Secondary network control traffic or delay/jitter-sensitive traffic
Expedited	EF	High-priority	Delay/jitter-sensitive traffic
High-2	H2	High-priority	Delay/jitter-sensitive traffic
Low-1	L1	Assured	Assured traffic
Assured forwarding	AF	Assured	Assured traffic
Low-2	L2	Best effort	Best-effort traffic
Best effort	BE	Best effort	Best-effort traffic

By default, the eight forwarding classes are grouped into three class types as shown in Table 6.1: high-priority, assured, and best effort. The assured and the best effort type forwarding classes are also collectively referred to as low-priority forwarding classes. Typically, high-priority forwarding classes are serviced before other forwarding classes (see Chapter 10 for more information about scheduling behavior). The high-priority classes are intended to be used for real-time traffic, that is, delay- or jitter-sensitive traffic. If the core network has sufficient bandwidth and is not oversubscribed with high-priority traffic, it is possible to effectively support the delay and jitter characteristics of high-priority traffic without utilizing traffic-engineered paths.

The assured-type forwarding classes provide services with a committed information rate (CIR) and a peak information rate (PIR), similar to Asynchronous Transfer Mode (ATM) variable bitrate (VBR) service categories or Frame-Relay. If the core service network has sufficient bandwidth along the path for the assured traffic, all aggregate high-queuing priority datagrams within an assured-type forwarding class will reach the service destination. When the network is congested, low-queuing priority datagrams within assured type forwarding classes can be discarded before discarding high-queuing priority datagrams within the class. Thus, this type of forwarding classes allow datagrams belonging to the same forwarding class to be further classified as being either high- or low-queuing priority and provide differential treatment to different queuing priority datagrams under a congested state.

The best-effort forwarding classes do not have delivery guarantees. Therefore, for queues configured to serve these classes, the CIR can be set to zero. All datagrams within these classes are treated, at best, as low-queuing priority datagrams within an assured-type forwarding class.

In essence at a queuing point under congestion, the queuing priority of a datagram plays an important role in determining if the datagram gets queued or dropped. More specifically, once the occupancy of a queue exceeds a certain threshold, low-queuing priority datagrams forwarded to the queue are dropped, whereas high-queuing priority datagrams forwarded to the queue are accepted. For further details about how the queuing priority of a datagram impacts its queuing possibilities, see Chapter 8.

On the other hand, the priority with which a datagram is scheduled out of a queue at a queuing point is determined by its forwarding class. For further details about scheduling, see Chapter 10.

> **Note:** The command line interface (CLI) of ALSRP refers to the forwarding classes using their abbreviated names. Although some of the forwarding class names resemble DSCP names (for example, EF forwarding class and EF DSCP), they are two different entities. At the ingress of a node, an IP packet marked with any one of the 64 DSCP markings (discussed in Chapter 3) can be mapped to any of the eight forwarding classes. By default all the IP packets, regardless of their DSCP marking, are mapped to the BE forwarding class. In addition to IP packets with DSCP markings, other traffic with or without a ToS marking can also be mapped to any of the forwarding classes based on user-specified matching criteria.

6.3 Profile States of Datagrams and Queues

The queuing priority of a datagram is often referred to as its *profile*. A high-queuing priority datagram is referred to as an *in-profile* datagram. A low-queuing priority datagram is referred to as an *out-of-profile* datagram.

ALSRP supports the concept of in-profile and out-of-profile states not only for datagrams but also for queues. There is a clear distinction between the profile state of a queue and the profile state of a datagram.

A queue is considered to be in-profile if the rate at which the queue is serviced is less than or equal to its configured CIR. A queue is considered to be out-of-profile if the rate at which the queue is serviced is greater than its CIR but less than its PIR. Thus, the profile state of a queue changes depending on its servicing rate. A queue's PIR is the maximum rate at which the queue can be serviced. The profile state of a queue impacts the queue's scheduling priority, as described in Chapter 10.

At access ingress, the queuing priority that a datagram receives as a part of the traffic classification process is a temporary one. As shown in Listing 6.1, the temporary queuing priority is simply referred to as `priority`. The queuing priority is said to be "temporary" because it is considered only at the access ingress queuing. When a datagram leaves its queue at the access ingress, its temporary queuing priority is replaced by a permanent one. The permanent queuing priority of a datagram is referred to as the datagram's profile. The datagram profile is considered at all the subsequent queuing points within the ALSRP network.

Overwriting a Temporary Queuing Priority with a Permanent One

Why is the queuing priority of a datagram that is determined during traffic classification, at access ingress, replaced by the one determined when the datagram is scheduled out of the access ingress queue?

Traffic entering a carrier's network through an access ingress port may or may not conform to the associated SLA. The queuing priority of a datagram, which in turn is the datagram's conformance to the CIR of the associated service contract, can be realistically assessed only when the datagram is scheduled out of the access ingress queue. However, just for queuing of datagrams at access ingress, which precedes the scheduling, end-user markings are trusted. Because different customer traffic is segregated at access ingress, trusting one end-user marking does not impact the other customers' traffic.

Listing 6.1 Display of example traffic classification statements of a SAP-ingress policy

```
dscp nc1 fc "nc" priority high
default-fc "be"
default-priority low
```

6.4 SAP-Ingress Policy and Traffic Mapping at Access Ingress

A SAP-ingress policy associated with a service access point specifies how to classify incoming traffic through the SAP. Listing 6.2 shows the options for creating a SAP-ingress policy. SAP-ingress QoS policies are identified through their policy ID, which is a number between 1 and 65535. The policy ID 1 is reserved for the default policy, which cannot be modified.

> **Best Practices:** In ALSRP, default policies cannot be modified. Therefore, the best practice is to always use custom made policies. Even if a default policy is sufficient for a given scenario, it is better to make a copy of the default policy and apply the copy instead. That way the applied policies can be changed whenever needed.

Listing 6.2 Command options for creating a SAP-ingress QoS policy

```
A:Pod1>config>qos# sap-ingress
  - no sap-ingress <policy-id>
  - sap-ingress <policy-id> [create]

 <policy-id>          : [1..65535]
 <create>             : keyword - mandatory while creating an entry.
```

Listing 6.3 shows the default SAP-ingress policy. A SAP-ingress policy has three functional segments: mapping traffic to forwarding classes, mapping forwarding classes to queues, and queue declarations.

Listing 6.3 Default SAP-ingress QoS policy

```
A:Pod1>config>qos# sap-ingress 1
A:Pod1>config>qos>sap-ingress# info detail
-------------------------------------------
            description "Default SAP ingress QoS policy."
            scope template
```

(continued)

```
        queue 1 priority-mode auto-expedite create
            no parent
            adaptation-rule pir closest cir closest
            rate max cir 0
            mbs default
            cbs default
            high-prio-only default
        exit
        queue 11 multipoint priority-mode auto-expedite create
            no parent
            adaptation-rule pir closest cir closest
            rate max cir 0
            mbs default
            cbs default
            high-prio-only default
        exit
        default-fc be
        default-priority low
```

In Listing 6.3, you see only two segments. The two queue declarations begin with `queue 1 priority-mode` and `queue 11 multipoint priority-mode`. The last two lines show the mapping of traffic to the forwarding classes; as shown in the code, the default SAP-ingress policy maps all the incoming traffic to the BE forwarding class and to low-queuing priority. You see neither the forwarding class declarations nor the mapping of any forwarding class to queues. The reason for that is, by default, all the forwarding classes of a SAP-ingress policy are mapped to queue 1 and queue 11. All the unicast traffic is mapped to queue 1, and all multipoint traffic is mapped to queue 11.

Chapter 8 includes a detailed discussion of the mapping of forwarding classes to queues and queue declarations.

All the QoS policies in ALSRP that map traffic to forwarding classes (SAP-ingress, SAP-egress, and Network) can be configured as either a `template` or an `exclusive`. If the `scope` of a policy is `template`, the policy can be applied any number of times. Whereas, if the `scope` of a policy is `exclusive`, the policy can be applied only once. The `scope` of the default SAP-ingress, SAP-egress, and Network policies is `template`. Listing 6.4 shows the command options for configuring the slope of a SAP-ingress policy.

```
A:Pod2>config>qos>sap-ingress# scope
  - no scope
  - scope {exclusive|template}

 <exclusive|template> : keywords - specify type of policy
```

ALSRP offers several criteria to map traffic to different forwarding classes. These criteria are mainly different Layer 2 to Layer 4 header fields. Respectively, Layers 4, 3, and 2 of the Open Systems Interconnection (OSI) reference model are Transport, Network, and Data Link layers.

Best Practices: Although the descriptions within policies or configuration entities are a nonfunctional part of the entities, proper descriptions of configuration entities help immensely during maintenance and troubleshooting of the configuration.

Listing 6.5 shows the top-level configuration options available under a SAP-ingress policy. Traffic classification options are highlighted with bold text in the listing. Each type of classification rule is interpreted with a specific priority. Table 6.2 lists the classification rule types in the order in which they are evaluated.

Listing 6.5 Top-level command options available to configure a SAP-ingress policy

```
A:Pod1>config>qos>sap-ingress#
  [no] default-fc      - Configure default forwarding class for this policy
  [no] default-priori* - Configure default priority for this policy
  [no] description     - Description for this policy
  [no] dot1p           - Specify 802.1 priority mappings
  [no] dscp            - Specify DSCP mappings
  [no] fc              + Configure forwarding-class to queue mappings
  [no] ip-criteria     + Configure IP match criteria
  [no] mac-criteria    + Configure MAC match criteria
  [no] prec            - Specify IP precedence mappings
  [no] queue           + Configure a queue
  [no] scope           - Specify scope of the policy
```

Table 6.2 Access Ingress Traffic Classification Criteria and Order of Evaluation

Step	Rule Type	Forwarding Class	Queuing Priority	Comments
1	`default-fc` `default-priority`	Set the policy's default forwarding class or subclass.	Set the policy's default queuing priority.	All datagrams match the default rule.
2	`dot1p <dot1p-priority>`	Set when an fc-name exists in the policy. Otherwise, retained from the previous match.	Set when the priority parameter is high or low. Otherwise, retained from the previous match.	Each `dot1p-priority` must be explicitly defined. Each frame can only match one `dot1p` rule.
3	`prec <ip-prec-value>`	Set when an fc-name exists in the policy. Otherwise, retained from the previous match.	Set when the priority parameter is high or low. Otherwise, retained from the previous match.	Each `ip-prec-value` must be explicitly defined. Each packet can only match one `prec` rule.
4	`dscp <dscp-name>`	Set when an fc-name exists in the policy. Otherwise, retained from the previous match.	Set when the priority parameter is high or low. Otherwise, retained from the previous match.	Each `dscp-name` must be explicitly defined. Each packet can only match one `dscp` rule.
5	`ip-criteria` (allows multiple entries per policy and multiple criteria per entry)	Set when an fc-name exists in the policy. Otherwise, retained from the previous match.	Set when the priority parameter is high or low. Otherwise, retained from the previous match.	When IP criteria are specified, entries are matched based on ascending order until the first match and then processing stops. A packet can only match one IP criterion entry.
6	`mac-criteria` (allows multiple entries per policy and multiple criteria per entry)	Set when an fc-name exists in the policy. Otherwise, retained from the previous match.	Set when the priority parameter is high or low. Otherwise, retained from the previous match.	When MAC criteria are specified, entries are matched based on ascending order until the first match and then processing stops. A frame can only match one MAC criterion entry.

In the section "Classifying Traffic Based on Multiple Field Values" later in this chapter, a SAP-ingress policy using multiple traffic classification criteria is listed and the order in which the different rules are evaluated is explained.

Changing the Default Forwarding Class and Default Priority

You saw an example of setting the default forwarding class and default priority in Listing 6.3, which shows the default SAP-ingress policy. The default forwarding class can be changed from BE to a different forwarding class. Likewise, the default priority can also be changed. Listings 6.6 and 6.7 show the options for configuring the default forwarding class and the default priority. Mapping traffic to a subclass is discussed in Chapter 7.

Listing 6.6 Configuring the default forwarding class within a SAP-ingress QoS policy

```
A:Pod1>config>qos>sap-ingress# default-fc
  - default-fc <fc>
  - no default-fc

  <fc>                  : <class>[.<sub-class>]
                          class     - be|l2|af|l1|h2|ef|h1|nc
                          sub-class - [29 chars max]
```

Listing 6.7 Configuring the default priority within a SAP-ingress QoS policy

```
A:Pod1>config>qos>sap-ingress# default-priority
  - default-priority {low|high}
  - no default-priority

  <low|high>            : keyword - specifies the priority
```

One of the scenarios, where configuring one of the high-priority forwarding classes as the default forwarding class would be useful, is when the SAP port is connected to a video server streaming broadcast television channels. In that scenario, configuring the default priority to be high would also be useful.

Classifying Traffic According to Standard ToS Field Values

Classifying traffic based on IEEE 802.1p bits, IP precedence, DSCP values, IP, and MAC criteria to forwarding classes is optional. Configuring traffic classification using 802.1p, IP precedence, and DSCP within a SAP-ingress policy is all similar, and all are single-line configurations. Listing 6.8 shows command options for mapping traffic to a forwarding class and setting a frame's queuing priority using the Ethernet ToS field, 802.1p.

Listing 6.8 Options to map traffic using 802.1p

```
A:Pod1>config>qos>sap-ingress# dot1p ?
  - dot1p <dot1p-priority> [fc <fc>] [priority {low|high}]
  - no dot1p <dot1p-priority>

<dot1p-priority>      : [0..7]
<fc>                  : <class>[.<sub-class>]
                        class      - be|l2|af|l1|h2|ef|h1|nc
                        sub-class  - [29 chars max]
<low|high>            : keyword - specifies the priority
```

Listing 6.9 exhibits an example configuration of traffic mapping using the 802.1p field. According to the configuration, frames whose 802.1p field is set to 7 are mapped to forwarding class NC, and their queuing priority is set to high. Similarly frames whose 802.1p field is set to 2 are mapped to forwarding class AF and their queuing priority is set to low. However, for the frames whose 802.1p field is set to 1, no explicit forwarding class is set, although their queuing priority is set to high. For these frames, the default-fc will be retained. For frames whose 802.1p field is set to 0, only the forwarding class is specified. Therefore, for these frames the forwarding class will be BE, and the default-priority would be retained. Explicitly mapping frames with the 802.1p field marked as 0 to forwarding class BE is redundant, although not an error, as the default-fc is already mapped to the class BE.

Listing 6.9 Examples of traffic classification using 802.1p

```
dot1p 0 fc "be"
dot1p 1 priority high
dot1p 2 fc "af" priority low
dot1p 7 fc "nc" priority high
default-fc be
default-priority low
```

Listing 6.10 shows command options for mapping traffic to a forwarding class and setting a packet's queuing priority using IP Precedence. Although the 6-bit DSCP is the current standard for marking the ToS field in an IP header, several legacy customer premise equipments (CPEs) continue to use the 3-bit IP precedence bits. Therefore, ALSRP offers the option of classifying traffic at access ingress using IP precedence bits.

Listing 6.10 Options to map traffic using IP precedence bits

```
A:Pod1>config>qos>sap-ingress# prec
  - no prec <ip-prec-value>
  - prec <ip-prec-value> [fc <fc-name>] [priority {low|high}]

 <ip-prec-value>      : [0..7]
 <fc>                 : <class>[.<sub-class>]
                        class     - be|l2|af|l1|h2|ef|h1|nc
                        sub-class - [29 chars max]
 <low|high>           : keyword - specifies the priority
```

Listing 6.11 exhibits an example configuration of traffic mapping using IP precedence bits.

Listing 6.11 Examples of traffic classification using IP precedence bits

```
prec 1 fc "af"
prec 2 fc "af" priority high
prec 5 fc "ef" priority high
```

Listing 6.12 shows command options for mapping traffic to a forwarding class and setting an IP packet's queuing priority using DSCP bits. Listing 6.13 exhibits an example configuration of traffic mapping using DSCP bits.

Listing 6.12 Options to map traffic using DSCP

```
A:Pod1>config>qos>sap-ingress# dscp
  - dscp <dscp-name> [fc <fc>] [priority {low|high}]
  - no dscp <dscp-name>

 <dscp-name>           : be|cp1|cp2|cp3|cp4|cp5|cp6|cp7|cs1|cp9|af11
                         |cp11|af12|cp13|af13|cp15|cs2|cp17|af21|cp1
                         9|af22|cp21|af23|cp23|cs3|cp25|af31|cp27|af
                         32|cp29|af33|cp31|cs4|cp33|af41|cp35|af42|c
                         p37|af43|cp39|cs5|cp41|cp42|cp43|cp44|cp45|
                         ef|cp47|nc1|cp49|cp50|cp51|cp52|cp53|cp54|c
                         p55|nc2|cp57|cp58|cp59|cp60|cp61|cp62|cp63
 <fc>                  : <class>[.<sub-class>]
                         class      - be|l2|af|l1|h2|ef|h1|nc
                         sub-class  - [29 chars max]
 <low|high>            : keyword - specifies the priority
```

Listing 6.13 Examples of traffic classification using DSCP

```
dscp nc1 fc "nc" priority high
dscp af21 fc "af" priority high
dscp af23 fc "af"
```

As illustrated in Listing 6.13, in order to classify traffic using DSCP, you need to be familiar with DSCP names and the value each name represents. If you are averse to playing guessing games and do not put much trust in your memory, you can seek help from the ALSRP nodes themselves on this. In ALSRP nodes, the command `show qos dscp-table` will list all the DSCP names and their corresponding values in decimal, binary, and hexadecimal. Listing 6.14 displays part of the table.

Listing 6.14 Part of the built-in DSCP table of ALSRP

```
A:Pod1# show qos dscp-table

===========================================================
DSCP Mapping
===========================================================
DSCP Name       DSCP Value      TOS (bin)       TOS (hex)
-
be              0               0000 0000       00
cp1             1               0000 0100       04
cp2             2               0000 1000       08
cp3             3               0000 1100       0C
cp4             4               0001 0000       10
cp5             5               0001 0100       14
cp6             6               0001 1000       18
cp7             7               0001 1100       1C
```

Classifying Traffic Based on IP or MAC Criteria

A SAP-ingress policy cannot have both IP criteria and MAC criteria. If you have an IP criteria configured in your SAP-ingress policy, you cannot configure a MAC criteria, and vice versa.

The IP and MAC criteria can be basic or detailed. Listing 6.15 shows the command options for creating an IP criteria; it also shows how to create an entry within an IP criteria. As shown in the code, both IP and MAC criteria are constructed from the policy entries. An entry is identified by a unique numerical entry ID. The entries are evaluated in numerical order based on the entry ID, from the lowest to highest ID value. The action for the first **entry** that matches all the criteria is performed. Once a match is found no further entries are evaluated.

Listing 6.15 Command options for creating an IP criteria entry

```
A:Pod1>config>qos>sap-ingress# ip-criteria
  - ip-criteria
  - no ip-criteria

 [no] entry           + Configure an IP based policy entry
      renum           - Renumber an entry

A:Pod1>config>qos>sap-ingress# ip-criteria entry
  - entry <entry-id> [create]
  - no entry <entry-id>

 <entry-id>           : [1..65535]
 <create>             : keyword - mandatory while creating an
                        entry.
```

Best Practices: As mentioned, IP and MAC criteria entries are evaluated in numerical order based on the entry ID, from the lowest to the highest ID value. Therefore, when you initially configure the entries, let the entry IDs be multiples of 5 or 10. This provides space for inserting new entries between two existing entries if needed later on, without the need for renumbering all the existing entries.

Listing 6.16 shows the command options available within an IP criterion. Within an IP criterion, **match** options indicate the fields of an IP header that have to be inspected and the field values that have to be met. If a packet successfully meets the matching criteria, the packet is mapped to the forwarding class and queuing priority specified in the action statement of the entry.

Listing 6.16 Command options available within an IP criterion entry

```
A:Pod1>config>qos>sap-ingress>ip-criteria>entry$
  [no] action          - Specify action queue and priority
  [no] description     - Description for this entry
  [no] match           + Specify IP match criteria for this policy
```

Listing 6.17 displays the options available to configure an action statement within an IP criterion entry.

Listing 6.17 Command options available for configuring an action statement within an IP criterion entry

```
A:Pod1>config>qos>sap-ingress>ip-criteria>entry$ action
  - action [fc <fc-name>] [priority {low|high}]
  - no action

  <fc>                 : <class>[.<sub-class>]
                         class      - be|l2|af|l1|h2|ef|h1|nc
                         sub-class  - [29 chars max]
  <low|high>           : keyword - specifies the priority
```

Command options available for creating IP and MAC criteria entries are the same, except for the match options. Listing 6.18 illustrates the match options available for creating IP criteria, and Listing 6.20 shows the match options available for creating MAC criteria.

Listing 6.18 Syntax of match options available for creating an IP criterion

```
A:Pod1>config>qos>sap-ingress>ip-criteria>entry# match
  - match [protocol <protocol-id>]
  - no match

  <protocol-id>        : [0..255] - protocol numbers accepted in DHB
```

(continued)

```
                              keywords -
                              none|crtp|crudp|egp|eigrp|encap|ether-ip|
                              gre|icmp|idrp|igmp|igp|ip|ipv6|ipv6-frag|ipv6-icmp|
                               ipv6-no-nxt|ipv6-opts|ipv6-route|isis|iso-ip|l2tp|
                              ospf-igp|pim|pnni|ptp|rdp|rsvp|stp|tcp|udp|vrrp
                                      - * (udp/tcp wildcard)


[no] dscp               - Specify DSCP match
[no] dst-ip             - Specify destination IP and mask match
[no] dst-port           - Specify destination TCP/UDP port match
[no] fragment           - Specify match criteria applies to IP fragments
[no] src-ip             - Specify source IP and mask match
[no] src-port           - Specify source TCP/UDP port match
```

The supported IP match criteria are:

- Source IP address/prefix

- Source port/range

- Destination IP address/prefix

- Destination port/range

- Protocol type (TCP, UDP, GRE, IPv6, PNNI, PIM, etc.)

- DSCP value

- IP fragment

For more information on these IP header fields, refer back to Chapter 3. A protocol to be matched can be specified using its Assigned Internet Protocol Number. The most common protocols can also be specified using the listed keywords.

Note: www.iana.org/assignments/protocol-numbers identifies the Assigned Internet Protocol Numbers and the associated protocols.

Traffic belonging to common applications can be targeted using their well-known port numbers.

Listing 6.19 exhibits an example of IP criteria. The example maps HTTP traffic to the forwarding class L2. A packet has to satisfy all the match conditions of an entry for the corresponding action to be performed on the packet. For example, to satisfy entry 10 shown in the listing, a packet must have the protocol field of its IP header set to UDP as well as have its destination port set to 80.

Listing 6.19 IP criteria mapping HTTP traffic to the L2 forwarding class

```
            entry 10 create
                description "Mapping UDP http traffic to L2"
                match protocol udp
                    dst-port eq 80
                exit
                action fc "l2" priority low
            exit
            entry 20 create
                description "Mappping TCP http traffic to L2"
                match protocol tcp
                    dst-port eq 80
                exit
                action fc "l2" priority high
            exit
```

Listing 6.20 shows the match options available for creating media access control (MAC) criteria.

Listing 6.20 Syntax of match options available for creating a MAC criterion

```
A:Pod1>config>qos>sap-ingress>mac-criteria>entry# match
  - match [frame-type {802dot3|802dot2-llc|802dot2-snap|ethernet-II}]
  - no match

 <frame-type>            : 802dot3|802dot2-llc|802dot2-snap|ethernet-II
```

(continued)

```
[no] dot1p       - Specify 802.1P priority and mask to match
[no] dsap        - Specify DSAP value and mask to match
[no] dst-mac     - Specify destination MAC address and mask to match
[no] etype       - Specify ethernet-type match
[no] snap-oui    - Specify snap-oui match
[no] snap-pid    - Specify snap-pid match
[no] src-mac     - Specify source MAC and mask to match
[no] ssap        - Specify SSAP value and mask to match
```

The supported MAC match criteria are:

- IEEE 802.1p value/mask
- Source MAC address/mask
- Destination MAC address/mask
- EtherType value
- IEEE 802.2 LLC SSAP value/mask
- IEEE 802.2 LLC DSAP value/mask
- IEEE 802.3 LLC SNAP OUI zero or non-zero value
- IEEE 802.3 LLC SNAP PID value

For more information on the above Ethernet header fields, refer back to Chapter 3. The MAC criteria that are evaluated for an Ethernet frame depend on the frame's format. Table 6.3 lists Ethernet frame formats and their descriptions.

Table 6.3 Ethernet Frame Formats

Ethernet Frame Format	Description
802dot3	IEEE 802.3 Ethernet frame
802dot2-llc	IEEE 802.3 Ethernet frame with an 802.2 LLC header
802dot2-snap	IEEE 802.2 Ethernet frame with 802.2 SNAP header
ethernet-II	Ethernet type II frame

Table 6.4 shows match conditions of MAC criteria applicable for different Ethernet frame formats.

Table 6.4 MAC Criteria Applicable for Different Ethernet Frame Formats

Frame Format	Src. MAC	Dest. MAC	IEEE 802.1p	Etype Values	LLC Header SSAP/DSAP Value/Mark	SNAP-OUI Zero Non-Zero Value	SNAP-PID Value
802dot3	Yes	Yes	Yes	No	No	No	No
802dot2-llc	Yes	Yes	Yes	No	Yes	No	No
802dot2-snap	Yes	Yes	Yes	No	No†	Yes	Yes
ethernet-II	Yes	Yes	Yes	Yes	No	No	No

† When a SNAP header is present, the LLC header is always set to AA-AA.

Listing 6.21 exhibits an example for MAC criteria. If you ever configure similar criteria within your enterprise network, unlike the descriptions in the example, you may want to be more discreet!

Listing 6.21 An example for MAC criteria

```
mac-criteria
    entry 10 create
        description "high priority for traffic originating from my PC"
        match
            src-mac 00-11-43-47-8d-db
        exit
        action fc "h2" priority high
    exit
    entry 20 create
        description "high priority for traffic destined to my PC"
        match
            dst-mac 00-11-43-47-8d-db
        exit
        action fc "h2" priority high
    exit
exit
```

Classifying Traffic Based on Multiple Field Values

Listing 6.22 displays an example SAP-ingress policy, which uses different types of traffic classification rules for classifying ingress traffic. As shown in the listing, when different types of traffic classification rules are used within a SAP-ingress policy, the rules are evaluated in the order listed in Table 6.2. The table lists the actual process followed within an ALSRP. However, it would be easier to remember the order of evaluation as stated in the following note.

Note: If traffic classification of a SAP-ingress policy is based on multiple field values, the fields are considered in the following order of precedence: `ip-criteria` or `mac-criteria`, `dscp`, `ip-prec`, `dot1p`, and `default`.

While using the SAP-ingress policy in Listing 6.22, the IP criteria takes the topmost precedence. Within the IP criteria, the entries are evaluated in ascending order based on their IDs. If an incoming IP packet satisfies the `match` conditions of an IP criteria `entry`, the packet is classified as specified in the `action` statement of the entry, and evaluation of further entries for the packet is terminated. However, if the packet does not satisfy any of the IP criteria entries, then listed DSCP rules are considered for the packet. If the DSCP classification rules also fail, then the IP precedence rule is attempted. If the incoming packet does not satisfy the IP precedence rule as well, or if the datagram is a non-IP Ethernet frame, then the 802.1p classification rule is evaluated. If all these classification rules fail, then the incoming datagram is assigned the default queuing priority and mapped to the default forwarding class. The listing does not show the default priority and forwarding class because these default values are not modified in the example.

Listing 6.22 An example SAP-ingress policy using multiple-field traffic classification

```
sap-ingress 200 create
    queue 1 create
    exit
    queue 11 multipoint create
    exit
    dot1p 7 fc "nc" priority high
    dscp af21 fc "af" priority high
    dscp af23 fc "af" priority low
    prec 5 fc "ef" priority high
    ip-criteria
        entry 10 create
```

(continued)

```
                    description "high priority for ping"
                    match protocol icmp
                    exit
                    action fc "h2" priority high
                exit
                entry 20 create
                    description "medium preference for ftp"
                    match protocol tcp
                        dst-port eq 21
                    exit
                    action fc "af" priority high
                exit
                entry 30 create
                    description "best effort for UDP"
                    match protocol udp
                    exit
                    action fc "be" priority low
                exit
            exit
        exit
```

Quick Quiz

Assuming that the traffic classification statements in the SAP-ingress policy shown in Listing 6.22 are valid in classifying the anticipated application traffic at the SAP ingress among appropriate forwarding classes, can you guarantee differential service for different application traffic at the access ingress? (Clue: If the SAP-ingress policy is used, the resulting traffic behavior would be analogous to seating the business, first, and economy class passengers of an airplane together.)

Although the SAP-ingress policy may be classifying different application traffic appropriately, all the unicast traffic is queued together in queue 1 and all the multipoint traffic is queued together in queue 11. Therefore, differentiated service for different application traffic is not possible at the access ingress. The only differentiation possible is between traffic classified as high-queuing priority and that classified as low-queuing priority, and this differentiation applies only if the access ingress is congested. However, if at subsequent queuing points the different forwarding classes are queued separately, then differentiated services are possible at those points.

Quick Quiz

You are anticipating UDP-based video traffic, whose IP precedence bits are marked with decimal value 5 at an access ingress point in your network. Using the SAP-ingress policy in Listing 6.21, can you map the video traffic to forwarding class EF? (Clue: Consider the order in which different traffic classification statements are evaluated.)

Although a traffic classification statement that considers the IP precedence bits would correctly map the traffic to forwarding class EF, IP criteria entry 30 takes priority over the precedence bits-based classification and maps the traffic to BE.

To fix this, create an IP criteria entry, whose ID is less than 30, to map the video traffic to EF. Alternatively, change IP criteria entry 30 to exclude the video traffic, while mapping User Datagram Protocol (UDP) traffic to BE.

6.5 Applying the SAP-Ingress Policy

As the name indicates, the SAP-ingress policy is applied under the ingress of the SAP(s) of a service configuration. For the Layer 2 services (VLL and VPLS), SAPs are directly configured under a service configuration. Listing 6.23 shows an example of a Layer 2 (VPLS) service configuration with the SAP-ingress QoS policy 200 applied to the SAP 1/2/2.

Listing 6.23 An example Layer 2 service configuration associated with a SAP-ingress policy

```
vpls 100 customer 1 create
    stp
        shutdown
    exit
    sap 1/2/2 create
        ingress
            qos 200
        exit
    exit
    spoke-sdp 2:100 create
    exit
    no shutdown
exit
```

Applying a SAP-ingress policy under a Layer 2 service is illustrated in Figure 6.2.

Figure 6.2 Application of a SAP-ingress Policy under a VPLS Service Configuration

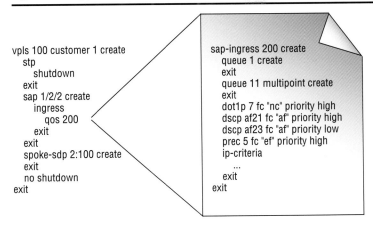

```
vpls 100 customer 1 create          sap-ingress 200 create
   stp                                  queue 1 create
      shutdown                          exit
   exit                                 queue 11 multipoint create
   sap 1/2/2 create                     exit
      ingress                           dot1p 7 fc "nc" priority high
         qos 200                        dscp af21 fc "af" priority high
      exit                              dscp af23 fc "af" priority low
   exit                                 prec 5 fc "ef" priority high
   spoke-sdp 2:100 create               ip-criteria
   exit                                    ...
   no shutdown                          exit
exit                                 exit
```

For the Layer 3 services (IES and VPRN) SAPs are configured under the interfaces, which in turn are configured under the service configuration. Listing 6.24 shows an example of a Layer 3 service (IES) configuration with the SAP-ingress QoS policy 200 applied to the SAP 1/2/3.

Listing 6.24 An example Layer 3 service configuration associated with a SAP-ingress policy

```
ies 200 customer 1 create
    interface "to-PC" create
        sap 1/2/3 create
            ingress
                qos 200
            exit
        exit
    exit
    no shutdown
exit
```

Applying a SAP-ingress policy under a Layer 3 service is illustrated in Figure 6.3.

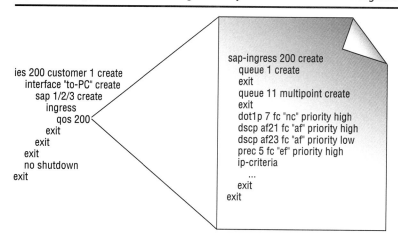

```
ies 200 customer 1 create
   interface "to-PC" create
      sap 1/2/3 create
         ingress
            qos 200
         exit
      exit
   exit
   no shutdown
exit
```

```
sap-ingress 200 create
   queue 1 create
   exit
   queue 11 multipoint create
   exit
   dot1p 7 fc "nc" priority high
   dscp af21 fc "af" priority high
   dscp af23 fc "af" priority low
   prec 5 fc "ef" priority high
   ip-criteria
      ...
   exit
exit
```

6.6 Network QoS Policy

Earlier in this chapter you learned that a SAP-ingress QoS policy has three functional segments and is applied for access (SAP) ingress. Network QoS policies,
however, have only two functional segments: (1) classifying traffic at network
ingress, and (2) marking the forwarding class and queuing priority of a datagram in
the datagram's header at network egress. Thus, the traffic classification functions of
a network port in either traffic direction are performed through the same Network
QoS policy.

The functional differences between a SAP-ingress QoS policy and a Network
policy essentially reflect the behavioral differences between a SAP and a network port
in terms of traffic handling. A SAP-ingress policy (and the corresponding SAP-egress
policy) is based on the service contract between a service provider and a customer,
whereas a Network policy is based on the business model of a service provider.

Best Practices: Using the same Network QoS policy throughout the network will
help eliminate unexpected traffic black holes in the network. It will also make network-
wide QoS troubleshooting and maintenance easier.

Use multiple Network QoS policies within a network only if the network design war-
rants it. Even under those conditions, try to minimize the number of different Network
QoS policies used.

A Network policy is created in the same way as a SAP-ingress policy. Listing 6.25 shows the outline of the default Network QoS policy. As evident from Listing 6.25, the two functional segments of a Network policy are readily distinguishable through segment headings—ingress and egress—and through their indentation. The remainder of the section first analyzes traffic marking at network egress and then traffic classification at network ingress.

Listing 6.25 Default Network QoS policy with functional segments of the policy indicated

```
A:Pod1>config>qos# network 1
*A:Pod1>config>qos>network# info detail
----------------------------------------------
            description "Default network QoS policy."
            scope template
            ingress
                default-action fc be profile out
                no ler-use-dscp
                dscp be fc be profile out
                ...
                dscp af43 fc h2 profile out
                lsp-exp 0 fc be profile out
                ...
                lsp-exp 7 fc nc profile in
            exit
            egress
                no remarking
                fc af
                    dscp-in-profile af11
                    dscp-out-profile af12
                    lsp-exp-in-profile 3
                    lsp-exp-out-profile 2
                    dot1p-in-profile 2
                    dot1p-out-profile 2
                exit
                ...
                fc nc
                    dscp-in-profile nc2
                    dscp-out-profile nc2
                    lsp-exp-in-profile 7
                    lsp-exp-out-profile 7
```

(continued)

```
                        dot1p-in-profile 7
                        dot1p-out-profile 7
                exit
        exit´
```

Traffic Marking at Network Egress

At the first network egress point of a network, the forwarding class and queuing priority of a datagram that are determined at the access ingress are typically marked on a ToS field of the datagram's encapsulation header. The marking of the datagrams removes the need for all the network ingress points along the network path to perform the extensive traffic classification task performed at access ingress. Once a datagram is marked, all the subsequent network ingress points only need to inspect one selected ToS field in the datagram's header to reclassify the datagram to their associated forwarding classes and queuing priorities.

Typically there is no need to re-mark a datagram at subsequent network egress points within a network. This is particularly true if the same Network policy is used throughout the network. Therefore, by default an ALSRP marks a datagram only at the first network egress point and does not do any re-marking at subsequent network egress points. However, if you need to mark a datagram at any subsequent network egress point, you must configure `remarking` (instead of `no remarking`) under the `egress` segment of the associated Network QoS policy.

As mentioned earlier, the ToS field used for marking at a network egress is selected, depending on the datagram's encapsulation within its network path, and in the following order of preference:

1. EXP field for MPLS encapsulated traffic
2. DSCP field in routed IP or a GRE tunneled network
3. 802.1p field for Ethernet encapsulated traffic

In order to fully differentiate both high- and low-queuing priorities for each of the eight forwarding classes the selected ToS field requires 16 different markings. The number of forwarding classes chosen for a network depends on the number of types of traffic with different service needs carried over the network. Even if all eight forwarding classes are required, typically you do not need to differentiate between high- and low-queuing priorities for all eight forwarding classes.

As discussed earlier in the chapter, because of the stringent time and throughput commitments associated with the traffic carried by the high-priority forwarding classes, all the datagrams carried by these forwarding classes (NC, H1, EF, and H2) are typically classified as high-queuing priority. For the best-effort traffic types, (L2 and BE), all the traffic can be classified as low-queuing priority. Only for assured forwarding classes (L1 and AF) do high- and low-queuing priority datagrams need to be differentiated. When all eight forwarding classes are used, and with these typical network practices applied, you need 10 different ToS field markings.

From the discussions in Chapter 3, you know that only DSCP offers 64 different markings, whereas both 802.1p and EXP only offer 8 different markings. This limited number of markings can be considered a setback of both 802.1p and EXP marking standards. Therefore, some marking compromises are required while using 802.1p or EXP fields for network QoS marking when all eight forwarding classes are used.

Table 6.5 summarizes the egress marking of the default Network QoS policy.

Table 6.5 Default Network Policy's Egress Marking Summary

ALSRP FC		Dot1P Marking (bin-dec)	Egress DSCP Marking		Egress LSP EXP Marking (bin-dec)
Label	Queuing Priority		Label	(bin–dec)	
NC	High/Low	111 – 7	NC2	111000 – 56	111 – 7
H1	High/Low	110 – 6	NC1	110000 – 48	110 – 6
EF	High/Low	101 – 5	EF	101110 – 46	101 – 5
H2	High	100 – 4	AF41	100010 – 34	100 – 4
	Low	100 – 4	AF42	100100 – 36	100 – 4
L1	High	011 – 3	AF21	010010 – 18	011 – 3
	Low	011 – 3	AF22	010100 – 20	010 – 2
AF	High	010 – 2	AF11	001010 – 10	011 – 3
	Low	010 – 2	AF12	001100 – 12	010 – 2
L2	High/Low	001 – 1	CS1	001000 - 8	001 – 1
BE	High/Low	000 – 0	BE	000000 - 0	000 – 0

When marking the DSCP field, the default Network QoS policy differentiates between high- and low-queuing priority for H2, L1, and AF forwarding classes. When marking the EXP field, the default Network QoS policy does not differentiate between L1 and AF forwarding classes, but does differentiate between high- and low-queuing priorities only within those two forwarding classes. When marking the 802.1p field, the default Network QoS policy does not differentiate between high- and low-queuing priorities within any of the forwarding classes.

The default Network QoS policy maps forwarding classes to the 802.1p and EXP markings in one of many possible ways. If the default policy doesn't suit the needs of a particular scenario, a different policy can be created. Regardless of the suitability of the default Network QoS policy, it is always preferable to use a custom created policy, as mentioned earlier.

As shown in Listing 6.25, within the `egress` segment of a Network QoS policy the traffic is marked under a forwarding class. Listing 6.26 shows the options available for marking traffic within a Network QoS policy. For configuration examples of marking traffic using the different ToS fields, see the default Network QoS policy shown in Listing 6.25.

Listing 6.26 Options for marking traffic within a Network QoS policy

```
A:Pod1>config>qos>network>egress>fc#
 [no] dot1p-in-profi* - Specify Dot1p in profile mapping
 [no] dot1p-out-prof* - Specify Dot1p out profile mapping
 [no] dscp-in-profile - Specify DSCP in profile mapping
 [no] dscp-out-profi* - Specify DSCP out profile mapping
 [no] lsp-exp-in-pro* - Specify LSP-EXP in profile mapping
 [no] lsp-exp-out-pr* - Specify LSP-EXP out profile mapping
```

For exceptions and additional features involved with network egress marking, see Chapter 7.

Traffic Mapping at Network Ingress

Compared to traffic mapping at access ingress, traffic mapping at network ingress is simple and straightforward. The order of precedence of the different traffic classification criteria at network ingress is: EXP, DSCP, and 802.1p. If none of the explicit mappings are matched, the datagram is given the default mapping.

Table 6.6 summarizes the DSCP-based ingress traffic classification in the default Network QoS policy. The first entry is the default mapping, which is used for all DSCP values for which there is no explicit forwarding class mapping. There is no explicit ingress dot1p to FC mapping in the default Network QoS policy. This means that if a datagram arrives with a particular dot1p marking, it will map to the default forwarding class (assuming that there is no DSCP or EXP marking).

Table 6.6 Summary of DSCP-Based Ingress Traffic Classification in the Default Network QoS Policy

Ingress DSCP		Traffic Classification	
Label	Value	FC	Queuing Priority
Default		BE	Low
AF11	001010 – 10	AF	High
AF12	001100 – 12	AF	Low
AF13	001110 – 14	AF	Low
AF21	010010 – 18	L1	High
AF22	010100 – 20	L1	Low
AF23	010110 – 22	L1	Low
AF31	011010 – 26	L1	High
AF32	011100 – 28	L1	Low
AF33	011110 – 30	L1	Low
AF41	100010 – 34	H2	High
AF42	100100 – 36	H2	Low
AF43	100110 – 38	H2	Low
EF	101110 – 46	EF	High
NC1	110000 – 48	H1	High
NC2	111000 – 56	NC	High

Table 6.7 summarizes the EXP-based ingress traffic classification in the default Network QoS policy.

Table 6.7 Summary of EXP-Based Ingress Traffic Classification in the Default Network QoS Policy

Ingress LSP EXP Value	Traffic Classification	
	FC	Queuing Priority
0	BE	Low
1	L2	High
2	AF	Low
3	AF	High
4	H2	High
5	EF	High
6	H1	High
7	NC	High

Listing 6.27 shows command options for configuring the default forwarding class and queuing priority within a Network QoS policy.

Listing 6.27 Options for configuring the default traffic classification in a Network policy

```
A:Pod1>config>qos>network>ingress# default-action
  - default-action fc {fc-name} profile {in|out}

<fc-name>          : be|l2|af|l1|h2|ef|h1|nc
<in|out>           : keywords - specify type of marking to be done
```

Listing 6.28 provides command options for mapping Ethernet frames to a forwarding class and to a queuing priority using 802.1p bits.

Listing 6.28 Options for configuring 802.1p-based traffic classification in a Network policy

```
A:Pod1>config>qos>network>ingress# dot1p
  - dot1p <dot1p-priority> fc {fc-name} profile {in|out}
  -  no dot1p

<dot1p-priority>   : [0..7]
<fc-name>          : be|l2|af|l1|h2|ef|h1|nc
<in|out>           : keywords - specify type of marking to be done
```

Listing 6.29 shows command options for mapping IP packets to a forwarding class and to a queuing priority using DSCP bits.

Listing 6.29 Options for configuring the DSCP-based traffic classification in a Network policy

```
A:Pod1>config>qos>network>ingress# dscp
  - dscp <dscp-name> fc {fc-name} profile {in|out}
  -  no dscp

 <dscp-name>            : be|cp1|cp2|cp3|cp4|cp5|cp6|cp7|cs1|cp9|af11|c
                         p11|af12|cp13|af13|cp15|cs2|cp17|af21|cp19|af
                         22|cp21|af23|cp23|cs3|cp25|af31|cp27|af32|cp2
                         9|af33|cp31|cs4|cp33|af41|cp35|af42|cp37|af43
                         |cp39|cs5|cp41|cp42|cp43|cp44|cp45|ef|cp47|nc
                         1|cp49|cp50|cp51|cp52|cp53|cp54|cp55|nc2|cp57
                         |cp58|cp59|cp60|cp61|cp62|cp63
 <fc-name>              : be|l2|af|l1|h2|ef|h1|nc
 <in|out>               : keywords - specify type of marking to be done
```

Best Practices: DSCP markings that differ only in terms of drop probability (for example, AF11, AF12, and AF13) should all be mapped to the same forwarding class to avoid reordering of datagrams belonging to an application. Only the queuing priority can be changed between these DSCP markings.

This best practice applies to both Network policy and SAP-ingress policy configuration.

Listing 6.30 provides command options for mapping MPLS traffic to a forwarding class and to a queuing priority using EXP bits.

Listing 6.30 Options for configuring the EXP-based traffic classification in a Network policy

```
A:Pod1>config>qos>network>ingress# lsp-exp
  - lsp-exp <lsp-exp-value> fc {fc-name} profile {in|out}
  - no lsp-exp

 <lsp-exp-value>        : [0..7]
 <fc-name>              : be|l2|af|l1|h2|ef|h1|nc
 <in|out>               : keywords - specify type of marking to be done
```

6.7 Applying Network QoS Policy

Network QoS policy is applied under the `interface`(s) of the `router` configuration of a node. Listing 6.31 shows an example `interface` configuration associated with a Network QoS policy.

Listing 6.31 An example interface configuration associated with a Network QoS policy

```
A:Pod1>config>router# info

#----------------------------------------------------
echo "IP Configuration"
#----------------------------------------------------
        interface "system"
            address 10.10.10.1/32
        exit
        interface "to-Pod2"
            address 10.10.1.2/24
            port 1/1/1
            qos 110
        exit
#----------------------------------------------------
```

Applying a Network policy under an `interface` configuration is illustrated in Figure 6.4.

Figure 6.4 Application of a Network QoS Policy under an Interface Configuration

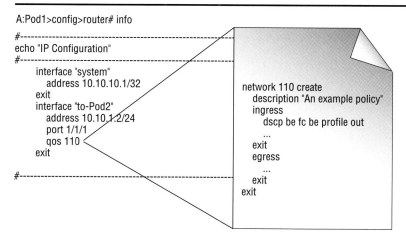

6.8 SAP-Egress Policy and Traffic Marking at Access Egress

A SAP-egress policy is created in a manner similar to a SAP-ingress or a Network QoS policy. Listing 6.32 shows the default SAP-egress policy. A SAP-egress policy has two functional segments: mapping forwarding classes to queues, and queue declarations.

Quick Quiz

Can you guess why there are no forwarding class declarations or mapping of any forwarding class as a part of the default SAP-egress policy?

If you guessed that by default all the forwarding classes of a SAP-egress policy are mapped to queue 1, you are correct.

Listing 6.32 Default SAP-egress QoS policy with functional segments of the policy

```
A:Pod1>config>qos>sap-egress# info detail
---------------------------------------------
        description "Default SAP egress QoS policy."
        scope template
        queue 1 auto-expedite create
            no parent
            adaptation-rule pir closest cir closest
            rate max cir 0
            cbs default
            mbs default
            high-prio-only default
        exit
---------------------------------------------
```

In a SAP-egress policy, traffic marking is configured as a part of the forwarding class declaration. By default, no traffic is marked at access egress. Listing 6.33 shows the command options for marking an 802.1p field under a forwarding class in a SAP-egress policy.

Listing 6.33 Options for marking the 802.1p field under a forwarding class in a SAP-egress policy

```
A:Pod1>config>qos>sap-egress>fc# dot1p
  - dot1p <dot1p-value>
  - no dot1p

 <dot1p-value>           : [0..7]
```

Listing 6.34 exhibits an example SAP-egress policy that marks the 802.1p field of two different forwarding classes.

Listing 6.34 An example of a SAP-egress policy illustrating 802.1p marking

```
        sap-egress 200 create
            description "An example for illustrating 802.1p marking"
            queue 1 create
            exit
            fc af create
                dot1p 2
            exit
            fc ef create
                dot1p 5
            exit
        exit
```

6.9 Applying a SAP-Egress Policy

A SAP-egress policy is applied under the **egress** segment of the SAP(s) of a service configuration. For the Layer 2 services (VLL and VPLS), SAP is directly configured under the service configuration. Listing 6.35 shows an example of a Layer 2 (VPLS) service configuration with the SAP-egress QoS policy 200 applied to the SAP 1/2/2.

Listing 6.35 An example Layer 2 service configuration associated with a SAP-egress policy

```
vpls 100 customer 1 create
    stp
        shutdown
    exit
    sap 1/2/2 create
        ingress
            qos 200
        exit
        egress
            qos 200
        exit
    exit
    spoke-sdp 2:100 create
    exit
    no shutdown
exit
```

Applying a SAP-egress policy under a Layer 2 service is illustrated in Figure 6.5.

Figure 6.5 Application of a SAP-Egress Policy under a VPLS Service Configuration

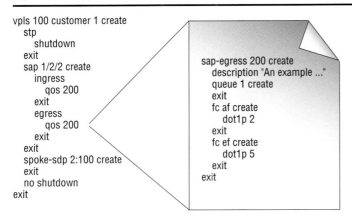

```
vpls 100 customer 1 create
    stp
        shutdown
    exit
    sap 1/2/2 create
        ingress
            qos 200
        exit
        egress
            qos 200
        exit
    exit
    spoke-sdp 2:100 create
    exit
    no shutdown
exit
```

```
sap-egress 200 create
    description "An example ..."
    queue 1 create
    exit
    fc af create
        dot1p 2
    exit
    fc ef create
        dot1p 5
    exit
exit
```

For Layer 3 services (IES and VPRN), SAP is configured under an `interface`, which in turn is configured under the service configuration. Listing 6.36 shows an example of a Layer 3 (IES) service configuration with the SAP-egress QoS policy 200 applied to the SAP 1/2/3.

Listing 6.36 An example Layer 3 service configuration associated with a SAP-egress policy

```
ies 200 customer 1 create
    interface "to-PC" create
        sap 1/2/3 create
            ingress
                qos 200
            exit
            egress
                qos 200
            exit
        exit
    exit
    no shutdown
exit
```

Applying a SAP-egress policy under a Layer 3 service is illustrated in Figure 6.6.

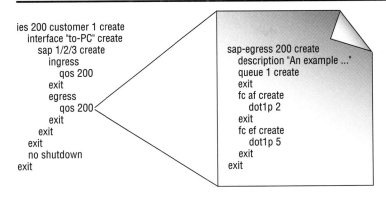

```
ies 200 customer 1 create
    interface "to-PC" create
        sap 1/2/3 create
            ingress
                qos 200
            exit
            egress
                qos 200
            exit
        exit
    exit
    no shutdown
exit
```

```
sap-egress 200 create
    description "An example ..."
    queue 1 create
    exit
    fc af create
        dot1p 2
    exit
    fc ef create
        dot1p 5
    exit
exit
```

6.10 Verification Commands for QoS Policy Application

So far in this chapter you have learned about the need for traffic classification at different network points and how to do the traffic classification in an ALSRP network using different QoS policies. In this section, you'll learn some of the ALSRP verification commands related to those topics.

Listing 6.37 provides the options available under **show qos**. These commands are helpful in verifying different aspects of the QoS policies and other QoS related information. You are already familiar with one of these commands: **show qos dscp-table**.

Listing 6.37 show qos commands of ALSRP

```
A:Pod1>show>qos#
     atm-td-profile  - Display ATM traffic descriptor profile information
     dscp-table      - Lookup DSCP Name-value mappings
     network         - Display Network policy information
     network-queue   - Display Network policy information
     sap-egress      - Display Sap Egress policy information
     sap-ingress     - Display Sap ingress policy information
     scheduler-hier* + Display Scheduler hierarchy information
     scheduler-name  - Display Scheduler policies which have this scheduler
     scheduler-poli* - Display Scheduler policy information
     scheduler-stats + Display Scheduler statistics information
     shared-queue    - Display Shared policy information
     slope-policy    - Display Slope policy information
```

This section leads you through the **show qos** commands associated with SAP-ingress, SAP-egress, and Network QoS policies. The **show qos** command syntax for these three policies are:

```
sap-ingress [<policy-id>] [association|match-criteria|detail]
sap-egress [<policy-id>] [association|detail]
network [<policy-id>] [detail]
```

As mentioned in the introduction, in the command syntax, square brackets indicate optional parameters of a command, angle brackets indicate that a substitution is required for the placeholder, and a pipe (|) indicates an either-or relationship between the parameters on either side of the pipe.

When a **policy-id** is specified in the commands, information regarding the specified policy is displayed. When no **policy-id** is specified in the commands, information regarding all the configured policies of the given type is displayed.

Without any optional parameters these commands (for example, **show qos sap-egress**) list the identifiers of all the configured policies along with some minimal details (scope and description in the case of access policies).

When multiple policies of a given type (SAP-ingress or SAP-egress) are applied for hundreds of SAPs, the **association** option is useful to verify the associated policy of each SAP. Listing 6.38 shows the output of the **show qos sap-ingress association** command.

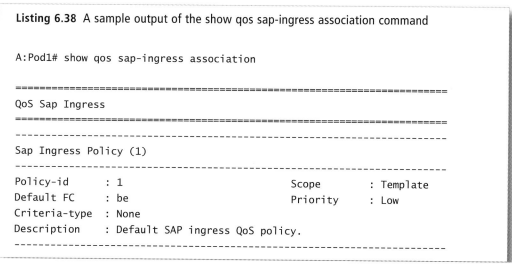

Listing 6.38 A sample output of the show qos sap-ingress association command

```
A:Pod1# show qos sap-ingress association

===========================================================================
QoS Sap Ingress
===========================================================================
---------------------------------------------------------------------------
Sap Ingress Policy (1)
---------------------------------------------------------------------------
Policy-id      : 1                        Scope       : Template
Default FC     : be                       Priority    : Low
Criteria-type  : None
Description    : Default SAP ingress QoS policy.
---------------------------------------------------------------------------
```

(continued)

```
Associations
-----------------------------------------------------------------------
No Associations Found.


-----------------------------------------------------------------------
Sap Ingress Policy (201)
-----------------------------------------------------------------------
Policy-id     : 201                        Scope      : Template
Default FC    : be                         Priority   : Low
Criteria-type : IP
-----------------------------------------------------------------------
Associations
-----------------------------------------------------------------------
Service-Id    : 100 (VPLS)                 Customer-Id  : 1
  - SAP : 1/2/2
Service-Id    : 200 (IES)                  Customer-Id  : 1
  - SAP : 1/2/3
=======================================================================
```

Adding the `detail` option to any of the `show qos` commands lists all the details about a policy, including its associations.

Summary

The chapter began by outlining how traffic is classified and marked at the four different types of networking points in an ALSRP network. At the access ingress, ALSRP can classify traffic not only based on standard ToS field values, but also based on the values of other header parameters such as port numbers, or the IP or Ethernet address of the source or destination. At the first network egress point, the QoS requirement of a datagram determined at access ingress is marked in the ToS field of the datagram's tunnel header. The marking of the datagrams removes the need for all the network ingress points along the network path to perform the extensive traffic classification task carried out at access ingress. Once a datagram is marked, all the subsequent network ingress points only need to inspect one selected ToS field in the datagram's header to reclassify the datagrams to their associated forwarding classes and queuing priorities. Typically, QoS markings used over a datagram within a service provider network are transparent to the downstream network. However, if a downstream network requests that the QoS markings of a datagram be visible, ALSRP allows marking the 802.1p ToS field of the datagram at access egress, provided that the datagram has an Ethernet encapsulation.

ALSRP can classify traffic into eight different forwarding classes. Traffic within each forwarding class can be further classified into high- and low-queuing priorities. When a queuing point is congested, the queuing priority of a datagram plays an important role in determining if the datagram gets queued or dropped. On the other hand, the priority with which a datagram is scheduled out of a queue at a queuing point is determined by its forwarding class.

The chapter also covered SAP-ingress, Network, and SAP-egress QoS policies, their default configurations, and how to apply these policies to the appropriate node entities. A SAP-ingress policy associated with a service access point specifies how to classify incoming traffic at the SAP. A Network QoS policy associated with a network interface is used both to classify traffic arriving at the network ingress and to mark traffic leaving through the network egress. Marking traffic at the first network egress point is important, but at subsequent network egress points it is optional and can be redundant. A SAP-egress policy associated with a service access point can be used to mark the 802.1p field of Ethernet frames leaving the SAP.

Advanced Traffic Classification

7

To meet traffic classification requirements in a wide range of network application scenarios, ALSRP offers a number of advanced traffic classification features.

Chapter Objectives

- To discuss access ingress subclasses

- To explain color-aware profiling and access ingress marking

- To describe trust state of interface and its impact on network egress marking

- To explore classifying and marking QinQ encapsulated Ethernet frames

- To discuss the tunnel termination QoS override

In the previous chapter, you learned how traffic is typically classified at access ingress and how the classification is maintained throughout an ALSRP network. This chapter discusses the special traffic classification needs of certain types of traffic and how to handle those requirements.

The chapter presents the need for color-aware traffic profiling and how to implement it in an ALSRP access node. The chapter then explains why and how to implement access ingress QoS marking of Internet Protocol (IP) packets. It moves on to address the trust nature of different types of interfaces and the impact of this trust nature over network egress marking. Next, it covers choosing the appropriate 802.1p field for traffic classification and marking in a frame with two or more IEEE 802.1Q VLAN (virtual local area network) tags. Finally, the chapter discusses tunnel termination QoS override.

In ALSRP, color-aware traffic profiling and access ingress marking are implemented using a common construct in a SAP-ingress policy called *forwarding subclasses*. Therefore, this chapter begins with a discussion of forwarding subclasses.

7.1 Forwarding Subclasses

In addition to its eight forwarding classes, ALSRP allows for the creation of up to 56 subclasses within a SAP-ingress QoS policy. For example, it is possible for one forwarding class to have 56 subclasses defined, or for each of the eight forwarding classes to have seven subclasses defined, or for any combination as long as the total number of subclasses defined does not exceed 56. A subclass association is relevant only within the context of access ingress QoS processing.

Each subclass retains the node behavior that is defined for the parent forwarding class and provides expanded ingress QoS classification actions. Subclasses are always associated with their parent class queues to prevent out-of-sequence forwarding. Any attempt to associate a queue within a subclass will fail.

Subclasses can be used for the following purposes:

- Color-aware profiling or explicit profiling of datagrams
- Access ingress marking of IP packets

Subclasses and their parent class can differ in terms of how they mark the profile of datagrams and how they mark the Type of Service (ToS) field of IP packets that flows through them.

The creation of a forwarding subclass is similar to the creation of a forwarding class within a SAP-ingress policy. In the previous chapter, we deferred full-fledged discussion on mapping forwarding classes to queues to Chapter 8. However, to help you better understand subclasses, here's a quick preview on creating forwarding classes and subclasses in a SAP-ingress policy.

Listing 7.1 shows the options for creating a forwarding class or a subclass within a SAP-ingress policy.

Listing 7.1 Options for creating a forwarding class/subclass within a SAP-ingress policy

```
A:Pod1>config>qos>sap-ingress# fc
  - fc <fc-name> [create]
  - no fc <fc-name>

 <fc>                   : <class>[.<sub-class>]
                         class     - be|l2|af|l1|h2|ef|h1|nc
                         sub-class - [29 chars max]
 <create>               : keyword - mandatory while creating an entry.
```

A forwarding class name must be the abbreviation of one of the eight ALSRP forwarding classes. A forwarding subclass name has two parts, joined by a dot. The first part must be the abbreviation of one of the eight ALSRP forwarding classes. The second part can be any string of 29 characters or less. The first part implicitly associates the subclass with the appropriate forwarding class.

Listing 7.2 shows a part of an example SAP-ingress policy in which a forwarding class and four forwarding subclasses are created. The subclass names in the listing show different character types that can be used for the second part of a subclass name. These example names do not provide any meaningful insight to the purpose of the subclasses.

Listing 7.2 Creating a forwarding class and subclasses

```
        fc "l1" create
        exit
        fc "l1.2$b" create
        exit
        fc "l1.234" create
        exit
        fc "l1.Ram" create
        exit
        fc "l1.Balakrishnan" create
        exit
```

The `no fc <fc-name.sub-class-name>` command removes a subclass from the SAP-ingress QoS policy. To successfully remove a subclass, all associations with the subclass in the classification commands within the policy must first be removed or assigned to another forwarding class or subclass. The optional `force` keyword on the classification commands automatically removes the subclass associations by reassigning the associations to the parent forwarding class of the subclass.

Best Practices: The second part of a subclass name can be any string with a maximum of 29 characters. However, as a best practice a subclass name should be such that it readily identifies the purpose of the subclass, and thus helps during troubleshooting and maintenance.

The subclass names Ram and Balakrishnan in the preceding example may please someone named Ram Balakrishnan. However, they are meaningless as far as the node configuration is concerned and hence useless when it comes to the maintenance or troubleshooting of the configuration.

Later in the chapter, examples of subclasses with meaningful names are shown.

7.2 Color-Aware Profiling

Typically, the profile state of all datagrams through the access ingress is determined as datagrams are scheduled out of the access ingress. This is referred to as *implicit profiling*. The profile state of a datagram determined at the access ingress is maintained throughout the network until the datagram leaves the provider network. The profile state of a datagram determines the queuing priority of the datagram at all the subsequent queuing points along its path that are experiencing congestion.

However, what if the end (virtual private network [VPN]) customer device or a node prior to the access ingress has already marked some of the datagrams as low-queuing priority? In such scenarios, it would not be wise to ignore those markings and ultimately give preference to low-queuing priority datagrams by dropping datagrams that are originally marked as high-queuing priority.

The solution to this problem is referred to as *color-aware profiling* or *explicit profiling*. ALSRP supports color-aware profiling. Within a SAP-ingress policy multiple subclasses can be created for a forwarding class and the subclasses can be used for the explicit profiling of datagrams flowing through them.

Color-aware profiling adds the ability to selectively treat packets received on a SAP as in-profile or out-of-profile regardless of the queue forwarding rate. This allows a customer or access device to color a packet out-of-profile with the intention of preserving in-profile bandwidth for higher priority packets.

Configuring Color-Aware Profiling

Listing 7.3 shows the configuration options within a forwarding class or a subclass of a SAP-ingress policy. For configuring color-aware profiling of datagrams we are particularly interested in the `profile` statement in Listing 7.3.

Listing 7.3 Configuration options within a forwarding class/subclass of a SAP-ingress policy

```
A:Pod1>config>qos>sap-ingress>fc#
 [no] broadcast-queue - Specify the broadcast-queue
 [no] in-remark       - Specify the in-profile remarking
 [no] multicast-queue - Specify the multicast-queue
 [no] out-remark      - Specify the out-profile remarking
 [no] profile         - Specify the profile to be assigned
 [no] queue           - Specify the unicast-queue
 [no] unknown-queue   - Specify the unknown-queue
```

The profile of a forwarding class or subclass can be explicitly stated as `in` or `out`. By stating that the profile of a forwarding class or subclass is in-profile, all the datagrams that flow through the class or subclass are marked as such. Similarly, by stating that the profile of a forwarding class or subclass is out-of-profile, all the datagrams that flow through the class or subclass are marked as out-of-profile. All the datagrams that are not explicitly profiled get temporarily treated as high-queuing priority for access ingress queuing and are profiled implicitly when scheduled out of the access ingress.

For the explicit profile statement of a forwarding class or subclass to be effective, the associated queue of the forwarding class must be in `profile` mode. Configuring queues and queue modes is discussed in Chapter 8. The default mode of a queue is `priority` mode and not `profile` mode. The two queue modes of access ingress queues are compared in Table 8-2.

Note: The default queues of a SAP-ingress policy (queue 1 for unicast packets and queue 11 for multicast packets) are configured as `priority` mode and cannot be changed.

Listing 7.4 illustrates a part of an example SAP-ingress policy, in which sub-classes are explicitly profiled.

Listing 7.4 Explicit profiling of forwarding class/subclass

```
...
fc "af" create
...
exit
fc "af.in" create
    profile in
exit
fc "af.out" create
    profile out
exit
dscp af31 fc "af.in"
dscp af33 fc "af.out"
```

7.3 Honoring the Three Drop Precedence of Assured Forwarding PHB

Listing 7.5 illustrates an example SAP-ingress QoS policy that shows how to honor all three drop precedences of AF PHB defined in RFC2597, which was presented in Chapter 3. The subclasses shown in this listing also follow the best practice on naming subclasses meaningfully.

Listing 7.5 Example SAP-ingress policy honoring AF PHB drop precedences

```
sap-ingress 613 create
    queue 1 create
    exit
    queue 3 profile-mode create
        rate max cir 100
    exit
    queue 11 multipoint create
    exit
    fc "af" create
        queue 3
    exit
```

(continued)

```
        fc "af.red" create
            profile out
        exit
        fc "af.green" create
            profile in
        exit
        fc "af.yellow" create
        exit
        dscp af31 fc "af.green"
        dscp af32 fc "af.yellow"
        dscp af33 fc "af.red"
    exit
```

The policy maps af31 (low drop) to the af.green subclass, af32 (medium drop) to the af.yellow subclass, and af33 (high drop) to the af.red subclass. The subclass af.green is explicitly profiled as in. Similarly, the subclass af.red is explicitly profiled as out, and the subclass af.yellow is not explicitly profiled. Therefore, all the datagrams forwarded through the af.yellow subclass will be implicitly profiled when they are scheduled out of their access ingress queue.

Because queue 3 is in profile-mode, all packets marked as af31 will be counted against the CIR of the queue. All the packets marked as af33 will be counted against the PIR (above CIR and less than PIR) forwarding rate of the queue. After these, whatever excess CIR of queue is available will be used for packets marked af32, and accordingly some of these packets will be marked as in-profile and others as out-of-profile.

7.4 Access Ingress Marking of IP Packets

The previous chapter discussed the need for traffic classification at access ingress and traffic marking at the first network egress. While this section may look like a repetition of that topic, it's not. ALSRP does permit both the classification of datagrams and the traffic marking of IP packets at the access ingress.

The Need for Access Ingress Packet Marking

If datagrams are going to be marked by default at the first network egress point, why do you need to mark packets at the access ingress?

Normally, original packets are transmitted untouched within a carrier network, and only the ToS field of the encapsulation added to packets within the carrier network is marked. Even in the case of a network core where packets are routed, the packets from VPN customers are transmitted untouched, as we will discuss later in the chapter.

Therefore, if marking the ToS fields of the original IP packet is a requirement within a carrier network, the options for marking them are available at access ingress.

The ToS fields (either the six differentiated service code point bits or the three precedence bits) of IP packets or IP routed frames can be marked at access ingress depending on the basis of the forwarding class or subclass. Because the ingress marking is for IP packets, the function is enforced only for Layer 3 services (IES and VPRN) and is ignored for Layer 2 services (VLL and VPLS).

Configuring Access Ingress Marking

Listing 7.3 showed the configuration options within a forwarding class or a subclass of a SAP-ingress policy. Within a forwarding class or subclass, `in-remark` and `out-remark` commands are used to mark IP packets. The commands impact packets regardless of whether their profile state is explicitly or implicitly determined.

Listing 7.6 shows an example SAP-ingress policy in which HTTP packets are marked at access ingress. In the example, the DSCP field of both in-profile and out-of-profile packets flowing through L2 forwarding class are respectively marked AF41 and AF43. However, for the packets flowing through the `l2.out` subclass, you will notice that only the DSCP field of out-of-profile packets is marked as AF43. Is this really a valid configuration?

Yes, the configuration is valid. The `l2.out` subclass is explicitly set to be out-of-profile. Therefore, it is of no use to specify the ToS marking for in-profile packets within the subclass. As there is no explicit profiling of datagrams flowing through the L2 forwarding class, the profile state of datagrams flowing through the L2 forwarding class will be implicitly determined when scheduled out of queue 2, depending on the profile state of the queue. Therefore, in this case, markings for both in-profile and out-of-profile packets have to be specified.

The IP ToS fields that are marked explicitly at the access ingress are not affected by any egress marking decision of the node. See the following section for information about egress marking.

Listing 7.6 Example SAP-ingress policy for highlighting access ingress marking

```
sap-ingress 425 create
    queue 1 create
    exit
    queue 2 profile-mode create
        rate max cir 1024
    exit
    queue 11 multipoint create
    exit
    fc "12" create
        queue 2
        in-remark dscp af41
        out-remark dscp af43
    exit
    fc "12.out" create
        out-remark dscp af43
        profile out
    exit
    ip-criteria
        entry 10 create
            description "Mapping UDP http traffic"
            match protocol udp
                dst-port eq 80
            exit
            action fc "12.out"
        exit
        entry 20 create
            description "Mapping TCP http traffic"
            match protocol tcp
                dst-port eq 80
            exit
            action fc "12" priority high
        exit
    exit
exit
```

7.5 The Trust Nature of Interfaces and Network Egress Marking

In the previous chapter, you learned about the need for marking traffic at its first network egress point, and learned that by default, traffic is not re-marked at subsequent network egress points. In order to re-mark traffic at a subsequent network egress point, the re-marking option within the associated Network policy of the egress point has to be enabled.

You also learned that, if required, the ToS field of original IP packets belonging to Layer 3 services can be marked at access ingress.

Unless requested specifically, it is not desirable to alter the ToS markings of original packets from customers receiving VPN services from the provider. In networks using Multi Protocol Label Switching (MPLS) or IP Generic Routing Encapsulation (GRE) tunnels within the core, the QoS markings at network egress points are made in tunnel encapsulation without affecting the original packets from the VPN customers.

However, what about the case of VPRN services over a network using routed IP core? In this scenario, to avoid altering the ToS marking on the original IP packets, ALSRP relies on the trust nature of interfaces.

Table 7.1 lists the different interface types and their default trust nature. As listed in the table, Layer 2 (VLL and VPLS) and IES interfaces are untrusted, whereas VPRN and network interfaces are trusted. By default, because VPRN interfaces are trusted the original packets belonging to the service are left unmarked even at the first network ingress point.

The trust nature of all interfaces, with the exception of Layer 2 interfaces, can be changed. Listings 7.7 through 7.9 show how to configure the trust state of different types of interfaces.

Table 7.1 Interface Types and Their Default Trust Nature

Interface Type	Trust State
IES	Untrusted
VLL	Untrusted and un-configurable
VPLS	Untrusted and un-configurable
VPRN	Trusted
Network	Trusted

Listing 7.7 Command options to configure the trust nature of an IES interface

```
A:Pod1>config>service>ies>if# tos-marking-state
  - no tos-marking-state
  - tos-marking-state {trusted|untrusted}

 <trusted|untrusted>  : keywords
```

Listing 7.8 Command options to configure the trust nature of a VPRN interface

```
A:Pod1>config>service>vprn>if$ tos-marking-state
  - no tos-marking-state
  - tos-marking-state {trusted|untrusted}

 <trusted|untrusted>  : keywords
```

Listing 7.9 Command options to configure the trust nature of a network interface

```
A:Pod1>config>router>if# tos-marking-state
  - no tos-marking-state
  - tos-marking-state {trusted|untrusted}

 <trusted|untrusted>  : keywords
```

In summary, the parameters that affect the decision to mark a datagram or not at a network egress are:

- The trust nature and the type of the interface from which the datagram is arriving
- The status of the re-marking option within the associated Network policy
- Access ingress marking

The field in which the QoS marking is made at a network egress depends on whether the network is using IP routing, MPLS, or GRE tunneling.

Table 7.2 summarizes the marking or re-marking rules adhered to at network egress points.

Table 7.2 Marking/Re-Marking Rules Adhered to at Network Egress Points

Ingress Interface Type	Ingress Interface Trust State	Premarking at Access Ingress	Result
VLL/VPLS SAP	Always untrusted	N/A	Regardless of re-marking, the parameter of the associated Network QoS policy tunnel header of the Layer 2 datagrams will always be marked at the first network egress point as specified in the Network policy: the experimental bits (EXP) field in the case of the MPLS core or the DSCP field in the case of GRE. The ToS field of the original IP headers, if any, is left untouched.
IES SAP	Untrusted (default)	None	Regardless of the re-marking parameter of the associated Network QoS policy, the ToS field of the (original) IP header will be marked at the first network egress point as specified in the Network policy. Any user-specified DSCP/IP precedence value is overwritten.
IES SAP	Trusted	None	With no re-marking, the IP ToS field is left untouched at the first network egress point. With re-marking, any user-specified DSCP/IP precedence value is overwritten at the first network egress point.
IES SAP	Trusted or untrusted	Yes	A packet belonging to an IES service marked at access ingress is left untouched at the first network ingress, regardless of the re-marking parameter of the associated Network QoS policy and the trust state of the ingress interface.
VPRN SAP	Trusted (default)	None	The original IP ToS field is left untouched at the first network egress point, irrespective of the re-marking parameter of the associated Network QoS policy. The tunnel header is marked at the first network ingress: the EXP field in the case of the MPLS core or the DSCP field in the case of GRE.
VPRN SAP	Untrusted	None	Regardless of the re-marking parameter of the associated Network QoS policy the packet will be re-marked at the first network egress point: the EXP field in the case of the MPLS core, the DSCP field in the case of GRE, or the DSCP field of the original IP header in the case of the routed network.

(continued)

Table 7.2 Marking/Re-Marking Rules Adhered to at Network Egress Points (*continued*)

Ingress Interface Type	Ingress Interface Trust State	Premarking at Access Ingress	Result
VPRN SAP	Trusted or untrusted	Yes	A packet belonging to a VPRN service marked at access ingress is left untouched at the first network ingress, irrespective of the re-marking parameter of the associated Network QoS policy and the trust state of the ingress interface.
			The tunnel header is marked at the first network ingress: the EXP field in the case of the MPLS core or the DSCP field in the case of GRE.
Network port	Trusted (default)	N/A	Traffic is not re-marked if it is configured so that there is no re-marking in the associated Network policy. Otherwise:
			The EXP/DSCP value of the tunnel header is re-marked as specified in the associated Network policy in the case of traffic belonging to VLL, VPLS, or VPRN services.
			The DSCP field of the original IP header of the packet belonging to IES services is re-marked.
Network port	Untrusted	N/A	Regardless of the re-marking parameter of the associated Network QoS policy, the datagram will be re-marked:
			The EXP/DSCP value of the tunnel header is re-marked as specified in the associated Network policy in the case of traffic belonging to VLL, VPLS, or VPRN services.
			The DSCP field of the original IP header of the packet belonging to IES services is re-marked.

7.6 Selecting a ToS Field in QinQ Encapsulated Frames

Chapter 3 discussed the different types of Ethernet frame encapsulation types and 802.1Q VLAN tagging. In this section, you'll learn about the "double-tagging" of Ethernet frames and how to choose a ToS field within the double-tags of a frame.

Just as IEEE 802.1Q tagging is referred to as *Q tagging*, IEEE 802.1Q-in-Q tagging is commonly referred to as *QinQ tagging*. The IEEE 802.1 Q-in-Q standard allows for the addition of an extra 802.1Q VLAN tag to a frame that is already Q-tagged, resulting in the double-tagging of frames.

Figure 7.1 shows how an Ethernet frame is tagged and double-tagged with 802.1Q tags.

Figure 7.1 The Tagging and Double-Tagging of Ethernet Frames

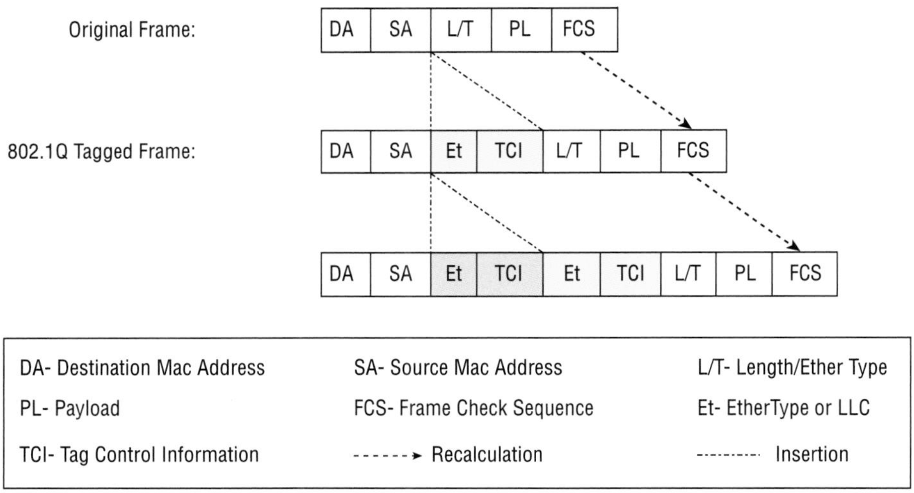

QinQ tagging can be used for several reasons:
- To increase VLAN ID (VID) space
- To preserve a customer's VLAN tags and associated ToS markings while transporting the traffic through a carrier network
- To allow service providers to transport multiple customer traffic that is VLAN-tagged over the same set of 802.1Q tunnels

Depending on the application, QinQ-tagged frames must be classified based on either the bottom or top Q tag. At access ingress, traffic classification can be based on either of the VLAN tag ToS markings. Similarly at access egress, ALSRP allows you to mark both the 802.1p fields used for QinQ tagging or to preserve the bottom Q tag.

> **Note:** The two Q tags of double-tagged frames are referred to differently in the networking industry. The first tag added to the frame is referred to as the customer, inner or bottom tag. The second tag added to the frame is referred to as the service, outer or top tag.
>
> It is easier to recognize these names when viewed from a node's perspective. A frame shown in Figure 7.1 is received within a node starting with the destination media access control (MAC) address and ending with the frame check sequence. The service, outer or the top tag is the one processed first when the frame is received by a node.

Port and SAP Configuration for 802.1Q Tagging

In ALSRP an Ethernet access port can be associated with one of the following encapsulation types in order to distinguish the services on the port or channel:

- null (no 802.1Q) tagging (this is the default)
- dot1q (single 802.1Q) tagging
- QinQ (double 802.1Q) tagging

Encapsulation types are not required for network ports. Listing 7.10 shows how to configure the encapsulation type of an Ethernet port.

Listing 7.10 Options for configuring the 802.1Q tagging type of an ethernet port

```
A:Pod1>config>port>ethernet# encap-type
  - encap-type {dot1q|null|qinq}
  - no encap-type

 <dot1q|null|qinq>    : keywords
```

Listing 7.11 exhibits two example Ethernet access port configurations. Port 1/2/1 is configured with single 802.1Q tagging, and port 1/2/2 is configured with double 802.1Q tagging.

Listing 7.11 Example ethernet port configurations with 802.1Q tagging associations

```
...
    port 1/2/1
        ethernet
            mode access
            encap-type dot1q
        exit
        no shutdown
    exit
    port 1/2/2
        ethernet
            mode access
            encap-type qinq
        exit
        no shutdown
    exit
...
```

When a port is associated with a single or double 802.1Q tagging, the corresponding SAPs can be configured to carry frames with specific VLAN tag identifiers. Listing 7.12 displays an example of a VPLS configuration with 802.1Q-associated SAPs.

Listing 7.12 Example VPLS configuration with 802.1Q associated SAPs

```
        vpls 100 customer 1 create
            stp
                shutdown
            exit
            sap 1/2/1:4000 create
            exit
            sap 1/2/1:* create
            exit
            sap 1/2/2:10.11 create
            exit
            sap 1/2/2:10.* create
            exit
            spoke-sdp 2:100 create
            exit
            no shutdown
        exit
```

In the VPLS example, SAP 1/2/1:4000 is configured to carry Q-tagged frames with VLAN ID (VID) 4000. SAP 1/2/1:* is configured to carry Q-tagged frames with any VID, except for VID 4000. SAP 1/2/2:10.11 is configured to carry QinQ frames with the top Q tag VID 10 and bottom Q tag VID 11. SAP 1/2/2:10.* is configured to carry QinQ frames with the top Q tag VID 10 and with any bottom Q tag VID, except for the bottom Q tag VID 11.

Traffic Classification of QinQ-Tagged Frames at Access Ingress

When a QinQ-tagged frame arrives at an access ingress point and if the traffic classification is based on the Ethernet ToS value, which tag is considered? Table 7.3 lists the 802.1p fields considered by default for a combination of different port/SAP Q tagging type associations and for incoming frames with different Q tags.

Table 7.3 ToS Field Selection of Ethernet Frames by Default

Port/SAP Type	Existing Packet Tags	802.1p Bits Used for Match
Null	None	None
Null	Dot1P (VLAN-ID 0)	Dot1P Pbits
Null	Dot1Q	Dot1Q Pbits
Null	TopQ BottomQ	TopQ Pbits
Null	TopQ (No BottomQ)	TopQ Pbits
Dot1Q	None (Default SAP)	None
Dot1Q	Dot1P (Default SAP VLAN-ID 0)	Dot1P Pbits
Dot1Q	Dot1Q	Dot1Q Pbits
QinQ/TopQ	TopQ	TopQ Pbits
QinQ/TopQ	TopQ BottomQ	TopQ Pbits
QinQ/QinQ	TopQ BottomQ	BottomQ Pbits

In ALSRP, a SAP can be forced to match 802.1p bits either from the top Q tag or bottom Q tag of incoming QinQ-tagged frames for traffic classification. Listings 7.13 and 7.14 show the options for forcing the choice of a specific ToS field of QinQ-tagged frames within a VPRN and a VLL service SAP, respectively. The options available under other service configurations are similar.

Listing 7.13 Options to choose the 802.1P field in QinQ-tagged frames within a VPRN service SAP

```
A:Pod1>config>service>vprn>if>sap>ingress# match-qinq-dot1p
  - match-qinq-dot1p {top|bottom}
  - no match-qinq-dot1p

<top|bottom>           : top|bottom
```

Listing 7.14 Options to choose the 802.1P field in QinQ-tagged frames within a VLL service SAP

```
A:Pod1>config>service>epipe>sap>ingress$ match-qinq-dot1p
  - match-qinq-dot1p {top|bottom}
  - no match-qinq-dot1p

<top|bottom>           : top|bottom
```

Table 7.4 lists the 802.1p field considered for use in various combinations of different port/SAP Q-tagging type associations and for incoming frames with different Q tags, when a SAP is forced to match its top Q tag ToS field.

Table 7.4 ToS Field Selection of Ethernet Frames When Forced to Match Top Q Tag Field

Port/SAP Type	Existing Packet Tags	802.1p Bits Used for Match
Null	None	None
Null	Dot1P (VLAN-ID 0)	Dot1P Pbits
Null	Dot1Q	Dot1Q Pbits
Null	TopQ BottomQ	TopQ Pbits
Null	TopQ (No BottomQ)	TopQ Pbits
Dot1Q	None (Default SAP)	None
Dot1Q	Dot1P (Default SAP VLAN-ID 0)	Dot1P Pbits
Dot1Q	Dot1Q	Dot1Q Pbits
QinQ/TopQ	TopQ	TopQ Pbits
QinQ/TopQ	TopQ BottomQ	TopQ Pbits
QinQ/QinQ	TopQ BottomQ	TopQ Pbits

Table 7.5 lists the 802.1p field considered by default for various combinations of different port/SAP Q-tagging type associations and for incoming frames with different Q tags, when a SAP is forced to match its bottom Q tag ToS field.

Table 7.5 ToS Field Selection of Ethernet Frames When Forced to Match Bottom Q Tag Field

Port/SAP Type	Existing Packet Tags	802.1p Bits Used for Match
Null	None	None
Null	Dot1P (VLAN-ID 0)	Dot1P Pbits
Null	Dot1Q	Dot1Q Pbits
Null	TopQ BottomQ	BottomQ Pbits
Null	TopQ (No BottomQ)	TopQ Pbits
Dot1Q	None (Default SAP)	None
Dot1Q	Dot1P (Default SAP VLAN-ID 0)	Dot1P Pbits
Dot1Q	Dot1Q	Dot1Q Pbits
QinQ/TopQ	TopQ	TopQ Pbits
QinQ/TopQ	TopQ BottomQ	BottomQ Pbits
QinQ/QinQ	TopQ BottomQ	BottomQ Pbits

Triple-Tagged Frames

Is it possible to have more than two Q tags on a frame? If so, how do you then choose the ToS field?

Yes, it is possible to have triple-tagged frames, although it is seldom the case. In such cases the outer two tags are considered for ToS field matching, as discussed in this section.

If the markings of the three ToS fields happen to be different, a service provider is responsible only for the service contract with his direct client, and hence it is logical to care about only the outer two ToS fields.

Marking QinQ-Tagged Frames at the Access Egress

If an access egress is required to mark the 802.1p field of QinQ-tagged frames, which tag does it mark? Table 7.6 lists which 802.1p field is marked by default, if the access egress if configured to mark frames.

Table 7.6 802.1p Field Marked by Default, if Marking Is Enabled at an Access Egress

SAP Type	Preserved 802.1p State of Frame	Marked (or Re-Marked) Pbits
Null	No preserved Dot1P bits	None
Null	Preserved Dot1P bits	Preserved tag Pbits re-marked using `dot1p` value
Dot1Q	No preserved Dot1P bits	New Pbits marked using `dot1p` value
Dot1Q	Preserved Dot1P bits	Preserved tag Pbits re-marked using `dot1p` value
TopQ	No preserved Dot1P bits	TopQ Pbits marked using `dot1p` value
TopQ	Preserved Dot1P bits (used as TopQ and BottomQ Pbits)	TopQ Pbits marked using `dot1p` value, BottomQ Pbits preserved
QinQ	No preserved Dot1P bits	TopQ Pbits and BottomQ Pbits marked using `dot1p` value
QinQ	Preserved Dot1P bits (used as TopQ and BottomQ Pbits)	TopQ Pbits and BottomQ Pbits marked using `dot1p` value

As listed in the table, in the case of QinQ-tagged frames both the top and bottom Q tags are marked by default. However, it is common that service providers are required to preserve the bottom Q tag's ToS marking even when the top Q tag's ToS field has to be re-marked. Therefore, ALSRP offers the flexibility to mark only the ToS field of the top Q tag. Listing 7.15 shows the options for configuring a SAP egress to mark the 802.1p field of only the top Q tag.

Listing 7.15 Options to enable access egress marking of the ToS field of only the top Q tag

```
A:Pod1>config>service>vpls>sap>egress# qinq-mark-top-only
  - no qinq-mark-top-only
  - qinq-mark-top-only
```

Table 7.7 lists which 802.1p field is marked, if a SAP egress is configured to mark only the Top Q tag's ToS field.

Table 7.7 802.1p Field Marked When a SAP Egress Is Configured to Mark Only the Top Q Tag

SAP Type	Preserved 802.1p State of Frame	Marked (or Re-Marked) Pbits
Null	No preserved Dot1P bits	None
Null	Preserved Dot1P bits	Preserved tag Pbits re-marked using `dot1p` value
Dot1Q	No preserved Dot1P bits	New Pbits marked using `dot1p` value
Dot1Q	Preserved Dot1P bits	Preserved tag Pbits re-marked using `dot1p` value
TopQ	No preserved Dot1P bits	TopQ Pbits marked using `dot1p` value
TopQ	Preserved Dot1P bits (used as TopQ and BottomQ Pbits)	TopQ Pbits marked using `dot1p` value, BottomQ Pbits preserved
QinQ	No preserved Dot1P bits	TopQ Pbits marked using `dot1p` value, BottomQ Pbits marked with zero
QinQ	Preserved Dot1P bits (used as TopQ and BottomQ Pbits)	TopQ Pbits marked using `dot1p` value, BottomQ Pbits marked using preserved value

7.7 Tunnel Termination QoS Override

In Chapter 6, we discussed the order of precedence of the different traffic classification criteria at network ingress: EXP, DSCP, and 802.1p. This order of precedence may not be suitable for a network ingress where an MPLS tunnel terminates.

For example, consider the scenario illustrated in Figure 7.2. In this scenario, a content provider has leased tunnel services to a number of locations from a network service provider to directly offer multiple application services to residential customers.

The content provider has purchased sufficient bandwidth throughout the tunnel. The network resources available at access points facing the residential customers are in accordance with the service agreement between the network provider and the individual residential customers.

According to the service contract in place with the content provider, the network provider need not offer differentiated service for different application traffic within the MPLS tunnel. Therefore, the network provider may use the same set of markings in the tunnel encapsulation for all the application traffic.

Figure 7.2 Tunnel Termination QoS Scenario

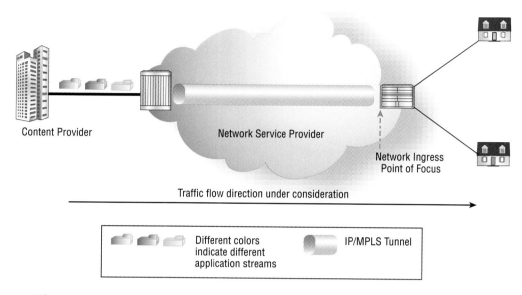

Content Provider

Network Service Provider

Network Ingress
Point of Focus

Traffic flow direction under consideration

Different colors
indicate different
application streams

IP/MPLS Tunnel

The access points corresponding to residential customers may not have adequate bandwidth if all the applications burst at the same time. Therefore, the network provider has to differentiate the services for different application traffic at the access egress facing residential customers. In order to provide differentiated service at the access egress, the network provider cannot classify traffic at the corresponding network ingress based on the tunnel encapsulation markings and instead has to rely on the DSCP markings on the packets' headers.

ALSRP supports the flexibility of this tunnel termination QoS override. The override applies only to routed IP packets after their tunnel encapsulation is removed. When the override is enabled, the traffic classification is based on the ToS field in the routed IP packets' header. If an explicit match entry is not found, the default QoS mapping is used. Regardless of whether the tunnel type is MPLS or IP GRE, the tunnel encapsulation ToS field is ignored. Non-IP routed packets in a terminating tunnel are not affected by the override. Similarly, the override has no impact at the network ingresses where there is no tunnel termination.

The tunnel termination QoS override is part of the ingress section of the Network QoS policy. Listing 7.16 shows the options for configuring the tunnel termination

QoS override. The command `ler-use-dscp` enables the tunnel termination QoS override, and the command `no ler-use-dscp` disables it.

Listing 7.16 Options for configuring the tunnel termination QoS override

```
A:Pod1>config>qos>network>ingress# ler-use-dscp
  - ler-use-dscp
  - no ler-use-dscp
```

Summary

This chapter started by introducing forwarding subclasses of ALSRP and explaining how and why to configure them. ALSRP allows for the creation of up to 56 subclasses within a SAP-ingress QoS policy. The subclasses can be divided among the eight forwarding classes in any combination. At one end of the continuum, one of the forwarding classes could have 56 subclasses. At the other end of the continuum, each of the eight forwarding classes could have up to seven subclasses.

Subclasses are used for two purposes: color-aware traffic profiling and access ingress marking of IP packets. Color-aware traffic profiling allows customers or other access devices to color a packet as out-of-profile with the intention of preserving in-profile bandwidth for higher-priority packets. Using color-aware traffic profiling in ALSRP, the three drop precedence of AF PHBs defined in RFC2597 can be honored.

Access ingress marking is useful if marking ToS fields of the original IP packets from customers is a requirement within a service provider network. Otherwise, original IP packets from customers are usually left untouched within a service provider network. ALSRP relies on the trust state of interfaces to avoid overwriting ToS values marked by VPN customers.

IEEE 802.1 QinQ tagging can be used for several reasons. Depending on the application, QinQ-tagged frames must be classified based on either the bottom or top Q tag ToS field. At the access ingress, ALSRP allows traffic classification based on either of the VLAN tag ToS markings. Similarly at the access egress, ALSRP permits either marking both the inner and outer 802.1p fields of QinQ tags or preserving the bottom Q tag.

At the network ingress of an IP/MPLS tunnel termination node, ALSRP allows overriding the default order of precedence of the different traffic classification criteria. The command `1er-use-dscp` within an associated Network QoS policy forces the network ingress to classify traffic arriving through IP/MPLS tunnels terminating at the node based on the DSCP value of the original IP header. The command impacts only Layer 3 service traffic and allows the bypassing of the tunnel header QoS marking.

Queuing and Buffer Management

8

Service providers can minimize datagram loss resulting from transient traffic spikes in a network through buffering. Buffer management helps to avoid network congestion and prevent buffer overflow.

Chapter Objectives

- To identify the different buffer partitions of an IOM

- To describe buffer-related queue parameters

- To explain Network-Queue QoS policy

- To discuss classical and dynamic buffer management techniques offered within ALSRP.

- To explain Slope QoS policy

Buffering and buffer management are vital aspects of the data path architecture of network nodes. Buffering helps minimize datagram loss resulting from transient traffic spikes in a network. Buffer partitioning helps distribute the buffering resources to traffic belonging to different flows, different classes of service, and different customers. Buffer management helps prevent network congestion and buffer overflow, while allowing an increase of network resource utilization.

This chapter discusses the ALSRP IOM buffer partitions and explains how their buffering space is allocated to traffic flows at different networking points. It also covers: quality of service (QoS) policies that address buffering, details regarding buffer-related queue parameters, and buffer management techniques.

8.1 Understanding Buffer Partitions

This section discusses hard-partitioned buffer units of an IOM, and how those buffer units are divided into buffer pools. A buffer pool is divided into two portions: a reserved portion and a shared portion. Queues are dynamically created within buffer pools, and a queue takes certain buffer space from the reserved portion and the rest from the shared portion.

Storage and Seating Partitions: Real-Life Counterparts of Buffer Partitions

Are you wondering why we need all these different buffer partitions? Here's a look at a couple of real-life examples to provide some insight regarding the use of optimal partitions to enhance the usage of a limited space. These examples will help you understand the similar use of buffer partitions to meet the different needs for storage space.

First, think about the different rooms in a house, the role played by the size of a room in its use; consider why we have closets and why closets are further divided into shelves. What are the benefits and disadvantages of bigger and smaller shelves?

As a second example, consider our favorite real-life example in this book: airplanes and airlines. A commercial airplane is typically hard-partitioned into a cockpit, passenger seating areas, a mechanical area, baggage area, and so on. A passenger area might be further hard- (there could be physical doors) or soft- (there could be curtains) partitioned into business class, first class, and economy class. Within a flying class there are a number of seats to accommodate numerous passengers. Within the physical constraints of a plane, it is a fact that the higher the number of (occupied) seats, the

(continued)

---

higher the revenue that can be generated during the flights. However, if the seat size is too narrow, passengers cannot be seated comfortably, which, in turn, could affect the revenue generation. Therefore, the number of seats and seat sizes (besides other weight and space constraints) have to be optimized in order to maximize the resources of a plane during its flights.

Figure 8.1 shows the hard-partitioned buffer units of an ALSRP IOM slot that takes in two media-dependent adapters (MDAs). As shown in Figure 8.1, there are two separate physical buffer units, one for each direction, for each MDA. As indicated in the figure, these two physical buffer units corresponding to each MDA are referred to as the ingress and egress buffer units of an MDA.

Figure 8.1 Hard-Partitioned Buffering Locations

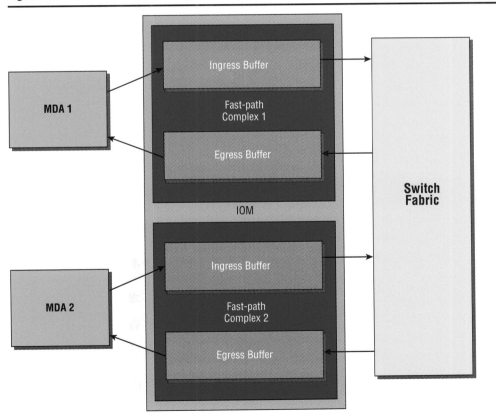

The Role of Buffer Pools

Each physical buffer unit is divided into a number of smaller buffer pools. For a port configured as `access` mode, two buffer pools—an access ingress pool and an access egress pool—are allocated for its exclusive use. For a port configured as `network` mode, only one buffer pool—the network egress pool—is allocated for its exclusive use. On the ingress side, all the network ports of an MDA share one mega pool—the network ingress pool—from the ingress buffer unit of the MDA.

It could be noticed that whether the port is in access or network mode, it always has one buffer pool exclusively allocated for its egress traffic. Why? If the egress traffic of all ports of an MDA were to share a common buffer pool, and if one of these ports gets congested, traffic belonging to the congested port could monopolize the buffer pool and let other ports starve.

The same reason explains why an exclusive buffer pool is allocated for the ingress traffic of each access port. If a buffer pool was shared among the ingress traffic of all access ports of an MDA, unregulated (bursty and nonconforming) traffic arriving through a port could monopolize the buffer pool. Still, to avoid allowing one or a few traffic flows to monopolize the utilization of network resources in their path, in the DiffServ QoS model, rate-limiting of all the incoming traffic is essential at its respective access ingress.

In that case, why is a mega buffer pool shared among the ingress traffic of all the network ports of an MDA? The answer is: to take advantage of statistical multiplexing gain. The traffic arriving through all the network ports of an MDA have been rate-limited (at their respective access ingress points of the network), and their profiles are marked according to their SLA conformance. Therefore, these regulated traffic flows can be allowed to share a buffer pool, without the fear of any of them monopolizing the entire buffer pool. The idea behind statistical multiplexing gain is that not all of the traffic streams traversing a network point would burst at the same time, and therefore, if these streams share a common bigger buffer space, bigger traffic bursts can be accommodated.

The size of buffer pools is automatically determined as a function of the MDA type and the port configuration (mode and port speed). As mentioned earlier, each buffer pool is partitioned into two portions: reserved and shared portions. The size distribution between reserved and shared portions can be configured either explicitly or implicitly.

Time Share Properties: An Example of Multiplexing Gain

The concept of time-share properties (as in resorts) is an example of a real-life multiplexing gain. For the amount a person pays to buy a time-share property, it is not feasible to own the property permanently. However, the intention is to use such a property only for a few days for a year or two. Therefore, several people with similar intentions pool their (small) amounts of money to buy the property and use it one after another.

The size of the reserved portion of an access ingress pool, access egress pool, or network egress pool can be explicitly configured as a part of the corresponding port configuration. Listing 8.1 shows the command options for explicitly configuring the reserved portion size of an access ingress pool. Configuring the reserved portion size of an access egress pool is similar to that of an access ingress pool. The reserved portion size of an access egress pool is configured under the egress section of a port access configuration.

Listing 8.1 Command options for configuring the reserved portion size of an access ingress buffer pool

```
A:Pod1>config>port>access>ingress>pool# resv-cbs
  - no resv-cbs
  - resv-cbs <percent-or-default>

 <percent-or-default> : [0..100|default]
```

Listing 8.2 shows the command options for explicitly configuring the reserved portion size of a network egress pool.

Listing 8.2 Command options for configuring the reserved portion size of a network egress buffer pool

```
A:Pod1>config>port>network>egress>pool# resv-cbs
  - no resv-cbs
  - resv-cbs <percent-or-default>

 <percent-or-default> : [0..100|default]
```

The size of the reserved portion of a network ingress buffer pool is configured directly under the MDA. Listing 8.3 displays the command options for explicitly configuring the reserved portion size of a network ingress pool.

Listing 8.3 Command options for configuring the reserved portion size of a network ingress buffer pool

```
A:Pod1>config>card>mda>network>ingress>pool# resv-cbs
  - no resv-cbs
  - resv-cbs <percent-or-default>

 <percent-or-default> : [0..100|default]
```

The default configuration of a buffer pool allows for the implicit configuration of the reserved portion size of the buffer pool. Under implicit configuration, the size of the reserved portion of a buffer pool is automatically determined as the sum of the committed burst size (CBS) of the queues instantiated within the buffer pool. Queues and queue parameters are discussed in the subsequent sections of this chapter.

Table 8.1 lists the implications of configuring the reserved portion size of a buffer pool explicitly and implicitly.

Table 8.1 Differences between Explicit and Implicit Configuration of a Buffer Pool Reserved Portion Size

Explicit Configuration	Implicit Configuration
Static.	Dynamic as the queues with CBS are created and deleted.
If the sum of the CBS of queues is less than the reserved portion threshold, the buffer pool can be underutilized.	Not applicable.
If the sum of the CBS of queues is greater than the reserved portion threshold, oversubscription of CBS of queues results, and queues cannot be guaranteed any buffer space.	CBS oversubscription occurs only if the sum of the CBS of queues exceeds the total pool size.
Like reserved portion size, the shared portion is also fixed.	Shared portion size varies along with the reserved portion size, and oversubscription of CBS results in no shared portion.

Buffer Pools and Queues

Queues are created within buffer pools. Queues can be used to isolate traffic belonging to different forwarding classes and different forwarding types. At access ingress, queues are also used to isolate traffic belonging to different SAPs that are configured within the same port.

Figure 8.2 shows a logical representation of queues created within a buffer pool. As shown in the figure, depending on their configuration, queues may take up their entire buffer space from the reserved portion, from the shared portion, or some from the reserved and the rest from the shared portion.

As the name indicates, the buffer space a queue takes from the reserved portion of a buffer pool is exclusively reserved for the traffic flowing through the queue. In contrast, the buffer space of the shared portion is not reserved for the exclusive use of any particular queues, but it is a common resource for all the queues. As discussed earlier, the purpose of having the shared buffer space is to take advantage of statistical multiplexing gain and accommodate bigger bursts.

Figure 8.2 A Logical Representation of Queues Created within a Buffer Pool

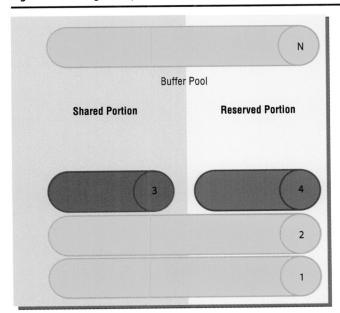

Buffering Aspect of the End-to-End Traffic Flow

Now that you have an understanding of the need for buffer partitions, and the relationships among buffer pools and queues, Figure 8.3 summarizes the end-to-end traffic flow from a buffering perspective.

Figure 8.3 Buffering Perspective of End-to-End Traffic Flow Summary

> **Access Ingress:** Traffic belonging to different ports is isolated. Traffic belonging to a SAP is queued separately from the traffic arriving through other SAPs. Traffic belonging to different FCs can be mapped to different queues.

> **Network Ingress:** Traffic arriving through all network ports of an MDA is buffered together. Traffic belonging to different FCs can be mapped to different queues.

> **General Note:** At all ingress queuing points, point-to-point traffic and multipoint traffic are forwarded to different sets of queues.

> **Network Egress:** Traffic belonging to different ports is isolated. Traffic belonging to different FCs can be mapped to different queues.

> **Access Egress:** Traffic belonging to different ports is isolated. Traffic belonging to a SAP is queued separately from the traffic leaving through other SAPs. Traffic belonging to different FCs can be mapped to different queues.

CPE-Left   Node1   Node2   Node3   CPE-Right

Traffic flow direction under consideration

Point-to-point and Multipoint Traffic

As explained in Chapter 1, ALSRP supports four different forwarding types: unicast, multicast, broadcast, and unknown-cast forwarding. Unicast is generally referred to as point-to-point forwarding. Multicast, broadcast, and unknown-cast are generally referred to as multipoint forwarding. Only virtual private LAN service (VPLS) supports all four forwarding types. Virtual leased line (VLL) service uses only unicast forwarding. Virtual private routed network (VPRN) and Internet-Enhanced Service (IES) support unicast and multicast forwarding.

The following bullets summarize the buffering process for the different queuing points.

- **Access ingress**—As mentioned earlier, each access port has an exclusively assigned access ingress buffer pool to isolate the ingress traffic of a port from other port traffic of the MDA. Moreover, each service access point (SAP) has its own set of queues. Based on the queues' configuration, the ingress traffic through a SAP can be held separately from other SAP traffic belonging to the same port. ALSRP forwards point-to-point traffic and multipoint traffic to different sets of queues at ingress (both access and network ingress) points. Within multipoint forwarding, through SAP-ingress policy configuration, traffic belonging to multicast, broadcast, and unknown-cast types can be forwarded to different sets of queues. Traffic belonging to different forwarding classes can also be mapped to different queues through the SAP-ingress policy configuration. The default SAP-ingress policy maps all the unicast traffic, irrespective of the forwarding classes, to queue 1. Similarly, it maps all the multipoint traffic to queue 11.

- **Network egress**—Each network port has an exclusively assigned network egress buffer pool to isolate the egress traffic of a port from other port traffic of the MDA. Traffic belonging to different forwarding classes can be mapped to different queues through a Network-Queue policy.

- **Network ingress**—All the network ports of an MDA share a common mega-buffer pool for ingress traffic to take advantage of statistical multiplexing gain. Traffic belonging to different forwarding classes can be mapped to different queues through the Network-Queue policy configuration. Point-to-point traffic and multipoint traffic are mapped to a different set of queues.

- **Access egress**—Each access port has an exclusively assigned access egress buffer pool to isolate the egress traffic of a port from other port traffic of the MDA. Moreover, each SAP has its own set of queues, and based on the queues' configuration the egress traffic through a SAP can be held separately from other SAP traffic belonging to the same port. Traffic belonging to different forwarding classes can be mapped to different queues through SAP-egress policy configuration. The default SAP-egress policy maps all the traffic, irrespective of the forwarding classes, to queue 1.

8.2 Buffer-Related Queue Parameters

A queue has the following three buffer-related parameters:

- Committed buffer size (CBS)
- Maximum buffer size (MBS)
- High priority only (HPO) buffer size

These parameters are discussed in the following sections.

Committed Buffer Size

The committed buffer size (CBS) specifies the buffer space that the queue can draw from the reserved buffer portion of the buffer pool in which the queue is created. ALSRP allows the oversubscribing of the reserved portion of a buffer pool. When the reserved portion of a buffer pool is not oversubscribed, the CBS of a queue configured within the buffer pool can be viewed as the queue's guaranteed buffer space.

For access queues, the CBS is specified in KB (kilobytes). The CBS for a network queue is defined as a percentage of the corresponding buffer pool size. A network queue CBS can be configured in hundredths of a percent, and the configuration range is 0.00 percent to 100.00 percent. If the CBS is zero, then there is no guaranteed buffer space for the queue, and all the buffer space for the queue is drawn from the shared portion of the buffer pool.

In network QoS designs, the CBS of a queue is usually expressed as a correlation to the configured committed information rate (CIR) of the queue. CIR is discussed in detail in Chapter 10. For this discussion, it is sufficient to know that the CIR is a parameter expressing a rate at which traffic flows through the queue and is expressed as Kbps (kilobits/sec). Expressing queue buffer sizes in absolute values does not provide any insight into their effectiveness in buffering the traffic flowing through the queue. For example, 64 KB of buffer is negligible buffer space for a queue rate of 1 Gbps (gigabits/sec) , whereas it is a considerable amount of buffer space for a queue rate of 1.5 Mbps (megabits/sec). Therefore, queue buffer sizes are better expressed as the product of the bandwidth times the delay (*bandwidth*delay*), where delay is a desired time interval for holding traffic bursts. In other words, the buffer size is expressed as how much of a time interval's worth of traffic the buffer space can hold at the configured rate of the traffic flow.

Equation 8.1 shows how to correlate CBS and CIR.

Equation 8.1 Correlation of CBS and CIR

$$CBS(KB) = \left(\frac{CIR(Kbps) * time(s)}{8} \right)$$

> **Note:** In order to guarantee buffer space for queues within a buffer pool, a network designer has to make sure that the sum of the CBS of queues created within the buffer pool does not oversubscribe the reserved portion of the pool.

Maximum Buffer Size

The parameter specifies the maximum size of the queue. The difference between the maximum buffer size (MBS) and the committed buffer size is the buffer space that the queue can draw from the shared portion of the buffer pool in which the queue is created. ALSRP allows oversubscribing of the shared portion of a buffer pool.

For access queues, the MBS is specified in KB. The MBS for a network queue is defined as a percentage of the corresponding buffer pool size. A network queue MBS can be configured in hundredths of a percent and the configuration range is 0.00 percent to 100.00 percent. The MBS of a queue can be correlated to the peak information rate (PIR) of the queue as shown in Equation 8.2.

Equation 8.2 Correlation of MBS and PIR

$$MBS(KB) = \left(\frac{PIR(Kbps) * time(s)}{8} \right)$$

If the occupancy of a queue is at its maximum buffer size, the incoming traffic to the queue is dropped. Therefore, if the MBS of a queue is configured as zero, no traffic can pass through the queue. If a queue's MBS = CBS > 0, then the queue draws all of its buffer space from the reserved portion of its buffer pool.

High Priority Only Buffer Size

The high priority only buffer space is reserved exclusively for high-queuing priority (in-profile) traffic. In other words, $MBS * (1 - HPO)$ is the queue occupancy threshold, beyond which all the low-queuing priority (out-of-profile) datagrams attempting to enter the queue will be dropped. The HPO (high priority only) reservation for a queue is defined as a percentage of the MBS value. The HPO default value is 10 percent of the MBS.

The following example explains how the CBS, MBS, and HPO of a queue, along with current queue occupancy, determine the queuing chances of an incoming datagram moving into the queue.

Access Queuing Example

The buffer parameters of an access queue are configured as follows: MBS = 10 KB, CBS = 8 KB, HPO = 30 percent. There is no oversubscription of the reserved portion of the buffer pool. Also there is no Slope policy (Slope policies are discussed later in this chapter) applied to the buffer pool. Given different rates of queue occupancy (X), the example calculates whether an incoming datagram will be queued or dropped.

- X = 5 KB: X < CBS < MBS. When an in-profile or out-of-profile datagram arrives, the datagram will be queued in the reserved portion.

- X = 7 KB: X < CBS < MBS. Because [MBS * (1– HPO)] = 7 KB (kilobytes), if an out-of-profile datagram arrives the datagram will be discarded. Because X < CBS, when an in-profile datagram arrives, it will be queued in the reserved portion.

- X = 9 KB: X < MBS. Because [MBS * (1– HPO)] = 7 KB, if an out-of-profile datagram arrives, the datagram will be discarded. Because X < MBS, when an in-profile datagram arrives, it will contend with other queues' traffic for shared buffer space. HPO restricts out-of-profile datagrams, and it does not guarantee that an in-profile datagram will get a buffer if the CBS is exceeded.

Best Practices: The best practice for traffic classification suggests that all high-priority forwarding class traffic be in-profile and all best-effort forwarding class traffic be out-of-profile. Under those conditions, configuring HPO for high-priority forwarding class queues is meaningless and is subject to designers' discretion. Similarly, not configuring HPO as 0 percent for low-priority forwarding class queues would result in buffer wastage. Therefore, configuring HPO appropriately only on queues mapped to assured forwarding classes helps to enhance the assured forwarding services.

If the HPO of a queue is configured as 100 percent, no low-queuing priority traffic can pass through the queue.

If the HPO of a queue is configured such that the threshold is within the CBS of the queue, certain queue space is guaranteed for the high-queuing priority datagram. Alternatively, if the HPO of a queue is configured such that the threshold is between the CBS and MBS of the queue, certain queue space is reserved for the high-queuing priority datagram, but not guaranteed.

8.3 Configuring Access Queues and Queue Mapping

Chapter 6 discussed the SAP-ingress and SAP-egress QoS policies, and examined the default SAP-ingress and SAP-egress policies containing queue configurations. This section addresses access queue creation, configuring buffer-related parameters in those queues, and mapping traffic to newly configured queues.

SAP-Ingress Queue Creation

Listing 8.4 shows the options for creating a queue within a SAP-ingress policy.

Listing 8.4 Options for creating a queue in a SAP-ingress policy

```
A:Pod1>config>qos>sap-ingress$ queue
  - no queue <queue-id>
  - queue <queue-id>[multipoint][<queue-type>][<queue-mode>][create]

 <queue-id>        : [1..32]
 <multipoint>      : keyword - mandatory while creating a
                     multipoint queue
 <queue-type>      : expedite|best-effort|auto-expedite - keywords
 <queue-mode>      : profile-mode|priority-mode - keywords
 <create>          : keyword - mandatory while creating an entry.
```

As indicated by the `queue-id` range in Listing 8.4, up to thirty-two queues can be created within a SAP-ingress policy. Thirty-two queues can be mapped to four different forwarding type classes and eight forwarding classes within each of the four different forwarding types. In order to map multipoint forwarding type traffic to a queue, the queue must have been created with the optional parameter `multipoint`.

The optional parameter `queue-type` indicates the type of hardware scheduler (arbitrator) associated with the queue. This scheduling-related parameter is covered in Chapter 10.

The optional parameter `queue-mode` is related to traffic classification, which was briefly discussed in Chapter 7. The two values of this parameter are `priority-mode` (the default value) and `profile-mode`. Table 8.2 compares the priority and profile modes of access ingress queues.

Table 8.2 Comparison of the Priority and Profile Modes of Access Ingress Queues

Priority Mode	Profile Mode
Default.	Has to be explicitly stated when creating a queue.
Recognizes queuing priority markings of the ingress traffic classification.	Ignores the queuing priority markings of the ingress traffic classification.
Ignores the explicitly specified profile states under a forwarding class or subclass.	Honors the explicitly specified profile states under a forwarding class or subclass.
Always determines the profile state of datagrams from the profile state of forwarding queues at the time of access ingress scheduling	Determines the profile state of datagrams that do not have any explicit profile markings from the profile state of forwarding queues at the time of scheduling.
Using the keyword `police` for real-time rate-limiting is possible. See Chapter 12.	Using the keyword `police` for real-time rate-limiting is not possible.

Note: Queue 1 and queue 11 are created by default while creating a SAP-ingress policy. Therefore, their `queue-type` and `queue-mode` cannot be changed.

Best Practices: Because creation options of the default queues cannot be changed, always map a low priority (more specifically, a best-effort type) forwarding class to these queues.

Mapping Traffic to SAP-Ingress Queues

By default, all point-to-point traffic is mapped to queue 1 within a SAP-ingress QoS policy. Similarly, all multipoint traffic is mapped to queue 11. In order to map a forwarding class's traffic to a different queue, both the forwarding class and the queue must be created. Once the forwarding class and the queue are created, the queue can be specified under the forwarding class to map the two entities. You saw how to create forwarding classes and subclasses in Chapter 7. In this chapter, you learn how to map forwarding class traffic to queues.

Listing 8.5 shows the configuration options available under a forwarding class within a SAP-ingress policy. The options: `broadcast-queue`, `multicast-queue`, `queue`, and `unknown-queue` are used to map different queues to the forwarding class.

Listing 8.5 Configuration options within a forwarding class of a SAP-ingress policy

```
A:Pod1>config>qos>sap-ingress>fc#
  [no] broadcast-queue - Specify the broadcast-queue
  [no] in-remark       - Specify the in-profile remarking
  [no] multicast-queue - Specify the multicast-queue
  [no] out-remark      - Specify the out-profile remarking
  [no] profile         - Specify the profile to be assigned
  [no] queue           - Specify the unicast-queue
  [no] unknown-queue   - Specify the unknown-queue
```

Listing 8.6 shows an example SAP-ingress policy in which forwarding class 12 is mapped to multiple queues as follows: Point-to-point (unicast) traffic flowing through the forwarding class is mapped to queue 2. Multicast, broadcast, and unknown-cast traffic of the forwarding class is respectively mapped to queues 10, 18, and 26.

Listing 8.6 An example SAP-ingress policy that illustrates the mapping of a forwarding class to queues

```
        sap-ingress 100 create
            description "Example: Mapping forwarding class to queues"
            queue 1 create
            exit
            queue 2 create
```

(continued)

```
            exit
            queue 10 multipoint create
            exit
            queue 11 multipoint create
            exit
            queue 18 multipoint create
            exit
            queue 26 multipoint create
            exit
            fc "l2" create
                queue 2
                broadcast-queue 18
                multicast-queue 10
                unknown-queue 26
            exit
            dot1p 1 fc "l2" priority low
        exit
```

Note: To prevent any out-of-sequence forwarding, queues can be mapped only within a forwarding class and not within a forwarding subclass.

Best Practices: To make troubleshooting easier, assign the same queue for a given forwarding class at all network points within a network. For example, map queue 5 to unicast EF traffic both in SAP and network policies in all the nodes within a network.

SAP-Egress Queue Creation

Listing 8.7 shows the options for creating a queue within a SAP-egress policy.

Listing 8.7 Options for creating a queue in a SAP-egress policy

```
A:Pod1>config>qos>sap-egress# queue
  - no queue <queue-id>
  - queue <queue-id> [<queue-type>] [create]

 <queue-id>          : [1..8]
 <queue-type>        : expedite|best-effort|auto-expedite - keywords
 <create>            : keyword - mandatory while creating an entry.
```

The notable differences in command line options for creating a queue within a SAP-egress policy as compared to a SAP-ingress policy are as follows:

- The `queue-id` range is limited to eight; indicating that only up to eight queues can be created within a SAP-egress policy (as opposed to thirty-two queues within a SAP-ingress policy).
- Absence of the keyword `multipoint`. At access egress only unicast forwarding is relevant.
- Absence of `queue-mode` options. Because no traffic classification is done at an egress point, `queue-mode` is not relevant within a SAP-egress policy.

The optional parameter `queue-type` indicates the type of hardware scheduler (arbitrator) associated with the queue. We will defer the discussion on the scheduling related parameter to Chapter 10.

Note: Queue 1 is created by default while creating a SAP-egress policy. Therefore, the `queue-type` of queue 1 cannot be changed.

Mapping Traffic to SAP-Egress Queues

Within a SAP-egress QoS policy, all traffic is mapped to queue 1 by default. As with a SAP-ingress queue, in order to map a forwarding class's traffic to a different queue, both the forwarding class and the queue must be created. Once the forwarding class and the queue are created, the queue can be specified under the forwarding class to map the two entities.

Listing 8.8 shows options for creating a forwarding class within a SAP-egress policy.

Listing 8.8 Options for creating a forwarding class within a SAP-egress policy

```
A:Pod1>config>qos>sap-egress# fc
  - fc <fc-name> [create]
  - no fc <fc-name>

 <fc-name>          : be|l2|af|l1|h2|ef|h1|nc - keywords
 <create>           : keyword - mandatory while creating an entry.
```

Listing 8.9 shows the configuration options available within a forwarding class of a SAP-egress policy.

Listing 8.9 Configuration options available within a forwarding class of a SAP-egress policy

```
A:Pod1>config>qos>sap-egress>fc#
 [no] dot1p          - Specify the dot1p value to be used
 [no] queue          - Specify the queue to forward this FC traffic
```

Chapter 6 discussed configuring the `dot1p` (802.1p) parameter within a forwarding class to mark the traffic at access egress. Configuring the `queue` parameter within a forwarding class, maps the forwarding class to the queue.

Listing 8.10 provides an example SAP-egress policy in which the forwarding class EF is mapped to queue 6.

Listing 8.10 An example SAP-egress policy that illustrates the mapping of a forwarding class to a queue

```
        sap-egress 100 create
            description "Example: Mapping forwarding class to queue"
            queue 1 create
            exit
            queue 6 create
            exit
            fc ef create
                queue 6
            exit
        exit
```

Configuring Buffer-Related Parameters of Access Queues

Once a queue is configured within an access QoS policy, configuring parameters within the queue are identical irrespective of whether it is a SAP-ingress or SAP-egress policy.

Listing 8.11 shows configurable parameters within a queue of a SAP-egress policy.

As mentioned earlier in the chapter, CBS and MBS are specified by kilobyte size in SAP-ingress and SAP-egress policies. HPO is always specified as a percentage of MBS. Listing 8.12 exhibits the configuration options for CBS, MBS, and HPO within an access policy.

Listing 8.12 Configuration options of buffer-related queue parameters within access QoS policies

```
A:Pod1>config>qos>sap-ingress>queue# cbs
  - cbs <size-in-kbytes>
  - no cbs

 <size-in-kbytes>     : [0..131072 | default]

A:Pod1>config>qos>sap-ingress>queue# mbs
  - mbs <size-in-kbytes>
  - no mbs

 <size-in-kbytes>     : [0..131072 | default]

A:Pod1>config>qos>sap-ingress>queue# high-prio-only
  - high-prio-only <percent>
  - no high-prio-only

 <percent>            : [0..100 | default]
```

8.4 Network-Queue Policy

A Network-Queue policy associated with a network port or MDA describes the network queues' configuration and mapping of forwarding classes to queues. Listing 8.13 shows the options for creating a Network-Queue policy.

Listing 8.13 Options for creating a Network-Queue policy

```
A:Pod1>config>qos# network-queue
  - network-queue <policy-name> [create]
  - no network-queue <policy-name>

 <policy-name>        : [32 chars max]
 <create>             : keyword - mandatory while creating an entry.
```

Unlike SAP-ingress, SAP-egress, and Network QoS policies, Network-Queue policies are identified by their policy name rather than by a `policy-id`. A policy name is a string of characters with a maximum limit of 32 characters.

Listing 8.14 shows the outline of the default Network-Queue policy. As shown in the code, there are two functional segments within a Network-Queue policy: mapping forwarding classes to queues, and queue configurations. In Listing 8.14, you can see the queue declarations in the two **queue** sections, and the mappings under the **fc** declarations.

Listing 8.14 Default Network-Queue policy with functional segments of the policy shown

```
A:Pod1>config>qos# network-queue default
A:Pod1>config>qos>network-queue# info detail
---------------------------------------------
          description "Default network queue QoS policy."
          queue 1 auto-expedite create
              rate 100 cir 0
              mbs 50
              cbs 1
              high-prio-only 10
          exit
          ...
```

(continued)

```
                queue 16 multipoint auto-expedite create
                    rate 100 cir 10
                    mbs 25
                    cbs 1
                    high-prio-only 10
                exit
                fc af create
                    multicast-queue 11
                    queue 3
                exit
                ...
                fc nc create
                    multicast-queue 16
                    queue 8
                exit
    ------------------------------------------------
```

A Network-Queue policy supports the configuration of up to 16 queues: 8 unicast queues and 8 multicast queues corresponding to 8 forwarding classes. Within a Network-Queue policy, no queues are available for broadcast and unknown-cast forwarding types, because these forwarding types are relevant for VPLS services only at access ingress queuing points. Tables 8.3 and 8.4, respectively, summarize the configuration of the unicast and multicast queues of the default Network-Queue policy.

Table 8.3 Configuration Summary of Unicast Queues of the Default Network-Queue Policy

Configuration %	High-Priority FCs				Low-Priority FCs				Sum
	NC Q8	H1 Q7	EF Q6	H2 Q5	L1 Q4	AF Q3	L2 Q2	BE Q1	
PIR	100	100	100	100	100	100	100	100	800
CIR	10	10	100	100	25	25	25	0	295
MBS	25	25	50	50	25	50	50	50	325
CBS	3	3	10	10	3	10	3	1	43
HPO	10	10	10	10	10	10	10	10	-

Table 8.4 Configuration Summary of Multicast Queues of the Default Network-Queue Policy

Configuration %	High-Priority FCs				Low-Priority FCs				Sum
	NC Q16	H1 Q15	EF Q14	H2 Q13	L1 Q12	AF Q11	L2 Q10	BE Q9	
PIR	100	100	100	100	100	100	100	100	800
CIR	10	10	100	100	5	5	5	0	235
MBS	25	25	50	50	25	50	50	50	325
CBS	1	1	1	1	1	1	1	1	8
HPO	10	10	10	10	10	10	10	10	-

As noted in Tables 8.3 and 8.4, the unit of all the queue parameters of a Network-Queue policy is given as a percentage of associated buffer pool size. As shown in the tables, the cumulative sum of the MBS of all the queues exceeds 100 percent and the cumulative sum of the CBS of all the queues is well below 100 percent. In other words, the Network-Queue policy overbooks the associated buffer pools in terms of MBS and underbooks the pools in terms of CBS.

Both overbooking buffer pools in terms of MBS and underbooking them in terms of CBS encourages optimal utilization of the buffer pools. Underbooking a buffer pool in terms of CBS guarantees the buffer space reserved by a queue through its CBS configuration. Overbooking buffer pools in terms of MBS enhances the statistical multiplexing gain of the shared partition of a buffer pool. In Chapter 10, you will learn more about issues associated with overbooking the CIR.

Listing 8.15 provides the top-level command options available to configure a Network-Queue policy.

Listing 8.15 Top-level command options available to configure a Network-Queue policy

```
A:Pod1>config>qos>network-queue$
  [no] description    - Description for this policy
  [no] fc             + Configure forwarding-class to queue mappings
  [no] queue          + Configure a queue
```

Listing 8.16 exhibits the configuration options available within a Network-Queue policy to create a forwarding class and map its traffic to queues. Before mapping a queue to a forwarding class, the queue must be created. As in the case of a SAP-ingress policy, multicast traffic can be forwarded only to queues that are created with the `multipoint` option.

Listing 8.16 Forwarding class configuration options available within a Network-Queue policy

```
A:Pod1>config>qos>network-queue$ fc
  - fc <fc-name> [create]
  - no fc <fc-name>

 <fc-name>              : <be|l2|af|l1|h2|ef|h1|nc> - keywords
 <create>               : keyword - mandatory while creating an entry.


 [no] multicast-queue - Specify the multicast-queue
 [no] queue           - Specify the unicast-queue
```

Listing 8.17 shows the options available within a Network-Queue policy to create and configure queues. As in a SAP-ingress policy, a queue can be created within a Network-Queue policy with the optional keyword of `multipoint` and an optional `queue-type` parameter. The optional keyword `multipoint` would make the queue capable of catering to the scheduling needs of multicast traffic.

Listing 8.17 Queue creation and configuration options available within a Network-Queue policy

```
A:Pod1>config>qos>network-queue$ queue
  - no queue <queue-id>
  - queue <queue-id> [multipoint] [<queue-type>] [create]

 <queue-id>             : [1..16]
 <multipoint>           : keyword - mandatory while creating a
                          multipoint queue
 <queue-type>           : expedite|best-effort|auto-expedite - keywords
 <create>               : keyword - mandatory while creating an entry.

 [no] adaptation-rule - Specify the CIR and PIR adaptation rules
 [no] cbs             - Specify CBS
 [no] high-prio-only  - Specify high priority only burst size
 [no] mbs             - Specify MBS
 [no] rate            - Specify rates (CIR and PIR)
```

As mentioned earlier in the chapter, CBS and MBS are specified as a percentage of the associated buffer pool size in a Network-Queue policy. HPO is always specified as a given percentage of MBS. Listing 8.18 shows the configuration options for CBS, MBS, and HPO within a Network-Queue policy.

Listing 8.18 Configuration options of buffer-related queue parameters within a Network-Queue policy

```
A:Pod1>config>qos>network-queue>queue# cbs
  - cbs <percentage>
  - no cbs

 <percentage>            : [0.00..100.00]

*A:Pod1>config>qos>network-queue>queue# mbs
  - mbs <percentage>
  - no mbs

 <percentage>            : [0.00..100.00]

*A:Pod1>config>qos>network-queue>queue# high-prio-only
  - high-prio-only <percent>
  - no high-prio-only

 <percent>               : [0..100 | default]
```

8.5 Applying a Network-Queue Policy

Earlier in the chapter, you saw that at network ingress, buffer pools are allocated at the MDA level, and at network egress, buffer pools are allocated at the port level. Consequently, for network ingress, a Network-Queue policy is applied under the MDA configuration, and for network egress a Network-Queue policy is applied under the port configuration.

Listing 8.19 shows the options for applying a Network-Queue policy under the configuration of an MDA.

Listing 8.19 Options for applying a Network-Queue policy under an MDA configuration

```
A:Pod1>config>card>mda>network>ingress# queue-policy
  - no queue-policy
  - queue-policy <name>

 <name>                    : [32 chars max]
```

Listing 8.20 shows an example of an MDA configuration in which the Network-Queue policy nq1 is associated with the network ingress buffer pool of the MDA. Note that the example policy name should be more descriptive according to the best practices.

Listing 8.20 An example MDA configuration highlighting a Network-Queue policy association

```
        mda 1
            mda-type m5-1gb-sfp
            network
                ingress
                    queue-policy "nq1"
                exit
            exit
        exit
```

Applying a Network-Queue policy under an MDA configuration is illustrated in Figure 8.4.

Options for applying a Network-Queue policy at a network egress point differ slightly depending on the port type.

Figure 8.4 Application of a Network-Queue Policy under an MDA Configuration

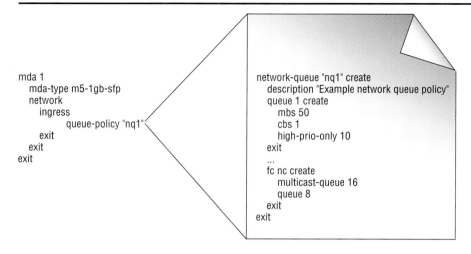

Ethernet Ports

Listing 8.21 shows the options for applying a Network-Queue policy under the configuration of an Ethernet port.

Listing 8.21 Options for applying a Network-Queue policy under an ethernet port

```
A:Pod1>config>port>ethernet>network# queue-policy
  - no queue-policy
  - queue-policy <name>

 <name>                 : [32 chars max]
```

Listing 8.22 provides an example Ethernet port configuration in which the Network-Queue policy **nq1** is associated with the network egress buffer pool of the port.

Listing 8.22 An example ethernet port configuration highlighting a Network-Queue policy association

```
port 1/2/5
    ethernet
        network
            queue-policy "nq1"
        exit
    exit
    no shutdown
exit
```

Applying a Network-Queue policy under an Ethernet port is illustrated in Figure 8.5.

Figure 8.5 Application of a Network-Queue Policy under an Ethernet Port Configuration

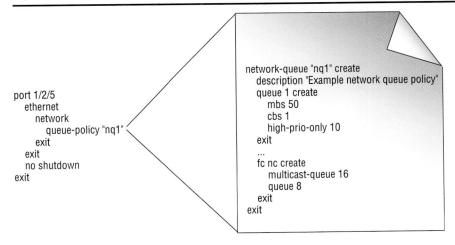

```
port 1/2/5
    ethernet
        network
            queue-policy "nq1"
        exit
    exit
    no shutdown
exit
```

```
network-queue "nq1" create
    description "Example network queue policy"
    queue 1 create
        mbs 50
        cbs 1
        high-prio-only 10
    exit
    ...
    fc nc create
        multicast-queue 16
        queue 8
    exit
exit
```

SONET/SDH Ports

Listing 8.23 shows the options for applying a Network-Queue policy under the configuration of a synchronous optional networking (SONET)/synchronous digital hierarchy (SDH) port.

Listing 8.23 Options for applying a Network-Queue policy under a SONET/SDH port

```
A:Pod1>config>port>sonnet-sdh>path>network# queue-policy
  - no queue-policy
  - queue-policy <name>

 <name>                  : [32 chars max]
```

Listing 8.24 shows an example SONET/SDH port configuration in which the Network-Queue policy **nq1** is associated with the network egress buffer pool of the port.

Listing 8.24 An example SONET/SDH port configuration highlighting a Network-Queue policy association

```
port 2/2/5
    sonnet-sdh
        path
            network
                queue-policy "nq1"
            exit
             no shutdown
          exit
      exit
      no shutdown
  exit
```

Applying a Network-Queue policy under a SONET/SDH port configuration is illustrated in Figure 8.6.

Figure 8.6 Application of a Network-Queue Policy under a SONET/SDH Configuration

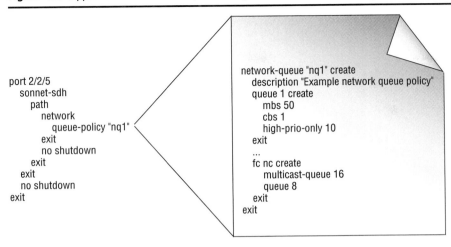

```
port 2/2/5                          network-queue "nq1" create
   sonnet-sdh                          description "Example network queue policy"
      path                             queue 1 create
         network                          mbs 50
            queue-policy "nq1"            cbs 1
         exit                             high-prio-only 10
         no shutdown                   exit
      exit                             ...
   exit                                fc nc create
   no shutdown                            multicast-queue 16
exit                                      queue 8
                                       exit
                                    exit
```

8.6 Buffer Management

So far in this chapter you have learned about buffer partitioning, queue creation and queue configuration. In this section, buffer management techniques will be addressed.

Buffer occupancy occurs when the ingress rate of a traffic stream at a queuing point is higher than its egress rate. Once the buffer occupancy of a traffic stream exceeds a certain threshold, the situation is referred to as congestion. Buffer management techniques are about how the datagrams of a traffic stream are handled once such congestion has set in.

Tail Drop Buffer Management

The simplest and most common buffer management technique is the *tail drop buffer management*. The tail drop buffer management technique drops incoming datagrams into a queue once the queue occupancy has reached a certain threshold. In ALSRP, the maximum size threshold of a queue is its MBS. Once a queue's occupancy has reached its MBS, all datagrams coming into the queue are dropped. The incoming datagrams are once again accepted into the queue only after the queue occupancy falls below the MBS threshold.

A slightly advanced version of tail drop buffer management technique recognizes queuing priorities among the datagrams flowing through a queue and offers multiple thresholds for dropping datagrams belonging to different priorities. ALSRP offers a configurable HPO threshold to drop low-queuing priority datagrams prior to dropping high-queuing priority datagrams at the MBS of a queue.

Tail drop buffer management is the default buffer management technique for both the shared and reserved portions of ALSRP. Figure 8.7 shows which buffer management technique is available in the shared and reserved portions of ALSRP. The Random Early Detection (RED) buffer management technique is optionally available only within the shared portion of a buffer pool. If RED is not configured, then the shared portion is also managed using the tail drop buffer management technique.

Figure 8.7 Buffer Management Techniques Available in Different Portions of a Buffer Pool

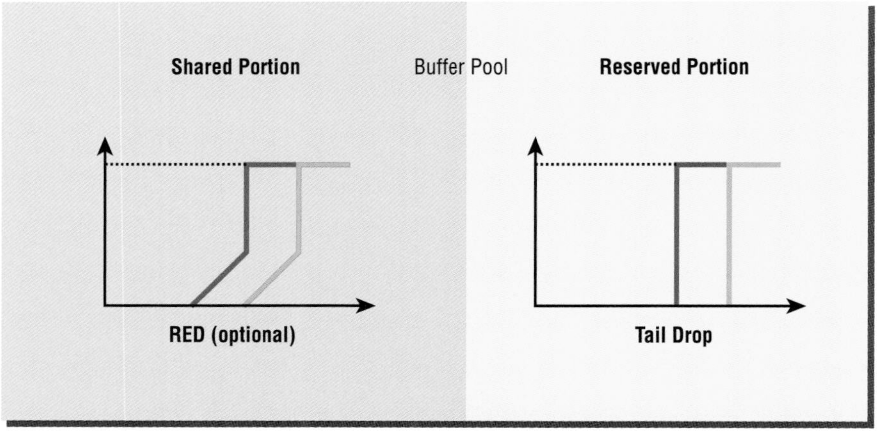

TCP Slow-Start Algorithm and the Need for RED

Transmission Control Protocol (TCP) is the predominant transport layer protocol for many Internet and intranet applications. Some of the common applications that use TCP are HTTP, Secure Shell, and FTP. TCP relies on a slow-start algorithm for controlling the amount of data segments transported across a network within a given transmission window. However, in modern high-speed networks this slow-start algorithm of TCP leads to suboptimal network bandwidth utilization.

In the initial exponential phase of a slow-start algorithm, TCP starts with one or two data segments within a transmission window and awaits acknowledgments. Once the acknowledgments for all the transmitted segments are received from the end-receiver system, the TCP doubles the number of data segments sent during the next transmission window. This process of exponential increase in the number of data segments transmitted in each subsequent transmission window repeats until a predefined slow-start threshold is reached or an acknowledgment for a transmitted segment is not received.

TCP assumes network congestion on failure to receive an acknowledgment, and as a result reduces the number of data segments transmitted during a transmission window to a small initial value.

Figure 8.8 shows the transmission behavior of TCP when a constant bandwidth is available for the transmissions in a network. The dotted line in the plot area indicates the bandwidth available for the transmission and the dashed line in the lower half of the plot area indicates the average bandwidth utilized. This figure illustrates that more than half of the network bandwidth is wasted by TCP.

Figure 8.8 Transmission Behavior of TCP

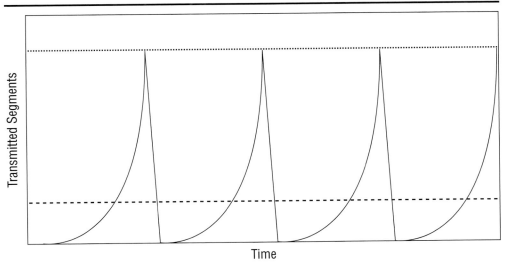

What would happen if several of these TCP streams were aggregated through a forwarding class and through a link segment within a network core? At first thought, you might assume that bandwidth multiplexing would happen, thus resulting in better network core bandwidth utilization. However, that is not the case. A phenomenon called *global synchronization* of TCP streams occurs, which results in further degradation of bandwidth utilization within the network core.

Figure 8.9 illustrates an example occurrence of global synchronization of three different TCP streams. In the example, different TCP streams start transmitting at different times and flow through a link segment within a network core. Because of the exponential increases in the traffic flow of the traffic streams, congestion sets in, and the streams contribute to the same queue occupancy. At time 9, the queue occupancy exceeds the MBS of the queue, and all further incoming datagrams into the queue are dropped by tail drop buffer management. As a result, all the TCP streams fail to receive acknowledgment for some of the segments transmitted within the window 9. Therefore, during time 10, all the TCP streams revert back to the small initial transmission value. From then on, all the TCP streams are synchronized; in other words, all the TCP streams go through the exponential increase and decrease cycles in sync, resulting in suboptimal utilization of network bandwidth throughout their data path.

Figure 8.9 Global Synchronization of TCP Streams as a Result of Tail Drop Buffer Management

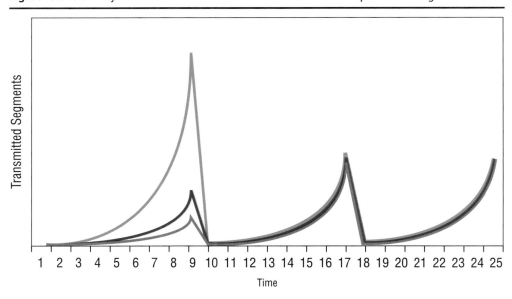

How can you solve the global synchronization of TCP streams problem and optimize the network bandwidth utilization of TCP streams? Instead of dropping datagrams from all the traffic streams at the same time, what if you drop datagrams from only one or a few of the TCP streams at a time? In that case, the streams, which lost their datagrams, would revert back to the initial transmission value, while the other streams would continue their exponential transmission. After a few transmission windows, if a few other TCP streams lost their datagrams, then, in turn, they would revert back to the initial transmission value. Thus, dropping datagrams from one or a few TCP streams at a time would result in bandwidth multiplexing. Figure 8.10 shows an ideal bandwidth multiplexing of three TCP streams. The more the TCP streams, the better the overall bandwidth utilization.

Random Early Detection is a buffer management technique that avoids congestion and optimizes bandwidth utilization of TCP streams as discussed here. Sally Floyd and Van Jacobson introduced RED in their article "Random Early Detection Gateways for Congestion Avoidance" (*IEEE/ACM Transactions on Networking,* August 1993).

Figure 8.10 An Ideal Bandwidth Multiplexing of TCP Streams

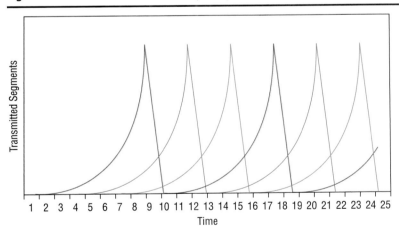

Random Early Detection

In a nutshell, Random Early Detection observes the average utilization of a buffer space. Once the utilization exceeds a certain start threshold, RED discards incoming datagrams into the buffer space, randomly using a given drop probability. As the average buffer utilization increases beyond the first threshold, the drop probability also increases. If the average buffer utilization exceeds a maximum threshold, all further incoming datagrams are dropped until the average buffer utilization falls below the maximum threshold.

ALSRP offers two independently configurable and optional RED slopes to manage traffic within the shared portion of buffer pools. The two RED slopes are `low-slope` and `high-slope`. The `low-slope` manages shared buffer access of the low-queuing priority traffic. The `high-slope` manages shared buffer access of the high-queuing priority traffic.

RED Slope Characteristics

Figure 8.11 shows a typical RED slope plotted in an X-Y graph. The *x*-axis is the percentage of shared buffer average utilization. The *y*-axis is the probability of packet discard.

Figure 8.11 RED Slope Characteristics

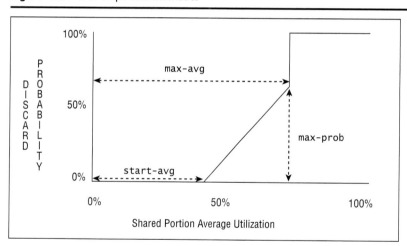

The RED curve has four regions:

1. (0, 0) to (`start-avg`, 0): When the shared buffer average utilization is between 0 and the `start-avg`, the datagram discard probability is zero and no datagrams are discarded by the RED slope.

2. (`start-avg`, 0) to (`max-avg`, `max-prob`): When the shared buffer average utilization is between `start-avg` and `max-avg`, the datagram discard probability is proportional to the average buffer utilization, and ranges from zero to the `max-prob`.

3. (`max-avg`, `max-prob`) to (`max-avg`, 100%): At the `max-avg` threshold, the datagram discard probability instantaneously increases from `max-prob` to 100 percent.

4. (`max-avg`, 100%) to (100%, 100%): When the shared buffer average utilization is between `max-avg` and 100 percent, the datagram discard probability is also 100 percent. Any incoming datagram that requests space in the shared buffer space will be discarded.

Note: If the `start-avg` and `max-avg` are configured such that they are equal to one another, the RED slope would act as a tail drop buffer management function.

The following list outlines the overall RED process:

1. The RED function keeps track of the average utilization of the shared portion space of the associated buffer pool.

2. When a datagram is received, the datagram discard probability is determined from the RED slope based on the existing average utilization.

3. A random number is generated and is compared to the discard probability of the datagram. The lower the discard probability, the lower the chances are that the random number is within the discard range.

4. If the random number is within the discard range, the datagram is discarded, which results in no change to the average utilization of the shared portion.

5. A datagram is also discarded if there is not enough space in the shared portion.

6. If the datagram is queued, a new shared portion average utilization is calculated using the time-average factor (TAF) for the buffer pool. The TAF is the relative weight of the previous shared portion average utilization result and the instantaneous shared portion utilization. (TAF is explained in detail in the following section.)

7. The new shared portion average utilization is used to determine the discard probability of the next incoming datagram.

8. If a datagram is removed from the shared portion of a queue, the shared portion utilization is reduced by the number of returned buffers.

Time-Average Factor

The *time-average factor* (TAF) parameter allows you to tune the weight provided between current utilization and the previous average utilization of the shared portion of the buffer pool while calculating a new average utilization of the shared portion.

Equation 8.3 shows how to calculate the average shared portion utilization.

Equation 8.3 Calculating a New Average Utilization of the Shared Portion of a Buffer Pool

$$SPAU_n = (SPU * \frac{1}{2^{TAF}}) + (SPAU_{n-1} * \frac{2^{TAF} - 1}{2^{TAF}})$$

where:

$SPAU_n$: Shared portion average utilization when the nth datagram arrives

SPU: Instantaneous shared portion utilization

$SPAU_{n-1}$: Shared portion average utilization when the n-1 datagram arrived

TAF: Time-average factor

The TAF is a configurable parameter that takes an integer value between 0 and 15 inclusively. The value is configured in the Slope policy and the same value applies to both high and low RED slopes.

The lower the TAF value, the higher the preference given to the instantaneous shared buffer utilization. Table 8.5 lists the weights distributed between the previous shared portion average utilization and the instantaneous shared buffer utilization for all the TAF values. The default TAF value is 7.

Table 8.5 Weight Distributed between Previous Average Utilization and Instantaneous Utilization for Different TAF Values

TAF	Weight	
	Previous Average Utilization	Instantaneous Utilization
0	0/1 = 0	1/1 = 1
1	1/2 = 0.5	1/2 = 0.5
2	3/4 = 0.75	1/4 = 0.25
3	7/8 = 0.875	1/8 = 0.125
4	15/16 = 0.9375	1/16 = 0.0625

(continued)

Table 8.5 Weight Distributed between Previous Average Utilization and Instantaneous Utilization for Different TAF Values *(continued)*

TAF	Weight	
	Previous Average Utilization	Instantaneous Utilization
5	31/32 = 0.96875	1/32 = 0.03125
6	63/64 = 0.984375	1/64 = 0.015625
7	127/128 = 0.9921875	1/128 = 0.0078125
8	255/256 = 0.99609375	1/256 = 0.00390625
9	511/512 = 0.998046875	1/512 = 0.001953125
10	1023/1024 = 0.9990234375	1/1024 = 0.0009765625
11	2047/2048 = 0.99951171875	1/2048 = 0.00048828125
12	4095/4096 = 0.999755859375	1/4096 = 0.00024414025
13	8191/8192 = 0.9998779296875	1/8192 = 0.0001220703125
14	16383/16384 = 0.99993896484375	1/16384 = 0.00006103515625
15	32767/32768 = 0.999969482421875	1/32768 = 0.000030517578125

Points to Ponder on RED Implementation

- RED is offered only within the shared portion and not in the reserved portion. The reason for this is that by definition, the reserved portion is guaranteed buffer space for different queues. Therefore, within that space there cannot be any random discards.

- You might expect that randomly discarding datagrams could lead to unfair service between different TCP streams, but this is not the case. The impact (number of datagrams dropped at a congestion point) felt by different TCP streams at a congestion point due to RED is proportional to the stream's contribution to the congestion.

- In the RED function, a moving average of shared portion utilization is used in determining datagram discard probability. Why is this so? The shared portion of a buffer pool is typically meant for the use of bursty traffic streams. As a result, instantaneous utilization of the shared portion can fluctuate drastically. Therefore, if the instantaneous shared portion utilization is used to determine the packet discard probability, the buffer management would be unstable. On the other hand, if higher preference is given to the previous shared portion average utilization, the changes in the calculation would become sluggish. As a result, the RED function may not effectively handle bursty traffic. Therefore, depending on the burstiness of the traffic handled, the TAF value must be configured appropriately.

(continued)

Points to Ponder on RED Implementation *(continued)*

- If TCP streams and UDP streams are managed by the same RED function, a TCP stream would regulate its bandwidth consumption as a result of dropping one of its datagrams, whereas a User Datagram Protocol (UDP) stream would not regulate its bandwidth consumption even if several of its datagrams were dropped. As a result of these different behaviors, UDP streams could run TCP streams dry. You can avoid this situation by regulating traffic coming from TCP streams using the high-slope of the RED function, and regulating traffic coming from UDP streams using the low-slope.

- Many real-time applications use User Datagram Protocol/Real-time Transport Protocol (UDP/RTP). Those applications cannot be entirely regulated by the low-slope of RED function. How do you address this situation? High-priority forwarding classes—the ones that would be used by real-time applications—would entirely use the reserved portion of a buffer pool to obtain guaranteed buffer space. Hence, that traffic would not be subjected to any RED buffer management. Moreover, the traffic belonging to high-priority forwarding classes typically tends to be well regulated and provided with adequate bandwidth; as a result they do not consume much buffer space.

8.7 Slope Policy

A Slope policy is used to configure RED parameters associated with a buffer pool. Listing 8.25 shows the command options for creating a Slope policy.

Listing 8.25 Command options for creating a Slope policy

```
A:Pod1>config>qos# slope-policy
  - no slope-policy <name>
  - slope-policy <name> [create]

 <name>              : [32 chars max]
 <create>            : keyword - mandatory while creating an entry.
```

Like Network-Queue policies, Slope policies are also identified through their policy name. A policy name is a string of characters with a maximum limit of 32 characters.

Listing 8.26 illustrates the default Slope policy configuration. As evident in the code, the `high-slope` and `low-slope` are `shutdown` in the default policy.

Listing 8.26 Default Slope policy

```
A:Pod1>config>qos# slope-policy default
A:Pod1>config>qos>slope-policy# info detail
---------------------------------------------
            description "Default slope policy."
            high-slope
                shutdown
                start-avg 70
                max-avg 90
                max-prob 80
            exit
            low-slope
                shutdown
                start-avg 50
                max-avg 75
                max-prob 80
            exit
            time-average-factor 7
---------------------------------------------
```

The `start-avg`, and `max-avg` are configured as a certain percentage of the shared portion size of a buffer pool. The `max-prob` is configured as a certain percentage of discard probability. Listing 8.27 provides the options for configuring RED slope parameters.

Listing 8.27 Options for configuring RED slope parameters

```
A:Pod1>config>qos>slope-policy>high-slope# start-avg
  - no start-avg
  - start-avg <percent>

 <percent>            : [0..100]

A:Pod1>config>qos>slope-policy>high-slope# max-avg
  - max-avg <percent>
```

(continued)

```
  - no max-avg

 <percent>              : [0..100]

A:Pod1>config>qos>slope-policy>high-slope# max-prob
  - max-prob <percent>
  - no max-prob

 <percent>              : [0..100]
```

Listing 8.28 shows the options for configuring the TAF within a Slope policy.

Listing 8.28 Options for configuring the TAF

```
A:Pod1>config>qos>slope-policy# time-average-factor
  - no time-average-factor
  - time-average-factor <value>

 <value>                : [0..15]
```

8.8 Applying Slope Policy

To make the association with access ingress, access egress, and network egress buffer pools, Slope policies are applied under a port configuration. To associate with a network ingress buffer pool, Slope policies are applied under an MDA configuration.

The command options available to associate a slope policy with a network ingress buffer pool is illustrated in Listing 8.29.

Listing 8.29 Options for applying a Slope policy under an MDA configuration

```
A:Pod1# configure card 1 mda 1 network ingress pool
A:Pod1>config>card>mda>network>ingress>pool# slope-policy
  - no slope-policy
  - slope-policy <name>

 <name>                 : [32 chars max]
```

Listing 8.30 shows an example MDA configuration in which the Slope policy sp1 is associated with the network ingress buffer pool of the MDA. The figure also shows the association of Network-Queue policy nq1 with the buffer pool.

Listing 8.30 An example MDA configuration highlighting a Slope policy association

```
mda 1
    mda-type m5-1gb-sfp
    network
        ingress
            pool
                slope-policy "sp1"
            exit
            queue-policy "nq1"
        exit
    exit
exit
```

Applying a Slope policy under an MDA configuration is illustrated in Figure 8.12.

Figure 8.12 Application of a Slope Policy under an MDA Configuration

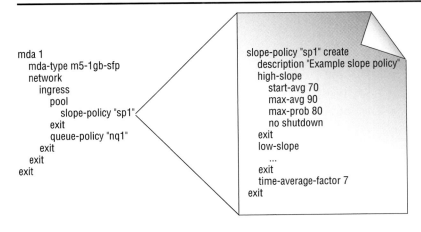

Listings 8.31, 8.32, and 8.33 show the options for associating a Slope policy with access ingress, access egress, and network egress buffer pools, respectively.

Listing 8.31 Options for associating a Slope policy with an access ingress buffer pool

```
A:Pod1>config>port>access>ingress>pool# slope-policy
  - no slope-policy
  - slope-policy <name>

 <name>              : [32 chars max]
```

Listing 8.32 Options for associating a Slope policy with an access egress buffer pool

```
A:Pod1>config>port>access>egress>pool# slope-policy
  - no slope-policy
  - slope-policy <name>

 <name>              : [32 chars max]
```

Listing 8.33 Options for associating a Slope policy with a network egress buffer pool

```
A:Pod1>config>port>network>egress>pool# slope-policy
  - no slope-policy
  - slope-policy <name>

 <name>              : [32 chars max]
```

8.9 Verification Commands for Buffer Management

So far in this chapter you have learned about buffer partitions, queuing, and buffer management within ALSRP. In this section, you will learn some of the related ALSRP verification and validation commands.

In Chapter 6, Listing 6.37 lists all the commands available under show qos. This section, overviews the show qos commands associated with Network-Queue and Slope policies. The show qos command syntax for these two polices is:

```
network-queue [<network-queue-policy-name>] [detail]
slope-policy [<slope-policy-name>] [detail]
```

When a policy-name is specified in the commands, information regarding the specified policy is displayed. When no policy-name is specified in the commands, information regarding all the configured policies of the given type is displayed.

Without any optional parameters these commands (for example, show qos slope-policy) simply list all the configured policies of the type along with their descriptions.

The detail option of the command lists all the details about a policy, including its associations. Listing 8.34 provides a sample output of the show qos network-queue <policy-name> detail command. Listing 8.35 displays a sample output of show qos slope-policy <policy-name> detail command.

Listing 8.34 A sample output of the show qos network-queue <policy-name> detail command

```
A:Pod1# show qos network-queue nq1 detail
===============================================================================
QoS Network Queue Policy
===============================================================================
-------------------------------------------------------------------------------
Network Queue Policy (nq1)
-------------------------------------------------------------------------------
Policy       : nq1
Description  : Example network queue policy
-------------------------------------------------------------------------------
Queue CIR       PIR      CBS      MBS     HiPrio
-------------------------------------------------------------------------------
1     0         100      1.00     50.00   10
2     25        100      3.00     50.00   10
3     25        100      10.00    50.00   10
4     25        100      3.00     25.00   10
```

(continued)

```
5       100     100     10.00  50.00   10
6       100     100     10.00  50.00   10
7       10      100     3.00   25.00   10
8       10      100     3.00   25.00   10
9       0       100     1.00   50.00   10
10      5       100     1.00   50.00   10
11      5       100     1.00   50.00   10
12      5       100     1.00   25.00   10
13      100     100     1.00   50.00   10
14      100     100     1.00   50.00   10
15      10      100     1.00   25.00   10
16      10      100     1.00   25.00   10
-------------------------------------------------------------------------
FC      UCastQ  MCastQ
-------------------------------------------------------------------------
be      1       9
l2      2       10
af      3       11
l1      4       12
h2      5       13
ef      6       14
h1      7       15
nc      8       16


-------------------------------------------------------------------------
Associations
-------------------------------------------------------------------------
MDA     : 1/1
Port-id : 1/2/5
=========================================================================
```

Listing 8.35 A sample output of the show qos slope-policy <policy-name> detail command

```
A:Pod1# show qos slope-policy sp1 detail
=========================================================================
QoS Slope policy
=========================================================================
Policy       : sp1
Description  : Example slope policy
Time Avg     : 7
```

(continued)

```
--------------------------------------------------------------------------
High Slope Parameters
--------------------------------------------------------------------------
Start Avg      : 70                   Admin State  : Enabled
Max Avg        : 90                   Max Prob.    : 80


--------------------------------------------------------------------------
Low Slope Parameters
--------------------------------------------------------------------------
Start Avg      : 50                   Admin State  : Enabled
Max Avg        : 75                   Max Prob.    : 80


--------------------------------------------------------------------------
Associations
--------------------------------------------------------------------------
Object Type Object Id    Application        Pool
--------------------------------------------------------------------------
MDA         1/1          Net-Ing            default
Port        1/1/2        Net-Egr            default
==========================================================================
```

Listing 8.36 shows another family of commands useful to verify and debug buffer-related configuration issues.

Listing 8.36 show pools family of commands

```
A:Pod2# show pools
  - pools <mda-id[/port]> [<access-app> [service <service-id>]]
  - pools <mda-id[/port]> [<network-app>]

 <mda-id[/port]>      : slot/mda[/port]
 <access-app>         : access-ingress|access-egress
 <network-app>        : network-ingress|network-egress
 <service-id>         : [1..2147483647]
```

The command `show pools <mda-id[/port]>` lists all the logical buffer pools associated with the specified entity (MDA or port), but provides actual pool size only for those physical buffer pools that are actually created for the entity.

When a specific buffer pool is mentioned along with `show pools <mda-id[/port]>`, the command lists the buffer management details of the pool along with the details of the queues configured within the buffer pool. Listing 8.37 shows a sample output of the `show pools <port-id> network-egress` command.

Listing 8.37 A sample output of the show pools <port-id> network-egress command

```
A:Pod2# show pools 1/1/1 network-egress

===============================================================================
Pool Information
===============================================================================
Port                 : 1/1/1
Application          : Net-Egr         Pool Name         : default
Resv CBS             : Sum
-------------------------------------------------------------------------------
Utilization                   State     Start-Avg    Max-Avg    Max-Prob
-------------------------------------------------------------------------------
High-Slope                    Up             70%        90%         80%
Low-Slope                     Up             50%        75%         80%

Time Avg Factor      : 7
Pool Total           : 10240 KB
Pool Shared          : 6144 KB         Pool Resv         : 4096 KB

High Slope Start Avg : 4096 KB         High slope Max Avg : 5120 KB
Low Slope Start Avg  : 3072 KB         Low slope Max Avg  : 4096 KB

Pool Total In Use    : 0 KB
Pool Shared In Use   : 0 KB            Pool Resv In Use  : 0 KB
WA Shared In Use     : 0 KB

Hi-Slope Drop Prob   : 0               Lo-Slope Drop Prob : 0
-------------------------------------------------------------------------------
FC-Maps                       ID        MBS      Depth  A.CIR     A.PIR
                                        CBS             O.CIR     O.PIR
-------------------------------------------------------------------------------
be                            1/1/1     5120     0      0         1000000
                                        96              0         Max
l2                            1/1/1     5120     0      250000    1000000
                                        256             250000    Max
```

(continued)

```
af                              1/1/1     5120        0      250000     1000000
                                          896                250000     Max
l1                              1/1/1     2560        0      250000     1000000
                                          256                250000     Max
h2                              1/1/1     5120        0      1000000    1000000
                                          896                Max        Max
ef                              1/1/1     5120        0      1000000    1000000
                                          896                Max        Max
h1                              1/1/1     2560        0      100000     1000000
                                          256                100000     Max
nc                              1/1/1     2560        0      100000     1000000
                                          256                100000     Max
==============================================================================
```

As evident in Listing 8.37, there are three parts to the `show pools` output: pool information, buffer management details, and details of all the queues created within the buffer pool.

Under the pool information, the value `sum` for `Resv CBS` indicates that no explicit distribution is specified between the reserved and shared partitions of the buffer pool, and the size of the reserved partition is automatically calculated as the sum of the CBS of the queues created within the buffer pool.

Under the buffer management details, the first three lines (starting with `High-Slope`, `Low-Slope`, and `Time Avg Factor`) lists the configuration details of the associated Slope policy. The next two lines (`Pool Total`, `Pool Shared`, and `Pool Resv`) list the actual size of the buffer pool and its partitions. The next two lines list the physical sizes of high- and low-slope thresholds. The next three lines list the current usage of different partitions of the buffer pool. `WA shared` refers to Weighted Average utilization of shared portion. `Hi-Slope` and `Low-Slope Drop Prob` values indicate respectively the drop probabilities calculated for the next incoming high- and low-queuing priority datagram.

The details listed for each queue created within the buffer pool include:

- CBS, MBS, and current utilization (`Depth`) in terms of KB.

- Administrative and operational CIR in terms of Kbps.

- Administrative and operational PIR in terms of Kbps.

The difference between actual and operational rates is explained in Chapter 10.

> **Note:** You may encounter small differences between allocated MBS and CBS sizes of a queue when compared to the configured values. Because the buffer is usually allocated as certain blocks, there could be a rounding off of differences.

If a `service-id` is specified in the following command, only queues belonging to the specified service will be listed in the output of the command:

```
show pools <mda-id[/port]> [<access-app> [service <service-id>]]
```

Summary

Buffer partitions within an IOM of ALSRP include hard and soft partitions. Soft partitions include buffer pools allocated for MDA and port entities. A buffer pool is further divided into reserved and shared portions. Queues are configured within buffer pools and a queue may take buffers from either or both of the reserved and shared portions of a buffer pool.

Each access port has an exclusively assigned access ingress and access egress buffer pool. Each SAP has its own set of queues both at access ingress and egress. At access ingress, traffic belonging to different forwarding classes and different forwarding types can be mapped to different queues through the associated SAP-ingress policy. At access egress, traffic belonging to different forwarding classes can be mapped to different queues through the associated SAP-egress policy.

Each network port has an exclusively assigned network egress buffer pool. At the ingress side, all the network ports of an MDA share a common mega-buffer pool to take advantage of statistical multiplexing gain. Both at network ingress and network egress, a common Network-Queue policy is used to map traffic to queues and to configure queue parameters. Both at network ingress and network egress, traffic belonging to different forwarding classes can be mapped to different queues. Additionally, at network ingress, unicast traffic and multicast traffic are mapped to different sets of queues.

An ALSRP queue has three buffer-related parameters: CBS, MBS, and HPO. The CBS of a queue is guaranteed buffer space for the queue, which is drawn from the reserved portion of the associated buffer pool. The MBS is the maximum size of a queue. The difference between the MBS and the CBS is the buffer space that the queue can draw from the shared portion of the buffer pool in which the queue is created. By sharing the space drawn from the shared portion of a buffer pool with other queues created within the pool, the queue takes advantage of statistical multiplexing gain. The HPO is the buffer space within a queue, which is reserved exclusively for high-queuing priority traffic.

By default, both the reserved and shared portions of a buffer pool are managed by the tail drop buffer management technique. Optionally, the shared portion of a buffer pool can be managed using the RED buffer management technique. ALSRP provides two individually configurable RED slopes for managing high- and low-queuing priority datagrams. A Slope policy is used to configure RED parameters associated with a buffer pool.

Hardware Queue Enabling Options at Access Ingress

9

For a provider edge device aggregating thousands of subscribers in a triple-play type application, optimizing the number of hardware queues allocated at the access ingress is important.

Chapter Objectives

- To demonstrate how to optimize multipoint SAP aggregation in an MDA in a PE device

- To explain the flexibility offered by ALSRP in scaling the number of hardware queues available at access ingress for servicing customer traffic

- To explain how the data path of traffic types changes with the different scaling options

Throughout this book, you have seen the flexibility offered by ALSRP's quality of service (QoS) features to adapt to different application needs. In this chapter, you will learn about the advanced flexibility of the ALSRP scaling options for access ingress queuing, which allow service providers to control the number of hardware queues created for a service at access ingress. In the rest of this chapter, the scaling options for access ingress queuing are simply referred to as the scaling options.

Why is controlling the number of hardware queues created for a service in an MDA at access ingress important?

- Depending on the network application, an MDA of a PE device can aggregate a number of SAPs, anywhere from a few to several thousands.

- According to one of the basic premises of the DiffServ model, incoming customer traffic has to be rate monitored before aggregating the microflows at the service provider edge. Two actions can result from rate monitoring the microflows: marking of packets in excess of committed information rate (CIR) with a higher drop preference within the same forwarding class (FC), and rate-limiting microflow packets to not exceed PIR. Therefore, at the access ingress each SAP's traffic is isolated by having a separate set of queues.

- In the ALSRP, depending on the service and the associated SAP-ingress policy, the number of queues required for a SAP varies anywhere from 1 to 32.

- For multipoint services (VPLS, VPRN, and IES) head-of-line blocking at access ingress, which can be caused due to destination MDA egress congestion, is prevented by isolating traffic destined to different MDA egress.

Thus, depending on the network application, the number of hardware queues required in the ingress direction of a PE device MDA can vary from a few queues to several thousands of queues. Therefore, depending on the network application, optimization of the number of queues created may be essential at access ingress.

For network applications like edge aggregation in triple-play service offerings, such optimization would help increase the scalability of customer aggregation.

9.1 Configuring the Scaling Options

ALSRP provides the following three scaling options for access ingress queuing:

1.   Service Queuing

2. Shared Queuing

3. Multipoint Shared Queuing

The default option is Service Queuing. The other two options have to be explicitly configured under service SAP configuration.

Listing 9.1 shows the command line syntax for selecting the scaling options for VPLS service. Selecting the options for the other multipoint services—VPRN and IES—is similar; except the SAPs are configured under an interface for VPRN and IES services. All three scaling options are also available for IES and VPLS subscriber SLA profile instance queuing.

Note: The IES and VPLS subscriber SLA profiles are explained in the *Triple-Play Guide*, which is part of the ALSRP product manuals.

Listing 9.1 Configuring the scaling option for a multipoint service

```
A:Pod1>config>service>vpls>sap>ingress# qos
  - no qos [<policy-id>]
  - qos <policy-id> [shared-queuing|multipoint-shared]

<policy-id>          : [1..65535]
<shared-queuing|mu*> : keywords
```

Listing 9.2 shows the syntax for selecting the scaling options for Epipe service. As mentioned in Chapter 1, Epipe is a type of virtual leased line (VLL) service. The other types of VLL services are Apipe, Fpipe, and Ipipe. Selecting the scaling options is similar for all the point-to-point services: Apipe, Fpipe, and Ipipe.

Listing 9.2 Configuring the scaling option for a point-to-point service

```
A:Pod2>config>service>epipe>sap>ingress$ qos
  - no qos [<policy-id>]
  - qos <policy-id> [shared-queuing]

<policy-id>          : [1..65535]
<shared-queuing>     : enables shared-queuing
```

As you may observe in Listing 9.2, the Multipoint Shared Queuing option is not available for point-to-point services. Also, the Multipoint Shared Queuing option is not available under the Routed-CO model, which does not support upstream (customer to service provider) multipoint traffic.

Note: The Routed-CO model is explained in the *Triple-Play Guide,* which is a part of the ALSRP product manuals.

9.2 An Example for Comparing the Scaling Options

To understand the differences among the three different scaling options, consider a VPLS service example, which aggregates three different SAPs. Listing 9.3 shows its configuration.

Listing 9.3 An example VPLS configuration using the Service Queuing option

```
vpls 100 customer 1 create
    shutdown
    stp
        shutdown
    exit
    sap 1/2/2:1001 create
        ingress
            qos 100
        exit
    exit
    sap 1/2/2:1002 create
        ingress
            qos 100
        exit
    exit
    sap 1/2/2:1003 create
        ingress
            qos 100
        exit
    exit
    spoke-sdp 12:100 create
    exit
exit
```

In the example VPLS configuration, three SAPs are configured in port 1/2/2 and a service distribution point (SDP) is configured under an interface in port 1/1/1. An SDP acts as a logical way to direct traffic from one ALSRP node to another through a unidirectional service tunnel. According to the configuration, any incoming traffic to the VPLS is forwarded to two different MDAs. Figure 9.1 shows a logical representation of the traffic forwarding. The logical representation shows only the required MDAs and ports.

Figure 9.1 Logical Representation of Traffic Flow through an Example VPLS Configuration

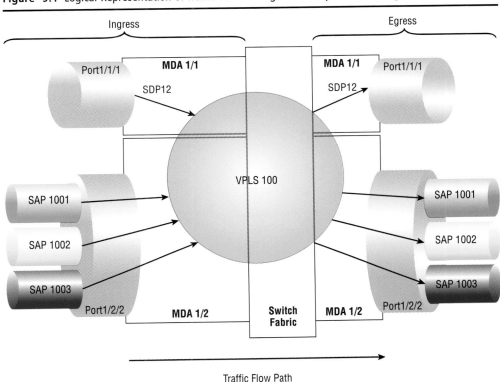

Traffic Flow Path

Listing 9.4 shows SAP-ingress policy 100 associated with the SAPs in the Listing 9.3 example service configuration. According to the QoS policy, the ingress traffic through each of the SAPs is associated with one of the two different FCs. Each FC in turn is mapped to a unicast queue and a separate multicast queue. In total, the SAP-ingress QoS policy associates four queues to each SAP.

```
sap-ingress 100 create
    queue 1 create
    exit
    queue 3 create
    exit
    queue 9 multipoint create
    exit
    queue 11 multipoint create
    exit
    fc "af" create
        queue 3
        multicast-queue 11
    exit
    fc "be" create
        queue 1
        multicast-queue 9
    exit
    ...
    #Traffic Mappings to FCs are not shown
    ...
exit
```

9.3 Service Queuing

As mentioned earlier, the default scaling option is Service Queuing. The configuration shown in Listing 9-3 invokes the default Service Queuing at the access ingress of the three SAPs (the ingress side of MDA 1/2 in the example).

Figure 9.2 shows queues created at the ingress of MDA 1/2 for the configuration. Note that the queues in Figure 9.2 are color-coded according to the FC they are mapped to and also according to the SAP they belong to. As shown in Figure 9.2, for each SAP, the Service Queuing option creates one set of unicast queues for each destination MDA involved in the service configuration. In addition, for each SAP a separate set of multipoint queues are created for servicing multipoint traffic destined for multiple destination MDAs.

Why do you need a separate set of unicast queues for each destination MDA? A separate set of unicast queues per SAP for each destination MDA is required to avoid head-of-line blocking at the ingress. Sorting data traffic on a per-switch fabric destination basis allows transmission to an uncongested destination even if one or more destinations experience congestion.

Figure 9.2 Hardware Queues Enabled while Using the Service Queuing Option

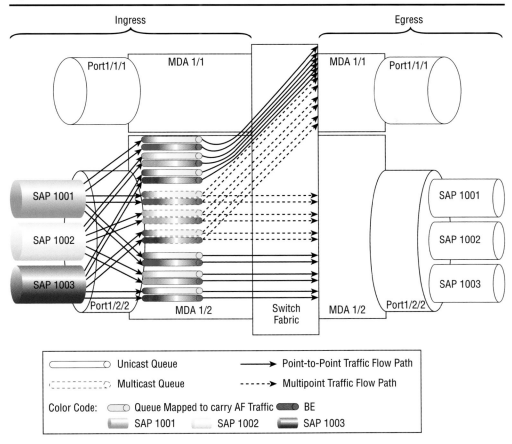

When the Service Queuing option creates multiple hardware queues corresponding to a single logical service queue configured through a SAP-ingress policy, the system automatically monitors the offered load and forwarding rate of each hardware queue such that their aggregate committed information rate (CIR) and peak information rate (PIR) reflects what is provisioned on the service queue through the SAP-ingress policy.

With the Service Queuing option, the incoming SAP traffic is queued only once at the access ingress. Consequently, there are no additional datagram processing requirements. However, by looking at Equation 9.1 and because of the fact that there is a finite number of hardware queues available to an MDA, you can infer that a high number of unicast queues, multicast queues, or destination MDAs would limit the number of SAPs associated with the service in one MDA.

Explanation through Equations

Equation 9.1 shows the formula for the number of hardware queues created at access ingress, when the Service Queuing option is chosen.

Equation 9.1 Number of Hardware Queues Created with the Service Queuing Option

$$HWQ = \sum_{S_i=SAP_1}^{SAP_n} [(SIPUCQ(S_i) * DMDA) + SIPMCQ(S_i)]$$

Where

HWQ: Number of hardware queues created

SAP_n: Total number of SAPs configured, in the MDA under consideration, for the service

$SIPUCQ(S_i)$: Number of unicast queues configured in the SAP-ingress policy associated with SAP S_i

$DMDA$: Number of destination MDA associated with the given service

$SIPMCQ(S_i)$: Number of multipoint queues configured in the SAP-ingress policy associated with SAP S_i

In the example under consideration,

$$HWQ = \sum_{S_i=1}^{3} [(SIPUCQ(S_i) = 2 * DMDA = 2) + SIPMCQ(S_i) = 2] = 18.$$

According to Equation 9.1, the number of SAPs aggregated in an MDA can be maximized by minimizing both the number of logical queues configured in the associated SAP-ingress and the number of destination MDAs associated with the multipoint service.

Minimizing the number of logical queues at access ingress does not necessarily imply lower granularity of traffic classification or a lower number of network and access egress queues. Careful QoS planning can maximize the number of SAPs of a multipoint service aggregated in an MDA by reducing the number of service ingress logical queues, while maintaining the granularity of classification.

Impact of Service Queuing over Point-to-Point Services

Point-to-point services map one ingress entity and one egress entity, so there is no question of scaling SAPs. Because there is only one egress entity, the DMDA for those services is always equal to 1. Once you substitute *DMDA* = 1 in Equation 9.1, the hardware queues created for each SAP would have one-to-one correspondence with the logical queues declared in the associated SAP-ingress policy. So Service Queuing does not have any bearing on the point-to-point services, and consideration is required only while using a multipoint service for network applications such as edge aggregation in triple-play service offerings.

Similarly, a good network design can minimize the number of destination MDAs associated with the multipoint service. In the case of multipoint services, configuring only one destination MDA (i.e., substituting DMDA = 1 in Equation 9.1) would result in hardware queues created for each SAP having one-to-one correspondence with the logical queues declared in the associated SAP-ingress policy. However, configuring only one destination MDA for a multipoint service or even reducing down to a few MDAs is not always possible, particularly when network redundancy is paramount.

When minimizing the number of service ingress logical queues or minimizing the number of destination MDAs associated with the service is not possible, or when the minimization does not sufficiently increase the number of SAPs aggregated in an MDA into the multipoint service, the Shared Queuing or Multipoint Shared Queuing options are the alternatives to consider.

9.4 Shared Queuing

As stated in Section 9.1, to choose the Shared Queuing option, the `shared-queuing` keyword has to be enabled while associating a SAP-ingress policy in the service configuration. For example, the VPLS service configuration illustrated in Listing 9-5 shows the modified configuration with the `shared-queuing` option enabled.

Figure 9.3 shows the hardware queues created in the ingress direction of MDA 1/2 by the Shared Queuing option. As shown in Figure 9.3, two stages of queues are created for unicast traffic. In the first stage, a set of unicast queues in one-to-one correspondence with the logical queues configured through the associated

SAP-ingress policy is created for each SAP. In the second stage, the system automatically creates eight queues (corresponding to the eight FCs) for each of the destination MDAs. The second stage queues are shared by all the SAPs sending traffic to a particular destination. The multipoint queues are not impacted by the Shared Queuing option.

Listing 9.5 An example VPLS configuration using the Shared Queuing option

```
vpls 100 customer 1 create
    shutdown
    stp
        shutdown
    exit
    sap 1/2/2:1001 create
        ingress
            qos 100 shared-queuing
        exit
    exit
    sap 1/2/2:1002 create
        ingress
            qos 100 shared-queuing
        exit
    exit
    sap 1/2/2:1003 create
        ingress
            qos 100 shared-queuing
        exit
    exit
    spoke-sdp 12:100 create
    exit
exit
```

The first stage queues are used for rate-limiting the customer traffic and to maintain service statistics. The second stage queues are used as ingress virtual output queues and prevent head-of-line blocking at the ingress as a result of congestion at one or more egress ports.

Figure 9.3 Hardware Queues Enabled while Using the Shared Queuing Option

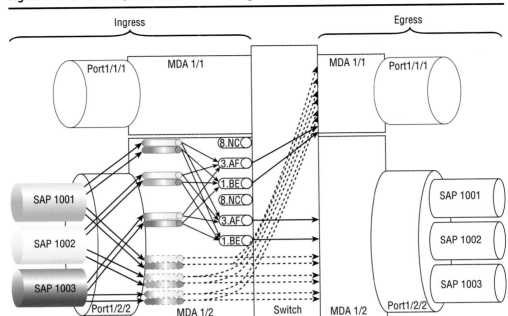

The second stage queues are subjected to the configuration of the default Shared-Queue QoS policy. The first stage queues created for each SAP have a one-to-one relationship with the queues provisioned in the associated SAP-ingress policy.

Table 9.1 lists the default configuration of the unicast queues of the Shared-Queue QoS policy. The rates are defined as a percentage of the associated port rate. The buffer sizes are defined as a percentage of the associated buffer pool size. The default unicast queues configuration of the default Shared-Queue QoS policy and Network-Queue QoS policy are identical.

Explanation through Equations

Equation 9.2 provides the formula for the number of hardware queues created in the first stage at access ingress, while using the Shared Queuing option.

Equation 9.2 Number of Hardware Queues Created in the First Stage with the Shared Queuing Option

---

$$FHWQ = \sum_{S_i=SAP_1}^{SAP_n} [SIPUCQ(S_i) + SIPMPQ(S_i)]$$

Where

$FHWQ$: Number of hardware queues created in the first stage

SAP_n: Total no. of SAPs configured, in the MDA under consideration, for the service

$SIPUCQ(S_i)$: Number of unicast queues configured in the SAP-ingress policy associated with SAP S_i

$SIPMPQ(S_i)$: Number of multipoint queues configured in the SAP-ingress policy associated with SAP S_i

In the example under consideration,

$$FHWQ = \sum_{S_i=1}^{3} [SIPUCQ(S_i) = 2] + [SIPMPQ(S_i) = 2] = 12.$$

The system uses a constant number of queues for the second stage. The number of second stage queues is dependent on the chassis type. Equation 9-3 shows the overall formula for the number of queues created, while using the Shared Queuing option.

(continued)

Equation 9-3 Number of Hardware Queues Created with the Shared Queuing Option

$$HWQ = FHWQ + (SHWQ = \delta_c)$$

On expanding the above equation we get:

$$HWQ = \sum_{S_i=SAP_1}^{SAP_n} [SIPUCQ(S_i) + SIPMPQ(S_i)] + \delta_c$$

Where

   HWQ: Number of hardware queues created

   $SHWQ$: Number of hardware queues created in the second stage

   δ_c: A chassis-dependent constant

Table 9.1 Default Configuration of Unicast Queues of the Default Shared-Queue QoS Policy

Configuration in %	High-Priority FCs				Low-Priority FCs			
	NC Q8	H1 Q7	EF Q6	H2 Q5	L1 Q4	AF Q3	L2 Q2	BE Q1
PIR	100	100	100	100	100	100	100	100
CIR	10	10	100	100	25	25	25	0
MBS	25	25	50	50	25	50	50	50
CBS	3	3	10	10	3	10	3	1
HPO	10	10	10	10	10	10	10	10

The default Shared-Queue QoS policy also defines 24 multipoint queues, besides the 8 unicast queues. These multipoint queues are neither instantiated nor applicable for the Shared Queuing option.

Because the Shared Queuing option creates only one (first stage) hardware queue for each SAP corresponding to each logical service queue configured in the associated SAP-ingress policy, the queue rates configured in the policy are directly imposed.

In order to evaluate the hardware queue optimization provided by the Shared Queuing option as compared to the Service Queuing option, compare Equation 9.1 with Equation 9.3.

For the Service Queuing option (Equation 9.1):

$$HWQ = \sum_{S_i=SAP_1}^{SAP_n} [(SIPUCQ(S_i) * DMDA) + SIPMCQ(S_i)]$$

For the Shared Queuing option (Equation 9.3):

$$HWQ = \sum_{S_i=SAP_1}^{SAP_n} [SIPUCQ(S_i) + SIPMPQ(S_i)] + \delta_c$$

The important difference between the two equations is the absence of the multiplicative factor DMDA for the Shared Queuing option. In other words, the Shared Queuing option does not create a set of unicast queues for each of the destination MDAs associated with the multipoint service. Therefore, when a multipoint service associated with multiple destination MDAs aggregates hundreds and thousands of SAPs in an MDA, the Shared Queuing option would help scale the application. In such a scenario, the number of second stage queues (δ_c) that the Shared Queuing option enables would be insignificant when compared to the queue optimization the option provides.

Because of dual-stage queue processing, under the Shared Queuing option unicast traffic datagrams are processed twice at the access ingress. However, because multipoint traffic flows only through a single stage of the ingress queue, there is no additional datagram processing.

9.5 Multipoint Shared Queuing

Similar to the Shared Queuing option, to choose the Multipoint Shared Queuing option, the `multipoint-shared` keyword has to be explicitly enabled while associating a SAP-ingress policy in the service configuration. For the VPLS service example under consideration, Listing 9.6 shows the modified configuration with the `multipoint-shared` queuing option enabled.

Listing 9.6 An example VPLS configuration using the Multipoint Shared Queuing option

```
vpls 100 customer 1 create
    shutdown
    stp
        shutdown
    exit
    sap 1/2/2:1001 create
        ingress
            qos 100 multipoint-shared
        exit
    exit
    sap 1/2/2:1002 create
        ingress
            qos 100 multipoint-shared
        exit
    exit
    sap 1/2/2:1003 create
        ingress
            qos 100 multipoint-shared
        exit
    exit
    spoke-sdp 12:100 create
    exit
exit
```

Figure 9.4 shows queues created at the ingress of MDA 1/2 by the Multipoint Shared Queuing option. As indicated in Figure 9.4, the Multipoint Shared Queuing option optimizes the number of hardware queues created at access ingress more than the Shared Queuing option. When the Multipoint Shared Queuing option is enabled, both the multipoint traffic and unicast traffic flow through the same two stages of queues. As a result, all the traffic is processed twice at the access ingress of the MDA.

Although multipoint and unicast traffic flow through the same set of queues, they conform to their respective queue configurations as given in their SAP-ingress and Shared-Queue policies.

Figure 9.4 Hardware Queues Enabled while Using the Multipoint Shared Queuing Option

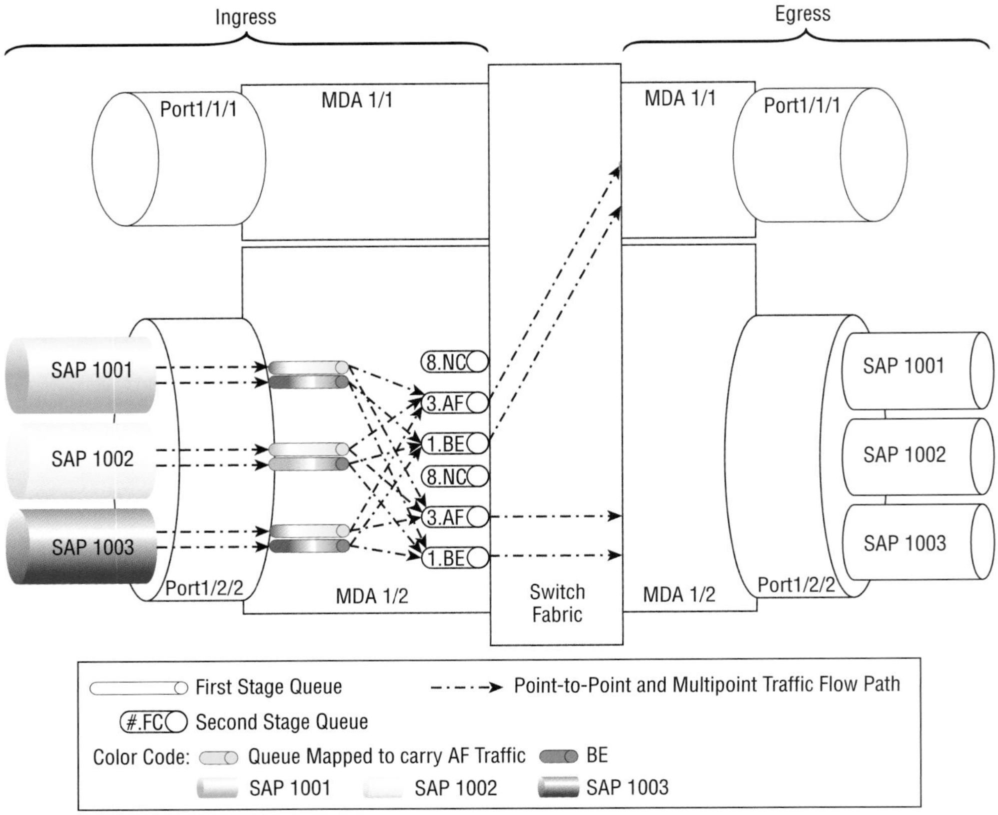

Explanation through Equations

Equation 9.4 shows the formula for the number of hardware queues created in the first stage at access ingress, when the Multipoint Shared Queuing option is chosen.

Equation 9.4 Number of Hardware Queues Created in the First Stage with the Multipoint Shared Queuing Option

$$FHWQ = \sum_{S_i=SAP_1}^{SAP_n} SIPUCQ(S_i)$$

(continued)

Where

 FHWQ: Number of hardware queues created in the first stage

 SAP$_n$: Total number of SAPs configured, in the MDA under consideration, for the service

 SIPUCQ(S$_i$): Number of unicast queues configured in the SAP-ingress policy associated with SAP S$_i$

In the example under consideration,

$$FHWQ = \sum_{S_i=1}^{3} [SIPUCQ(S_i) = 2] = 6$$

The system automatically creates a constant number of queues for the second stage. The number of second stage queues is dependent on the chassis type. Equation 9.5 shows the overall formula for the number of queues created.

Equation 9.5 Number of Hardware Queues Created with the Multipoint Shared Queuing Option

---

$$HWQ = \sum_{S_i=SAP_1}^{SAP_n} [SIPUCQ(S_i)] + \delta_c$$

Where

 δ_c : A chassis-dependent constant

Table 9.2 lists the default configuration of all the queues defined in the default Shared-Queue QoS policy.

Table 9.2 Default Shared-Queue QoS Policy-Configuration of All Queues

Configuration %	High-Priority FCs				Low-Priority FCs			
	NC	H1	EF	H2	L1	AF	L2	BE
Unicast Queues	Q8	Q7	Q6	Q5	Q4	Q3	Q2	Q1
Multicast Queues	Q16	Q15	Q14	Q13	Q12	Q11	Q10	Q9
Broadcast Queues	Q24	Q23	Q22	Q21	Q20	Q19	Q18	Q17
Unknown-Cast Queues	Q32	Q31	Q30	Q29	Q28	Q27	Q26	Q25
PIR	100	100	100	100	100	100	100	100
CIR	10	10	100	100	25	25	25	0
MBS	25	25	50	50	25	50	50	50
CBS	3	3	10	10	3	10	3	1
HP-Only	10	10	10	10	10	10	10	10

9.6 Comparing the Scaling Options

Figure 9.5 shows the relative optimization provided by the three scaling options in terms of the number of hardware queues and data processing requirement. The direction of the arrows in the figure indicates greater optimization. For the purpose of the figure, the constant number of second stage queues involved with Shared Queuing and Multipoint Shared Queuing options is assumed to be negligible.

Figure 9.5 Relative Optimization Provided by the Scaling Options

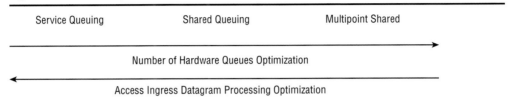

For a large number of SAP aggregations within a multipoint service at an access ingress involving multiple destination MDAs, Multipoint Shared Queuing provides the best optimization of the three options in terms of the number of hardware queues enabled at the access ingress. The Shared Queuing option also reduces the number of hardware queues enabled under this scenario, compared to Service Queuing, but it does not result in as many reductions as Multipoint Shared Queuing.

In terms of datagram processing capacity optimization in the ingress direction of the service traffic, the Service Queuing option provides the best possible optimization. The Service Queuing option does not need any additional datagram processing. The Shared Queuing option only processes unicast traffic flowing through the service ingress queues twice. Multipoint Shared Queuing processes all the traffic flowing through the service ingress queues twice.

9.7 Verification Commands Associated with the Scaling Options

Listing 9.7 shows an example output of the show qos shared-queue default command. The associations displayed as part of the command lists all the services and their associated SAPs that are enabled with second stage hardware queues. In addition, the list shows the scaling option configured with each SAP.

Listing 9.7 An example output of the show qos shared-queue default command

```
A:Pod1# show qos shared-queue default
===============================================================
QoS Shared Queue Policy
===============================================================
---------------------------------------------------------------
Shared Queue Policy (default)
---------------------------------------------------------------
Policy        : default
Description   : Default Shared Queue Policy
---------------------------------------------------------------
Associations
---------------------------------------------------------------
Service : 100           SAP : 1/2/2:1002 (shared Q)
Service : 100           SAP : 1/2/2:1003 (multipoint-shared Q)
===============================================================
```

For the purpose of the output display in Listing 9.7, each SAP of the VPLS configuration shown in Listing 9.3 is configured with a different scaling option. Listing 9.7 does not list SAP 1/2/2:1001 in the VPLS service 100, because the default Service Queuing option (which was configured with the SAP) does not involve any second stage shared queues. In order to list all the SAPs associated with a service, use the following command:

```
show service id <service_id> sap
```

Associating Different SAPS of a Service with Different Scaling Options for Access Ingress Queuing

The configuration exercise for getting the output display shown in Listing 9.7 is good from an educational point of view, but how about from the MDA resource optimization point of view?

From the MDA resource optimization point of view, this is a poor configuration. The configuration results not only in suboptimal use of the ingress hardware queues of the MDA but also in suboptimal ingress datagram processing at the MDA. Also, mixing different scaling options within a service will make troubleshooting very difficult. Therefore, as a best practice, avoid using different scaling options with different SAPs of a service.

The `show pools <port_id> access-ingress` command displays all the first stage hardware queues of the buffer pool and their associated configuration. Listings 9.8, 9.9, and 9.10 show the output of the command respectively for the configurations listed in Listings 9.3, 9.7, 9.9.

Listing 9.8 Queues created for the Service Queuing option configuration

```
A:Pod1# show pools 1/2/2 access-ingress
===============================================================================
Pool Information
===============================================================================
Port             : 1/2/2
Application      : Acc-Ing          Pool Name         : default
...
-------------------------------------------------------------------------------
Name                       FC-Maps        MBS      HP-Only A.PIR    A.CIR
                                          CBS      Depth   O.PIR    O.CIR
-------------------------------------------------------------------------------
100->1/2/2:1001->11
                           be l2 af l1    1280     256     1000000  0
                           h2 ef h1 nc    0        0       Max      0
100->1/2/2:1001->9
                           be             1280     256     1000000  0
                                          0        0       Max      0
100->1/2/2:1002->11
                           be l2 af l1    1280     256     1000000  0
                           h2 ef h1 nc    0        0       Max      0
100->1/2/2:1002->9
                           be             1280     256     1000000  0
                                          0        0       Max      0
100->1/2/2:1003->11
                           be l2 af l1    1280     256     1000000  0
                           h2 ef h1 nc    0        0       Max      0
100->1/2/2:1003->9
                           be             1280     256     1000000  0
                                          0        0       Max      0
```

(continued)

```
100->1/2/2:1001->3
                      af           1280      256      1000000   0
                                   0         0        Max       0
100->1/2/2:1001->3
                      af           1280      256      1000000   0
                                   0         0        Max       0
100->1/2/2:1001->1
                      be l2 l1 h2  1280      256      1000000   0
                      ef h1 nc     0         0        Max       0
100->1/2/2:1001->1
                      be l2 l1 h2  1280      256      1000000   0
                      ef h1 nc     0         0        Max       0
100->1/2/2:1002->1
                      be l2 l1 h2  1280      256      1000000   0
                      ef h1 nc     0         0        Max       0
100->1/2/2:1002->1
                      be l2 l1 h2  1280      256      1000000   0
                      ef h1 nc     0         0        Max       0
100->1/2/2:1002->3
                      af           1280      256      1000000   0
                                   0         0        Max       0
100->1/2/2:1002->3
                      af           1280      256      1000000   0
                                   0         0        Max       0
100->1/2/2:1003->1
                      be l2 l1 h2  1280      256      1000000   0
                      ef h1 nc     0         0        Max       0
100->1/2/2:1003->1
                      be l2 l1 h2  1280      256      1000000   0
                      ef h1 nc     0         0        Max       0
100->1/2/2:1003->3
                      af           1280      256      1000000   0
                                   0         0        Max       0
100->1/2/2:1003->3
                      af           1280      256      1000000   0
                                   0         0        Max       0
=================================================================
```

Listing 9.9 First stage queues created for the Shared Queuing option configuration

```
A:Pod1# show pools 1/2/2 access-ingress

================================================================================
Pool Information
================================================================================
Port              : 1/2/2
Application       : Acc-Ing          Pool Name       : default
Resv CBS          : Sum
--------------------------------------------------------------------------------
Utilization                    State    Start-Avg   Max-Avg   Max-Prob
--------------------------------------------------------------------------------
High-Slope                     Down        70%        90%        80%
Low-Slope                      Down        50%        75%        80%

Time Avg Factor   : 7
Pool Total        : 32768 KB
Pool Shared       : 20480 KB          Pool Resv       : 12288 KB

Pool Total In Use  : 0 KB
Pool Shared In Use : 0 KB            Pool Resv In Use  : 0 KB
WA Shared In Use   : 0 KB

Hi-Slope Drop Prob : 0               Lo-Slope Drop Prob : 0
--------------------------------------------------------------------------------
Name                           FC-Maps      MBS       HP-Only A.PIR   A.CIR
                                            CBS       Depth   O.PIR   O.CIR
--------------------------------------------------------------------------------
100->1/2/2:1001->11
                               be l2 af l1  1280      256     1000000 0
                               h2 ef h1 nc  0         0       Max     0
100->1/2/2:1001->9
                               be           1280      256     1000000 0
                                            0         0       Max     0
100->1/2/2:1002->11
                               be l2 af l1  1280      256     1000000 0
                               h2 ef h1 nc  0         0       Max     0
100->1/2/2:1002->9
                               be           1280      256     1000000 0
                                            0         0       Max     0
```

(continued)

```
100->1/2/2:1003->11
                       be l2 af l1   1280      256      1000000   0
                       h2 ef h1 nc   0         0        Max       0
100->1/2/2:1003->9
                       be            1280      256      1000000   0
                                     0         0        Max       0
100->1/2/2:1001->3
                       af            1280      256      1000000   0
                                     0         0        Max       0
100->1/2/2:1001->1
                       be l2 l1 h2   1280      256      1000000   0
                       ef h1 nc      0         0        Max       0
100->1/2/2:1002->1
                       be l2 l1 h2   1280      256      1000000   0
                       ef h1 nc      0         0        Max       0
100->1/2/2:1002->3
                       af            1280      256      1000000   0
                                     0         0        Max       0
100->1/2/2:1003->1
                       be l2 l1 h2   1280      256      1000000   0
                       ef h1 nc      0         0        Max       0
100->1/2/2:1003->3
                       af            1280      256      1000000   0
                                     0         0        Max       0
===============================================================================
```

Listing 9.10 First stage queues created for the Multipoint Shared Queuing option configuration

```
A:Pod1# show pools 1/2/2 access-ingress

===============================================================================
Pool Information
===============================================================================
Port            : 1/2/2
Application     : Acc-Ing           Pool Name        : default
Resv CBS        : Sum
-------------------------------------------------------------------------------
Utilization               State     Start-Avg   Max-Avg    Max-Prob
-------------------------------------------------------------------------------
```

(continued)

```
High-Slope                  Down            70%        90%        80%
Low-Slope                   Down            50%        75%        80%

Time Avg Factor    : 7
Pool Total         : 32768 KB
Pool Shared        : 20480 KB        Pool Resv         : 12288 KB

Pool Total In Use  : 0 KB
Pool Shared In Use : 0 KB            Pool Resv In Use   : 0 KB
WA Shared In Use   : 0 KB

Hi-Slope Drop Prob : 0               Lo-Slope Drop Prob : 0
--------------------------------------------------------------------------
Name                        FC-Maps     MBS     HP-Only A.PIR    A.CIR
                                        CBS     Depth   O.PIR    O.CIR
--------------------------------------------------------------------------
100->1/2/2:1001->3
                            af          1280    256     1000000  0
                                        0       0       Max      0
100->1/2/2:1001->1
                            be l2 l1 h2 1280    256     1000000  0
                            ef h1 nc    0       0       Max      0
100->1/2/2:1002->1
                            be l2 l1 h2 1280    256     1000000  0
                            ef h1 nc    0       0       Max      0
100->1/2/2:1002->3
                            af          1280    256     1000000  0
                                        0       0       Max      0
100->1/2/2:1003->1
                            be l2 l1 h2 1280    256     1000000  0
                            ef h1 nc    0       0       Max      0
100->1/2/2:1003->3
                            af          1280    256     1000000  0
                                        0       0       Max      0
==========================================================================
```

Summary

This chapter introduced the following three different scaling options for access ingress queuing:

- Service Queuing
- Shared Queuing
- Multipoint Shared Queuing

The Service Queuing option is the default, while the other two have to be explicitly configured under service SAP configuration.

Shared Queuing and Multipoint Shared Queuing offer scalability of customer aggregation, in applications such as edge aggregation in triple-play service offerings. Under the Shared Queuing option, similar to the Service Queuing option, the data paths for unicast and multipoint traffic are different (the traffic flows through different sets of queues). Under the Multipoint Shared Queuing option the data paths for unicast and multipoint traffic are the same at access ingress.

Shared Queuing and Multipoint Shared Queuing options involve two stages of access ingress queuing that are automatically created by the system. These second stage queues are subjected to default Shared-Queue QoS policy.

Multipoint Shared Queuing provides the best optimization of the three options in terms of the number hardware queues enabled at the access ingress. The Shared Queuing option also reduces the number of hardware queues enabled under the scenario, compared to Service Queuing, but it does not result in as many reductions as Multipoint Shared Queuing.

In terms of datagram processing optimization in the ingress direction of the service traffic, the Service Queuing option does not need any additional datagram processing. The Shared Queuing option only processes unicast traffic flowing through the service ingress queues twice. Multipoint Shared Queuing processes all the traffic flowing through the service ingress queues twice.

Scheduling

10

Scheduling determines the order in which queues that are mapped to different forwarding classes are serviced. Scheduling also governs the distribution of bandwidth to traffic within different forwarding classes.

Chapter Objectives
- To explain the basic scheduling behavior of ALSRP
- To identify the scheduling-related parameters of a queue
- To explain the adaptation rule options of a queue
- To discuss the implications of choosing the queue-type parameter
- To clarify the difference between the single and dual arbitrator modes of basic scheduling

Scheduling can be described as the order in which queues that are mapped to different forwarding classes are serviced. It also determines the bandwidth provided to traffic within different forwarding classes (FCs). Thus, scheduling performs the ultimate job of service differentiation.

In ALSRP input/output module's (IOM) fast-path complexes there are a number of hardware-related scheduling entities called *arbitrators*. An arbitrator can take datagrams out of any number of queues and send them toward any one destination. In the ingress direction, arbitrators send datagrams toward their destination media-dependent adapter (MDA). In the egress direction, arbitrators send datagrams toward their destination port. The collective action of all the ingress arbitrators constitutes the ingress scheduling of an MDA traffic. Similarly, the collective action of all the egress arbitrators constitutes the egress scheduling of an MDA traffic.

This chapter explains the basic scheduling options available in ALSRP, the scheduling-related queue parameters, and the commands used for verifying and validating the scheduling configuration.

10.1 Scheduling-Related Queue Parameters

A queue has the following four scheduling-related parameters:
- Committed information rate (CIR)
- Peak information rate (PIR)
- Adaptation rule
- Arbitrator association rule

Normally, the committed information rate (CIR) of a queue is the minimum guaranteed rate at which the queue will be serviced. The peak information rate (PIR) is the maximum rate at which a queue can be serviced. The CIR and PIR that are configured using a QoS policy are referred to as *administrative rates*. The adaptation rule associates an administrative rate to the underlying hardware scheduling rates referred to as *operational rates*. The arbitrator association rule of a queue specifies the type of arbitrator for servicing the queue. These parameters are discussed in detail in the following subsections.

The Committed Information Rate

Aside from being the minimum guaranteed service rate of a queue, the CIR of a queue performs two distinct functions:

- **Prioritizing the queue scheduling**—Arbitrators prioritize the servicing of the queues associated with them based on the profile state of the queues. Queues that operate below their CIR are considered to be in-profile and are always serviced before queues that operate above their CIR, which are considered to be out-of-profile. This function of the CIR is discussed in detail later in this chapter.

- **Determining profile markings of datagrams**—As you learned in Chapters 6 and 8, when an access ingress queue is configured to be in `priority-mode`, datagrams scheduled out of the queue are marked as in-profile or out-of-profile based on the queue's CIR state. If the current service rate of the queue is below its CIR threshold, the datagrams transmitted out of it are marked as in-profile. If the current service rate of the queue is above its CIR threshold, the datagrams transmitted out of it are marked as out-of-profile.

For an access queue the CIR is specified in Kbps (kilobits/sec). For a network queue the CIR is defined as a percentage of the network interface bandwidth.

The Peak Information Rate

The peak information rate (PIR) of a queue defines the maximum rate at which datagrams are allowed to exit a queue. The PIR does not specify the maximum rate at which datagrams can enter a queue; this is determined by the queue's ability to absorb bursts and is defined by its maximum burst size.

For an access queue the PIR is specified in Kbps. For a network queue the PIR is defined as a percentage of the network interface bandwidth. In the command-line interface of an ALSRP node, the PIR of a queue is simply referred to as `rate`.

The Adaptation Rule

As mentioned earlier in the chapter, the configured CIR and PIR values of a queue are only administrative values. The operational CIR and PIR values, which may vary slightly from administrative values, depend on the administrative values, the specified adaptation rule, and the hardware scheduling rates supported by ALSRP for the associated MDA. The possible values to the adaptation rule parameters are max, min, and closest. The default value is closest.

The adaptation rule is independently configured for CIR and PIR. The adaptation rule dictates how the configured administrative value is matched to one of the supported hardware-scheduling rates, when the exact rate match is not available. The hardware scheduling rates depend on the associated MDA. Table 10.1 lists the hardware scheduling rates supported for the majority of the MDAs.

Table 10.1 The ALSRP Hardware Scheduling Rates Supported for the Majority of the MDAs.

H/W Rate Steps	Rate Range (Rate Step * 0 to Rate Step * 250)
1 Kb	0 to 250 Kbps
8 Kb	0 to 2 Mbps
10 Kb	0 to 2.5 Mbps
50 Kb	0 to 12.5 Mbps
100 Kb	0 to 25 Mbps
500 Kb	0 to 125 Mbps
1 Mb	0 to 250 Mbps
5 Mb	0 to 1.25 Gbps
10 Mb	0 to 2.5 Gbps
50 Mb	0 to 12.5 Gbps
100 Mb	0 to 25 Gbps
500 Mb	0 to 125 Gbps

Before learning the impact of the adaptation rule, consider how the hardware scheduling and the rate-selection process works. Imagine that each of the hardware rate steps listed in Table 10.1 is a scheduling wheel (analogous to the water wheel shown in Figure 10.1). The 12 rate steps listed in the table are analogous to water wheels of 12 different sizes. The bytes of data scheduled (volume of water released) by each wheel in one rotation is proportional to its hardware rate step value listed in Table 10.1 (liters or gallons in the place of Kb for water). A 1-Kb wheel is capable of servicing 1 Kb of data in one rotation (one step). Similarly, a 500-Mb wheel is capable of servicing 500 Mb of data in one rotation. Each wheel can be rotated anywhere from

0 to 250 rotations per second, and fractions of a rotation are not possible. If the 1-Kb wheel is rotated 4 times per second, it will service 4 Kbps.

Figure 10.1 Water Wheel Illustration

To schedule traffic out of a queue at the configured PIR and CIR rates, the queue has to be associated with one of the scheduling wheels. Because a queue can be associated with only one scheduling wheel, the same wheel has to be used to achieve both CIR and PIR of the queue. Achieving an operational PIR as close as possible to the administrative PIR takes precedence. In other words, the wheel that provides the closest match for the configured PIR is chosen.

Here's an example: A queue has to be scheduled at a PIR of 255 Mbps (megabits/sec) and a CIR of 126 Mbps. In this example, you would choose the 5 Mb scheduling wheel as it provides an exact match for the PIR value considered. The wheel would be rotated 51 times/sec to achieve the configured PIR. However, how many times does the wheel have to be rotated to achieve the configured CIR? If the wheel is rotated 25 times we can achieve 125 Mbps, which is the closest that we can get to the administrative CIR value.

In this example, is achieving 125 Mbps of operational CIR in the place of 126 Mbps of administrative CIR good enough? It all depends on the SLA a service provider has in place with their client. This is where the adaptation rule comes into play. The three adaptation rule values are as follows:

- The default adaptation rule of `closest` tries to find an operational rate that is as close as possible to the administrative rate, irrespective of whether the operational rate is greater or smaller compared to the administrative rate.

- The adaptation rule of `min` means the operational rate must be at *least* equal to the configured administrative rate. In other words, if the adaptation rule is `min`, an operational rate equal to or slightly greater than the administrative rate is achieved.

- The adaptation rule of max means the operational rate must not *exceed* the configured administrative rate. In other words, if the adaptation rule is max, an operational rate equal to or slightly less than the administrative rate is achieved.

The following sidebar shows an example for determining operational rates from administrative rates for different adaptation rules.

Operational PIR and CIR Determination Example

The queue administrative attributes are: CIR = 201 Mbps, PIR = 403 Mbps, and Adaptation Rule (for both PIR and CIR) = X.

According to Table 10.1, the PIR value of the queue is in the range of 0 to 1.25 Gbps (gigabits/sec). Therefore, the 5 Mb scheduling wheel is used.

If X = min: The operational CIR will be 205 Mbps and the operational PIR will be 405 Mbps. These operational values were selected because these are the native hardware rates greater than or equal to the administrative CIR and PIR values.

If X = max: The operational CIR will be 200 Mbps, and the operational PIR will be 400 Mbps. These operational values were selected because these are the native hardware rates less than or equal to the administrative CIR and PIR values.

If X = closest: The operational CIR and PIR values will be 200 Mbps and 405 Mbps, respectively. These operational values were selected because these are the closest matching native hardware rates to the administrative CIR and PIR values.

The Arbitrator Association Rule

The arbitrator association rule of a queue, as its name indicates, allows for the selection of the type of underlying *arbitrator* to service the traffic flowing through the queue. The parameter is applicable only in the case of dual arbitrator mode of scheduling. Under single arbitrator mode of scheduling the parameter configuration is ignored. Read further to learn about single and dual arbitrator modes of scheduling.

In the command line interface of ALSRP, the arbitrator association rule is referred to as `queue-type`. The possible values for the parameters are `expedite`, `best-effort`, and `auto-expedite`. The default value is `auto-expedite`.

The arbitrator association rule is explained further, at the end of the next section.

10.2 Scheduling Modes

Usually arbitrators are paired to service all traffic flowing to a given destination within a node. This mode of scheduling with paired arbitrators is referred to as *dual arbitrator mode*. This mode applies to all MDAs of ALSRP with the exception of the M60-10/100eth-TX MDA.

Pairing arbitrators is not possible in the case of scheduling egress traffic toward M60-10/100eth-TX (60 port Ethernet) MDAs because of the large number of ports in the MDA. Therefore, in this case unpaired individual arbitrators are used to serve 60 destination ports. This mode of scheduling is referred as *single arbitrator mode*.

Single Arbitrator Mode of Scheduling

Single arbitrator mode is used only for egress scheduling of M60-10/100eth-TX MDA. However, learning how this mode of scheduling works is important for two reasons:

1. M60-10/100eth-TX is one of the commonly used MDAs.
2. Learning how the single arbitrator mode operates is a convenient stepping stone for understanding the dual arbitrator mode.

An arbitrator is a pair of scheduling loops. The first loop is for scheduling the queues that are in in-profile state, and the second loop is for scheduling the queues that are in out-of-profile state. See Chapter 6 for a discussion of in-profile and out-of-profile queue states.

In the single arbitrator mode, one arbitrator is assigned to each of the 60 destination ports of M60-10/100eth-TX MDA. The arbitrator assigned to a port schedules all the traffic destined to leave through that particular port.

Figure 10.2 shows the scheduling operation of single arbitrator mode. In the figure, for all the green queues, PIR is equal to CIR and CIR is greater than zero. For all the queues that are partially green and partially red, PIR is greater than CIR and CIR is greater than zero. For all the red queues, PIR is greater than CIR and CIR is equal to zero.

Figure 10.2 The Scheduling Operation of the Single Arbitrator Mode

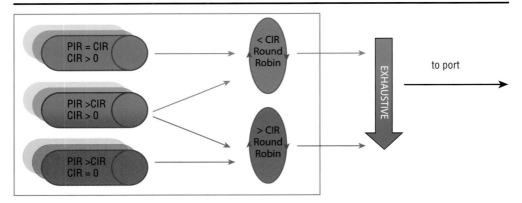

The arbitrator starts its scheduling operation with its first loop of scheduling. During the first loop the arbitrator services traffic from the queues that are operating within their CIR, in a round robin manner. The queues whose CIR is equal to zero are not part of this first loop. As the round robin servicing continues, queues reach their operational CIR and leave the first loop of scheduling. In other words, during the round robin progression of first loop, a queue that has transmitted up to its CIR stops transmitting further during a scheduling window. The first loop of the arbitrator concludes when either all the queues are serviced up to their CIR or the available scheduling bandwidth is exhausted.

Within a scheduling window, if additional bandwidth is available after the conclusion of the first scheduling loop, the second scheduling loop starts. During the second loop, the arbitrator services traffic from the queues whose PIR is greater than their CIR. The queues whose PIR is equal to their CIR are not part of this second loop. As the round robin servicing continues, queues reach their operational PIR and leave the second scheduling loop within a scheduling window. The second loop of the arbitrator concludes when either the available scheduling bandwidth is exhausted or all the queues are serviced up to their PIR.

Best Practices: To honor service commitments it is important not to overbook the CIR of queues. To maximize the network bandwidth utilization, the PIR of queues may be overbooked.

The following sidebar shows how bandwidth is distributed between two queues under single arbitrator scheduling mode.

Dual Arbitrator Mode of Scheduling

Dual arbitrator mode is used for all the ingress scheduling of ALSRP. The mode is also used for all the egress scheduling except for the egress scheduling of the M60-10/100eth-TX MDA. As mentioned earlier, in the dual arbitrator mode, arbitrators are paired to service datagrams to a given destination.

For servicing all the ingress traffic arriving through an MDA, a pair of arbitrators is assigned for each of the possible destination MDAs, and a pair of arbitrators is assigned to schedule all the multipoint traffic, regardless of its destination. To service all the egress traffic of an MDA, a pair of arbitrators is assigned for each of the destination ports.

Figure 10.3 shows the scheduling operation of paired arbitrators. As shown in the figure, one of the paired arbitrators is referred to as the *high-priority arbitrator* and the other one as the *low-priority arbitrator*. With paired arbitrators, four scheduling loops are available and they schedule traffic to a destination in the following order:

- In-profile queues associated with the high-priority arbitrator.
- In-profile queues associated with the low-priority arbitrator.
- Out-of-profile queues associated with both the high- and the low-priority arbitrators.

When a scheduling loop serves more than one queue, the queues are serviced in a round robin manner. The out-of-profile queue loops of the paired arbitrators have been combined to provide *biased round robin scheduling* for all the out-of-profile queues. A loop concludes either when it has served the required bandwidth to all the associated queues or when the bandwidth is exhausted for the scheduling window.

Figure 10.3 The Dual Arbitrator Scheduling Mode Operation

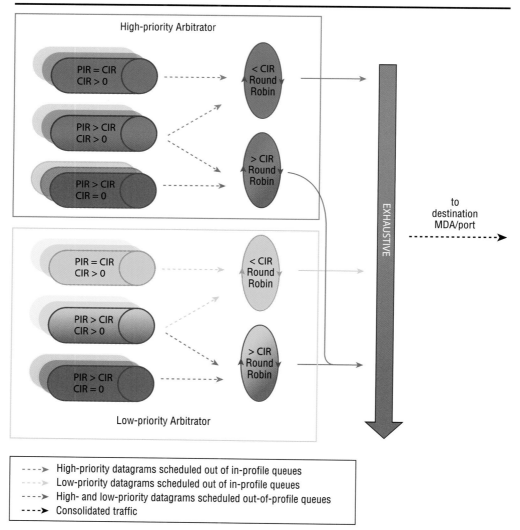

Here's how the biased round robin scheduling, illustrated in Figure 10.3, works. In the dual arbitrator mode, queues in the in-profile state and associated with the high-priority arbitrator are serviced first. Once these queues have been serviced up to their CIR, or if they become empty, queues in the in-profile state and associated with the low-priority arbitrator are serviced. Once those queues have been serviced up to their CIR, or if they become empty, all the queues in the out-of-profile state, regardless of the queue's association to high- or low-priority arbitrators, are serviced. If traffic arrives in the queues that are in the in-profile state while the scheduler is in the process of executing the lower loops, the scheduler will temporarily stop the current loop and service those higher-priority queues (that is, perform the first and second loop of scheduling). When it finally resumes its third loop scheduling, it always starts with the queues associated with the high-priority arbitrator; this is the reason that the third loop is considered a *biased* round robin. In biased round robin, the scheduling of queues in the out-of-profile state are done in a round robin fashion, but with a slight bias toward the queues associated with the high-priority arbitrator.

The sidebar on the following page shows bandwidth distribution between three queues under dual arbitrator scheduling mode.

The following subsection explains how the queues become associated with one of the arbitrators.

Associating Queues to High- or Low-Priority Arbitrators

The association of a queue to an arbitrator is determined by the value assigned to the arbitrator association rule (queue-type) of the queue. The default arbitrator association rule is auto-expedite. According to the default arbitrator association rule, a queue is associated to either the high- or low-priority arbitrator based on the forwarding classes mapped to the queue. If one or more high-priority forwarding classes (NC, H1, EF, or H2) are mapped to a queue, the queue is associated with the high-priority arbitrator. On the other hand, if even one of the assured types or best-effort forwarding classes (L1, AF, L2, or BE) is mapped to a queue, the queue is associated with a low-priority arbitrator.

Dual Arbitrator Mode Bandwidth Distribution Example

Three ingress queues, Q1, Q2, and Q3, of a M60-10/100th-TX MDA are sending traffic to a single destination MDA. In other words, the three queues are serviced using the dual arbitrator scheduling mode. Q1's operational CIR is 1 Mbps, its operational PIR is 3 Mbps, and it is associated with the high-priority arbitrator. Q2's operational CIR is 2 Mbps, its operational PIR is 5 Mbps, and it is associated with the low-priority arbitrator. Q3's operational CIR is 0, its operational PIR is 10 Mbps, and it is associated with the low-priority arbitrator. Assume that all the three queues have enough traffic to consume all the available scheduling bandwidth, which is denoted as X. Consider how the bandwidth would be distributed between the three queues in the steady state given different values of X. Excess bandwidth distribution to queues in the out-of-profile state using biased round robin scheduling depends heavily on the traffic flow dynamics. Therefore, the numbers listed below, particularly those including excess bandwidth distribution, are only an approximation.

- X = 1 Mbps: Q1 gets 1 Mbps; Q2 and Q3 get none.
- X = 2 Mbps: Q1 gets 1 Mbps; Q2 gets 1 Mbps; and Q3 gets none.
- X = 3 Mbps: Q1 gets 1 Mbps; Q2 gets 2 Mbps; and Q3 gets none.
- X = 7 Mbps: Q1 gets 3 Mbps; Q2 gets 3 Mbps; and Q3 gets 1 Mbps.
- X = 9 Mbps: Q1 gets 3 Mbps; Q2 gets 4 Mbps; and Q3 gets 2 Mbps.
- X = 11 Mbps: Q1 gets 3 Mbps; Q2 gets 5 Mbps; and Q3 gets 3 Mbps.
- X = 15 Mbps: Q1 gets 3 Mbps; Q2 gets 5 Mbps; and Q3 gets 7 Mbps.
- X = 20 Mbps: Q1 gets 3 Mbps; Q2 gets 5 Mbps; and Q3 gets 10 Mbps.

For example, if EF, H1, and H2 forwarding classes are mapped to the same queue, according to the default arbitrator association rule, the queue gets associated to the high-priority arbitrator. However, if EF, H2, and L1 forwarding classes are mapped to the same queue, according to the default value of the rule, the queue is associated to the low-priority arbitrator. Regardless of the forwarding classes mapped to a queue, if you want the queue to be associated with the high-priority arbitrator, you need to configure the arbitrator association rule (`queue-type`) of the queue to be `expedite`. Similarly you can associate a queue forcefully with the low-priority arbitrator, irrespective of the forwarding classes mapped to the queue, by configuring the arbitrator association rule of the queue to be `best-effort`.

10.3 Nodal Scheduling: Putting It All Together

The previous two sections explained the single and dual arbitrator modes of scheduling. In those sections, you saw the scheduling behavior of one or two arbitrators in isolation. This section shows you the interaction between ingress and egress schedulers of a node using the example shown in Figure 10.4.

Figure 10.4 shows a logical view of an ALSRP node with two MDAs. As an example, assume M1-10gb-XFP MDA is configured under MDA slot 1/1 and M10-1gb-SFP MDA is configured under MDA slot 1/2. Three SAPs—201, 202, and 203—are configured under port 1/2/2. Only point-to-point traffic is considered in the example; therefore, an arbitrator pair for serving multipoint traffic is not shown in the figure. Also, only unidirectional traffic is considered: traffic flowing from the three service access points (SAPs) towards service distribution points (SDPs) configured in ports 1/1/1, 1/2/1, and 1/2/10.

Figure 10.4 Example of End-to-End Scheduling within a Node

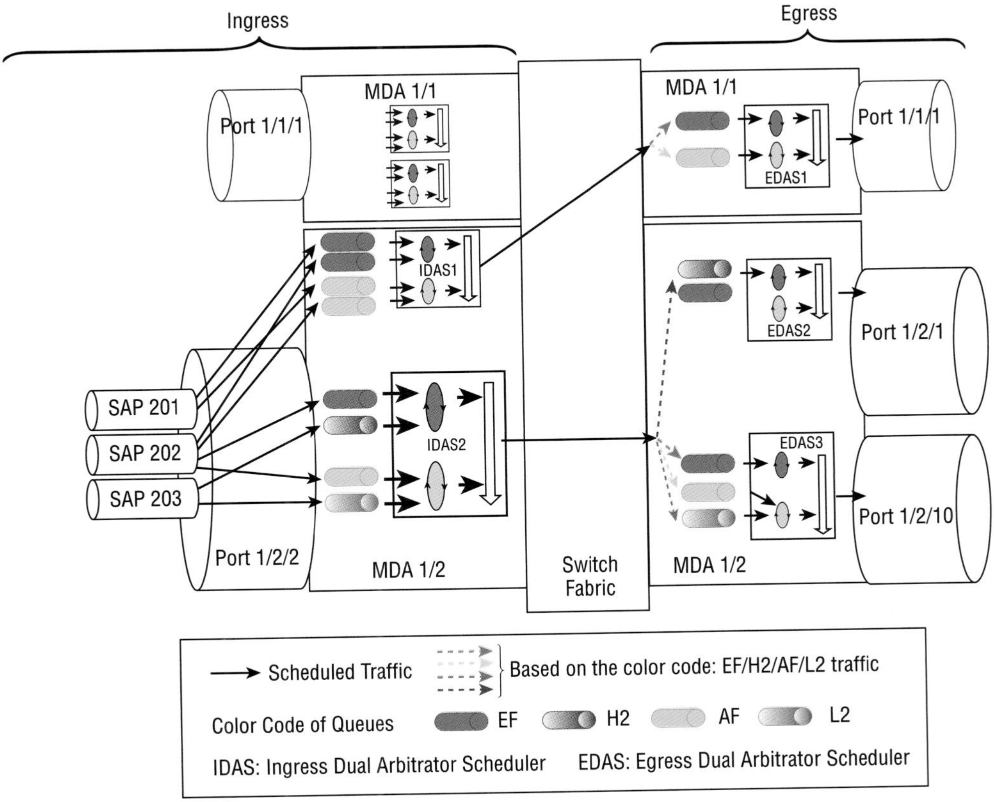

The incoming traffic through SAP 201 is destined to an SDP configured under port 1/1/1. The incoming traffic through SAP 201 is mapped to two different forwarding classes: EF and AF. The incoming traffic through SAP 202 is also mapped to EF and AF forwarding classes. However, the traffic arriving through SAP 202 has multiple destinations: port 1/1/1 (configured under MDA 1/1) and port 1/2/10 (configured under MDA 1/2). Traffic arriving through SAP 203 is mapped to the H2 and L2 forwarding classes. H2 traffic arriving through SAP 203 is destined to port 1/2/1 and L2 traffic arriving through the SAP is destined to port 1/2/10.

In the example, forwarding classes are mapped to queues on a one-on-one basis both at ingress and egress. As discussed in Chapter 8, the queues belonging to different SAPs are isolated from each other at the access ingress. At the egress, queues belonging to different ports are isolated.

Traffic arriving through SAP 202 can be either destined to port 1/1/1 (MDA 1/1) or port 1/2/10 (MDA 1/2). Therefore, as discussed in Chapter 9, the default Service Queuing option creates a separate set of unicast queues at access ingress for each destination MDA the SAP serves.

Traffic arriving through MDA 1/2 is flowing toward two different destination MDAs. Therefore, two dual-arbitrator schedulers (IDAS1 and IDAS2) serve the traffic toward their destination in the ingress direction of the MDA. The example assumes the default arbitrator association rule of **auto-expedite**. Therefore, the high-priority arbitrator of IDAS1 serves the traffic from the EF queues of both SAP 201 and SAP 202 toward destination MDA 1/1. The low-priority arbitrator of IDAS1 serves the traffic from the AF queues of both SAP 201 and SAP 202 toward destination MDA 1/1. Similarly, the high-priority arbitrator of IDAS2 serves the traffic from the EF queue of SAP 202 and the H2 queue of SAP 203 toward destination MDA 1/2. The low-priority arbitrator of IDAS2 serves the traffic from the AF queue of SAP 202 and the L2 queue of SAP 203 toward destination MDA 1/2.

The dual-arbitrator schedulers (in the example IDAS1 and IDAS2) function independently of one another. As a result of this independence of the ingress dual-arbitrator schedulers and separate ingress queuing for each of the destination MDAs, congestion occurring at one destination MDA does not impact the rest.

At the egress side of MDA 1/1, all the traffic flows through port 1/1/1. Therefore, only one dual-arbitrator scheduler (EDAS1) is required to schedule all the traffic flowing toward port 1/1/1. The high-priority arbitrator of EDAS1 serves the traffic from the EF queue and the corresponding low-priority arbitrator serves the traffic from the AF queue.

At the egress side of MDA 1/2, the traffic flows through ports 1/2/1 and 1/2/10. Therefore, two dual-arbitrator schedulers (EDAS2 and EDAS3) are subjected to schedule the traffic flowing toward the ports. The high-priority arbitrator of EDAS2 serves the traffic from the H2 queue that is destined to port 1/2/1. The high-priority arbitrator of EDAS3 serves the traffic from the EF queue that is destined to port 1/2/10. The low-priority arbitrator of EDAS3 serves the traffic from the AF and L2 queues that are destined to port 1/2/10.

Similar to ingress dual-arbitrator schedulers, the egress dual-arbitrator schedulers (and also single-arbitrator schedulers) serving traffic to different ports function independently of one another. As a result of this independence, congestion occurring at one port does not impact traffic flow to the other ports of an MDA.

10.4 Configuring Scheduling Parameters of Access Queues

In this section, you'll add the scheduling parameters configuration of access queues to what you already know about a SAP-ingress and a SAP-egress policies.

Any changes to the default arbitrator association rule, must be specified while creating the queue itself. Once the queue has been created, the arbitrator association rule cannot be changed.

Listing 10.1 shows examples for configuring the arbitrator association rule while creating queues in a SAP-ingress and a SAP-egress policies. In the listing code, queue 2 and queue 3 are created within a SAP-ingress policy. Queue 2 is created with the default arbitrator association rule, which is `auto-expedite`. The arbitrator association rule for queue 3 is explicitly configured as `expedite`. Queue 4 is created within a SAP-egress policy, and its arbitrator association rule is explicitly configured as `best-effort`.

Listing 10.1 Example queue creations within SAP-ingress and SAP-egress policies highlighting the arbitrator association rule configuration

```
A:Pod1>config>qos>sap-ingress$ queue 2 create
A:Pod1>config>qos>sap-ingress>queue$ exit
A:Pod1>config>qos>sap-ingress# queue 3 expedite create
A:Pod1>config>qos>sap-ingress>queue$ exit
A:Pod1>config>qos>sap-ingress# info detail
...
            queue 2 priority-mode auto-expedite create
...
            queue 3 priority-mode expedite create
...
A:Pod1>config>qos# sap-egress 425 create
A:Pod1>config>qos>sap-egress$ queue 4 best-effort create
A:Pod1>config>qos>sap-egress>queue$ exit
A:Pod1>config>qos>sap-egress# info detail
...
            queue 4 best-effort create
...
```

Listing 10.2 provides the options for configuring the adaptation rule of a queue within a SAP-egress policy; the options available in a SAP-ingress policy are identical.

Listing 10.2 Options for configuring the adaptation-rule of access queues

```
A:Pod1>config>qos>sap-egress>queue# adaptation-rule
  - adaptation-rule [pir <adaptation-rule>] [cir <adaptation-rule>]
  - no adaptation-rule

 <adaptation-rule>    : max|min|closest
```

Listing 10.3 displays the options for configuring the PIR and the CIR of a queue within a SAP-ingress policy. Listing 10.4 illustrates the options for configuring the PIR and the CIR of a queue within a SAP-egress policy. The rate parameters are configured in terms of Kbps in access policies. The options for configuring rate parameters within a SAP-ingress and a SAP-egress policy are the same, except that a SAP-ingress policy provides the option of declaring the keyword `police` instead of CIR in a queue rate configuration. The keyword `police` is a rate-limiting declaration; it is discussed in detail in Chapter 12.

Listing 10.3 Options for configuring the rate parameters of a queue in a SAP-ingress policy

```
A:Pod1>config>qos>sap-ingress>queue# rate
  - no rate
  - rate <pir-rate> [cir <cir-rate>]
  - rate <pir-rate> police

<pir-rate>            : [1..100000000|max]
<cir-rate>            : [0..100000000|max]
<police>             : keyword
```

Listing 10.4 Options for configuring the rate parameters of a queue in a SAP-egress policy

```
A:Pod1>config>qos>sap-egress>queue# rate
  - no rate
  - rate <pir-rate> [cir <cir-rate>]

<pir-rate>            : [1..100000000|max]
<cir-rate>            : [0..100000000|max]
```

10.5 Configuring Scheduling Parameters of Network Queues

The queue configurations of unicast and multipoint queues of the default Network-Queue policy were covered in the "Network-Queue Policy" section of Chapter 8. Here you will learn about the scheduling parameters of those queues.

Tables 10.2 and 10.3 (reprints of Table 8.3 and 8.4, respectively) summarize the configuration of unicast and multicast queues of the default Network-Queue policy.

Table 10.2 Configuration Summary of Unicast Queues of the Default Network-Queue Policy

Configuration %	High-Priority FCs				Low-Priority FCs				Sum
	NC Q8	H1 Q7	EF Q6	H2 Q5	L1 Q4	AF Q3	L2 Q2	BE Q1	
PIR	100	100	100	100	100	100	100	100	800
CIR	10	10	100	100	25	25	25	0	295
MBS	25	25	50	50	25	50	50	50	325
CBS	3	3	10	10	3	10	3	1	43
HPO	10	10	10	10	10	10	10	10	-

Table 10.3 Configuration Summary of Multicast Queues of the Default Network-Queue Policy

Configuration %	High-Priority FCs				Low-Priority FCs				Sum
	NC Q16	H1 Q15	EF Q14	H2 Q13	L1 Q12	AF Q11	L2 Q10	BE Q9	
PIR	100	100	100	100	100	100	100	100	800
CIR	10	10	100	100	5	5	5	0	235
MBS	25	25	50	50	25	50	50	50	325
CBS	1	1	1	1	1	1	1	1	8
HPO	10	10	10	10	10	10	10	10	-

In a Network-Queue policy, the PIR and CIR of a queue are configured as certain percentages of the associated network interface bandwidth. From the tables, it is obvious that both the PIR and CIR of queues have been overbooked when compared to their associated network interface bandwidth. Overbooking the PIR of queues can help maximize network bandwidth utilization. However, overbooking the CIR of network queues could result in no guaranteed bandwidth. According to Table 10.3, there is no guaranteed bandwidth for all the application traffic. Even to guarantee bandwidth for high-priority applications at least the sum of the CIR of queues that are serviced by the high-priority arbitrator should not be overbooked.

Why then has the default Network-Queue policy overbooked the CIR of queues? ALSRP is customizable for a wide range of applications, from a pan-continental carrier class network to a simple vertical market network, from an advanced triple-play network to multipoint VPN over a single network infrastructure. Therefore, it is difficult to configure default QoS policies that are applicable for all the anticipated applications. A careful consideration of all the default QoS policies reveals that the policies are configured such that ALSRP by default would behave like a classical router by providing best-effort service. To provide service differentiation in a network scenario, QoS design has to be planned as a part of network deployment.

Best Practices: To maximize multi-service routing benefits of ALSRP, customize QoS policies according to the applications, SLAs and business objectives.

Configuring the arbitrator association rule of a network queue is similar to configuring the arbitrator association rule of an access queue and is done while creating the queue. Listing 10.5 shows examples of configuring the arbitrator association rule of network queues.

Listing 10.5 Examples of configuring the arbitrator association rule of network queues

```
A:Pod1>config>qos>network-queue$ queue 2 expedite create
A:Pod1>config>qos>network-queue>queue$ exit
A:Pod1>config>qos>network-queue# queue 3 best-effort create
A:Pod1>config>qos>network-queue>queue$ exit
```

Listing 10.6 provides the options for configuring the adaptation rule of a network queue.

Listing 10.6 Options for configuring the adaptation rule of a queue in a Network-Queue policy

```
A:Pod2>config>qos>network-queue>queue# adaptation-rule
  - adaptation-rule [pir <adaptation-rule>] [cir <adaptation-rule>]
  - no adaptation-rule

 <adaptation-rule>    : max|min|closest
```

Listing 10.7 shows the options for configuring rate parameters of a network queue.

```
A:Pod1>config>qos>network-queue>queue# rate
  - no rate
  - rate <percent> [cir <percent>]

 <percent>          : [0..100]
 <percent>          : [0..100]
```

10.6 Verification Commands for Scheduling

The final section of this chapter explores the verification commands related to scheduling.

The show pools family of commands discussed in "Verification Commands for Buffer Management" section in Chapter 8 lists all the queues configured within a buffer pool. The list entries show administrative and operational PIR and CIR values. In addition to all the uses already discussed in Chapter 8, the verification command is also useful to determine whether the adaptation rule configuration of a queue is valid.

Verifying Traffic on Ports

The command show port <port-id> detail is useful to see how much traffic has traversed through different queues of a port. This information is displayed under the title Queue Statistics. All the statistics in the command display are accumulated values from the time the port statistics are previously cleared. Therefore, prior to using the command, you may want to clear the statistics of the port using the command clear port <port-id> statistics. Listing 10.8 displays a sample output show port <port-id> detail command. The sample output in the listing belongs to an Ethernet port. Instead, if the command is used over an SONET/SDH port, SONET related information will be displayed along with the port and queue statistics.

Listing 10.8 Sample output of the show port <port-id> detail command

```
A:Pod2# clear port 1/1/1 statistics
A:Pod2# show port 1/1/1 detail


===============================================================================
Ethernet Interface
===============================================================================
Description       : 1-Gig Ethernet SFP
Interface         : 1/1/1                    Oper Speed        : 1 Gbps
...
===============================================================================
Traffic Statistics
===============================================================================
                                       Input                Output
-------------------------------------------------------------------------------
Octets                                 27478              97632442
Packets                                  276                 70700
Errors                                     0                     0
===============================================================================
Ethernet Statistics
===============================================================================
Broadcast Pckts  :         0  Drop Events        :               0
Multicast Pckts  :       122  CRC/Align Errors   :               0
Undersize Pckts  :         0  Fragments          :               0
Oversize Pckts   :         0  Jabbers            :               0
Collisions       :         0

Octets                        :         97659920
Packets                       :            70976
Packets of 64 Octets          :                0
Packets of 65 to 127 Octets   :              444
Packets of 128 to 255 Octets  :                0
Packets of 256 to 511 Octets  :                0
Packets of 512 to 1023 Octets :                0
Packets of 1024 to 1518 Octets :           70532
Packets of 1519 or more Octets :               0
===============================================================================
```

(continued)

```
==================================================================
Port Statistics
==================================================================
                                    Input              Output
------------------------------------------------------------------
Unicast Packets                       231               70645
Multicast Packets                      63                  63
Broadcast Packets                       0                   0
Discards                                0                   0
Unknown Proto Discards                  0
==================================================================


==================================================================
Ethernet-like Medium Statistics
==================================================================

Alignment Errors :        0  Sngl Collisions  :              0
FCS Errors       :        0  Mult Collisions  :              0

...
==================================================================
Queue Statistics
==================================================================

------------------------------------------------------------------
Ingress Queue  1        Packets              Octets
    In Profile  forwarded :   0                  0
    In Profile  dropped   :   0                  0
    Out Profile forwarded :   0                  0
    Out Profile dropped   :   0                  0
...
Ingress Queue  9        Packets              Octets
    In Profile  forwarded :   0                  0
    In Profile  dropped   :   0                  0
    Out Profile forwarded :   716                79230
    Out Profile dropped   :   0                  0
...
Ingress Queue 16        Packets              Octets
    In Profile  forwarded :   0                  0
    In Profile  dropped   :   0                  0
    Out Profile forwarded :   0                  0
    Out Profile dropped   :   0                  0
```

(continued)

```
Egress Queue  1                   Packets              Octets
    In Profile  forwarded :     0                   0
    In Profile  dropped    :     0                   0
    Out Profile forwarded :     0                   0
    Out Profile dropped   :     0                   0
...
Egress Queue  6                   Packets              Octets
    In Profile  forwarded :     72695               100315222
    In Profile  dropped    :     0                   0
    Out Profile forwarded :     0                   0
    Out Profile dropped   :     0                   0
Egress Queue  7                   Packets              Octets
    In Profile  forwarded :     0                   0
    In Profile  dropped    :     0                   0
    Out Profile forwarded :     0                   0
    Out Profile dropped   :     0                   0
Egress Queue  8                   Packets              Octets
    In Profile  forwarded :     475                 40220
    In Profile  dropped    :     0                   0
    Out Profile forwarded :     0                   0
    Out Profile dropped   :     0                   0
```

To check the rate at which traffic traverses through a port, use the `monitor port` family of commands shown in Listing 10.9. As illustrated in the code, the command family can also be used to see the absolute value, instead of the rate, of traffic that traversed through the port during a specified interval. Listing 10.10 shows some sample output of the `monitor port <port-id> rate` command. By default, the `monitor port <port-id> rate` command outputs the statistics every 10 seconds and repeats the output 10 times in total.

Listing 10.9 Options for the monitor port family of commands

```
A:Pod2# monitor port
port <port-id> [<port-id>...(up to 5 total)] [interval <seconds>]
   [repeat <repeat>] [absolute|rate]

 <port-id>            : slot/mda/port[.channel]
...
 <seconds>            : [3..60] - default 10
 <repeat>             : [1..999] - default 10
 <absolute|rate>      : keywords - default mode delta
```

Listing 10.10 Sample output of the monitor port <port-id> rate command

```
A:Pod2# monitor port 1/1/1 rate

===============================================================================
Monitor statistics for Port 1/1/1
===============================================================================
                                              Input              Output
-------------------------------------------------------------------------------

-------------------------------------------------------------------------------
At time t = 0 sec (Base Statistics)
-------------------------------------------------------------------------------
Octets                                       721992          1589762998
Packets                                        7104             1152291
Errors                                            0                   0


-------------------------------------------------------------------------------
At time t = 10 sec (Mode: Rate)
-------------------------------------------------------------------------------
Octets                                           70              634483
Packets                                           1                 459
Errors                                            0                   0
Utilization (% of port capacity)             ~0.00                0.50


-------------------------------------------------------------------------------
At time t = 20 sec (Mode: Rate)
-------------------------------------------------------------------------------
Octets                                          196              742442
Packets                                           2                 537
Errors                                            0                   0
Utilization (% of port capacity)             ~0.00                0.59
...
```

Verifying Traffic on SAPs

The show service id <service-id> all and show service id <service-id>
sap <sap-id> detail commands are useful for checking the absolute amount of
traffic received at and transmitted from a SAP. To clear a service's statistics, use the
clear service statistics id <service-id> counters command. Listing 10.11

exhibits a sample output of the `show service id <service-id> all` command. The code includes the values `Off. HiPriro` (offered high-priority traffic), `Off. LoPrio` (offered low-priority traffic), `Dro. HiPrio` (dropped high-priority traffic), `Dro. LoPrio` (dropped low-priority traffic), `For. InProf` (forwarded in-profile traffic), and `For. OutProf` (forwarded out-of-profile traffic).

Listing 10.11 Sample output of the show service id <service-id> all command

```
A:Pod2# clear service statistics id 100 counters
A:Pod2# show service id 100 all
===============================================================================
Service Detailed Information
===============================================================================
Service Id          : 100          Vpn Id             : 0
Service Type        : VPLS
Customer Id         : 1
Last Status Change: 06/15/2007 15:24:46
Last Mgmt Change  : 06/15/2007 15:24:26
Admin State         : Up           Oper State         : Up
MTU                 : 1514         Def. Mesh VC Id    : 100
SAP Count           : 1            SDP Bind Count     : 1
Send Flush on Fail: Disabled       Host Conn Verify   : Disabled
-------------------------------------------------------------------------------

...
-------------------------------------------------------------------------------
Sap Statistics
-------------------------------------------------------------------------------
Last Cleared Time     : 06/15/2007 16:17:10

                        Packets             Octets
Forwarding Engine Stats
Dropped               : 0                   0
Off. HiPrio           : 172                 16669
Off. LowPrio          : 0                   0
Off. Uncolor          : 56319               76706478

Queueing Stats(Ingress QoS Policy 100)
Dro. HiPrio           : 0                   0
Dro. LowPrio          : 0                   0
For. InProf           : 56491               76723147
```

(continued)

```
For. OutProf         : 0                    0

Queueing Stats(Egress QoS Policy 1)
Dro. InProf          : 0                    0
Dro. OutProf         : 0                    0
For. InProf          : 0                    0
For. OutProf         : 600                  54216
-------------------------------------------------------------------------
Sap per Queue stats
-------------------------------------------------------------------------
                       Packets              Octets

Ingress Queue 1 (Unicast) (Priority)
Off. HiPrio          : 0                    0
Off. LoPrio          : 0                    0
Dro. HiPrio          : 0                    0
Dro. LoPrio          : 0                    0
For. InProf          : 0                    0
For. OutProf         : 0                    0

Ingress Queue 3 (Unicast) (Profile)
Off. ColorIn         : 0                    0
Off. ColorOut        : 0                    0
Off. Uncolor         : 61382               83602284
Dro. ColorOut        : 0                    0
Dro. ColorIn & Uncolor: 0                   0
For. InProf          : 61382               83602284
For. OutProf         : 0                    0

Ingress Queue 11 (Multipoint) (Priority)
Off. HiPrio          : 181                  17533
Off. LoPrio          : 0                    0
Dro. HiPrio          : 0                    0
Dro. LoPrio          : 0                    0
For. InProf          : 181                  17533
For. OutProf         : 0                    0

Egress Queue 1
For. InProf          : 0                    0
For. OutProf         : 619                  56008
Dro. InProf          : 0                    0
Dro. OutProf         : 0                    0

-------------------------------------------------------------------------
...
```

To check the rate at which traffic flows through a SAP, you can use the `monitor service` family of commands shown in Listing 10.12. As shown in the code, the command family can also be used to see the absolute value, instead of the rate, of traffic traversed through the SAP during a specified interval. Listing 10.13 shows a sample output of the `monitor service id <service-id> sap <sap-id> rate` command.

Listing 10.12 Options for the monitor service family of commands

```
A:Pod2# monitor service id <service-id> sap
  - sap <sap-id> [interval <seconds>] [repeat <repeat>] [absolute|rate]

 <sap-id>               : null      - <port-id|bundle-id|lag-id|aps-id>
 ...
 <seconds>              : [11..60] - default 11
 <repeat>               : [1..999] - default 10
 <absolute|rate>        : keywords - default mode delta
```

Listing 10.13 Sample output of the monitor service id <service-id> sap <sap-id> rate command

```
A:Pod2# monitor service id 100 sap 1/2/2 rate
===============================================================================
Monitor statistics for Service 100 SAP 1/2/2
===============================================================================
-------------------------------------------------------------------------------
At time t = 0 sec (Base Statistics)
-----------------------------------------------------------------------...
-------------------------------------------------------------------------------
At time t = 11 sec (Mode: Rate)
-------------------------------------------------------------------------------
-------------------------------------------------------------------------------
Sap Statistics
-------------------------------------------------------------------------------
 ...
```

(continued)

```
--------------------------------------------------------------------
Sap per Queue Stats
--------------------------------------------------------------------
                        Packets              Octets              % Port
                                                                 Util.


Ingress Queue 1 (Unicast) (Priority)
Off. HiPrio          : 0                    0                   0.00
Off. LoPrio          : 0                    0                   0.00
Dro. HiPrio          : 0                    0                   0.00
Dro. LoPrio          : 0                    0                   0.00
For. InProf          : 0                    0                   0.00
For. OutProf         : 0                    0                   0.00

Ingress Queue 3 (Unicast) (Profile)
Off. ColorIn         : 0                    0                   0.00
Off. ColorOut        : 0                    0                   0.00
Off. Uncolor         : 442                  601595              0.48
Dro. ColorOut        : 0                    0                   0.00
Dro. ColorIn & Uncolor: 0                   0                   0.00
For. InProf          : 442                  601595              0.48
For. OutProf         : 0                    0                   0.00

Ingress Queue 11 (Multipoint) (Priority)
Off. HiPrio          : 0                    29                  ~0.00
Off. LoPrio          : 0                    0                   0.00
Dro. HiPrio          : 0                    0                   0.00
Dro. LoPrio          : 0                    0                   0.00
For. InProf          : 0                    29                  ~0.00
For. OutProf         : 0                    0                   0.00


Egress Queue 1
For. InProf          : 0                    0                   0.00
...
```

Extending Flexibility and Customization to Queue Scheduling

ALSRP has a wide range of applications. There are networks that are based on a single ALSRP node, and networks that span across continents using hundreds of ALSRP nodes. Such a wide range of applications is possible only if the nodes are customizable according to the needs of the service provider.

A careful analysis of the QoS architecture of ALSRP shows that it is fully configurable. Any application traffic can be mapped to any of the 8 forwarding classes or 54 subclasses. Any (one or more) forwarding classes can be associated with any of the possible queues at each queuing point. The queue sizes and rates are fully configurable. The arbitrator type associated with a queue can also be configured. In order to maintain the flexibility in customizing the nodes according to the needs of the applications supported, the basic scheduling is deliberately kept simple but configurable.

ALSRP allows network designers to choose how many queues have to be exhaustively serviced over one another and how many queues have to be serviced with a specified priority, but with different weights. Moreover, with ALSRP it is possible to prioritize queues belonging to one customer over another. Because of the flexibility in scheduling provided by the ALSRP, service providers can either sell bandwidth for different services or multiple services within a set bandwidth. Chapter 11 shows you how to design hierarchical scheduling in ALSRP.

Summary

ALSRP uses a hardware-related entity called an arbitrator for scheduling. An arbitrator is a pair of scheduling loops. The first loop is for scheduling the queues that are in in-profile state, and the second loop is for scheduling the queues that are in out-of-profile state.

There are four scheduling-related parameters common to all queues: CIR, PIR, adaptation rule, and arbitrator type selector. While CIR of queues is not over booked, a queue is guaranteed to be serviced at its CIR. At access ingress the CIR of a queue performs two functions: determining the profile of the datagram scheduled out of a queue that is configured in priority mode, and determining the profile state of the queue while scheduling. At all other queuing points, the CIR determines only the profile state of the queue while scheduling. PIR is the maximum rate at which a queue can be serviced. The CIR and PIR configured using a QoS policy are referred to as administrative rates. The adaptation rule associates an administrative rate with the underlying hardware scheduling rates referred to as operational rates. The arbitrator association rule of a queue specifies the type of the arbitrator for servicing the queue.

There are two basic scheduling modes in ALSRP: single arbitrator scheduling mode and dual arbitrator scheduling mode. Single arbitrator scheduling mode is applicable only to the egress scheduling of M60-10/100eth-TX MDA, and dual arbitrator scheduling mode applies everywhere else. In single arbitrator scheduling mode, there are two scheduling loops: In the first loop all in-profile queues are serviced, and in the second loop all the out-of-profile queues are serviced. In dual arbitrator scheduling mode, there are four scheduling loops; the out-of-profile queue loops of the paired arbitrators are combined to provide biased round robin scheduling for all the out-of-profile queues. In dual arbitrator scheduling mode, traffic going to a destination is scheduled in the following order:

- In-profile queues associated with the high-priority arbitrator.
- In-profile queues associated with the low-priority arbitrator.
- Out-of-profile queues associated with both the high- and low-priority arbitrators

Hierarchical Scheduling

11

In ALSRP, hierarchical scheduling can be used to customize scheduling at an access interface, and thereby dynamically distribute bandwidth between different applications or different customer sites.

Chapter Objectives

- To describe the hierarchical scheduling related parameters

- To explain how a virtual scheduler works, and how it calculates the bandwidth to allocate to queues

- To explain the Scheduler policy construct

- To demonstrate how to apply a Scheduler policy to a SAP and to a `multi-service-site`

Hierarchical scheduling is commonly referred to as hierarchical quality of service, or HQoS. Using a hierarchy of virtual schedulers, the ALSRP HQoS can both customize the access scheduling according to the needs of an application, and dynamically allocate bandwidth to queues according to their overall bandwidth usage.

Using hierarchical scheduling, a service provider can redistribute unused bandwidth of one application to another in triple-play-type service offerings, or they can redistribute unused bandwidth of one site to another of a multi-service site, as long as the connection to both sites terminates on the same input/output module (IOM) of an ALSRP node. Such bandwidth redistribution is similar to a corporation buying a common pool of cell phone talk time for its employees.

HQoS can customize scheduling and dynamically allocate bandwidth between:

- Multiple queues belonging to a SAP.
- Multiple SAPs belonging to a customer on a port.
- Multiple SAPs belonging to a single customer, spread across different ports within a media-dependent adapter (MDA).
- Multiple SAPs belonging to a single customer, spread across different ports of two different MDAs that are in the same IOM.

Applying HQoS to Regulate Different End-Customer Traffic

If an HQoS construct can only regulate traffic belonging to multiple SAPs of a single customer, how can it be used to schedule traffic flowing through different SAPs belonging to different customers in a triple-play like application?

HQoS or a Scheduler policy can be applied for a SAP or multiple SAPs belonging to a single customer. However, "customer" as referred to here is a configurable entity in ALSRP. For a triple-play-type application, you can configure a common customer entity for all the residential customers and use a common Scheduler policy for those residential customer SAPs.

A hierarchical scheduler is configured using a Scheduler policy. The virtual schedulers, which are the building blocks of a Scheduler policy, are tied to each other and to the queues declared in a SAP-ingress or SAP-egress policy through parent-child relationships.

To implement hierarchical scheduling of the queues of a SAP, you must apply a Scheduler policy as well as the associated SAP-ingress or SAP-egress policy to the SAP. For hierarchical scheduling of the queues of more than one SAP, the Scheduler policy has to be applied under a `multi-service-site` within a `customer` configuration.

This chapter begins by describing the parameters associated with hierarchical scheduling and explains the basics of a virtual scheduler. Then it discusses the design process of a Scheduler policy and the application of hierarchical scheduling to service entities. Finally, the chapter presents verification commands related to hierarchical scheduling.

11.1 Hierarchical Scheduling Parameters

Like a queue, a virtual scheduler also has the two rate parameters: peak information rate (PIR) and committed information rate (CIR). The `parent` declaration command of a child (within a queue or virtual scheduler) consists of the following four additional hierarchical scheduling-related parameters:

- `level`
- `cir-level`
- `weight`
- `cir-weight`

The `level` and `weight` parameters are associated with the PIR, while the `cir-level` and `cir-weight` are associated with the CIR.

You are already familiar with the functions of PIR (`rate`) and CIR parameters. The difference in configuring the rate parameters of a virtual scheduler as compared with configuring these parameters in access queues is that the CIR parameter of a virtual scheduler can be configured to be `sum`. The value `sum` is the default value, and it implies that the CIR of a virtual scheduler is the sum of the CIRs of its children.

The `level` and `cir-level` parameters refer to the priority a child has compared with other children, for receiving the bandwidth from their parent scheduler. The `cir-level` parameter specifies the priority of a child during the committed bandwidth distribution cycle. The `level` parameter specifies the priority of a child during the excess bandwidth distribution cycle. The value range of a `cir-level` parameter is from 0 to 8, and the value range of a `level` parameter is 1 to 8. If the `cir-level` of a child is configured as 0, then the child will not be considered in the committed bandwidth distribution cycle.

The `cir-weight` parameter specifies the relative weight of a child compared with other children that are in the same priority level during the committed bandwidth distribution cycle. Similarly, the `weight` parameter specifies the relative weight of a child compared with other children that are in the same priority level during the excess bandwidth distribution cycle. The value range of the `cir-weight` and `weight` parameters is from 0 to 100.

11.2 Virtual Scheduler Bandwidth Distribution

A Scheduler policy defines virtual schedulers and can arrange them into up to three different tiers: tier 1 (top level) through tier 3 (bottom level). Tier 1 virtual schedulers are the root schedulers. A queue can be a child to any one virtual scheduler in any tier. A virtual scheduler can be a child to any other virtual scheduler in a higher level (lesser tier number). A (single) parent virtual scheduler is responsible for the bandwidth distribution to all its children; consequently a child cannot have a parent-child relationship with more than one virtual scheduler (in other words, the "marriage" of two virtual schedulers is forbidden in the world of virtual schedulers and everyone must be single!).

Figure 11.1 summarizes the possible relationships in hierarchical scheduling. The figure shows four virtual schedulers and six queues. Line arrows in the figure indicate parent-child relationships. The tier 1 scheduler is the root scheduler, and it has three children: Scheduler 3A, Queue 3, and Scheduler 2A. Scheduler 2A has two children: Queue 4 and Scheduler 3B. Scheduler 3A has two children: Queue 1 and Queue 2. Scheduler 3B also has two children: Queue 5 and Queue 6.

Bandwidth available for a tier 1 virtual scheduler in the egress side is limited by the bandwidth of the port to which traffic is forwarded, by the number of competing entities that forward traffic to the port and by the amount of traffic offered by those entities. Similarly, bandwidth available for a tier 1 virtual scheduler in the ingress side is limited by the forwarding capacity provided for the destination MDA to which the traffic is forwarded and by the amount of traffic from different sources destined for the destination MDA.

Figure 11.1 Virtual Scheduler Hierarchical Organization

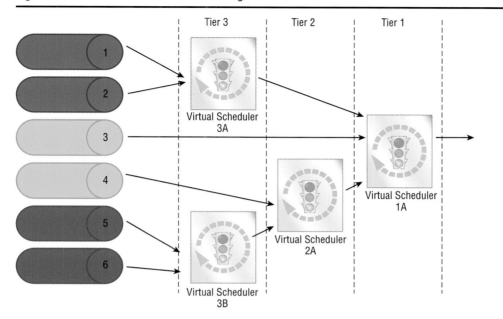

A virtual scheduler distributes all the bandwidth it receives from its parent among its children in two passes: a *committed bandwidth distribution pass* and an *excess bandwidth distribution pass*. During the committed bandwidth distribution pass, the CIR-related parameters of the children (`cir`, `cir-level`, and `cir-weight`) are considered for the bandwidth distribution. During the excess bandwidth distribution pass, the PIR-related parameters of the children (`rate`, `level`, and `weight`) are considered for the bandwidth distribution.

A virtual scheduler distributes bandwidth among its children during a committed bandwidth distribution as follows:

- The bandwidth distribution starts among the children with the highest `cir-level` and continues with the children, who have decreasing `cir-level`s.

- If more than one child has the same `cir-level`, the bandwidth is distributed among the children using `cir-weight`s in a weighted round robin fashion. As each child reaches its CIR for the scheduling window, the child is taken out of contention from the committed bandwidth distribution pass.

- The pass concludes when either all the children are serviced up to their CIR or the bandwidth is exhausted.

If a virtual scheduler has excess bandwidth after its committed bandwidth distribution pass, it goes through the excess distribution pass. A virtual scheduler distributes bandwidth among its children during an excess bandwidth distribution pass as follows:

- The bandwidth distribution starts among the children with the highest level and continues with the children, who have decreasing levels.
- If more than one child has the same level, the bandwidth is distributed among the children using weights in a weighted round robin fashion. As each child reaches its PIR for the scheduling window, the child is taken out of contention from the excess bandwidth distribution pass.
- The pass concludes when either all the children are serviced up to their PIR or the bandwidth is exhausted.

A virtual scheduler is smart enough to keep track of the actual throughput of each of its children during a scheduling window and to redistribute any unused bandwidth from one child to another that needs more bandwidth. A scheduling window span is in the order of a few milliseconds. Thus, the bandwidth allocated to each child changes dynamically.

11.3 Examples of Virtual Scheduler Bandwidth Distribution

This section offers several specific examples to better illustrate how a virtual scheduler allocates bandwidth to its children. A complete case study on designing a hierarchical scheduling is presented in Chapter 15. For the examples presented in this section assume that every child of a virtual scheduler consumes all the bandwidth allocated to it (so that you do not need to worry about the dynamics of change in bandwidth allocation).

Simple Bandwidth Distribution Examples

Example 1: In the first example, illustrated in Figure 11.2, there is one virtual scheduler, with two queues as its children. The rates and hierarchical scheduling-related parameters of the queues are shown within the rectangular boxes in the queues.

Figure 11.2 Virtual Scheduler Bandwidth Distribution Example 1

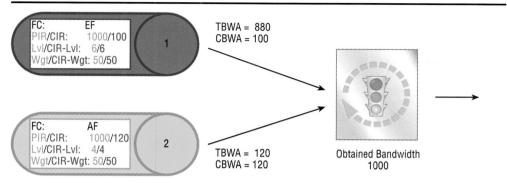

The virtual scheduler obtains 1000 Kbps (kilobits/sec) and in turn allocates the bandwidth to its two children through the committed and excess bandwidth passes. During the committed bandwidth pass, the virtual scheduler first looks at the `cir-levels` of its children. The `cir-level` of the top queue is 6 and the `cir-level` of the bottom queue is 4. The top queue has a higher priority to receive committed bandwidth, and it receives 100 Kbps, the CIR bandwidth it requested. The virtual scheduler is left with 900 Kbps, sufficient to allocate 120 Kbps (the CIR requested) to the bottom queue. After allocating the committed bandwidth to both of its children, the virtual scheduler concludes its committed bandwidth distribution pass and is still left with an excess bandwidth of 780 Kbps. Because of the excess bandwidth available, the virtual scheduler goes through an excess bandwidth distribution pass. During the excess bandwidth pass the virtual scheduler first looks at the `levels` of its children. Again, the `level` of the queue in the top is 6 and the level of the queue in the bottom is 4. The top queue has a higher priority to receive excess bandwidth. Its PIR is 1000 Kbps, which means that it requires an additional 900 Kbps to attain its PIR. However, as there are only 780 Kbps remaining, it receives all of it. Because the bandwidth is exhausted, the virtual scheduler concludes its excess bandwidth distribution pass. Hence, although both queues are configured with a PIR of 1000 Kbps, there isn't enough excess bandwidth available to enable them to achieve their PIR. However, if at any time, the top queue does not utilize all the bandwidth allocated to it, the virtual scheduler will redistribute the excess bandwidth it had previously allocated to the top queue to the bottom queue.

The committed bandwidth (CBWA) and the total bandwidth (TBWA) assigned to each queue are shown next to the queues.

Example 2: Figure 11.3 shows a second example of bandwidth distribution by a virtual scheduler. The only difference between this example and the previous one is that the `level` of the top queue is 3 instead of 6. Therefore, the top queue gets a lower priority during the excess bandwidth pass.

Figure 11.3 Virtual Scheduler Bandwidth Distribution Example 2

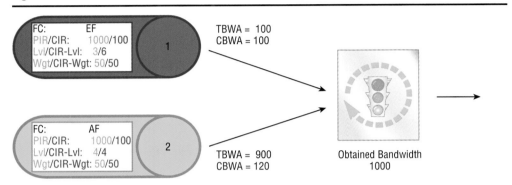

Example 3: Figure 11.4 shows a third example of bandwidth distribution by a virtual scheduler. In this example, the CIR of both the queues is 100, and their `level` is 4. During the excess bandwidth distribution pass, the virtual scheduler realizes that both the queues have equal priority and therefore looks at their weight to determine how to distribute the bandwidth. The `weight` of the top queue is 30, and the `weight` of the bottom queue is 10. The available excess bandwidth is 800 Kbps. Therefore, during the excess bandwidth pass, the virtual scheduler distributes 3 Kb (kilobits) for the top queue for every 1 Kb (kilobits) distributed to the bottom queue. In other words, during the excess bandwidth pass, the bandwidth is distributed in a 3:1 ratio between the top and bottom queues, reflecting the 3:1 ratio in their `weight`s. Therefore, the top queue receives 600 Kbps of the available bandwidth, and the bottom queue receives 200 Kbps.

Figure 11.4 Virtual Scheduler Bandwidth Distribution Example 3

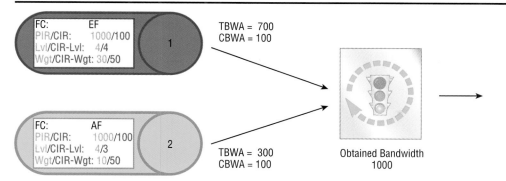

In this example, you saw how a virtual scheduler distributes bandwidth among its children based on their weights. The proportional rate at which bandwidth is distributed by a virtual scheduler for children that are in the same level, using their weights, can be formalized as follows. Let there be n children of the virtual scheduler that are in the same level. Let W_i be the **weight** of the ith child and $EBWPR_i$ be the proportional rate at which the child receives the excess bandwidth. $EBWPR_i$ can be defined as:

$$EBWPR_i = \frac{W_i}{\displaystyle\sum_{j=1}^{n} W_j}$$

During the progression of the excess bandwidth distribution pass, as each child gets bandwidth up to its PIR, the child is taken out of contention for receiving bandwidth from the pass. As each child is taken out, the **weight** of the child is removed from the denominator of the above equation.

As an exercise, substitute the values from the preceding Example 3 in the equation and determine the proportional rate at which Queue 2 will receive excess bandwidth:

$$EBWPR(Q2) = \frac{10}{(30+10)} = \frac{1}{4}$$

This explanation is equally applicable for bandwidth distribution during a committed bandwidth pass, but instead of `weight` and $EBWPR_i$, it will be `cir-weight` and $CBWPR_i$.

Example 4: In the fourth example, illustrated in Figure 11.5, the `level` parameters of both queues are configured to be identical. Therefore, the `weight` parameters of the queues gain significance in distributing the bandwidth. However, the `weight` and `cir-weight` of the bottom queue are configured to be zero.

When the `cir-weight` of a child is zero, the child obtains bandwidth during the committed bandwidth distribution only after all its siblings with the same `cir-level` and with non-zero `cir-weight` have received their committed bandwidth. Similarly when the `weight` of a child is zero, the child gets bandwidth during the excess bandwidth distribution only after all its siblings with the same `level` and with non-zero `weight` have received their excess bandwidth. When there are multiple children at the same level with zero weight, the children are treated with equal priority and bandwidth is assigned to them in round robin fashion, when their turn arrives.

Figure 11.5 Virtual Scheduler Bandwidth Distribution Example 4

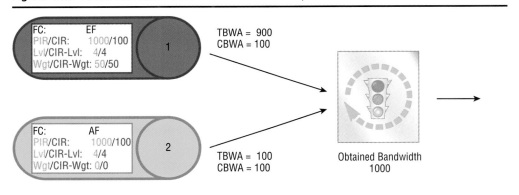

Best Practices: Complex hierarchical schedulers can be difficult to debug and maintain. Therefore, the hierarchical structure within a Scheduler policy should be optimized using the minimum number of virtual schedulers, and the policy should be well documented.

More Complex Examples of Bandwidth Distribution

Now that you have mastered how a virtual scheduler allocates bandwidth to its children, let's increase the complexity and see how bandwidth is allocated to queues through a two-tiered Scheduler policy.

The two-tiered scheduler policies considered in this section are not necessarily optimized (the resulting hierarchical scheduling can be easily achieved using just one virtual scheduler), and hence should be considered only for example purposes.

Example 5: Figure 11.6 shows the implementation structure of a two-tiered Scheduler policy. In the structure, there are two virtual schedulers: one configured under tier-1 and the other configured under tier-2. The structure also shows four queues on the left-hand side. Only one forwarding class is mapped to each of the four queues; for convenience, we'll refer to the queues by the forwarding classes mapped to them.

Figure 11.6 Virtual Scheduler Bandwidth Distribution Example 5

```
FC:         EF
PIR/CIR:    1000/100        6      TBWA = 800
Lvl/CIR-Lvl:  6/6                  CBWA = 100
Wgt/CIR-Wgt: 50/50

                                                        Tier 1
                                                        Obtained
FC:         L1                                          Bandwidth
PIR/CIR:    1000/150        4      TBWA = 120           1000
Lvl/CIR-Lvl:  4/4                  CBWA = 120
Wgt/CIR-Wgt: 33/60

FC:         AF                     TBWA = 80
PIR/CIR:    1000/120        3      CBWA = 80
Lvl/CIR-Lvl:  4/4                                       TBWA = 200
Wgt/CIR-Wgt: 33/40                                      CBWA = 200

FC:         BE                                    Tier 2
PIR/CIR:    1000/10         1      TBWA = 0        PIR/CIR:     1000/200
Lvl/CIR-Lvl:  4/4                  CBWA = 0        Lvl/CIR-Lvl:   4/4
Wgt/CIR-Wgt: 33/0                                 Wgt/CIR-Wgt: 50/50
```

The tier 1 scheduler is the root scheduler. The root scheduler has two children: the EF queue and the tier 2 virtual scheduler. The tier-2 scheduler has three children: the L1 queue, the AF queue, and the BE queue.

The root scheduler begins the bandwidth distribution with the committed bandwidth distribution pass. The root scheduler inspects the `cir-level` of its two children. Realizing that the EF queue has higher priority, the root scheduler offers the committed bandwidth of 100 Kbps to the queue. Then the root scheduler provides the committed bandwidth of 200 Kbps to the tier-2 scheduler. At this point, the committed bandwidth distribution pass of the root scheduler is complete and the root scheduler has 700 Kbps of bandwidth remaining.

To distribute the excess bandwidth, the root scheduler initiates the excess bandwidth distribution pass. Again in the excess bandwidth distribution pass, the EF queue gets higher priority, and it requests an excess bandwidth of 900 Kbps. The root scheduler only has an excess bandwidth of 700 Kbps. So the root scheduler provides all the available excess bandwidth to the EF queue and terminates the excess bandwidth distribution pass. Hence, the EF queue obtains its configured CIR of 100 Kbps and a total bandwidth of 800 Kbps.

The tier-2 scheduler obtains a total bandwidth of 200 Kbps. The tier-2 scheduler in turn distributes the bandwidth to its three children through its own committed and excess bandwidth distribution passes. During the committed bandwidth distribution pass, the tier-2 scheduler inspects the `cir-level`s of its three children. The `cir-level` all three children is the same (4). Therefore, the tier-2 scheduler inspects the `cir-weight` of its children. Respectively, the `cir-weight`s of L1, AF, and BE queues are 60, 40, and 0. Because the `cir-weight` of the BE queue is 0, its priority level is lower than the other two queues. The bandwidth available with the tier-2 scheduler is distributed between the L1 and AF queue in a 3:2 (60:40) ratio. The L1 queue receives 120 Kbps, and the AF queue receives 80 Kbps. The available bandwidth with the tier-2 scheduler gets exhausted before the scheduler can provide the configured CIR bandwidth to any of its children. Because the available bandwidth is exhausted, the committed bandwidth distribution pass is concluded, and the excess bandwidth distribution pass is skipped. Thus, according to the deliberate configuration of the example, the BE queue does not receive any bandwidth, while all other queues are utilizing the TBWA allocated to them.

In the BE queue, the incoming datagrams will begin to queue up and could eventually be dropped. The example is considered again later in the section to discuss when the BE queue will be serviced.

Example 6: Figure 11.7 shows the implementation structure of another two-tiered Scheduler policy. The structure is the same as the previous example, and only the queue parameters have changed.

Figure 11.7 Virtual Scheduler Bandwidth Distribution Example 6

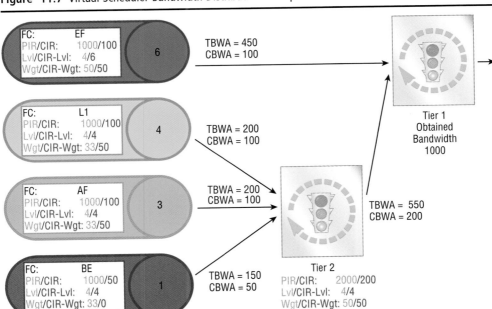

During the committed bandwidth distribution pass of the root scheduler the EF queue gets a higher priority compared with the tier-2 scheduler. Therefore, the EF queue gets its committed bandwidth of 100 Kbps first and then the tier-2 scheduler gets its committed bandwidth of 200 Kbps. The root scheduler is left with 700 Kbps of bandwidth for the excess bandwidth distribution pass.

During the excess bandwidth distribution pass of the root scheduler, the EF queue and the tier-2 scheduler have equal priority. Therefore, their `cir-weight`s are considered. Because their `cir-weight`s are equal, the excess bandwidth is shared equally. Thus, the EF queues ends up with a total bandwidth of 450 Kbps, and the tier-2 scheduler ends up with a total bandwidth of 550 Kbps.

Because the `cir-level` of the L1, AF, and BE queues are the same, during the committed bandwidth distribution pass of the tier-2 scheduler the `cir-weight`s of the queues are considered. Respectively, the `cir-weight`s of L1, AF, and BE queues are 50, 50, and 0. Therefore, the L1 and AF queues get their committed bandwidth first. Then the BE queue gets its committed bandwidth. There is sufficient bandwidth available for all three queues to obtain their respective committed bandwidths. After the conclusion of the committed bandwidth distribution pass, the tier-2 scheduler is left with an excess bandwidth of 300 Kbps.

Because the `level` of the L1, AF, and BE queues are the same, during the excess bandwidth distribution pass of the tier-2 scheduler the `weight` of each queue is considered. Because the weights of all three queues are the same, all three queues get an equal share of the excess bandwidth of the tier-2 scheduler. Hence, each queue receives an additional 100 Kbps of bandwidth to give them a respective total bandwidth of 200 Kbps, 200 Kbps, and 150 Kbps.

Dynamics of Virtual Scheduler Bandwidth Distribution

In all the examples shown so far, we assumed that every child of a virtual scheduler consumes all the bandwidth allocated to it. The assumption led to static bandwidth distribution; there would be no change in the bandwidth distributed by a virtual scheduler to its children from one scheduling window to another. However, in reality this assumption would not be valid, as the various applications' flows would not necessarily be continuously transmitting at a constant burst. Thus, when one of the applications ceases to be active or utilizes less than the allocated bandwidth, the virtual scheduler redistributes the excess bandwidth to its other children.

Look back at Example 5 and consider what happens if a child does not consume all the bandwidth allocated to it by a virtual scheduler. The EF queue in the example receives a total bandwidth of 800 Kbps. Assume that the EF queue used only 100 Kbps out of the assigned 800 Kbps within a scheduler window. The tier 1 root scheduler measures this actual bandwidth usage of the EF queue and allocates the unused bandwidth of 700 Kbps of the EF queue to the tier-2 virtual scheduler in the following scheduling window. The tier-2 virtual scheduler in turn allocates this excess bandwidth to its children according to the standard rules. Conversely, if the measured bandwidth usage of the EF queue has increased again in this scheduling window, the tier 1 scheduler will assign the additional bandwidth in the next scheduling window to the EF queue.

11.4 Creating and Configuring a Scheduler Policy

As mentioned earlier in the chapter, the Scheduler policy is where virtual schedulers are defined and configured. These schedulers are defined as tier 1, 2, or 3 schedulers, and their hierarchical relationships are also specified within the Scheduler policy.

Listing 11.1 shows the command line options for creating a Scheduler policy. Like Network-Queue and Slope policies, a Scheduler policy is also identified through the policy name.

Listing 11.1 Options for creating a Scheduler policy

```
A:Pod2>config>qos# scheduler-policy
  - no scheduler-policy <scheduler-policy-name>
  - scheduler-policy <scheduler-policy-name> [create]

 <scheduler-policy-*> : [32 chars max]
 <create>             : keyword - mandatory while creating an entry.
```

Note: There is no default Scheduler policy.

Listing 11.2 displays the top-level command options available to configure a Scheduler policy.

Listing 11.2 Top-level command options available to configure a Scheduler policy

```
A:Pod2>config>qos>scheduler-policy#
 [no] description     - Description for this policy
 [no] tier            + Configure schedulers in a particular tier
```

Specifying a description for a Scheduler policy is not mandatory, but is an essential best practice. Following the description, a tier level of 1 to 3 has to be specified before creating a virtual scheduler. Listing 11.3 illustrates the options for specifying a scheduler tier level.

Listing 11.3 Options for configuring a scheduler tier and an example tier creation

```
A:Pod2>config>qos>scheduler-policy# tier
  - no tier <tier>
  - tier <tier>

 <tier>                 : [1..3]
A:Pod2>config>qos>scheduler-policy# tier 1
A:Pod2>config>qos>scheduler-policy>tier#
```

Listing 11.4 shows the options for creating and configuring virtual schedulers. You are already familiar with the `description` and `rate` (PIR and CIR) parameters. You have seen the `description` parameter under every QoS policy, and also under other configuration entities such as services, port, and so on. You have seen the `rate` parameters within a queue configuration.

Listing 11.4 Options for creating and configuring virtual schedulers

```
A:Pod2>config>qos>scheduler-policy>tier# scheduler
  - no scheduler <scheduler-name>
  - scheduler <scheduler-name> [create]

 <scheduler-name>       : [32 chars max]
 <create>               : keyword - mandatory while creating an entry.


 [no] description       - Description for this policy
 [no] parent            - Specify the scheduler to which this scheduler
                          feeds
 [no] rate              - Specify rates (CIR and PIR)
```

As mentioned earlier in the chapter, the `cir` parameter available under a `scheduler` has one difference when compared with configuration possibilities under a queue. The `cir` parameter available under a `scheduler` can be configured as `sum`, which is the default value. Listing 11.5 provides the options for configuring the `rate` parameters under a `scheduler`. When configured as `sum`, the CIR of the virtual scheduler is equal to the sum of the CIR of the children of the virtual scheduler.

Listing 11.5 Options for configuring the rate parameters under a virtual scheduler

```
A:Pod2>config>qos>scheduler-policy>tier>scheduler# rate
  - no rate
  - rate <pir-rate> [cir <cir-rate>]

 <pir-rate>            : [1..100000000|max]
 <cir-rate>            : [0..100000000|sum|max]
```

Listing 11.6 shows the options for configuring the `parent` parameters under a scheduler. The `parent` parameters can also be configured for a queue, in order to associate the queue with a virtual scheduler. The configuration options for the `parent` parameters available under a queue are the same as those listed in Listing 11.6.

Listing 11.6 Options for configuring the parent parameters under a virtual scheduler

```
A:Pod2>config>qos>scheduler-policy>tier>scheduler# parent
  - parent <scheduler-name> [weight <weight>] [level <level>]
    [cir-weight <cir-weight>] [cir-level <cir-level>]
  - no parent

 <scheduler-name>     : [32 chars max]
 <weight>             : [0..100]
 <level>              : [1..8]
 <cir-weight>         : [0..100]
 <cir-level>          : [0..8]
```

Listing 11.7 exhibits an example Scheduler policy, and Listing 11.8 exhibits an example SAP-egress policy. The queues within the SAP-egress policy have parent-child relationships with the virtual schedulers defined within the Scheduler policy. Together the Scheduler policy of Listing 11.7 and the SAP-egress policy of Listing 11.8 form a hierarchical scheduling relationship reflecting the logical representation shown in Figure 11.7.

Listing 11.7 An example Scheduler policy

```
scheduler-policy "vsp1" create
    tier 1
        scheduler "root" create
            description "right most one in the logical representation"
            rate 1000 cir 1000
        exit
    exit
    tier 2
        scheduler "t2" create
            description "the one closer to queues in the logical representation"
            parent "root" level 4 weight 50 cir-level 4 cir-weight 50
            rate 1000 cir 200
        exit
    exit
exit
```

Listing 11.8 Example SAP-egress policy with queues

```
sap-egress 100 create
    description "Example association with a scheduler policy"
    queue 1 create
        parent "t2" level 4 weight 33 cir-level 4 cir-weight 0
        rate 1000 cir 50
    exit
    queue 3 create
        parent "t2" level 4 weight 33 cir-level 4 cir-weight 50
        rate 1000 cir 100
    exit
    queue 4 create
        parent "t2" level 4 weight 33 cir-level 4 cir-weight 50
        rate 1000 cir 100
    exit
    queue 6 create
        parent "root" level 4 weight 50 cir-level 6 cir-weight 50
        rate 1000 cir 100
    exit
    fc af create
```

(continued)

```
        queue 3
    exit
    fc be create
        queue 1
    exit
    fc ef create
        queue 6
    exit
    fc l1 create
        queue 4
    exit
exit
```

11.5 Applying a Scheduler Policy

A Scheduler policy can be applied either directly under a SAP to schedule the queues of the SAP, or under a `multi-service-site` configuration of a `customer` to schedule multiple SAPs and their queues belonging to the customer. In ALSRP, `multi-service-site` is a configurable entity, which acts as an anchor point to map ingress or egress hierarchical virtual schedulers to multiple SAPs assigned to the `multi-service-site`. Configuring a `multi-service-site` is explained later in this section.

Note: The Scheduler policy must be applied to the SAP or `multi-service-site` configuration of a customer in order for the queues defined in the SAP-ingress or SAP-egress policy to be associated with the virtual schedulers defined in the Scheduler policy. If a queue is configured with a parent scheduler association but a Scheduler policy containing that scheduler has not been applied to the SAP or `multi-service-site` configuration of a customer, the queue will be scheduled as per the basic scheduling mechanism. In other words, hierarchical scheduling will not take effect unless the Scheduler policy has been applied to the appropriate entity.

Applying a Scheduler Policy under a SAP

Figure 11.8 is a conceptual diagram showing the application of a Scheduler policy to an individual SAP. By applying a Scheduler policy to a SAP, the queues belonging to the SAP can be serviced by the hierarchical virtual schedulers of the

Scheduler policy. Thus, in turn the traffic arriving or leaving through the SAP can be hierarchically scheduled using the Scheduler policy.

Figure 11.8 Concept of Applying a Scheduler Policy to an Individual SAP

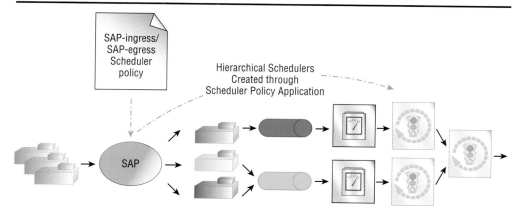

A Scheduler policy can be applied both under the ingress and egress configuration of a SAP. Listing 11.9 shows the options for applying a Scheduler policy under the ingress configuration of a SAP. The options for applying a Scheduler policy under the egress configuration of a SAP are similar.

Listing 11.9 Options for applying a Scheduler policy under the ingress configuration of a SAP

```
A:Pod2>config>service>vpls>sap>ingress# scheduler-policy
  - no scheduler-policy
  - scheduler-policy <scheduler-policy-name>

 <scheduler-policy-*> : [32 chars max]
```

Listing 11.10 exhibits an example service configuration with a Scheduler policy and an associated SAP-egress policy applied under the egress configuration of a SAP.

Listing 11.10 Example service configuration with a Scheduler policy applied under the egress configuration of a SAP

```
      vpls 100 customer 1 create
          stp
```

(continued)

```
            shutdown
        exit
        sap 1/2/2 create
            egress
                scheduler-policy "vsp1"
                qos 100
            exit
        exit
        spoke-sdp 1:100 create
        exit
        no shutdown
    exit
```

Applying a Scheduler policy directly under a SAP configuration is illustrated in Figure 11.9.

Figure 11.9 Application of a Scheduler Policy under a SAP Configuration

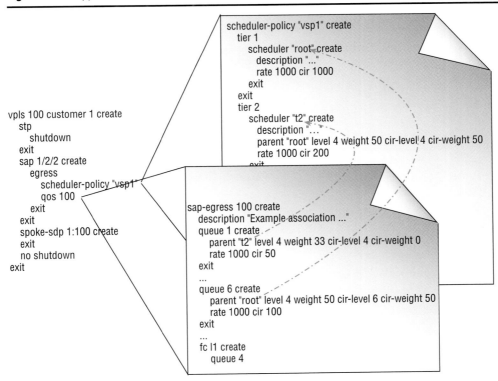

As illustrated in Figure 11.9, for a hierarchical scheduler to be effective with respect to ingress or egress traffic of a SAP, the following mappings have to be valid:

- Queues configured in a SAP-ingress or SAP-egress policy must have parent-child relationships with the virtual schedulers declared in a Scheduler policy.
- The SAP-ingress or the SAP-egress policy should be applied under the SAP configuration.
- The Scheduler policy should be applied under the SAP configuration along with the SAP-ingress or SAP-egress policy.

Applying a Scheduler Policy under a Multi-Service-Site Configuration

Figure 11.10 is a conceptual diagram showing the application of a Scheduler policy to a `multi-service-site`. In this way, all the SAP's queues assigned to the `multi-service-site` can be serviced by the hierarchical schedulers of the Scheduler policy.

Figure 11.10 Concept of Applying a Scheduler Policy to a multi-service-site

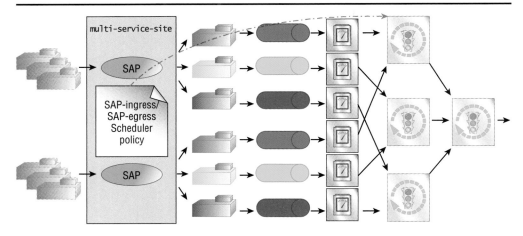

In essence, by applying a Scheduler policy to a `multi-service-site`, all the SAP queues of a customer within a port, within multiple ports of an MDA, or within two different MDAs of an IOM slot can be serviced by the hierarchical schedulers of the Scheduler policy.

Listing 11.11 shows the command options for creating a `multi-service-site`. Like a Scheduler policy, a `multi-service-site` is also identified by its name. The `tod-suite` option in the listing is not required for the current discussion, so let's defer that discussion to Chapter 13.

Listing 11.11 Options for creating a multi-service-site

```
A:Pod2>config>service>cust# multi-service-site
  - multi-service-site <customer-site-name> [create]
  - no multi-service-site <customer-site-name>

 <customer-site-name> : [32 chars max]
 <create>               : keyword - mandatory while creating an entry.


 [no] assignment       - Specify the port for the multi-service
 [no] description       - Description for this customer
      egress           + Specify egress parameters/policies
      ingress          + Specify ingress parameters/policies
 [no] tod-suite         - Configure a time-of-day suite for this multi-service
                          site
```

Listing 11.12 provides the options for configuring an `assignment` statement under a `multi-service-site` configuration. As shown in Listing 11.12, the assignment can be as simple as an individual channel or an entire IOM slot, which takes in two MDAs. The assignment to a `multi-service-site` can also be a port, Inverse Multiplexing for ATM (IMA) bundle, Link Aggregation Group (LAG), Automatic Protection Switching (APS), or point-to-point protocol (PPP) bundle. The entity mapped through the assignment statement must already be pre-provisioned on the system. LAG is explained in detail in Chapter 13.

Listing 11.12 Options for a multi-service-site assignment configuration

```
A:Pod2>config>service>cust>multi-service-site# assignment
  - assignment {port <port-id>|card <slot-number>}
  - no assignment

 <port-id>                : slot/mda/port[.channel]

                  aps-id          - aps-<group-id>[.channel]
```

(continued)

```
                              aps          - keyword
                              group-id     - [1..16]

                         bundle-<type>-slot/mda.<bundle-num>
                              bundle       - keyword
                              type         - ima|ppp
                              bundle-num   - [1..128]

                         ccag-id      - ccag-<id>.<path-id>[cc-type]
                              ccag         - keyword
                              id           - [1..8]
                              path-id      - [a|b]
                              cc-type      - [.sap-net|.net-sap]

                         lag-id       - lag-<id>
                              lag          - keyword
                              id           - [1..64]
         <slot-number>       : [1..10]
```

Listing 11.13 shows the options configurable under ingress of a
multi-service-site. As shown in the listing, a Scheduler policy can be
applied under ingress of a multi-service-site. The scheduler-override
option shown in the listing is not required for the current discussion and its
coverage is deferred to Chapter 13.

Listing 11.13 Ingress multi-service-site assignment configuration

```
A:Pod2>config>service>cust>multi-service-site# ingress
  - ingress

 [no] scheduler-over* + Apply a scheduler override
 [no] scheduler-poli* - Specify a scheduler-policy
```

Listing 11.14 displays the options configurable under egress of a multi-service-
site. The options available under egress of a multi-service-site are similar
to the ingress options, but in addition the agg-rate-limit option is available.
This option is also available under egress of a SAP. When configured under a
multi-service-site, the agg-rate-limit defines a maximum total rate for all
egress queues of all the SAPs of the multi-service-site. When applied under a

SAP, it defines a maximum total rate for all egress queues of the SAP. The `agg-rate-limit` command is mutually exclusive with the egress Scheduler policy. When an egress Scheduler policy is defined, the `agg-rate-limit` command will fail. If the `agg-rate-limit` command is specified, any attempt to bind a Scheduler policy to the `multi-service-site` or the SAP will fail.

Listing 11.14 Egress multi-service-site assignment configuration

```
A:Pod2>config>service>cust>multi-service-site# egress
  - egress

 [no] agg-rate-limit  - Configure the aggregate rate limit
 [no] scheduler-over* + Apply a scheduler override
 [no] scheduler-poli* - Specify a scheduler-policy
```

Listing 11.15 exhibits an example customer configuration. In the example, the Scheduler policy `vsp1` is assigned to the ingress of `multi-service-site Kirkland`, and the Scheduler policy `vsp2` is assigned to the egress of `multi-service-site Seattle`.

Listing 11.15 Example customer configuration highlighting Scheduler policy application under a multi-service-site

```
    customer 425 create
        multi-service-site "Kirkland" create
            assignment port 1/2/5
            egress
                scheduler-policy "vsp2"
            exit
        exit
        multi-service-site "Seattle" create
            assignment card 1
            ingress
                scheduler-policy "vsp1"
            exit
        exit
        description "QoS testing permitted"
        contact "Sir Edmund Hillary or Sherpa Tenzing Norgay"
        phone "123-456-7890"
    exit
```

Under the `multi-service-site Kirkland` a port 1/2/5 is assigned. According to this configuration, any SAP-egress policy that is assigned to the SAPs belonging to customer 425 and that is within port 1/2/5 can seek a parental relationship with virtual schedulers declared within the Scheduler policy `vsp2`.

Under the `multi-service-site Seattle`, an IOM slot 1 is assigned. According to this configuration, any SAP-ingress policy that is assigned to the SAPs belonging to customer 425 and that is within MDA 1/1 or 1/2 can seek a parental relation with virtual schedulers declared within the Scheduler policy `vsp1`.

Listing 11.16 exhibits an example service configuration, in which a `multi-service-site` is declared under a SAP.

Listing 11.16 Example service configuration to highlight declaration of a multi-service-site under a SAP

```
vpls 425 customer 425 create
    stp
        shutdown
    exit
    sap 1/2/2 create
        multi-service-site "Seattle"
        ingress
            qos 425
        exit
    exit
    ...
    spoke-sdp 1:425 create
    exit
    no shutdown
exit
```

Applying a Scheduler policy through a `multi-service-site` configuration is illustrated in Figure 11.11.

As illustrated in Figure 11.11, for a hierarchical scheduler to be effective with respect to ingress or egress traffic of a `multi-service-site`, the following mappings have to be valid:

• Queues configured in a SAP-ingress or SAP-egress policy must have parent-child relationships with the virtual schedulers declared in a Scheduler policy.

Figure 11.11 Application of a Scheduler Policy through a multi-service-site Configuration

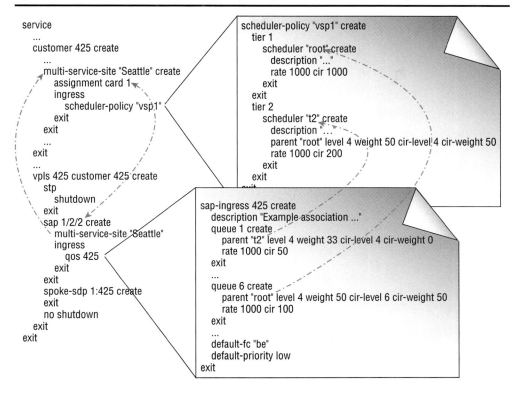

- The SAP-ingress or SAP-egress policy must be applied under the SAP configuration.
- The Scheduler policy must be applied under the `multi-service-site` configuration.
- The associated SAP, port, MDA or slot must be assigned under the `multi-service-site`.
- Under the SAP the `multi-service-site` must be declared.

Note: When applied under a `multi-service-site` configuration, a Scheduler policy is valid only within the entity that has been assigned to the `multi-service-site`. Furthermore, the policy is valid only in the direction—ingress or egress—under which the policy is applied.

11.6 Verification Commands for Hierarchical Scheduling

There are several `show qos` commands related to a Scheduler policy. These commands can be classified into the following four families of commands:

- `scheduler-name`
- `scheduler-policy`
- `scheduler-hierarchy`
- `scheduler-stats`

Show Scheduler Name

The `scheduler-name` command takes the name of a scheduler as an input and lists all the Scheduler policies in which a scheduler with that name exists. Note that two schedulers defined in two different scheduler policies, with different parameters can actually have the same name. Listing 11.17 shows the syntax and an example usage of the command. As can be seen, both Scheduler policies have been configured with a scheduler called **root**. However, the parameters of the schedulers called **root** may be different in each Scheduler policy.

Listing 11.17 Syntax and an example for the show qos scheduler-name command

```
A:Pod2>show>qos# scheduler-name
  - scheduler-name <scheduler-name>

 <scheduler-name>      : [32 chars max]

A:Pod2>show>qos# scheduler-name root


===============================================================
Scheduler : root
===============================================================
Scheduler Policy    : vsp1
Scheduler Policy    : vsp1-copy
===============================================================
```

With this command it is not possible to know whether the root schedulers defined in each policy are configured with the same parameters or not. Use the show qos scheduler-policy <scheduler-policy-name> command, described in the following subsection, to see the parameters of all schedulers defined within a Scheduler policy.

Show Scheduler Policy

Listing 11.18 provides the syntax of the show qos scheduler-policy command. The command can be used to see the details of a Scheduler policy or to see the list of entities to which a Scheduler policy is applied. Most importantly, the command can be used to see the hierarchical relationship between virtual schedulers of a Scheduler policy and queues of a SAP-ingress or a SAP-egress policy.

Listing 11.18 Syntax of the show qos scheduler-policy command

```
A:Pod2>show>qos# scheduler-policy
  - scheduler-policy [<scheduler-policy-name>]
    [association|sap-ingress <policy-id>|sap-egress <policy-id>]

<scheduler-policy-*> : [32 chars max]
<association>        : keyword - display associations
<policy-id>          : [1..65535]
<policy-id>          : [1..65535]
```

Listing 11.19 exhibits an example usage of the show qos scheduler-policy <scheduler-policy-name> command. As shown in the listing, the command displays the configuration summary of all the virtual schedulers within the specified Scheduler policy.

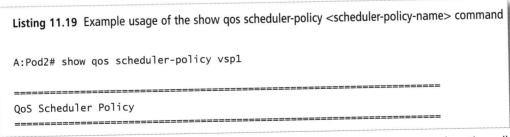

Listing 11.19 Example usage of the show qos scheduler-policy <scheduler-policy-name> command

```
A:Pod2# show qos scheduler-policy vsp1


===============================================================
QoS Scheduler Policy
===============================================================
```

(continued)

```
Policy-Name     : vsp1


-----------------------------------------------------------------
Tier/Scheduler                  Lvl/Wt    Rate      Parent
                                CIR Lvl/Wt CIR
-----------------------------------------------------------------
1 root                          1/1       1000      None
                                0/1       1000
2 t2                            4/50      1000      root
                                4/50      200
=================================================================
```

Listing 11.20 shows an example usage of the show qos scheduler-policy
<scheduler-policy-name> sap-egress <policy-id> command. The output of
the command shows the hierarchical relationship between queues of the SAP-
egress policy 100 and virtual schedulers of the Scheduler policy vsp1. As shown
in Figure 11.7, there are two schedulers defined in the Scheduler policy: a tier 1
scheduler called root and a tier 2 scheduler called t2. The scheduler root is the
parent of scheduler t2 and of queue 6 defined in the SAP-egress policy 100. The
scheduler t2 is the parent of queues 1, 3, and 4.

Listing 11.20 Example Usage of the show qos scheduler-policy <scheduler-policy-name> sap-
egress <policy-id> command

```
A:Pod2>show>qos# scheduler-policy vsp1 sap-egress 100


=================================================================
Compatibility : Scheduler Policy vsp1 & Sap Egress 100
=================================================================
Orphan Queues :
None Found


Hierarchy    :
Root
|
|---(S) : root
|   |
|   |---(S) : t2
|   |   |
```

(continued)

```
|    |    |---(Q) : 1
|    |    |
|    |    |---(Q) : 3
|    |    |
|    |    |---(Q) : 4
|    |
|    |---(Q) : 6
================================================================
```

Show Scheduler Hierarchy

The `scheduler-hierarchy` command also shows the hierarchical structure of virtual schedulers and queues. However, unlike the hierarchical structure shown in Listing 11.20, the `scheduler-hierarchy` command does not show hierarchical structures that are only configured, just the ones that are actually applied under a SAP, `multi-service-site`, or `subscriber` entity.

Listing 11.21 illustrates the different ways with which the command can be invoked. If a Scheduler policy is directly applied under a SAP, the `scheduler-hierarchy` command can be invoked using the SAP. If a Scheduler policy is applied through a `multi-service-site`, the `scheduler-hierarchy` command can be invoked using the `customer` option. Alternatively, if it is used in a triple-play service using subscriber entities, the `scheduler-hierarchy` command can be invoked using the `subscriber` option.

Note: Subscriber configuration is explained in *Triple-Play Guide*, which is part of the ALSRP product manuals.

Listing 11.21 High-level options for the show qos scheduler-hierarchy family of commands

```
A:Pod2>show>qos# scheduler-hierarchy
  - scheduler-hierarchy

      customer        - Display the scheduler hierarchy per
                        customer multi-service-site
      sap             - Display the scheduler hierarchy per SAP
      subscriber      - Display the scheduler hierarchy per
                        subscriber
```

Listing 11.22 exhibits an example usage of invoking the `show qos scheduler-hierarchy sap <sap-id> ingress` command. You can specify that the scheduling hierarchy for either the ingress or egress direction be shown. If neither direction is explicitly specified, then both will be shown.

Listing 11.22 Example for invoking the show qos scheduler-hierarchy command using a SAP and ingress options

```
A:Pod2# show qos scheduler-hierarchy sap 1/2/2 ingress

=======================================================================
Scheduler Hierarchy - Sap 1/2/2
=======================================================================
Root (Ing)
| slot(1)
|--(S) : root
|   |
|   |--(S) : t2
|   |   |
|   |   |--(S) : AccessIngress:425->1/2/2->4
|   |   |   |
|   |   |   |--(Q) : 425->1/2/2->4 1/1
|   |   |   |
|   |   |   |--(Q) : 425->1/2/2->4 1/2
|   |   |   |
|   |   |--(S) : AccessIngress:425->1/2/2->3
|   |   |   |
|   |   |   |--(Q) : 425->1/2/2->3 1/1
|   |   |   |
|   |   |   |--(Q) : 425->1/2/2->3 1/2
|   |   |   |
|   |   |--(S) : AccessIngress:425->1/2/2->1
|   |   |   |
|   |   |   |--(Q) : 425->1/2/2->1 1/1
|   |   |   |
|   |   |   |--(Q) : 425->1/2/2->1 1/2
|   |   |   |
|   |
|   |--(S) : AccessIngress:425->1/2/2->6
|   |   |
```

(continued)

```
|   |   |--(Q) : 425->1/2/2->6 1/1
|   |   |
|   |   |--(Q) : 425->1/2/2->6 1/2
|   |   |

=====================================================================
```

Listing 11.23 shows an example of invoking the show qos scheduler-hierarchy sap <sap-id> egress detail command. The output on the listing is obtained immediately after applying a Scheduler policy and a SAP-egress policy under the egress configuration of SAP 1/2/5, prior to sending any traffic through the SAP. The Scheduler policy is configured with only one virtual scheduler (root). The SAP-egress policy is configured with three queues having a parent-child relationship with the root scheduler.

Listing 11.23 Example for invoking the show qos scheduler-hierarchy command using SAP, egress, and detail options

```
A:Pod2# show qos scheduler-hierarchy sap 1/2/5 egress detail

=====================================================================
Scheduler Hierarchy - Sap 1/2/5
=====================================================================
Legend :
(*) real-time dynamic value
(w) Wire rates
---------------------------------------------------------------------

Root (Egr)
| slot(1)
|--(S) : root
|   |     AdminPIR:1000        AdminCIR:1000
|   |
|   |
|   |     [Within CIR Level 0 Weight 0]
|   |     Assigned:0           Offered:0
|   |     Consumed:0
|   |
|   |     [Above CIR Level 0 Weight 0]
```

(continued)

```
|   |      Assigned:0              Offered:0
|   |      Consumed:0
|   |
|   |
|   |      TotalConsumed:0
|   |      OperPIR:1000
|   |
|   |      [As Parent]
|   |      Rate:1000
|   |      ConsumedByChildren:0
|   |
|   |
|   |--(Q) : 500->1/2/5->1
|   |   |      AdminPIR:1000           AdminCIR:50
|   |   |      CBS:1                   MBS:64
|   |   |      Depth:0                 HiPrio:8
|   |   |
|   |   |      [Within CIR Level 4 Weight 0]
|   |   |      Assigned:50             Offered:0
|   |   |      Consumed:0
|   |   |
|   |   |      [Above CIR Level 4 Weight 33]
|   |   |      Assigned:1000           Offered:0
|   |   |      Consumed:0
|   |   |
|   |   |      TotalConsumed:0
|   |   |      OperPIR:1000            OperCIR:50
|   |
|   |--(Q) : 500->1/2/5->3
|   |   |      AdminPIR:1000           AdminCIR:100
|   |   |      CBS:1                   MBS:64
|   |   |      Depth:0                 HiPrio:8
|   |   |
|   |   |      [Within CIR Level 4 Weight 50]
|   |   |      Assigned:100            Offered:0
|   |   |      Consumed:0
|   |   |
|   |   |      [Above CIR Level 4 Weight 33]
|   |   |      Assigned:1000           Offered:0
|   |   |      Consumed:0
|   |   |
|   |   |      TotalConsumed:0
|   |   |      OperPIR:1000            OperCIR:100
```

(continued)

```
|   |
|   |--(Q) : 500->1/2/5->6
|   |   |       AdminPIR:1000        AdminCIR:100
|   |   |       CBS:1                 MBS:64
|   |   |       Depth:0               HiPrio:8
|   |   |
|   |   |       [Within CIR Level 6 Weight 50]
|   |   |       Assigned:100          Offered:0
|   |   |       Consumed:0
|   |   |
|   |   |       [Above CIR Level 4 Weight 50]
|   |   |       Assigned:1000         Offered:0
|   |   |       Consumed:0
|   |   |
|   |   |       TotalConsumed:0
|   |   |       OperPIR:1000          OperCIR:100
|   |
====================================================================
```

The command output not only summarizes the hierarchical scheduling relationship between the queues and the virtual scheduler under the SAP, but also summarizes the `parent` statement configuration of both the queue and the virtual scheduler. The command also shows the bandwidth assigned to each child during the committed bandwidth distribution pass (referred to as `Within CIR` in the output) and the excess bandwidth distribution pass (referred to as `Above CIR` in the output). Because none of the children consumed any of the bandwidth assigned to them, the hierarchical scheduler was able to assign the maximum bandwidth requested by each of the children.

In the output, `offered` refers to the incoming traffic rate of the associated entity. In the output string 500->1/2/5->1, the 500 refers to the id of the service, 1/2/5 refers to the SAP, and 1 refers to the ID of the queue that is configured in the associated SAP-egress policy.

Show Scheduler Stats

The `scheduler-stats` command, as the name implies, lists the statistics of traffic scheduled by each of the virtual schedulers used by a given entity. As with the `scheduler-hierarchy` command, the `scheduler-stats` command can also be invoked in three different ways, as shown in Listing 11.24. The invoking options for the command are identical to that of the `scheduler-hierarchy` families of command.

Listing 11.24 High-level options for the show qos scheduler-stats family of commands

```
A:Pod2>show>qos# scheduler-stats
  - scheduler-stats

        customer        - Display the scheduler stats per customer
                          multi-service-site
        sap             - Display the scheduler stats per SAP
        subscriber      - Display the scheduler stats per subscriber
```

Listing 11.25 exhibits an example of invoking the `show qos scheduler-stats` command using the `customer` option. Note that you can specify either the ingress or egress direction statistics. Both are shown if the direction is not explicitly specified.

Listing 11.25 Example for invoking the show qos scheduler-stats command using the customer option

```
A:Pod2>show>qos# scheduler-stats customer 425 site Seattle

===============================================================
Scheduler Stats
===============================================================
Scheduler                Forwarded Packets      Forwarded Octets
---------------------------------------------------------------
Ingress Schedulers

root                     17056030               18022410140
t2                       16480680               17238783440

Egress Schedulers

No Matching Entries
===============================================================
```

The values displayed by the command are the total number of packets and octets forwarded by the schedulers, either since the first time schedulers were applied to the entity, or since the last time they were cleared. In order to get the schedulers' statistics for a specific duration, you may want to clear their statistics prior to using the `show qos scheduler-stats` command. To clear a scheduler's statistics, use the `clear qos scheduler-stats` command. The `clear qos scheduler-stats` command can be invoked with the same options as the `show qos scheduler-stats` command. Listing 11.26 displays an example of invoking the `clear qos scheduler-stats` command using the `customer` option.

Listing 11.26 Example for invoking the clear qos scheduler-stats command using the customer option

```
A:Pod2# clear qos scheduler-stats customer 425 site Seattle ingress
A:Pod2# show qos scheduler-stats customer 425 site Seattle ingress


===================================================================
Scheduler Stats
===================================================================
Scheduler                Forwarded Packets      Forwarded Octets
-------------------------------------------------------------------
root                     137171                 147327218
t2                       124999                 130748954
===================================================================
```

Monitor Scheduler Stats

To check the rate at which traffic travels through virtual schedulers, use the `monitor qos scheduler-stats` family of commands shown in Listing 11.27. The command family can also be used to see the absolute quantity of traffic that traversed through the virtual schedulers during a given interval, instead of the rate.

Listing 11.27 High-level options for the monitor qos scheduler-stats family of commands

```
A:Pod2# monitor qos scheduler-stats
  - scheduler-stats

      customer          - Monitor scheduler statistics per customer
                          multi-service-site
      sap               - Monitor scheduler statistics for a SAP
      subscriber        - Monitor scheduler statistics for a subscriber
```

Listing 11.28 shows an example of the `monitor qos scheduler-stats` command along with `sap`, `ingress`, and `rate` options. When the command begins monitoring the statistics of the scheduler, it sets its display clock as time t = 0 seconds. At t = 0 sec, the total number of packets and octets forwarded by the schedulers, since the last time they were cleared, are displayed. At further display intervals (e.g., t = 11 sec) the rate at which packet and octets forwarded by the schedulers are shown. The command allows you to change the interval between displays and also the number of times the command is repeated.

Listing 11.28 Sample output of the monitor qos scheduler-stats command when Invoked using the SAP, ingress, and rate options

```
A:Pod2# monitor qos scheduler-stats sap 1/2/2 ingress rate


=======================================================================
Monitor Scheduler Statistics
=======================================================================
Scheduler                    Forwarded Packets     Forwarded Octets
-----------------------------------------------------------------------
-----------------------------------------------------------------------
At time t = 0 sec (Base Statistics)
-----------------------------------------------------------------------
Ingress Schedulers
root                         1025668               1092739664
t2                           962722                1007007212


-----------------------------------------------------------------------
At time t = 11 sec (Mode: Rate)
-----------------------------------------------------------------------
```

(continued)

```
Ingress Schedulers
root                     6761                7252535
t2                       6191                6475786


---------------------------------------------------------------
...
```

Summary

Hierarchical scheduling, otherwise referred to as HQoS, can be used to customize the access ingress and access egress scheduling according to the needs of an ALSRP application, and to dynamically allocate bandwidth to queues according to their bandwidth consumption. HQoS can be used to redistribute unused bandwidth of one application to another within a SAP, or to redistribute unused bandwidth of one site to another belonging to a `multi-service-site` configuration.

A hierarchical scheduler is configured using a Scheduler policy. The virtual schedulers, which are the building blocks of a Scheduler policy, are tied to each other and to the queues declared in a SAP-ingress or SAP-egress policy through parent-child relationships. A Scheduler policy can arrange the virtual scheduler in up to three different tiers: tier 1 (top level) through tier 3 (bottom level). Tier 1 virtual schedulers are the root schedulers. A queue can be a child to any one virtual scheduler in any tier. A virtual scheduler can be a child to any other virtual scheduler in a higher level. A parent virtual scheduler is responsible for the bandwidth distribution to all its children.

Similar to a queue, a virtual scheduler also has the two rate parameters: PIR and CIR. A parent-child relationship can be established within a queue or a virtual scheduler using the `parent` declaration command. In a parent statement, the name of the parent virtual scheduler is specified along with the following four HQoS related parameters:

- `level`
- `cir-level`
- `weight`
- `cir-weight`

The level and weight parameters are associated with the PIR, while the cir-level and cir-weight are associated with the CIR. The level and cir-level parameters refer to the priority a child has compared with other children for receiving bandwidth from their parent scheduler. A virtual scheduler distributes all the bandwidth it receives from its parent among its children in two passes: a committed bandwidth distribution pass and an excess bandwidth distribution pass. The cir-weight parameter specifies the relative weight of a child compared with other children that are in the same priority level during the committed bandwidth distribution cycle. Similarly, the weight parameter specifies the relative weight of a child compared with other children that are in the same priority level during the excess bandwidth distribution cycle.

A Scheduler policy can be applied either directly under a SAP to schedule the queues of the SAP, or under a multi-service-site configuration to schedule multiple SAPs and their queues belonging to the multi-service-site. In other words, through a customer multi-service-site a Scheduler policy can be applied to an entire port, an MDA, or an IOM slot.

Traffic Rate-Limiting

12

Unregulated traffic flowing through a network can cause network congestion, degrade the overall quality of service of the network, and lead to denial of service. Therefore, for any QoS model, and more particularly for a Diff-Serv model, regulating network traffic flow is essential.

Chapter Objectives

- To explain common rate-limiting techniques, their characteristics, and their importance

- To demonstrate how to implement different rate-limiting techniques in ALSRP

- To identify which rate-limiting techniques are most suitable for different application traffic

Regulating traffic flow is referred to as *rate-limiting*. By employing suitable rate-limiting approaches for different classes of service, service providers can ensure that service commitments to all the classes of services are honored. They can also ensure that their network resource utilization is maximized without causing congestion or resources overflow.

There are two elements to a rate-limiting approach: metering the rate at which a traffic stream flows, and action taken to handle excessive traffic. *Metering* involves measuring the temporal properties of traffic flows and is the common aspect for all the rate-limiting approaches. As discussed in Chapter 6, metering on microflows is done during scheduling at access ingress in ALSRP, and datagrams are marked as in-profile or out-of-profile accordingly. Rate-limiting approaches differ by the different types of actions they take to handle excessive traffic. The most suitable rate-limiting approach for a given scenario depends on the network point and class of service.

As discussed in Chapter 10, the stringent time commitments associated with high-priority forwarding class traffic are satisfied by providing priority in scheduling for such traffic over the traffic belonging to other forwarding classes. Because of the high scheduling priority provided to high-priority forwarding class traffic, allowing nonconforming traffic bursts over these streams can lead to starvation of other forwarding class traffic. Therefore, at access ingress, excessive traffic of high-priority forwarding classes should be dropped. This rate-limiting approach of dropping excessive traffic is referred to as *policing by discarding*.

Service providers allow excessive traffic flowing through assured-type and best-effort forwarding classes to maximize the network resource utilization. Therefore, this excessive traffic is not dropped and instead gets tagged as low-queuing priority. As discussed in Chapter 8, datagrams tagged as low-queuing priority are dropped prior to dropping any high-queuing priority datagrams within a forwarding class at a queuing point under congestion. This rate-limiting approach of tagging excessive traffic is referred to as *policing by tagging*.

Chapter 8 introduced Random Early Detection (RED), a popular congestion avoidance mechanism, and explained how RED helps rate-limit TCP traffic streams by influencing TCP's slow-start algorithm. In addition to being a buffer management technique, RED is also a rate-limiting technique. RED reacts to excessive traffic by notifying Transmission Control Protocol (TCP) stream sources to reduce their transmission rate. Thus, RED helps avoid congestion.

Another rate-limiting approach is *shaping*, which is commonly used at an access egress point to ensure that traffic from a forwarding class flows through policers downstream, without being dropped. Unlike a policing function, instead of dropping or tagging excessive bursts, shaping attempts to transform a nonconforming burst into a conforming burst.

This chapter discusses the common rate-limiting approaches (other than RED), their characteristics, the type of traffic and network point to which each can be best applied, and how to implement them in ALSRP.

In ALSRP, most of the common rate-limiting approaches (with the exception of RED) can be implemented by configuring the different queue parameters in certain relationships to each other. Through the underlying arbitrator, as discussed in Chapter 9, each ALSRP queue is associated with two standard leaky buckets: one for metering the CIR and one for metering the PIR. The leaky bucket implementation is used to control the rates at which a queue is serviced. The state of the CIR bucket at access ingress determines the profile of the datagram. The state of the PIR bucket is used to decide whether or not to service the next datagram. As discussed in Chapter 8, at all queuing points beyond the HPO threshold, further incoming out-of-profile (low-queuing priority) datagrams are dropped, and beyond MBS all incoming datagrams are dropped.

All the rate-limiting approaches discussed in this chapter refer to a *specified rate*. For access ingress queues, these are guaranteed rates specified in the corresponding service level agreement (SLA) for the microflows mapped to the queues. For network queues, the specified rate is the aggregate rate allocated for the corresponding forwarding class during the network QoS design. Chapter 14 introduces the steps involved in developing a QoS design for an IP/MPLS network.

12.1 Policing Network Traffic

In order to guarantee the service commitments of the various traffic streams belonging to different forwarding classes in a network, it is essential to police all incoming traffic entering into a service-oriented network at their respective access ingress points. Policing of a traffic flow is primarily intended to achieve the following objectives:

- Ensure that traffic flows conform to their traffic SLA.
- Provide isolation between traffic flows, so that conforming (high-queuing priority) traffic flows are not starved of bandwidth/buffer-space by nonconforming (low-queuing priority) flows.

As mentioned earlier, there are two approaches to policing: discarding and tagging. *Policing by discarding* occurs when the arrival rate of a microflow exceeds a specified rate and the excess datagrams are then dropped. *Policing by tagging* occurs when the excess datagrams are tagged (as having high drop probability under congestion) rather than being dropped. Policing by discarding is a technique consistent with Napoleon Bonaparte's ideology of policing: "The act of policing is, in order to punish less often, to punish more severely." Excess datagrams are simply not allowed to enter the queue, so that the rest of the traffic can proceed without interruption. On the other hand, policing by tagging is a model similar to certain stand-by tickets offered by the airline industry: There is no guarantee that you will reach your final destination as planned; however, at this segment there are enough resources for you to proceed to the next node. If there is any congestion in segments down the path, you would be among the first to be dropped (not dropped, but further delayed in the case of air travel with stand-by tickets).

The following sections explain these policing techniques in detail.

Policing by Discarding

In ALSRP, any queue (access or network) can enforce policing by discarding if the queue parameters are configured with the following set of values:

PIR = CIR = specified rate. CBS = 0 and MBS = 1.

When PIR = CIR = specified rate, only traffic flow less than or equal to the specified rate is allowed to pass through. Recall that in ALSRP the PIR is the maximum rate at which a queue is drained. Because the allocated buffer sizes for the queues are very low and insignificant, excess datagrams of any incoming flow that exceed the specified rate are dropped. This model emulates a 1-rate 2-color-marker (also referred to as a 1-bucket 2-color-marker), illustrated in Figure 12.1.

Note: If MBS = 0, no traffic can flow through the queue.

Depending on whether the policing option is configured in a SAP-ingress policy or a Network-Queue policy, the option can be applied to a microflow or to an aggregated flow.

Figure 12.1 1-Rate 2-Color-Marker

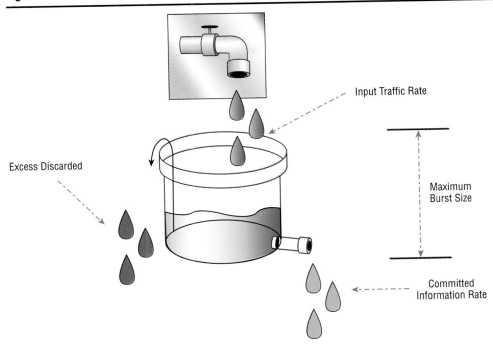

Input Traffic Rate

Excess Discarded

Maximum
Burst Size

Committed
Information Rate

Even though MBS is configured as 1 KB (kilobyte) for an access queue, typically buffers are allocated in certain blocks. Moreover, some of the underlying chipsets adopt a parallel memory input process to increase the efficiency of datagram queuing. Therefore, the actual MBS allocated to a queue is typically in the order of a few tenths of KBs, which is insignificant for flows with higher flow rates but significant for microflows with smaller flows rates like T1/E1 or sub-T1/E1 rates. The delay caused as a result of the minimum MBS buffering can be as high as a few tenths of milliseconds for T1/E1 rates.

For the microflows with smaller flow rates there is a special queue rate configuration option available in the SAP-ingress policy. SAP-ingress policy permits configuring a queue `rate` with a special keyword, `police`. Listing 12.1 revisits the command options for configuring the rate parameters of a queue in a SAP-ingress policy from Chapter 10, with the focus on the keyword `police`. The use of the keyword `police` is mutually exclusive with the configuration of a CIR value in the rate declaration statement. Also, only queues created in the default `priority-mode` can use the keyword `police` in their `rate` declaration statement. Attempting to use the keyword `police` in the `rate` declaration statement for queues created in the `profile-mode` will result in an error message.

Listing 12.1 Options for configuring rate parameters of a queue in a SAP-ingress policy

```
A:Pod1>config>qos>sap-ingress>queue# rate
  - no rate
  - rate <pir-rate> [cir <cir-rate>]
  - rate <pir-rate> police

<pir-rate>        : [1..100000000|max]
<cir-rate>        : [0..100000000|max]
<police>          : keyword
```

When the keyword `police` is used, the rate parameter value becomes the specified rate (recall that for the option CIR = PIR = specified rate), and any configured buffer sizes are irrelevant (as suggested for the option). Once the traffic arrival rate into the queue exceeds the specified rate, the excess datagrams are dropped without any buffering. All the datagrams that are allowed to pass through are tagged as in-profile.

Although configurable both in access and network queues, policing by discarding approach is more suitable at the access ingress for real-time and high-priority traffic. This rate-limiting approach is consistent with the policing function recommended in RFCs 3246 and 3247 for EF PHB. Refer to Chapter 3 for the discussion on EF PHB.

Note: Only a queue created in the default `priority-mode` can use the keyword `police` in its `rate` declaration statement.

Listing 12.2 shows an example SAP-ingress policy in which the queues' rates are configured using the keyword `police`.

Best Practices: The use of the keyword police in a rate declaration statement is recommended only when dealing with T1/E1 or sub-T1/E1 rates.

Appropriateness of Policing by Discarding for Access Ingress

Why is the keyword police available only in a SAP-ingress policy, and not in Network-Queue and SAP-egress policies?

The keyword police enforces the policing by discarding function over microflows with T1/E1 or sub-T1/E1 rates. The policing by discarding function is used to let only complaint traffic pass through. If excessive traffic is going to be dropped, it is better that this is done as close as possible to the source. Moreover, by discarding excess traffic at the entry points of a network, the service provider can conserve network resources.

Policing by Tagging

In ALSRP, access ingress queues can enforce policing by tagging if the queue parameters are configured according to the following relationship:

PIR > CIR = specified rate. MBS > CBS ∝ CIR and 0 < HPO < 100%.

As discussed in Chapters 6 and 10, at access ingress, datagrams scheduled out of a queue are tagged in-profile when the scheduling rate is less than its CIR. Similarly, datagrams scheduled out of a queue are tagged out-of-profile when the scheduling rate is greater than its CIR, but less than its PIR. Therefore, under this configuration, datagrams in excess of the specified rate may be permitted but would be tagged as out-of-profile. We discussed in Chapter 8 that a non-zero HPO value at any queuing point results in discarding of out-of-profile datagrams prior to discarding in-profile datagrams under congestion. Thus, the configuration emulates a 2-rate 3-color-marker (also referred to as a 2-bucket 3-color-marker), as illustrated in Figure 12.2. The implementation conforms to RFC 2698. This approach gives preferential treatment for well-behaving queues, while reducing the datagram discard probability for bursty traffic.

Figure 12.2 2-Rate 3-Color-Marker

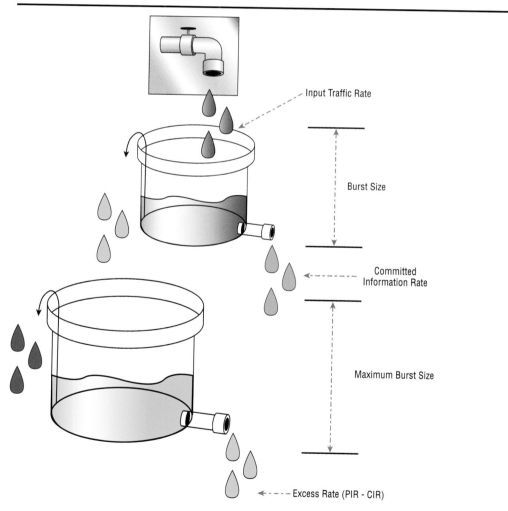

According to the configuration, bursts of datagrams longer than MBS at a rate greater than PIR will experience tail discarding.

This approach is appropriate for non-real-time assured-type forwarding class traffic at access ingress. To adopt the approach for best-effort traffic, configure CIR = specified rate = 0. As discussed in Chapter 6, by configuring CIR = 0 for best-effort traffic, at access ingress all the datagrams belonging to the flow are marked as out-of-profile.

Soft Policing

The policing by tagging approach is tailored to maximize network resource utilization by tagging nonconformance bursts belonging to non-real-time traffic as out-of-profile, instead of dropping them. The objective of tagging datagrams is, under congestion, to drop out-of-profile datagrams before dropping any in-profile datagrams belonging to the same forwarding class. This objective can be extended to other queuing points by configuring these queues with the same set of values suggested for enforcing policing by tagging function in access ingress queues:

PIR > CIR = specified rate. MBS > CBS $\propto$ CIR and 0 < HPO < 100%.

However, queues other than the ones at access ingress cannot tag datagrams, but can make use of the tagging done at access ingress. The approach can assure guaranteed service for in-profile datagrams, because CIR = specified rate. The guarantee is valid only if the sum of the CIR of the queues at the queuing point is not overbooked beyond the available bandwidth at the point. This approach allows the traffic flow to utilize excess bandwidth when available due to the configuration PIR > CIR. The approach can also mitigate temporary congestion by buffering datagrams in the space provided by MBS > CBS $\propto$ CIR. Under sustained congestion, out-of-profile datagrams will be dropped before dropping in-profile datagrams because 0 < HPO < 100%.

This approach is suitable for all non-real-time traffic (belonging to both assured and best-effort type forwarding classes) at all queuing points subsequent to access ingress, provided the traffic will not be subjected to a downstream policer.

Unlike the case of policing by tagging, CIR does not need to be configured as zero to adopt the approach for best-effort traffic. The condition is relaxed, because queuing points subsequent to access ingress do not tag datagrams, instead they rely on the tagging done at access ingress. Moreover, by configuring the CIR of the queues mapped to best-effort type forwarding classes to be slightly above zero and by not overbooking the sum of the CIR of the queues at the queuing point beyond available bandwidth, the requirement of best-effort PHB not to let the BE traffic starve, can be satisfied. BE PHB is defined in RFC 2474, which was discussed in Chapter 3.

12.2 Rendering Traffic Conforming by Using Shaping

Shaping buffers excessive traffic and dequeues it at a specified rate. Thus, shaping can make occasional nonconforming bursts become conforming.

If policing is important for the security of a network and to ensure that service commitments to all the forwarding classes are honored, then shaping is vital to preserve the integrity of individual traffic streams. Buffering and datagram processing, the two fundamental functions of network nodes, induce variable latency to traffic flowing through. The variable latency can cluster short bursts of otherwise conforming traffic streams and render them nonconforming. The shaping function can buffer the short bursts and render a stream conforming all over again. Thus, the shaping function is essential to ensure that traffic streams pass through rigorous downstream policers.

ALSRP queues inherently shape traffic. To shape traffic flowing into a queue at a specified rate, configure the queue parameters with the following relationship:

PIR = CIR = specified rate. MBS ≥ CBS ∝ CIR.

In ALSRP, PIR is the maximum rate at which queues can be serviced. By configuring PIR = CIR = specified rate, the queue cannot exceed the specified rate. However, intermittent bursts are buffered in the space provided by MBS ≥ CBS ∝ CIR. When the traffic arrival rate falls below the specified rate, the queue occupancy is depleted and as a result the queue gets ready to accommodate the next nonconforming burst. A higher MBS can accommodate bigger bursts and vice versa. Therefore, you should configure the MBS depending on the expected burst size. Although the approach can render traffic with occasional nonconforming bursts into conforming traffic, datagrams belonging to streams that consistently exceed the specified rate will eventually be dropped when their queue occupancy goes past MBS.

Shaping is essential at access egress, but it can also be used at network ingress and network egress for non-real-time assured-type forwarding class traffic, provided the traffic will be subjected to a downstream policing function. If real-time application traffic has some tolerance for network latency and if it is subjected to a downstream policer, then the traffic can be shaped at access egress.

12.3 Shapeless Policing

The days are gone when real-time applications were a little tolerant of traffic latency, but completely intolerant of traffic jitter. The reason for those service requirements was the lack of bigger buffer space to accommodate bigger bursts in the application products. To compensate for the lack of buffer space, the applications required network nodes to shape their traffic at access egress. Shaping introduced additional latency.

Today's network application products come packed with huge buffers. These applications no longer need network nodes to shape their traffic at access egress, and also they are becoming increasingly intolerant of traffic latency. This is especially true of online gaming applications and interactive video applications. The key strength of service routers is their flexibility in configuring them to accommodate diverse service needs of drastically divergent application traffic.

One way to accommodate these new service requirements is not to rate-limit such traffic but rather to provide them with the highest scheduling priority. However, this would be an open invitation to network insecurity and instability. So how can the requirements of these new services be met without compromising network security? This balancing act requires creativity from network design engineers. One such approach is *shapeless policing*.

In ALSRP, any queue (access or network) can enforce shapeless policing if the queue parameters are configured according to the following relationship:

PIR = Line rate > CIR = specified rate. HPO = 100% and MBS = CBS ∝ CIR*.

*Keep the buffer sizes to the minimum required.

The HPO = 100 percent requirement will drop all the out-of-profile datagrams; therefore, only conforming traffic can pass through the queuing point. CIR = specified rate guarantees the minimal required bandwidth for the stream. PIR = line rate (this does not need to be the line rate, any rate, which is sufficiently higher than the specified rate would do) provides additional bandwidth, if required for in-profile traffic. Because almost all additional bandwidth required is provided, typically there is no need for much of a buffer space. Therefore, to handle occasional random bursts of high-priority traffic a small buffer space is sufficient.

A logical question that might arise from reading the previous statement is, why do we need to configure PIR = line rate in order to handle only the in-profile datagrams?

Configuring CIR = specified rate would be sufficient to provide adequate bandwidth to handle conforming and well behaving in-profile datagrams. However, as we mentioned earlier, even a well-behaving stream may be rendered a bit bursty as the stream passes through network nodes because of minor variations in processing and queuing delays. Because of the induced burstiness, if a datagram of the stream misses a CIR scheduling window, it need not wait till the next CIR scheduling window, but can be scheduled out because of PIR = line rate.

Shapeless policing is recommended for real-time traffic at all the network ingress and egress queuing points. Provided that there is no downstream policer, the approach is also recommended for access egress.

12.4 Traffic Rate-Limiting: Putting It All Together

Table 12.1 summarizes the different rate-limiting approaches discussed in this chapter. The table specifies: how to configure queues in ALSRP nodes for different rate-limiting approaches and which rate-limiting approach would be suitable for different forwarding classes at different network points.

The rate-limiting approaches suggested in this chapter and summarized in Table 12.1 are only recommendations. Specific needs of different application traffic may vary, and the configurations may have to be tailored accordingly.

Table 12.1 Rate-Limiting Approaches Suitable for Different Types of Traffic and for Different Network Points

Rate-Limiting Approach	Parameter Relationship	Effect on Datagrams	Traffic Type Suitable to Regulate	Network Point to Apply	Comments
Policing by discarding	PIR = CIR = SpR $\newline$ CBS = 0 and MBS = 1	Traffic is strictly policed at the specified rate (SpR). All the excess datagrams are dropped.	Real time	Access ingress	For T1/E1 rates or for rates less than that, use the police keyword option.
Policing by tagging	PIR > CIR = SpR $\newline$ MBS > CBS $\propto$ CIR $\newline$ 0 < HPO < 100%	Excessive datagrams are tagged as out-of-profile, and conforming datagrams are tagged as in-profile.	Assured-type and best-effort-type forwarding classes	Access ingress	For adopting the approach for best-effort traffic, configure CIR = 0 so that all the datagrams of the traffic type will be tagged as out-of-profile.
Soft policing	PIR > CIR = SpR $\newline$ MBS > CBS $\propto$ CIR $\newline$ 0 < HPO < 100%	Drops out-of-profile datagrams before dropping in-profile datagrams under congestion.	Assured-type and best-effort-type forwarding classes	Network egress $\newline$ Network ingress $\newline$ Access egress	Although the queue parameters' relationship is the same as that of the policing by tagging approach, recall only access ingress queues have the ability to tag datagrams, and queues at other network points rely on tagging done by access ingress queues.
Shaping	PIR = CIR = SpR $\newline$ MBS $\geq$ CBS $\propto$ CIR	Shapes traffic to the specified rate.	Assured-type forwarding class	Network egress $\newline$ Network ingress $\newline$ Access egress	Suggested only if the flow will be subjected to a downstream policer.
Shapeless policing	PIR = LR* > CIR = SpR $\newline$ MBS = CBS $\propto$ CIR** $\newline$ HPO = 100% $\newline$ * PIR need not be LR, but should be sufficiently larger than SpR. $\newline$ ** Keep the buffer sizes to the minimum required.	Expedites datagrams' delivery without shaping.	Real-time	Network egress $\newline$ Network ingress $\newline$ Access egress	Provided that the traffic will not be subjected to a downstream policer.

Summary

Unregulated traffic can lead to denial of service within a network. By employing suitable rate-limiting approaches for different classes of service, service providers can ensure that service commitments to all the classes of services are honored, and maximize the network resource utilization without congesting or letting the resources overflow.

Because of the high scheduling priority provided to the high-priority forwarding class traffic, allowing nonconforming traffic bursts over these streams can lead to starvation of other forwarding classes' traffic. Therefore, at access ingress, excessive traffic of high-priority forwarding classes should be dropped. The policing by discarding approach is suitable at access ingress for high-priority forwarding classes. For policing microflows with T1/E1 or sub-T1/E1 rates, use the `police` keyword in a SAP-ingress policy queue configuration.

Service providers allow excessive traffic flowing through assured-type and best-effort forwarding classes to maximize the network resource utilization. Therefore, this excessive traffic is not dropped and instead is tagged as low-queuing priority. Datagrams tagged as low-queuing priority are dropped prior to dropping any high-queuing priority datagrams within a forwarding class at a queuing point under congestion. This rate-limiting approach is referred to as policing by tagging.

In addition to being a buffer management technique, RED is also a rate-limiting technique. RED reacts to excessive traffic by notifying TCP stream sources to reduce their transmission rates. Thus, RED helps avoid congestion.

If policing is important for the security of a network and to ensure that service commitments to all the classes of services are honored, then shaping is vital to preserve the integrity of individual traffic streams. The shaping function can buffer nonconforming short bursts within a flow and render the flow conforming all over again. Thus, the shaping function is essential to ensure that traffic streams pass through rigorous downstream policers.

Real-time applications, such as online gaming and interactive video applications, are becoming increasingly intolerant of traffic latency. To rate-limit this type of traffic, a shapeless policing approach is recommended. This approach expedites delivery of in-profile datagrams without any shaping.

Special Topics

13

ALSRP offers advanced QoS features, which enhance the quality of experience of end users, and which provide service differentiation factors for service providers.

Chapter Objectives

- To introduce the Link Aggregation Group and its QoS adaptation

- To explain Link Fragmentation and Interleaving

- To discuss the purpose of and ways to override QoS policies

- To introduce the Service Assurance Agent and explain how to routinely monitor the health of a network

- To explain how to adapt QoS configuration based on time

This chapter covers a wide variety of QoS related advanced features of ALSRP. These topics are either common for multiple traffic management features that were discussed in more than one previous chapter or available for special scenarios. The sections in this chapter are independent of each other and can be read in any order or on an as-needed basis.

The chapter begins with a discussion on Link Aggregation Group (LAG) and how to adapt service level agreements (SLAs) over access LAGs. The chapter then discusses Link Fragmentation and Interleaving (LFI) and how this feature avoids excessive delay to high-priority and delay-sensitive traffic over a low-speed link. The chapter next explains the QoS policy override and the flexibility offered by this feature to allow customization and exceptions while applying template access QoS and Scheduler policies. The following section describes the Service Assurance Agent (SAA), which allows service providers to determine the quality of service experienced by different application traffic within their network. Finally, the chapter discusses time-based QoS, with which ALSRP offers advanced flexibility to adapt traffic management features according to the changing needs of different applications over the course of a period.

13.1 Link Aggregation Group and QoS Adaptation

According to the IEEE 802.3ad standard, multiple Ethernet ports between two network nodes can be aggregated and used in parallel to form a *Link Aggregation Group*. All physical links in a given LAG combine to form one logical interface.

Configuring a LAG can be useful for two reasons:

- To increase the bandwidth available between the two network devices, beyond the limits of any one port or link. For example, when a segment of a network often experiences sustained congestion, increasing its bandwidth is the only way to improve QoS metrics of all the application traffic flowing through the segment. For an Ethernet-based segment, where spare ports are available, configuring LAGs may be the least disruptive way to increase the bandwidth of the segment.

- To provide redundancy in the event of failure of one or more participating links, ports, media-dependent adapter (MDAs), or input/output modules (IOMs).

Listing 13.1 shows the options for configuring a LAG. For more detail on these options, refer to the *Interface Guide*, which is part of the ALSRP product manuals.

Listing 13.1 Options for configuring a LAG

```
A:Pod2>config# lag
 - lag <lag-id>
 - no lag <lag-id>

 <lag-id>               : [1..64]

     access            + Configure access params
 [no] description      - Add/remove a text description for the link
                         aggregation group
 [no] dynamic-cost     - Enable/disable OSPF costing of a link
                         aggregation group
 [no] encap-type       - Configure encapsulation method
 [no] hold-time        - Configure hold-time for event reporting
 [no] lacp             - Enable/disable the LACP protocol
 [no] lacp-xmit-inte*  - Configure the timer interval for periodic
                         transmission of LACP packets
 [no] lacp-xmit-stdby  - Enable/disable LACP message transmission on
                         standby links
 [no] mac              - Configure a static MAC address for the link
                         aggregation group
 [no] mode             - Configure the mode of the link aggregation
                         group
 [no] port             - Add/remove ports from a link aggregation
                         group
 [no] port-threshold   - Configure the behavior for the LAG if the
                         number of operational links is equal to or
                         below a threshold level
 [no] selection-crit*  - Configure selection criteria to select the
                         active LACP sub-group
 [no] shutdown         - Shutdown the LAG port
```

ALSRP supports the provisioning of LAGs on both network and access ports. A LAG can be configured to be **access** or **network** by configuring its mode; the default mode is **network**. Listing 13.2 exhibits the options for configuring the mode of a LAG.

Listing 13.2 Options for configuring the mode of a LAG

```
A:Pod2>config>lag# mode
  - mode {access|network}
  - no mode

 <access|network>     : keywords
```

Once created, an access LAG can be used in place of an access port for config-uring service access points (SAPs). Listing 13.3 displays an example service configuration in which a LAG in **access** mode is used as a SAP. Similarly, once created, a **network** LAG can be used in place of a network port.

Listing 13.3 A service example using a LAG as a SAP

```
        vpls 100 customer 1 create
            stp
                shutdown
            exit
            sap 1/2/2 create
            exit
            sap lag-7 create
            exit
            spoke-sdp 1:100 create
            exit
            no shutdown
        exit
```

Enforcing SLAs over Access LAG

If all the active links of a LAG are restricted to the ports of the two MDAs within an IOM, then SLAs specified for the LAG (using a SAP-ingress, SAP-egress, or Scheduler policy) can be enforced seamlessly. For example, if the Scheduler policy associated with the SAP of a LAG restricts the overall peak information rate (PIR) of the SAP to be 100 Mbps (megabits/sec), then overall bandwidth used by all the links of the LAG can be restricted to 100 Mbps irrespective of how the flows are distributed between the links.

Best Practices: In order to increase the scope of the redundancy, distribute the participating ports of a LAG over as many IOM slots and MDAs as possible, and thereby minimize the impact that an MDA or IOM failure has on the performance of the LAG.

The QoS requirement to enforce the SLA across the links of a LAG directly contradicts the above best practice. IOM redundancy can be paramount to the LAG configuration in certain network design scenarios. Therefore, to resolve the conflict there are two different options available to enforce SLAs when the links of an access LAG are configured under more than one IOM:

- `distribute`—Divide the SLA among the IOMs, based on their share of the LAG group. For example, for a LAG with two links on IOM A and three links on IOM B, out of a PIR of 100 Mbps, IOM A would get 40 Mbps and IOM B would get 60 Mbps. The advantage of this method is that the overall SLA can be enforced. The downside is that a single flow cannot exceed the IOM's share of the SLA.
- `link`—Each port gets the full SLA. With the example above, each port would get a PIR of 100 Mbps. The advantage of this method is that a single flow can consume the entire SLA. The downside is that the overall SLA can be exceeded if the flows span multiple ports.

Enforcing SLAs over a LAG Based on Flow Diversity

In which scenarios should you use the `link` and `distribute` options for QoS adaptation of an access LAG?

When there is enough flow diversity (for example several flows with different source and destination IP addresses), the load will be uniformly balanced across multiple links of a LAG. In such cases, using the `distribute` option will help enforce the overall SLA on the LAG.

The `link` option is appropriate for cases where there is not enough flow diversity (mostly the same source and destination IP addresses), or where a single flow should be allowed to use the entire bandwidth permitted by the associated SLA.

Diversification based on additional parameters, such as User Datagram Protocol (UDP) and Transmission Control Protocol (TCP) port numbers, can be introduced for load balancing by using the command `configure system l4-load-balancing` from the root prompt of ALSRP.

Because the appropriate option depends on the network scenario under consideration, in ALSRP the service provider can select either option. The default option is `distribute`. Listing 13.4 shows the syntax to choose one of these options.

Listing 13.4 Options for configuring SLA enforcement over access LAG

```
A:Pod2>config>lag# access adapt-qos
  - adapt-qos <type>

 <type>                   : [link|distribute] - keywords
```

Listing 13.5 displays an example LAG configuration. In the example configuration, the two ports are configured in two different IOMs, and SLA enforcement is accomplished using the `link` option.

Listing 13.5 An example LAG configuration

```
    lag 7
        mac 00:6a:01:01:00:03
        mode access
        port 1/1/3
        port 2/2/3
        access
            adapt-qos link
        exit
        no shutdown
    exit
```

The command **adapt-qos** is available only for LAGs configured in **access** mode in order to enforce customer SLAs. When a LAG group is configured in the **network** mode, by default the **distribute** option is enabled.

Maintaining IOM Redundancy in a LAG without Compromising SLA Enforcement

LAG is used not only to provide higher bandwidth but also to protect against hardware failure. LAG members are typically distributed across different IOMs to eliminate a single point of failure. At the same time, QoS SLA enforcement is required. Is there a way to enforce SLA absolutely, while achieving IOM redundancy in a LAG?

Enforcing QoS policies across links attached to different IOMs is not possible, and therefore it is desirable that traffic always flows through a single IOM. This can be achieved by selecting only links of a single IOM as active LAG members and keeping all other LAG members in stand-by condition.

In case of a link failure, the switch-over mechanism must take into account the above QoS restriction. This means that all LAG members connected to the same IOM as the failing link will become stand-by, and LAG members connected to other IOMs will become active. This way, QoS enforcement constraints are respected, while the maximum number of available links are utilized.

The Link Aggregation Control Protocol (LACP) is based on the IEEE 802.3ad standards. It allows active LAG member selection based on particular constraints and makes the selection predictable. In an ALSRP node, LACP parameters can be configured under a LAG configuration. For further information on configuring LACP parameters in ALSRP, refer to the *Interface Guide*, which is a part of ALSRP product manuals.

Verification Commands for LAG

The show lag family of commands can be used to see the statistics, details, and entities associated with a LAG. The syntax of the command family is:

```
show lag [<lag-id>] [detail] [statistics]
show lag <lag-id> associations
```

In the first syntax, if a lag-id is specified as the part of a command, information only about the specific LAG is displayed. If no lag-id is specified, then information about all the configured LAGs is displayed.

Listing 13.6 shows a sample output of the `show lag <lag-id> detail` command.

Listing 13.6 Sample output of the show lag <lag-id> detail command

```
A:Pod2# show lag 7 detail

===============================================================================
LAG Details
===============================================================================
Description:

-------------------------------------------------------------------------------
Details
-------------------------------------------------------------------------------
Lag-id              : 7                 Mode              : access
Adm                 : up                Opr               : down
Thres. Exceeded Cnt : 0                 Port Threshold    : 0
Thres. Last Cleared : 09/04/2007 19:25:59  Threshold Action : down
Dynamic Cost        : false             Encap Type        : null
Configured Address  : 00:6a:01:01:00:03 Lag-IfIndex       : 1342177287
Hardware Address    : 00:6a:ff:00:01:47 Adapt Qos         : link
Hold-time Down      : 0.0 sec
LACP                : disabled


-------------------------------------------------------------------------------
Port-id      Adm    Act/Stdby Opr    Primary  Sub-group   Forced   Prio
-------------------------------------------------------------------------------
1/1/3        up     active    down   yes      1           -        32768
2/2/3        down   active    down            1           -        32768
===============================================================================
```

13.2 Link Fragmentation and Interleaving

Link Fragmentation and Interleaving (LFI) is an essential QoS feature for low-speed point-to-point protocol (PPP) links. The feature provides the ability to interleave high-priority traffic within a stream of fragmented lower-priority traffic. The main purpose of the feature is to avoid excessive delay to high-priority and delay-sensitive traffic over a low-speed link when lower-priority traffic with larger frame sizes uses the link.

The Value of Interleaving

In order to appreciate the purpose of the LFI feature, consider the following real-life scenario: Your colleague is printing an entire book on a shared printer, while you are waiting to print a one-page report on the printer, and the printer has no option to stop a started printing process. Moreover, your CEO is depending on the report for a board meeting that has already begun. Now imagine how good it would be if the printer could fragment the process of printing a book into subprocesses, printing one page at a time, and hence interleave the small process of printing the one-page memo.

Consider the following networking example: A T1 (or E1) link is used to transport both Voice over IP (VoIP) traffic and best-effort Internet traffic. Although a scheduler can give preference for scheduling VoIP traffic over the Internet traffic, once the transmission of a frame has started the scheduler is helpless in prioritizing further incoming high-priority traffic. In this situation, using LFI helps to fragment the jumbo-sized frame (such as FTP traffic frames) before transmitting it and interleaves the high-priority smaller packets in between the fragments.

Figure13.1 illustrates the conceptual procedure of LFI.

Figure 13.1 Conceptual Procedure of LFI

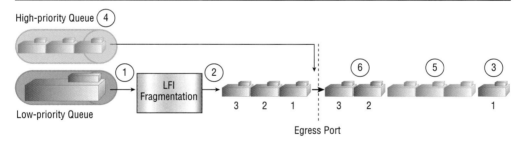

In the figure, there are two queues: a high-priority queue shown on the top-left side and a low-priority queue shown on the bottom-left side. The datagrams flowing through the high-priority queue are smaller frames shown in green. The datagrams flowing through the low-priority queue are bigger frames shown in red. The circled numbers in the figure identify the sequence of events, which are:

1. A low-priority frame arrives in the low-priority queue. At this particular instant, there are no frames in the high-priority queue, so the low-priority frame is dequeued and passed to the LFI fragmenting mechanism.

2. The original low-priority frame is divided into n fragments (3 in the example) based on the size of the frame and the fragment threshold configuration.

3. The fragments are then transmitted out through the egress port.

4. After the transmission of the fragments has begun, high-priority frames arrive in the high-priority queue.

5. The transmission of the remaining fragments stops and the high-priority packets are transmitted out through the egress interface. Note that high-priority packets are not fragmented.

6. After the high-priority traffic is transmitted, the remaining lower-priority fragments are transmitted.

Listing 13.7 shows the command options for choosing the fragment size threshold. Any frame whose size exceeds the fragment threshold is fragmented.

Listing 13.7 Commands to choose the fragment size threshold

```
A:Pod2>config>port# multilink-bundle fragment-threshold
  - fragment-threshold <fragment-threshold>
  - no fragment-threshold

 <fragment-threshold> : 128 to 512 bytes inclusive for MLPPP bundles
                        128 bytes for IMA bundles
```

Listing 13.8 displays the command options for enabling interleaving.

Listing 13.8 Commands to enable interleaving high-priority frames between fragments

```
A:Pod2>config>port# multilink-bundle interleave-fragments
  - interleave-fragments
  - no interleave-fragments
```

Listing 13.9 exhibits an example configuration for LFI.

Listing 13.9 An example configuration for LFI

```
port 1/1/2
    sonet-sdh
        clock-source node-timed
        path sts1-1
            no shutdown
        exit
    exit
    tdm
        ds3 1
            channelized ds1
            no shutdown
        exit
        ds1 1.9
            channel-group 1
                encap-type ipcp
                timeslots 1-24
                no shutdown
            exit
            no shutdown
exit

port bundle-ppp-1/1.10
    multilink-bundle
        fragment-threshold 256
        interleave-fragments
        member 1/1/1.1.9.1
    exit
    no shutdown
exit
```

13.3 QoS Policy Overrides

Providing services to thousands of customers cannot be easily achieved using only a small number of service-related policies to enforce SLAs. While services are supposed to be the same, exceptions and customizations creep in. For example, bandwidth has to be increased, or traffic priority may have to be changed, on a customer request basis.

Typically, these exceptions are implemented by configuring additional QoS policies or filter policies. Technically, there is nothing wrong with doing that. However, if the exceptions are too many and each one is unique, the result is numerous QoS policies. Too many QoS policies are difficult to maintain and make troubleshooting problematic.

To make maintenance and troubleshooting easier, ALSRP provides the flexibility to override the access queue parameters and virtual scheduler rates of a template policy under a SAP configuration (or under SLA-profile and Subscriber-profile if Enhanced Subscriber Management is used) within a service configuration. Enhanced Subscriber Management, SLA-profile and Subscriber-profile are triple-play service-specific features of ALSRP. For further information about these features, refer to the *Triple-Play Guide* of the ALSRP manuals. Such QoS policy overrides can be configured under the SAPs of all service types.

> **Note:** Only the QoS policies configured as `template` can be subjected to QoS policy overrides.

As mentioned in Chapter 6, among the access policies only SAP-ingress and SAP-egress policies have the `scope` configuration. Configuring the `scope` of these policies either as `template` or `exclusive` is also discussed in Chapter 6.

QoS policy overrides are particularly helpful in the following situations when:

- Only a few SAPs need minor exceptions from a generally applied QoS policy.
- There are many unique QoS exceptions.
- A QoS exception is temporary.

A QoS policy override under a SAP configuration permits altering only the parameters of the queues that are declared in the associated SAP-ingress or SAP-egress template policies. Similarly, an override is permitted for the rates of the virtual schedulers declared in the associated Scheduler policy of a SAP.

Listing 13.10 shows the syntax for queue override available at access ingress. The syntax for an access egress queue override is similar to that of access ingress. The following queue parameters can be overridden: scheduling rates (CIR and PIR), the adaptation rule, and buffer parameters (CBS, MBS, and HPO).

Listing 13.10 Access ingress queue override options

```
A:Pod1>config>service>ies>if>sap>ingress# queue-override queue
  - no queue <queue-id>
  - queue <queue-id> [create]

 <queue-id>             : [1..32]
 <create>              : keyword - mandatory while creating an entry.


 [no] adaptation-rule - Specify the CIR and PIR adaptation rules
 [no] cbs             - Specify CBS
 [no] high-prio-only  - Specify high priority only burst size
 [no] mbs             - Specify MBS
 [no] rate            - Specify rates (CIR and PIR)
```

Listing 13.11 displays the syntax for scheduler override available at access ingress. The syntax for an access egress scheduler override is similar to that of access ingress.

Listing 13.11 Access ingress scheduler override options

```
A:Pod1>config>service>ies>if>sap>ingress# scheduler-override scheduler
  - no scheduler <scheduler-name>
  - scheduler <scheduler-name> [create]

 <scheduler-name>      : [32 chars max]
 <create>             : keyword - mandatory while creating an entry.


 [no] rate            - Specify rates (CIR and PIR)
```

In order to understand the usefulness of the QoS policy override's flexibility, consider the following example: A service provider offering a standard High Speed Internet service for residential customers aggregates all the customer SAPs into a virtual private LAN service (VPLS). One of the customers (connected through SAP 1/2/2:1001) temporarily wants to host an Internet server and wants to have a guaranteed uploading speed of 3 Mbps compared to the regular uploading speed of 512 Kbps (kilobits/sec) offered by the service provider.

Listing 13.12 exhibits the service configuration of the service provider. The service provider uses the queue override option to override the queue configuration in the associated SAP-ingress policy and thereby increase the ingress rate to 3 Mbps.

Listing 13.12 VPLS configuration using the queue override

```
vpls 100 customer 1 create
    stp
        shutdown
    exit
    sap 1/2/2:100 create
        ingress
            qos 100
        exit
        egress
            qos 100
        exit
    exit
    ...
    sap 1/2/2:1001 create
        ingress
            qos 100
            queue-override
                queue 1 create
                    adaptation-rule pir min cir min
                    rate 3072 cir 3072
                exit
            exit
        exit
        egress
            qos 100
        exit
    exit
    spoke-sdp 2:100 create
    exit
    no shutdown
exit
```

QoS Policy Override Logic

Why is a QoS policy override recommended only for temporary overrides or in limited cases? Consider a triple-play service provider. The service provider offers VoIP, video, and three different data services (Lightening, Express+, and Express). By combining different services, the service provider offers eight different service packages. To offer the eight different service packages, does the service provider need eight different SAP-ingress and SAP-egress policies? Alternatively, can the service provider configure just one SAP-ingress and one SAP-egress policy and derive the rest of the package offering limitations using QoS policy overrides?

The purpose of a QoS policy override is to reduce the number of QoS policies configured within a node and thereby to make maintenance and troubleshooting of the node configuration easier.

In the triple-play type services, using QoS policy override to derive one or more service packages' limitations from the QoS policies of another service package is not recommended for the following reasons:

- A service package may be subscribed to by hundreds or thousands of residential customers. If QoS policy overrides are used to implement the package, the overrides have to be configured for each subscriber subscribing to the service package. In this scenario, the total number of override configuration statements would be several orders of magnitude higher than the number statements from configuring independent QoS policies for the service package. As a result, node configuration maintenance will become more complicated.

- If QoS policy overrides are used to derive one service package from the QoS policies belonging to another service package, then overrides configured for a subscriber can be as big as QoS policies themselves, thus rendering them ineffective in the best case.

- If any enhancement is made to the derived service package, modifications have to be made to several instances of overrides (for each subscriber), thus rendering the whole configuration difficult to maintain and troubleshoot.

13.4 Service Assurance Agent

Along with the different QoS features discussed so far in this book, you have also seen the verification commands related to those features. However, how do you verify the overall service quality experienced by different application traffic traversing a network?

ALSRP offers the Service Assurance Agent (SAA), which can measure the overall service quality experienced by different applications as well as raise alarms if the QoS metrics cross certain thresholds. SAA can measure the service quality experienced by different application traffic in terms of packet loss, flow latency, and jitter. These measurements can be either one-way or round trip. SAA results can be used to troubleshoot network problems, and for problem prevention and network topology planning. Also, SAA alarms can be used to alert the provider for timely intervention. In ALSRP, SAA results are stored in Simple Network Management Protocol (SNMP) tables, and these results can be queried either through the command line interface (CLI) or from a management system.

SAA tests are configured under `config saa` prompt of the CLI of an ALSRP node. Listing 13.13 displays the options for configuring an SAA `test`. To have an operational SAA test, all the following conditions must be satisfied:

- The type of the test has to be configured.
- At least one of the three listed events has to be configured.
- The test has to be administratively enabled by configuring it to be `no shutdown`.

Listing 13.13 Options for configuring an SAA test

```
A:Pod2>config>saa# test
  - no test <test-name> [owner <test-owner>]
  - test <test-name> [owner <test-owner>]

 <test-name>         : [32 chars max]
 <test-owner>        : [32 chars max] Default - "TiMOS CLI"


 [no] description    - Description for this SAA test
 [no] jitter-event   - Configure jitter event threshold
 [no] latency-event  - Configure latency event threshold
```

(continued)

```
[no] loss-event        - Configure loss event threshold
[no] shutdown          - Administratively enable/disable the SAA test
[no] type              + Configure type of SAA test
```

SAA Test Type

SAA tests are constructed over Operation and Maintenance (OAM) utilities, which in turn supplement the basic IP ping and traceroute operations with diagnostics specialized for the different levels in the service delivery model. The SAA test type indicates which OAM utility is to be used as the probe for the SAA test.

> **Note:** This book does not serve as a primer on network connections, paths, or related topics, and you may encounter some unfamiliar terms in this section. Many of these terms are defined in the glossary of this book. However, if you need more detailed information, please refer to the *Service Guide* of the ALSRP product manuals.

Listing 13.14 shows the different SAA `test type` options available. As shown in the code, there are diagnostics for MPLS label switched paths (LSPs), service distribution points (SDPs), media access control (MAC), Internet Control Message Protocol (ICMP), Virtual Circuit Connectivity Verification (VCCV) for virtual leased line (VLL) services, virtual private routed network (VPRN) services, customer premises equipment (CPE) and Domain Name System (DNS) entities.

Listing 13.14 Different SAA test types available

```
A:Pod2>config>saa>test# type
  - no type
  - type

      cpe-ping       - Configure CPE ping test
      dns            - Configure DNS name resolution test
      icmp-ping      - Configure ICMP ping test
      icmp-trace     - Configure ICMP traceroute test
      lsp-ping       - Configure LSP ping test
      lsp-trace      - Configure LSP trace test
```

(continued)

```
mac-ping         - Configure MAC ping test
mac-trace        - Configure MAC trace test
sdp-ping         - Configure SDP ping test
vccv-ping        - Configure VCCV ping test
vprn-ping        - Configure VPRN ping test
vprn-trace       - Configure VPRN trace test
```

Table 13.1 summarizes the different types of SAA tests and their purposes.

Table 13.1 Summary of Underlying OAM Utilities of SAA Tests and Their Purposes

Test Type	Purpose
cpe-ping	Data plane or control plane utility to determine connectivity to a given IP address within a VPLS.
dns	Two-way time measure request from this node to the specified DNS server. This is done by performing an address request followed by an immediate release of the acquired address once the time measurement has been performed.
icmp-ping	Regular ping sending ICMP "echo request" packets to the target host and listening for ICMP "echo response" replies to test whether the specified host is reachable across the network.
icmp-trace	Regular traceroute to determine the route taken by packets across the network to the specified host.
lsp-ping	Data plane LSP ping utility to verify LSP connectivity.
lsp-trace	Data plane LSP traceroute utility to determine the hop-by-hop path for an LSP.
mac-ping	Data plane or control plane utility to determine the existence of an egress SAP binding of a given MAC within a VPLS.
mac-trace	Data plane or control plane utility to determine the hop-by-hop path for a destination MAC address within a VPLS.
sdp-ping	Tests an SDP for data plane unidirectional or round-trip connectivity with a round trip time estimate.
vccv-ping	Data plane VCCV ping utility to verify a VLL connectivity.
vprn-ping	Data plane or control plane VPRN ping to verify a VPRN prefix.
vprn-trace	Data plane or control plane VPRN trace to determine the hop-by-hop path for a VPRN prefix.

Table 13.2 summarizes the most common parameters used to configure SAA test type commands.

Table 13.2 Summary of Most Common Parameters Used to Configure the SAA Test Types

Parameters	Details
service <service-id>	ID of the service to diagnose or manage.
send-control	Keyword—Send request using the control plane instead of the data plane.
return-control	Keyword—Send reply using the control plane instead of the data plane.
fc <fc-name>	Forwarding class (FC)—By specifying a particular FC and profile, the QoS experienced by traffic flowing through FC with the specified profile can be assessed.
profile <in|out>	Profile (queuing priority) of the datagram—By specifying a particular FC and profile, the QoS experienced by traffic flowing through FC with the specified profile can be assessed.
interval <interval>	The minimum amount of time, expressed in seconds, that must expire between sending out two consecutive requests. If the interval is set to 1 second and the timeout value is set to 10 seconds, then the maximum time between message requests is 10 seconds and the minimum is 1 second. The actual time depends upon the receipt of a message reply corresponding to the outstanding message request.
timeout <timeout>	The maximum amount of time, expressed in seconds, the router will wait for a message reply after sending the message request. On expiration of timeout, the requesting router assumes that the message response is lost, and any response received after the timeout will be silently discarded.
count <send-count>	The number of message requests to send.
ttl <vc-label-ttl>	The time to live (TTL), expressed as an integer, is a limit on the number of hops that the packet can go through before it is discarded.
min-ttl <min-label-ttl>	The minimum number of hops that the packet should go through.
max-ttl <max-label-ttl>	The maximum number of hops that the packet can go through.
size <octets>	The request payload size in octets, expressed as a decimal integer.

The command options for configuring all the different SAA test types are shown in the following listings.

CPE Testing

Listing 13.15 shows the command options for configuring the SAA test type cpe-ping. The source IP address can be any available valid IP address to which the CPE would respond. In other words, the source IP address should be in the routing table of the CPE so that the CPE will reply back to the router.

Listing 13.15 Command options for configuring the SAA test type cpe-ping

```
A:Pod2>config>saa>test>type$ cpe-ping
  - cpe-ping service <service-id> destination <ip-address> source <ip-address>
    [source-mac <ieee-address>] [fc <fc-name> [profile <in|out>]] [ttl
    <vc-label-ttl>] [count <send-count>] [send-control] [return-control]
    [interval <interval>]

  <service-id>        : [1..2147483647]
  <ip-address>        : a.b.c.d
  <vc-label-ttl>      : [1..255]
  <return-control>    : keyword - receives on the control plane
  <ieee-address>      : xx:xx:xx:xx:xx:xx or xx-xx-xx-xx-xx-xx
                        All zero and multicast not allowed
  <interval>          : [1..10]
  <send-count>        : [1..100]
  <send-control>      : keyword - sends via the control plane
  <fc-name>           : be|l2|af|l1|h2|ef|h1|nc - Default: be
  <in|out>            : keywords - Default: out
```

DNS Testing

Listing 13.16 illustrates the command options for configuring the SAA test type dns. The command is used to test the DNS name resolution.

ICMP Testing

Respectively, Listings 13.17 and 13.18 show the command options for configuring the SAA test types icmp-ping and icmp-trace. These are the standard ping and traceroute diagnostics defined by RFC 792 as an integral part of the Internet Protocol suite.

As shown in the listings, the diagnostics implementation allows one to refer to a destination system based either on its IP address or on its domain name (if one is available). In both the test commands, the option router <router-instance> allows targeting of a particular service or the management plane within a destination router. The commands allow the specification of a decimal value for the 8-bit ToS field of the IP header of the test messages.

In the icmp-ping command options, shown in Listing 13.17, the optional keyword rapid generates test packets as soon as possible instead of the default 1 per second, and detail displays diagnostics information in detail. The option pattern <pattern> allows the specification of a value for the date portion of a ping packet.

Listing 13.17 Command options for configuring the SAA test type icmp-ping

```
A:Pod2>config>saa>test>type$ icmp-ping
  - icmp-ping <ip-address|dns-name> [rapid|detail] [ttl <time-to-live>] [tos
    <type-of-service>] [size <bytes>] [pattern <pattern>] [source
    <ip-address>] [interval <seconds>] [{next-hop <ip-address>}|{interface
    <interface-name>}|bypass-routing] [count <requests>] [do-not-fragment]
```

(continued)

```
        [router <router-instance>] [timeout <timeout>]

<ip-address|dns-na*> : ipv4-address    - a.b.c.d
                       ipv6-address    - x:x:x:x:x:x:x:x[-interface]
                                         x:x:x:x:x:x:d.d.d.d[-interface]
                                         x - [0..FFFF]H
                                         d - [0..255]D
                                         interface - 32 chars max, mandatory
                                         for link local addresses
                       dns-name        - [63 chars max]
<rapid|detail>       : keywords
<time-to-live>       : [1..128]
<type-of-service>    : [0..255]
<bytes>              : [0..16384]
<pattern>            : [0..65535]
<ip-address>         : ip-address
<seconds>            : [1..10000]
<ip-address>         : ipv4-address    - a.b.c.d
                       ipv6-address    - x:x:x:x:x:x:x:x   (eight 16-bit
                                         pieces)
                                         x:x:x:x:x:x:d.d.d.d
                                         x - [0..FFFF]H
                                         d - [0..255]D
<bypass-routing>     : keyword
<requests>           : [1..100000]
<do-not-fragment>    : keyword
<interface-name>     : [32 chars max]
<router-instance>    : <router-name>|<service-id>
                       router-name     - "Base"|"management"|"vpls-management"
                                         Default - Base
                       service-id      - [1..2147483647]
<timeout>            : [1..10] seconds
```

In the `icmp-trace` command options, shown in Listing 13.18, the `wait` option is the same as the `timeout` option in most other SAA `test type` commands, but it is expressed in milliseconds instead of seconds.

Listing 13.18 Command options for configuring the SAA test type icmp-trace

```
A:Pod2>config>saa>test>type$ icmp-trace
  - icmp-trace <ip-address|dns-name> [ttl <ttl>] [wait <milli-seconds>] [source
    <ip-address>] [tos <type-of-service>] [router <router-instance>]

 <ip-address|dns-na*> : ipv4-address   - a.b.c.d
                        ipv6-address   - x:x:x:x:x:x:x:x
                                         x:x:x:x:x:x:d.d.d.d
                                         x - [0..FFFF]H
                                         d - [0..255]D
                        dns-name       - [63 chars max]
 <ttl>                : [1..255]
 <milli-seconds>      : [1..60000]
 <ip-address>         : ipv4-address   - a.b.c.d
                        ipv6-address   - x:x:x:x:x:x:x:x   (eight 16-bit
                                         pieces)
                                         x:x:x:x:x:x:d.d.d.d
                                         x - [0..FFFF]H
                                         d - [0..255]D
 <type-of-service>    : [0..255]
 <router-instance>    : <router-name>|<service-id>
                        router-name    - "Base"|"management"|"vpls-management"
                                         Default - Base
                        service-id     - [1..2147483647]
```

LSP Testing

LSP ping verifies whether the packet reaches the egress label edge router (LER), while in LSP traceroute mode the packet is sent to the control plane of each transit label switched router (LSR). In both LSP ping and LSP traceroute the reply node cross checks the data and control planes for the tested LSP. LSP ping and LSP traceroute diagnostics are based on RFC 4379, *Detecting Multi Protocol Label Switched (MPLS) Data Plane Failures.*

Listing 13.19 displays the command options for configuring the SAA `test type lsp-ping`. Among the command options, `<lsp-name>` identifies an LSP to send the request message. The `path <path-name>` is an LSP path name along which the LSP ping or trace request is sent. The default path is the active LSP path. The `prefix <ip-prefix/mask>` specifies the IP address prefix and subnet mask of the destination node.

Listing 13.19 Command options for configuring the SAA test type lsp-ping

```
A:Pod2>config>saa>test>type$ lsp-ping
  - lsp-ping {{<lsp-name> [path <path-name>]}|{prefix <ip-prefix/mask>}} [fc
    <fc-name> [profile {in|out}]] [size <octets>] [ttl <label-ttl>]
    [send-count <send-count>] [timeout <timeout>] [interval <interval>]
    [path-destination <ip-address>[interface <if-name>|next-hop <ip-address>]]

    <lsp-name>          : [32 chars max]
    <octets>            : [84..65535]
    <label-ttl>         : [1..255]
    <timeout>           : [1..10] seconds
    <interval>          : [1..10] seconds
    <fc-name>           : be|l2|af|l1|h2|ef|h1|nc - Default: be
    <in|out>            : keywords - Default: out
    <send-count>        : [1..100]
    <path-name>         : [32 chars max]
    <ip-prefix/mask>    : ip-prefix a.b.c.d
                          mask [value MUST be 32]
    <ip-address>        : ipv4 address    a.b.c.d
    <if-name>           : [32 chars max]
```

Listing 13.20 illustrates the command options for configuring the SAA `test type lsp-trace`. The `max-fail <no-response-count>` is the maximum number of consecutive MPLS echo requests sent without receiving a reply before the trace operation is declared to have failed. The default `no-response-count` is 5.

Listing 13.20 Command options for configuring the SAA test type isp-trace

```
A:Pod2>config>saa>test>type$ lsp-trace
  - lsp-trace {{<lsp-name> [path <path-name>]}|{prefix <ip-prefix/mask>}} [fc
    <fc-name> [profile {in|out}]] [max-fail <no-response-count>] [probe-count
    <probes-per-hop>] [size <octets>] [min-ttl <min-label-ttl>] [max-ttl
    <max-label-ttl>] [timeout <timeout>] [interval <interval>]
```

(continued)

```
        [path-destination <ip-address>[interface <if-name>|next-hop <ip-address>]]

<lsp-name>              : [32 chars max]
<octets>                : [104..65535]
<min-label-ttl>         : [1..255]
<max-label-ttl>         : [1..255]
<no-response-count>     : [1..255]
<probes-per-hop>        : [1..10]
<timeout>               : [1..60] seconds
<interval>              : [1..10] seconds
<fc-name>               : be|l2|af|l1|h2|ef|h1|nc - Default: be
<in|out>                : keywords - Default: out
<path-name>             : [32 chars max]
<ip-prefix/mask>        : ip-prefix - a.b.c.d (host bits must be 0)
                          mask [0..32]
<ip-address>            : ipv4 address     a.b.c.d
<if-name>               : [32 chars max]
```

MAC Testing

MAC ping provides an end-to-end test to identify the customer-facing port through which a CPE is connected. MAC ping can also be used with a broadcast MAC address to identify all egress points of a service for the specified broadcast MAC. MAC trace provides the ability to trace a specified MAC address hop by hop until the last node in the service domain is reached.

Respectively, Listings 13.21 and 13.22 show the command options for configuring the SAA test types mac-ping and mac-trace. The destination <ieee-address> is the destination MAC address to be pinged or traced. The source <ieee-address> is the source MAC address from which the OAM MAC request originates; by default, the system MAC address for the chassis is used.

Listing 13.21 Command options for configuring the SAA test type mac-ping

```
A:Pod2>config>saa>test>type$ mac-ping
  - mac-ping service <service-id> destination <dst-ieee-address> [source
    <src-ieee-address>] [fc <fc-name> [profile <in|out>]] [size <octets>] [ttl
    <vc-label-ttl>] [count <send-count>] [send-control] [return-control]
```

(continued)

```
        [interval <interval>] [timeout <timeout>]

<service-id>          : [1..2147483647]
<dst-ieee-address>    : xx:xx:xx:xx:xx:xx or xx-xx-xx-xx-xx-xx
                        All zero not allowed
<octets>              : [1..65535]
<vc-label-ttl>        : [1..255]
<send-control>        : keyword - sends via the control plane
<return-control>      : keyword - receives on the control plane
<src-ieee-address>    : xx:xx:xx:xx:xx:xx or xx-xx-xx-xx-xx-xx
                        All zero and multicast not allowed
<interval>            : [1..10] seconds
<send-count>          : [1..100]
<timeout>             : [1..10] seconds
<fc-name>             : be|l2|af|l1|h2|ef|h1|nc - Default: be
<in|out>             : keywords - Default: out
```

Listing 13.22 Command options for configuring the SAA test type mac-trace

```
A:Pod2>config>saa>test# type mac-trace
  - mac-trace service <service-id> destination <ieee-address> [source
    <ieee-address>] [fc <fc-name> [profile <in|out>]] [size <octets>] [min-ttl
    <vc-label-ttl>] [max-ttl <vc-label-ttl>] [probe-count <send-count>]
    [send-control] [return-control] [interval <interval>] [timeout <timeout>]

<service-id>          : [1..2147483647]
<ieee-address>        : xx:xx:xx:xx:xx:xx or xx-xx-xx-xx-xx-xx
                        All zero not allowed
<octets>              : [1..65535]
<vc-label-ttl>        : [1..255]
<send-control>        : keyword - sends via the control plane
<return-control>      : keyword - receives on the control plane
<send-count>          : [1..10]
<interval>            : [1..10]
<timeout>             : [1..60] seconds
<fc-name>             : be|l2|af|l1|h2|ef|h1|nc - Default: be
<in|out>             : keywords - Default: out
```

SDP Testing

SDP ping performs data plane unidirectional or round-trip connectivity tests on SDPs. The SDP ping OAM packets are sent over a data plane, with tunnel encapsulation, so it will follow the same path as traffic within the service. For a round-trip test, SDP ping uses a local egress SDP ID and an expected remote SDP ID. Because SDPs are unidirectional tunnels, the remote SDP ID must be specified and must exist as a configured SDP ID on the far end ALSRP node. Listing 13.23 shows the command options for configuring the SAA `test type sdp-ping`.

Listing 13.23 Command options for configuring the SAA test type `sdp-ping`

```
A:Pod2>config>saa>test>type$ sdp-ping
  - sdp-ping <orig-sdp-id> [resp-sdp <resp-sdp-id>] [fc <fc-name> [profile
    <in|out>]] [size <octets>] [count <send-count>] [timeout <timeout>]
    [interval <interval>]

 <orig-sdp-id>       : [1..17407]
 <resp-sdp-id>       : [1..17407]
 <fc-name>           : be|l2|af|l1|h2|ef|h1|nc - Default: be
 <in|out>            : keywords - Default: be
 <timeout>           : [1..10] seconds
 <interval>          : [1..10] seconds
 <octets>            : [40..9198]
 <send-count>        : [1..100]
```

VLL Connectivity Testing

VCCV ping is used to check connectivity of a VLL in-band. It provides a cross-check between the data plane and the control plane. The VCCV ping message is sent using the same encapsulation and along the same path as user packets in that VLL. This is equivalent to the LSP ping for a VLL service. VCCV ping reuses an LSP ping message format and can be used to test a VLL configured over an MPLS or Generic Routing Encapsulation (GRE) SDP. Listing 13.24 illustrates the command options for configuring the SAA `test type vccv-ping`.

If the ping is across two or more pseudowire segments, the `sdp-id`, `src-ip-address`, `dst-ip-address`, `ttl`, and `pw-id` parameters are to be used where:

- The `pw-id` is the VC ID of the last pseudowire segment.
- The `vc-label-ttl` must have a value equal to or higher than the number of pseudowire segments.

```
A:Pod2>config>saa>test>type# vccv-ping
  - vccv-ping <sdp-id:vc-id> [src-ip-address <ip-addr> dst-ip-address
    <ip-addr> pw-id <pw-id>][reply-mode {ip-routed|control-channel}][fc
    <fc-name> [profile {in|out}]] [size <octets>] [count <send-count>]
    [timeout <timeout>] [interval <interval>][ttl <vc-label-ttl>]>

  <sdp-id:vc-id>        : sdp-id - [1..17407]
                          vc-id  - [1..4294967295]
  <ip-routed|control*> : keywords - specify reply mode
                          Default: control-channel
  <fc-name>             : be|l2|af|l1|h2|ef|h1|nc - Default: be
  <in|out>              : keywords - Default: out
  <octets>              : [88..9198] octets - Default: 88
  <send-count>          : [1..100] - Default: 1
  <timeout>             : [1..10] seconds - Default: 5
  <interval>            : [1..10] seconds - Default: 1
  <ip-addr>             : a.b.c.d
  <vc-label-ttl>        : [1..255]
  <pw-id>               : [0..4294967295]
```

VPRN Testing

Listing 13.25 shows the command options for configuring the SAA test type vprn-ping.

Listing 13.25 Command options for configuring the SAA test type vprn-ping

```
A:Pod2>config>saa>test>type$ vprn-ping
  - vprn-ping <service-id> source <ip-address> destination <ip-address> [fc
    <fc-name> [profile <in|out>]] [size <size>] [ttl <vc-label-ttl>] [count
    <send-count>] [return-control] [timeout <timeout>] [interval <seconds>]

  <service-id>          : [1..2147483647]
  <ip-address>          : a.b.c.d
  <size>                : [1..65535]
```

(continued)

```
<vc-label-ttl>        : [1..255]
<return-control>      : keyword - receives on the control plane
<interval>            : [1..10] seconds
<send-count>          : [1..100]
<timeout>             : [1..100] seconds
<fc-name>             : be|l2|af|l1|h2|ef|h1|nc - Default: be
<in|out>              : keywords - Default: out
```

Listing 13.26 displays the command options for configuring the SAA `test type vprn-trace`.

Listing 13.26 Command options for configuring the SAA test type vprn-trace

```
A:Pod2>config>saa>test# type vprn-trace
  - vprn-trace <service-id> source <ip-address> destination <ip-address> [fc
    <fc-name> [profile <in|out>]] [size <size>] [min-ttl <vc-label-ttl>]
    [max-ttl <vc-label-ttl>] [probe-count <send-count>] [return-control]
    [timeout <timeout>] [interval <interval>]

<service-id>          : [1..2147483647]
<ip-address>          : a.b.c.d
<size>                : [1..65535]
<vc-label-ttl>        : [1..255]
<return-control>      : keyword - receives on the control plane
<send-count>          : [1..10]
<interval>            : [1..10] seconds
<timeout>             : [1..100] seconds
<fc-name>             : be|l2|af|l1|h2|ef|h1|nc - Default: be
<in|out>              : keywords - Default: out
```

Event Configuration

As shown earlier in Listing 13.13, there are three events for determining the three QoS metrics: `jitter-event`, `latency-event`, and `loss-event`. Listing 13.27 shows the command options for configuring the `latency-event`. The command options available for the other events are similar, except that the rising and falling thresholds of `loss-event` are configured in terms of the number of packets instead of in milliseconds.

Listing 13.27 Command options for configuring the SAA test latency-event

```
A:Pod2>config>saa>test# latency-event
  - latency-event rising-threshold <threshold> [falling-threshold <threshold>]
    [<direction>]
  - no latency-event

 <threshold>        : [0..2147483647] milliseconds
 <direction>        : inbound|outbound|roundtrip
```

At the termination of an SAA test, the obtained QoS measurement value is evaluated against the configured thresholds. If the observed value of an event is greater than the configured rising threshold of the event, an alarm is raised. The alarm is cleared when the observed value for the event in a subsequent test run falls below the configured falling threshold for the event. The alarms and the alarm clearance generated by these events are logged in the default system log (log-id 99). These alarms and alarm clearances can also be flagged into a network management system (Alcatel-Lucent 5620 SAM) through SNMP traps.

Best Practices: The rising threshold of an SAA test event should be configured such that it is well above the normally observed values for the event and should be well below any related SLAs.

Configuring the threshold well above normally observed values prevents any false alarms. Configuring the threshold well below any related SLAs means that the service provider would get timely warning to improve network conditions and to avoid customers observing any service deterioration.

The falling threshold of an SAA test event should be configured such that it is barely above the normally observed values for the event.

Listing 13.28 exhibits an example SAA test. The example test uses the sdp-ping OAM utility and measures the latency of low-queuing priority traffic belonging to the BE forwarding class. According to the configuration, 20 ping request packets are sent. The size of the packets is 1024 bytes and the interval between two consecutive packets is at least 2 seconds. The rising-threshold of the latency-event is 600 milliseconds and the falling-threshold is 500 milliseconds.

Listing 13.28 An example SAA test configuration using the sdp-ping `type`

```
test "sdp-2-data"
    description "Check latency on SDP 2 for data (FC: BE)"
    type
        sdp-ping 2 resp-sdp 1 interval 2 size 1024 count 20
    exit
    latency-event rising-threshold 600 falling-threshold 500
    no shutdown
exit
```

The ALSRP SAA test configuration permits configuring more than one event within a `test`. However there can be only one `test type` within an SAA `test`. Listing 13.29 exhibits an example SAA test in which all three events are configured. The test uses the `cpe-ping` OAM utility.

Listing 13.29 An example SAA test configuration using the cpe-ping `type`

```
test "CPE-PC"
    description "SLA conformance check for CPE PC"
    type
        cpe-ping service 100 source 192.168.0.110 destination
            192.168.0.105 fc "be" profile in count 15 interval 2
    exit
    jitter-event rising-threshold 100 falling-threshold 50
    loss-event rising-threshold 5 falling-threshold 1
    latency-event rising-threshold 500 falling-threshold 400
    no shutdown
exit
```

Triggering and Verifying SAA Tests

ALSRP keeps track of the results of each execution of SAA tests, until they are cleared. Therefore, you may sometimes need to clear any of the previous results obtained for an SAA test before executing the test again. Listing 13.30 shows the command options for clearing the results history of an SAA test. The code also shows examples for executing the `clear` command.

```
A:Pod1# clear saa
  - saa [<test-name> [owner <test-owner>]]

 <test-name>           : [32 chars max]
 <owner>               : [32 chars max] Default - "TiMOS CLI"


A:Pod1# clear saa CPE-PC
A:Pod1# clear saa sdp-2-data
```

Listing 13.31 displays the command options for executing an SAA test, along with an example execution. As shown in the code, an SAA test can be started or stopped under **oam saa**. An SAA test will automatically stop after completing the specified number of test counts. However, if a test has to be stopped in the middle before it completes the specified number of test counts, the following command can be used:

```
oam saa <test-name> [owner <test-owner>] stop
```

Listing 13.31 Command options and example for executing an SAA test

```
A:Pod1# oam saa
  - saa <test-name> [owner <test-owner>] {start|stop}

 <test-name>           : [32 chars max]
 <test-owner>          : [32 chars max] Default - "TiMOS CLI"
 <start|stop>          : keyword


A:Pod1# oam saa CPE-PC start
```

Listing 13.32 shows the command options for viewing the results of an SAA test.

Listing 13.33 shows the results of the executions of an example SAA test. The results are obtained after executing the SAA test twice.

During the first run (indicated as run #13 in the listing), the test CPE was held busy and forced to delay the ping responses. The delay in ping responses forced the round-trip latency to often exceed the rising threshold of the `latency-event`, and at times even to exceed the response wait time of the ping messages.

During the second run (indicated as run #14), the test CPE was held relatively free. As a result, the ping responses arrived well within the falling threshold of the `latency-event`.

Listing 13.33 The results of the execution of an example SAA test

```
A:Pod1# show saa CPE-PC


===============================================================================
SAA Test Information
===============================================================================
Test name                   : CPE-PC
Owner name                  : TiMOS CLI
Description                 : SLA conformance check for CPE PC
Administrative status       : Enabled
Test type                   : cpe-ping service 100 source 192.168.0.110
                              destination 192.168.0.105 fc "be" profile in
                              count 15 interval 2
Test runs since last clear  : 2
Number of failed test runs  : 1
Last test result            : Success
```

(continued)

```
--------------------------------------------------------------------------------
Threshold
Type         Direction Threshold  Value   Last Event             Run #
--------------------------------------------------------------------------------
Jitter-in    Rising    None       None    Never                  None
             Falling   None       None    Never                  None
Jitter-out   Rising    None       None    Never                  None
             Falling   None       None    Never                  None
Jitter-rt    Rising    100        None    Never                  None
             Falling   50         0       10/08/2007 15:40:34 13
Latency-in   Rising    None       None    Never                  None
             Falling   None       None    Never                  None
Latency-out  Rising    None       None    Never                  None
             Falling   None       None    Never                  None
Latency-rt   Rising    500        1940    10/08/2007 15:40:37 13
             Falling   400        10      10/08/2007 15:43:29 14
Loss-in      Rising    None       None    Never                  None
             Falling   None       None    Never                  None
Loss-out     Rising    None       None    Never                  None
             Falling   None       None    Never                  None
Loss-rt      Rising    5          6       10/08/2007 15:41:03 13
             Falling   1          0       10/08/2007 15:44:02 14


================================================================================
Test Run: 13
Total number of attempts: 15
Number of requests that failed to be sent out: 0
...
```

Using SAA Tests to Routinely Check Network Health

The quality of service of a network can dynamically change because of the dynamic nature of the traffic flowing through the network. Therefore, to routinely assess the health of a network, ALSRP permits the execution of SAA tests periodically either using a network management system or using time triggered actions.

Executing an SAA test periodically using a time-triggered action is discussed in detail in the following section.

ALSRP nodes raise a warning every time the observed results of an SAA test cross any of the configured event's thresholds. Each time a warning is raised, it is logged in the system log (`log-id 99`) of the node. Listing 13.34 shows a sample output of system log of an ALSRP node containing SAA test warnings.

Listing 13.34 Warnings raised by SAA test runs are recorded in the system log of the ALSRP node

```
A:Pod1# show log log-id 99

===============================================================================
Event Log 99
===============================================================================
Description : Default System Log
Memory Log contents  [size=500   next event=9  (not wrapped)]

8 2007/10/08 15:44:01.70 UTC MINOR: OAM #2101 Base SAA ping crossed Threshold
"OAM SAA ping test "CPE-PC" created by "TiMOS CLI" run #14 crossed falling
rtLoss threshold 1 with value 0"

7 2007/10/08 15:43:28.57 UTC MINOR: OAM #2101 Base SAA ping crossed Threshold
"OAM SAA ping test "CPE-PC" created by "TiMOS CLI" run #14 crossed falling
rtLatency threshold 400 with value 10"

6 2007/10/08 15:41:02.56 UTC MINOR: OAM #2101 Base SAA ping crossed Threshold
"OAM SAA ping test "CPE-PC" created by "TiMOS CLI" run #13 crossed rising
rtLoss threshold 5 with value 6"

5 2007/10/08 15:40:37.30 UTC MINOR: OAM #2101 Base SAA ping crossed Threshold
"OAM SAA ping test "CPE-PC" created by "TiMOS CLI" run #13 crossed rising
rtLatency threshold 500 with value 1940"

...
```

13.5 Time-Based QoS

The flexibility to allocate more resources to different services at different times helps the service provider to optimize the network resource utilization around the clock and maximize service revenues. For the end customer, the feature results in "pay while you use" model and a better network experience at the time of need.

With the help of time-of-day policies, for example, a service provider can allocate the majority of network resources for business use during the standard work hours and reallocate the majority of network resources for residential customers in the evenings and weekends. Thus, the service provider can maximize the network utilization around the clock.

Having time-of-day policies to maximize network utilization is similar to running a manufacturing plant with huge capital investment around the clock with different shifts to maximize the production and thereby maximize the profit.

ALSRP provides time dependencies for the following QoS features:

- SAP-ingress QoS policy
- SAP-egress QoS policy
- Scheduler QoS policy
- Service Assurance Agent
- Filters (Access Control Lists [ACLs])

The time dependency requirement for engaging a QoS policy or a filter policy is different from the one required to trigger an SAA test or any other scripts. To engage a policy, you must specify a time period, with a starting and an ending time. To execute a script only a time trigger (or a time pulse) is required.

ALSRP supports time triggers in the form of `schedule` and time period in the form of `time-range`. A `schedule` provides time triggers for the occurrence of an `action`. Besides triggering SAA tests, the `schedule` time dependencies can also be used to trigger connectivity checks, reboots, running scripts, and other OAM events. A `time-range` is a period during which an associated policy is held active.

System Time

Although configuring `system time` is part of the basic initial configuration of a node, it is briefly covered here for the sake of completeness in the discussion on configuring time dependencies.

The `system time` configuration of an ALSRP node can be displayed using the command `show system time`. Listing 13.35 displays a sample output of the `show system time` command.

Listing 13.35 A sample output of the show system time command

```
A:Pod2# show system time

===============================================================================
Date & Time
===============================================================================
Current Date & Time : 2007/09/17 15:49:43    DST Active            : yes
Current Zone        : PDT                    Offset from UTC       : -7:00
-------------------------------------------------------------------------------
Non-DST Zone        : PST                    Offset from UTC       : -8:00
Zone type           : standard
-------------------------------------------------------------------------------
DST Zone            : PDT                    Offset from Non-DST   : 0:60
Starts              : second sunday in march 02:00
Ends                : first sunday in november 02:00
===============================================================================
```

To adjust the system time of an isolated node, use the `admin set-time` command. Listing 13.36 shows the options of the `admin set-time` command.

Listing 13.36 Options to set the system time of an isolated node

```
A:Pod2# admin set-time
  - set-time <date> <time>

 <date>                 : YYYY/MM/DD
 <time>                 : hh:mm[:ss]
```

Time-zone-related information and daylight saving time schedule information can be configured under `system time`. Listing 13.37 illustrates the options available for configuring `system time`. Listing 13.38 displays an example of configuring time zone and daylight schedule information under `system time`.

Listing 13.37 Options for configuring time-related information

```
A:Pod2>config>system>time#
  [no] dst-zone      + Configure summer time settings
  [no] ntp           + Configure parameters for NTP protocol
  [no] sntp          + Configure parameters for SNTP protocol
  [no] zone          - Configure time zone and time offset for system
```

Listing 13.38 An example system time configuration

```
        time
            sntp
                shutdown
            exit
            dst-zone PDT
                start second sunday march 02:00
                end first sunday november 02:00
            exit
            zone PST
        exit
```

In order to maintain the system time of a network consisting of more than one node, use of the Network Time Protocol (NTP) or Simple Network Time Protocol (SNTP) is recommended. NTP is defined in RFC 1305. SNTP is defined in RFC 2030. As shown in Listing 13.37, NTP and SNTP parameters can also be configured under `system time`. For further information regarding configuring NTP and SNTP parameters in ALSRP, refer to the *System Basics Guide* of the ALSRP product manuals.

> **Best Practices:** Even if no time-dependent feature is configured in a node, synchronizing all the network nodes' system time using NTP or SNTP is recommended. Nodes with synchronized system times will have time-synchronized logs, and as a result it is easier to troubleshoot.

Time-Triggered Actions

All the time dependencies are configured under `cron`. Listing 13.39 shows the top-level options available under the `cron` configuration.

Does cron Sound Greek to You?

cron is a time-based scheduling service traditionally offered in a Unix environment. The etymological basis of cron is the Greek word *chronos*, meaning time.

Listing 13.39 Options available under cron

```
A:Pod2>config>cron#
  [no] action        + Configure action parameters for a script
  [no] schedule      + Configure CRON schedule
  [no] script        + Configure CRON script
  [no] time-range    + Configure a time range
  [no] tod-suite     + Configure a time-of-day Suite
```

A time triggered action is implemented in four parts:

1. The creation of a `schedule` object, which includes configuring time triggers and associating an `action` object to the time triggers.
2. The creation of an `action` object, which includes configuring the action-related parameters and associating a script object.
3. The creation of a `script` object, which includes specifying the location of the script file.
4. The creation of the script file at the specified location.

   Listing 13.40 displays the command options available to create a schedule.

```
A:Pod2>config>cron# schedule
  - no schedule <schedule-name> [owner <schedule-owner>]
  - schedule <schedule-name> [owner <schedule-owner>]

 <schedule-name>      : [32 chars max]
 <schedule-owner>     : [32 chars max] Default - "TiMOS CLI"

 [no] action          - Action parameters for this schedule
 [no] count           - Number of times to repeat periodic schedule run
 [no] day-of-month    - Configure the days of the month for CRON schedule
 [no] description     - Description for this CRON schedule
 [no] end-time        - Configure time to stop CRON schedule
 [no] hour            - Configure hour for CRON schedule
 [no] interval        - Interval between each periodic schedule run
 [no] minute          - Configure minute for CRON schedule
 [no] month           - Configure month for CRON schedule
 [no] shutdown        - Administratively enable/disable the CRON schedule
      type            - Type of schedule
 [no] weekday         - Configure week day for CRON schedule
```

The `action` command under a schedule is used to associate an `action` object to the schedule. An `action` object itself is configured under the `cron` prompt, which is shown in Listing 13.39.

The `type` command specifies the triggering nature of a schedule. The three values of the `type` command are:

- `periodic`—The `schedule` runs periodically at a given interval. This is the default behavior. When both `end-time` and `count` commands are configured, the condition that arrives earlier is applied.

- `calendar`—The `schedule` runs based on a calendar. Multiple commands can be specified in combination, and every time all the commands are satisfied the associated `action` is executed.

- `oneshot`—The schedule runs one time only. Once the associated `action` is executed the `schedule` enters an operationally down (finished) state.

If commands not compatible to a defined `type` are specified within a `schedule`, those commands are ignored. Obviously, the commands `action`, `description`, `shutdown` and `type` are relevant for all the `schedule` types. Table 13.3 summarizes the configuration command relevant for only certain types of `cron` schedules.

Table 13.3 Configuration Commands Relevant for Different Types of cron schedules

Periodic	Calendar/Oneshot
interval	month
count	day-of-month
end-time	weekday
	hour
	minute
	end-time

Listing 13.41 shows an example for a `periodic schedule`. According to the example, the associated action will be executed two times in two-minute intervals. If the specified `end-time` arrives before completing the execution of the associated action twice, the schedule will be put into a finished state and the schedule will not invoke the associated action further.

Listing 13.41 An example for a periodic schedule

```
schedule "example1"
    description "An example for periodic schedule"
    interval 120
    count 2
    action "Test_BE"
    end-time 2007/09/26 15:30
    no shutdown
exit
```

Listing 13.42 exhibits an example for a `calendar type schedule`. According to the example, the associated action will be executed in the month of July at 9:30 on Wednesdays. In the configuration, the hour is expressed using a 24-hour clock.

Listing 13.42 An example of a calendar type schedule

```
schedule "example2"
    description "An example for calendar schedule"
    action "Test_Video"
    type calendar
    day-of-month all
    hour 9
    minute 30
    month july
    weekday wednesday
    no shutdown
exit
```

Listing 13.43 shows an example of a `oneshot type schedule`. According to the example, the associated action will be executed only once at 10:00 either on October 2 or 14, whichever arrives first.

Listing 13.43 An example of a oneshot type schedule

```
schedule "example3"
    shutdown
    description "An example for oneshot schedule"
    action "Test_Filter_Block"
    type oneshot
    day-of-month 2 14
    hour 10
    month october
exit
```

Listing 13.44 displays the command options for configuring an `action` object. The commands `expire-time`, `lifetime`, and `max-completed` are related to statistics maintained regarding the `action` and displayed while using the command `show cron action <action-name>`. The command `results` is used to specify a filename and the location to store the output generated as a result of executing the associated script object. The command `script` is used to associate a `script` object to the action.

Listing 13.44 Command options for creating an action object

```
A:Pod2>config>cron# action
 - action <action-name> [owner <action-owner>]
 - no action <action-name> [owner <action-owner>]

<action-name>      : [32 chars max]
<action-owner>     : [32 chars max] Default - "TiMOS CLI"


      expire-time  - Maximum amount of time to keep the run history status
                     entry from a script run
      lifetime     - Maximum amount of time the script may run
      max-completed - Maximum number of script run history status entries to
                     keep
 [no] results      - Location to receive CLI output display of a script run
 [no] script       - Script to run
 [no] shutdown     - Administratively enable/disable CRON action
```

Listing 13.45 shows an example `action` object. ALSRP appends date and time stamps along with the extension `.out` to the specified name while creating a result file. An example of a result file created for the action shown in Listing 13.45 is `BEQoSResults_20070927-023112.out`, where 20070927 stands for 2007 September 27, and 023112 stands for 02:31:12 Coordinated Universal Time (UTC). The results can be either stored in a flash drive of ALSRP, or as shown in Listing 13.45, sent to any reachable device with an IP address and running a FTP or TFTP demon.

Listing 13.45 An example action object

```
        action "Test_BE"
            results "ftp://pod2:meena@192.168.0.100/./pod2/BEQoSResults"
            script "BEQoSTest"
            no shutdown
        exit
```

Note: Date and time stamps appended to a result file created while executing a `cron action` object is based on UTC and not based on the local time, even if local time is configured in the system. The reason behind using UTC is that a network can span multiple time zones.

Listing 13.46 illustrates the command options available for creating a `script` object. Listing 13.47 shows an example `script` object.

Listing 13.46 Command options for creating a script object under the config cron

```
A:Pod2>config>cron# script
  - no script <script-name> [owner <script-owner>]
  - script <script-name> [owner <script-owner>]

<script-name>       : [32 chars max]
<script-owner>      : [32 chars max] Default - "TiMOS CLI"

[no] description    - Description for this CRON script
[no] location       - Location of script to be scheduled
[no] shutdown       - Administratively enable/disable the CRON script
```

Listing 13.47 An example script object

```
script "BEQoSTest"
    description "Ensure the ftp server demon is running on the PC"
    location "ftp://pod2:meena@192.168.0.100/./pod2/BEQoSTest.txt"
    no shutdown
exit
```

Listing 13.48 shows the content of the example script `BEQoSTest.txt`. The contents are a list of ALSRP commands. The commands execute the SAA object `CPE-PC` and display the result.

Listing 13.48 Content of the example script BEQoSTest.txt

```
oam saa CPE-PC start
sleep 30
show saa CPE-PC
show system time
```

Time of Day Policies

A Time of Day policy is implemented in three steps:

1. Configure a `time-range`
2. Configure a Time of Day suite (`tod-suite`) to associate QoS policies with the `time-range`
3. Apply the Time of Day suite

Listing 13.49 shows the command options for creating a `time-range`.

Listing 13.49 Time-range creation options

```
A:Pod2>config>cron# time-range
  - no time-range <name>
  - time-range <name> [create]

 <name>              : [32 chars max]
 <create>            : keyword - mandatory while creating a time-range

 [no] absolute    - Configure an absolute time interval in the time-range
 [no] daily       - Configure a daily time interval in the time-range
 [no] description - Specify a description for this time-range
 [no] weekdays    - Configure a time interval for weekdays in the time-range
 [no] weekend     - Configure a time interval for every weekend day in the
                    time-range
 [no] weekly      - Configure a weekly periodic interval in the time-range
```

Among the `time-range` creation options shown in Listing 13.49, `daily`, weekdays, weekend, and weekly are recursive commands. The weekdays are Monday through Friday. The **weekend** days are Saturday and Sunday. The configuration of **daily**, **weekdays**, and **weekend** are similar to one another in the sense that you configure all three of them with a **start** and an **end** time.

Listing 13.50 exhibits an example configuration of a **time-range** using **weekdays** and **weekend**.

Listing 13.50 An example of a time-range configuration using weekdays and weekend

```
time-range "home-time" create
    description "evening and weekend special"
    weekdays start 00:00 end 06:00
    weekdays start 20:00 end 23:59
    weekend start 00:00 end 23:59
exit
```

In the weekly option in the place of just a starting and an ending time of day, you need to specify a starting and an ending time of week. To specify a starting or an ending time of week, you need to specify a day and time. Listing 13.51 illustrates an example configuration of a **time-range** using the **weekly** command.

Listing 13.51 An example of a time-range configuration using the weekly command

```
time-range "cmpt101Lab" create
    weekly start tue,18:00 end tue,20:00
    weekly start thu,18:00 end thu,20:00
exit
```

For **absolute** time, you need to specify absolute (Gregorian) calendar-based times as start and end time. Listing 13.52 shows an example configuration of an **absolute** **time-range**.

Listing 13.52 An example of an absolute time-range configuration

```
time-range "Olympics08" create
    absolute start 2008/08/08,00:00 end 2008/08/24,23:59
exit
```

Listing 13.53 displays the command options available for configuring a
`tod-suite`.

Listing 13.53 Command options for configuring a tod-suite

```
Pod2>config>cron# tod-suite
  - no tod-suite <tod-suite-name>
  - tod-suite <tod-suite-name> [create]

 <tod-suite-name>      : [32 chars max]
 <create>              : keyword - mandatory while creating a new tod-suite


 [no] description      - Specify a description for this tod-suite
      egress           + Configure tod suite egress parameters
      ingress          + Configure tod suite ingress parameters
```

Listing 13.54 shows the command options available for configuring the
`ingress` parameters of `tod-suite`. The options available for configuring the
`egress` parameters are identical to the ones shown in Listing 13.54.

Listing 13.54 Command options for configuring the ingress parameters of a tod-suite

```
A:Pod2>config>cron>tod-suite$ ingress
  - ingress

 [no] filter          - Specify an ingress filter for this tod-suite
 [no] qos             - Specify an ingress qos policy for this tod-suite
 [no] scheduler-poli* - Specify an ingress scheduler policy for this tod-suite
```

Table 13.4 summarizes the policies and filters that are applicable under the
`ingress` and the `egress` of a `tod-suite`.

Table 13.4 Policies/Filters Applicable under a tod-suite

Ingress	Egress
IP filter	IP filter
IPv6 filter	IPv6 filter
MAC filter	MAC filter
SAP-ingress policy	SAP-egress policy
Scheduler policy	Scheduler policy

Listing 13.55 exhibits an example configuration for `tod-suite`. While mapping a filter or a policy either under ingress or egress of a `tod-suite`, optionally an existing time-range and an optional priority value can be specified. The priority value ranges from 1 through 10, and the default value is 5.

Listing 13.55 An example configuration for tod-suite

```
tod-suite "ResidentialFocus" create
    egress
        qos 4663 time-range "home-time"
    exit
    ingress
        filter ip 4663 time-range "home-time" priority 3
        qos 4663 time-range "home-time"
        scheduler-policy "homeIngress" time-range "home-time"
    exit
exit
```

If no `time-range` is specified, the policy is always applied (as if directly applying under the ingress or egress configurations of a SAP). The optional priority range helps to tie-break when multiple conflicting policies are mapped. The lower the priority value, the higher the preference the associated policy has.

A `tod-suite` can be applied either under any service SAP configuration or under a customer `multi-service-site` configuration. Listing 13.56 shows an example service configuration in which a `tod-suite` is applied under a SAP.

Listing 13.56 An example of a tod-suite applied under a service SAP

```
vpls 100 customer 1 create
    stp
        shutdown
    exit
    sap 1/2/2 create
        tod-suite "ResidentialFocus"
    exit
    spoke-sdp 1:100 create
    exit
    no shutdown
exit
```

Listing 13.57 exhibits a customer configuration in which a tod-suite is applied under a multi-service-site.

Listing 13.57 An example of a tod-suite applied under a customer multi-service-site configuration

```
customer 5419 create
    multi-service-site "Blackwillow" create
        assignment port 1/1/2
        tod-suite "ResidentialFocus"
    exit
    description "Metcalfe Networks"
    contact "Ramesh"
exit
```

Verification Commands for Time-Based Policies

Listing 13.58 shows the high-level command options available under show cron. These commands can be invoked without any optional parameters. For example, the command show cron action will list information about all the action instances configured under cron. Alternatively, these commands can be invoked along with the name of a specific instance. For example, the command show cron action can be invoked along with the name of an action instance to get information about that specific instance, as in the case of show cron action Test_BE.

Listing 13.59 displays a sample output of the command show cron schedule
<schedule-name>. As evident in the sample output, the listed information
includes details about the associated action and script of the schedule. The
field, Administrative status, indicates whether the schedule has been enabled
by configuring it to be no shutdown. The Operational status indicates if the
schedule has completed the scheduled runs or not.

Listing 13.59 A sample output of the show cron schedule <schedule-name> command

```
A:Pod2# show cron schedule example2

===============================================================================
CRON Schedule Information
===============================================================================
Schedule                  : example2
Schedule owner            : TiMOS CLI
Description               : An example for periodic schedule
Administrative status     : enabled
Operational status        : finished
Action                    : Test_BE
Action owner              : TiMOS CLI
Script                    : BEQoSTest
Script Owner              : TiMOS CLI
Script source location    : ftp://*:*@192.168.0.100/./pod2/BEQoSTest.txt
Script results location   : ftp://*:*@192.168.0.100/./pod2/BEQoSResults
Schedule type             : periodic
Interval                  : 0d 00:02:00 (120 seconds)
Repeat count              : 2
```

(continued)

```
Next scheduled run        : None - periodic schedule has completed
End time                  : 2007/09/26 15:30
Weekday                   : none
Month                     : none
Day of month              : none
Hour                      : none
Minute                    : none
Number of schedule runs   : 2
Last schedule run         : 2007/09/26 15:17:37
Number of schedule failures : 0
Last schedule failure     : no error
Last failure time         : never


===============================================================================
```

Listing 13.60 shows the three different syntaxes supported by the show cron time-range family of commands.

Listing 13.60 Syntaxes supported by the show cron time-range command family

```
A:Pod2>show>cron# time-range
  - time-range [<name>]
  - time-range <name> associations
  - time-range [<name>] detail

 <name>            : [32 chars max]
 <detail>          : keyword
 <associations>    : keyword
```

Listing 13.61 displays a sample output of the show cron time-range <time-range-name> associations command. As evident from the sample output, the command lists all the entities with which the specified time-range is specified.

```
A:Pod2>show>cron# time-range home-time associations
===============================================================================
Cron time-range associations
===============================================================================
Name           : home-time                State: Inactive
Description :
evening and weekend special
-------------------------------------------------------------------------------
IP Filter associations
-------------------------------------------------------------------------------
IP filter Id: 4565, entry 10
-------------------------------------------------------------------------------
MAC Filter associations
-------------------------------------------------------------------------------
None
-------------------------------------------------------------------------------
Tod-suite associations
-------------------------------------------------------------------------------
ToD-suite: ResidentialFocus, for Ingress Ip Filter 4663
ToD-suite: ResidentialFocus, for Ingress Qos Policy 4663
ToD-suite: ResidentialFocus, for Ingress Scheduler Policy homeIngress
ToD-suite: ResidentialFocus, for Egress Qos Policy 4663
===============================================================================
```

Listing 13.62 shows the three different syntaxes supported by the show cron tod-suite family of commands.

Listing 13.62 Syntaxes supported by the show cron tod-suite command family

```
A:Pod2>show>cron# tod-suite
  - tod-suite [<tod-suite-name>] [detail]
  - tod-suite [<tod-suite-name>] associations
  - tod-suite [<tod-suite-name>] failed-associations

<tod-suite-name>    : [32 chars max]
<detail>            : keyword
<associations>      : keyword
<failed-associatio*> : keyword
```

Listing 13.63 exhibits a sample output of the `show cron tod-suite <tod-suite-name> detail` command. As listed in the sample output, the command shows all the filters and polices configured within the `tod-suite`, `time-range` and the priority associated with each filter/policy, and whether the filter/policy is active at the time of invoking the `show` command.

Listing 13.63 A sample output of the show cron tod-suite <tod-suite-name> detail command

```
A:Pod2>show>cron# tod-suite ResidentialFocus detail
===============================================================================
Cron tod-suite details
===============================================================================
Name         : ResidentialFocus
Type / Id                      Time-range                  Prio  State
-------------------------------------------------------------------------------
Ingress Ip Filter
  4663                         home-time                     3    Inact
Ingress Qos Policy
  4663                         home-time                     5    Inact
Ingress Scheduler Policy
  homeIngress                  home-time                     5    Inact
Egress Qos Policy
  4663                         home-time                     5    Inact
  1                            NO-TIME-RANGE                  1    Activ
===============================================================================
```

Listing 13.64 shows a sample output of the `show cron tod-suite <tod-suite-name> associations` command. The command lists all the entities with which the `tod-suite` is associated.

Listing 13.64 A sample output of the show cron tod-suite <tod-suite-name> associations command

```
A:Pod2>show>cron# tod-suite ResidentialFocus associations


===============================================================================
Cron tod-suite associations for suite ResidentialFocus
===============================================================================

Service associations
```

(continued)

```
-----------------------------------------------------------------------
Service Id  : 100                      Type    : VPLS
   SAP 1/2/2
-----------------------------------------------------------------------
Number of SAP's : 1

Customer Multi-Service Site associations
-----------------------------------------------------------------------
Multi Service Site: Blackwillow
-----------------------------------------------------------------------
Number of MSS's: 1
=======================================================================
```

Summary

This chapter began with a discussion on LAG and SLA adaptation over an access LAG. Multiple Ethernet ports between two network nodes are aggregated and used in parallel to form a LAG. LAGs are configured for two main reasons: to increase bandwidth between the connecting two nodes and to provide redundancy in the event of failure of one or more participating links, ports, MDAs, or IOMs. However, when an access LAG spreads over more than one IOM, any SLA associated with the LAG had to be adapted to the components links of the LAG. There are two types of such adaptation: link and distribute. Under link adaptation each link gets a full share of the SLA, whereas under distribute adaptation the SLA would be distributed among the participants IOM proportional to their bandwidth share in the LAG.

Link Fragmentation and Interleaving is an important QoS feature for low-speed links, particularly when both high-priority traffic and a jumbo-sized low-priority traffic use the same link. A high-priority datagram would experience an excessive delay if it arrived at the egress interface of a low-speed link just when transmission of a jumbo-sized datagram started over the link. In order to avoid such an excessive delay with a high-priority datagram, the LFI feature fragments the jumbo-sized low-priority datagram and interleaves the high-priority datagram over the low-speed links.

QoS policy overrides provide the flexibility of having exceptions and customization of SLAs for some of the customers in applications such as a triple-play service without creating custom access QoS policies or Scheduler policies.

The Service Assurance Agent helps the service provider in determining the quality of service experienced by different application traffic in the different segments of a network. SAA can raise alarms and warn the service provider before customers experience any deterioration of network service.

Finally, you learned about time-based QoS. ALSRP offers two types of time dependencies: time-triggered actions and time range. Time-triggered actions trigger scripts at configured times and, from a QoS perspective, can help to run SAA periodically. Time ranges are helpful for enabling QoS and filter policies for a specified period of time.

Designing Quality of Service

3

Part 3 introduces you to some of the best practices and principles related to designing QoS, and to the service requirements of common application traffic. They include a step-by-step approach for designing QoS in a multi-service network, and case studies on how to evaluate different design options.

QoS Design Principles and Service Requirements

14

A QoS design should reinforce and enhance the characteristics of a good network design. The QoS design for a commercial network should both enhance the quality of experience of the subscribers and maximize the revenue generated out of the network.

Chapter Objectives

- To explain the principles of designing QoS for an IP/MPLS network
- To describe the service requirements of common application traffic
- To explain the approach to designing QoS for an IP/MPLS network

Part 2 of this book described a wide spectrum of QoS features, including traffic classification, buffering, scheduling, and rate-limiting. You have learned about the need for these features, how they function, how they impact different sets of traffic classes, how to configure the features in ALSRP, and the commands to verify their performance. Building on the knowledge from the previous chapters, this chapter provides an overview of QoS design in an IP/MPLS network using ALSRP to demonstrate the configuration and implementation of the design.

This chapter is only an introduction to the much larger topic of QoS design, which includes:

- Analyzing best practices and principles.
- Understanding the service requirements of different application traffic and designing to meet their needs.
- Configuring QoS features according to a node's role (CPE, PE, or P-node within a LAN, WAN, VPN or triple-play network).
- Optimizing for a balance between network resource utilization and network redundancy, protecting networks against malicious attacks.

The details of these topics could fill an entire book.

14.1 Understanding QoS Design Principles

Throughout Part 2 of the book, we noted the best practices related to individual QoS features. This section discusses the best practices related to the design of a network as a whole.

Best Practices for Designing QoS to Substantiate the Characteristics of a Good Network Design

A QoS design should reinforce and enhance the characteristics of a good network design:

- A network design should be able to offer and deliver all the services requested by users.
- A network design should honor the offered service level agreements (SLAs) of different application traffic. The essence of enabling QoS features within a network is to satisfy this characteristic. In order to enhance the service delivery of

one application, do not compromise the service commitments of another application's traffic under normal operating conditions. However, under extreme conditions (such as link or node failures), it may not be possible to fully satisfy the service requirements of all the application traffic. In such conditions, preference should be given to the service requirements of high-priority and critical application traffic.

- A network's performance should be predictable. Not only should the performance and the behavior of the network be predictable, but so should its configuration. In other words, the configuration choices should be consistent and intuitive in all the nodes of a network. For example, you should use the same set of queues (same identification numbers) for a given forwarding class at all queuing points throughout the network. Another example of consistency is to match a SAP-ingress policy ID to its corresponding SAP-egress policy ID wherever possible.

- A network should be scalable. A scalable network is capable of adequately supporting growth without having to drastically redesign it. Scalability considerations should be reflected in both the macro and micro levels of design choices. For example, at the macro level, opting for the Differentiated Services (DiffServ) QoS model is better in terms of scalability than the IntServ QoS model. As an example at the micro level, try to match a subnet address in an `ip-criteria` configured within a SAP-ingress policy, instead of matching all the individual addresses of the subnet.

- A network should be robust. A robust network is capable of withstanding a variety of link/node failures and malicious attacks. The QoS design must take into account the reliability mechanisms implemented in the network so that the QoS design works in the different failure scenarios considered for the network. For example, in case of link failure, traffic will be rerouted to other links, and even with the additional traffic, those segments should strive to meet service requirements of different application traffic flowing through them.

- A network should be cost-efficient. The business objectives of a network should merit the choices of the components of the network. Moreover, having QoS features helps reduce the operational cost of the network and support network convergence. The objective of an optimal QoS design is to satisfy service requirements of different application traffic, while maximizing the network resource utilization.

- A network should be easy to maintain and troubleshoot. There are many aspects of QoS design that either enhance or impact the maintenance and ease of troubleshooting of the configuration. Examples of such elements are noted throughout the chapter.

Successful QoS Design for Commercial Networks

A successful QoS design for a commercial network has to strive to achieve the following two goals:

- Enhancing the end customer network experience
- Maximizing the revenue generated from the network

In order to enhance the end customer experience, the network must first and foremost be reliable. Furthermore, the service commitments for all the services offered through the network should be honored, if not exceeded, at all times.

The service requirements of end customers may change very often, sometimes multiple times within the same day! Therefore, a successful QoS design should be readily adaptable to changes, and the means to make the QoS changes should be easy and timely. As you learned from Chapter 13, adapting QoS at the time of need will also benefit the service providers.

In order to maximize the revenue generated from a network, the business case that drives the QoS design has to take into consideration the following service categories, services that:

- Generate maximum profit
- Generate the most revenue
- Are most heavily used
- Are essential and unavoidable
- Consume a lot of bandwidth

To maximize the revenue generated by a network, the QoS design should not only strive to maximize the network resource utilization but also to optimize the resource allocation for the above five service categories.

Successful QoS Design for Enterprise/Organizational Networks

The successful implementation of a QoS design for an enterprise/organizational network may require more than just technical resources; political stakes may also play a role. In an enterprise/organizational network, differential service treatment may put some departments at a disadvantage. Different departments may use different applications; thus, preferential treatment of one department's application traffic may occur at the cost of another department's traffic. More explicitly, an enterprise/organization may give priority to the network needs of one department over the network needs of another department.

If there is no consensus on the differential treatment achieved by QoS design, the design may not be implemented successfully for nontechnical reasons. Therefore, in such cases it is preferable to obtain consensus or executive backing before implementing a QoS design.

Best Practices for Enhancing Ease of Maintenance and Troubleshooting

The following list indicates Best Practices for QoS design that make it easy to maintain and troubleshoot your network:

- A predictable and intuitive configuration is easy to maintain and troubleshoot. The KISS principle ("keep it short and simple") applies to any network design, and is of particular importance to QoS design. Complex designs are difficult to understand, maintain, and troubleshoot. Follow the KISS principle when it comes to choosing QoS features for a network and when configuring QoS features.

- Not all the QoS features may be required for a QoS design. Use only those QoS features that would enhance the quality of the service delivery of the network under consideration.

- Always use the most straightforward form of a configuration. For example, if a Scheduler policy (or a SAP-ingress, SAP-egress, filter policy) is always going to be active, apply it directly under a SAP instead of applying the policy through a `tod-suite`.

- The importance of good documentation cannot be overstressed. Internal documentation is written as a part of the command line configuration. Internal documentation should be concise, yet provide sufficient relevant details to be clear when read by network Operation and Maintenance personnel who may not have been involved with the initial design. External documentation should describe the network design considerations in detail, and it should be thorough. Often the initial documentation effort is thorough, but later modifications are not captured in the documentation. Therefore, in order to keep the documentation effective, the documents should be updated with any modifications done to the network and to the configuration of the nodes within the network.

- Not only are active field nodes often used as lab nodes to test out configurations, but these test configurations are usually left to accumulate in the nodes. These unnecessary configurations residing in a node add complications to the troubleshooting activities done on the node. Furthermore, using in-service equipment to test a new configuration is always risky, as an incorrect configuration could have undesirable consequences, affecting service.

Validating before Deployment

Before implementing a QoS design on a production network, you should perform a proof-of-concept (POC) test in a lab and validate the design.

Once the POC has passed, implementation of the design can begin. However, a QoS design can be implemented in stages, and each stage can be validated before proceeding to the next stage.

14.2 Service Requirements of Common Application Traffic

This section describes the service requirements of the common application traffic of a multi-service network. Network control, voice, video, gaming, and data applications are some of the common multi-service network application traffic considered.

Network Control Traffic Service Requirements

The control plane traffic includes protocol (such as RIP, OSPF, IS-IS, BGP, LDP, RSVP, PIM) traffic and management (such as Telnet, SNMP, SSH, FTP) traffic. Without control plane protocol traffic a network cannot function, and without control plane management traffic the network cannot be managed. Therefore, it is crucial to have proper QoS configuration for this traffic.

As you learned in Chapter 3, RFC 791 recommended IP precedence value 7 for network control traffic and value 6 for internetwork control traffic. Later, RFC 2474 mapped IP precedence values 7 and 6 to differentiated service code point (DSCP) values NC2 (CS7) and NC1 (CS6), respectively. In ALSRP, by default NC2 and

NC1 DSCP values are mapped to NC and H1 forwarding classes, respectively. Consistent with the RFCs, all the internetwork control traffic is internally marked with a DSCP marking of NC1.

Mapping network management traffic to the H2 forwarding class with a DSCP marking of AF41 is suggested. Therefore, all the network management packets are internally marked with a DSCP marking of AF41 and mapped to the H2 forwarding class by the default Network QoS policy.

Network protocol traffic is time and loss sensitive. Network management traffic requires assured forwarding. Therefore, for both the classes of traffic adequate bandwidth should be committed.

Often Operation and Maintenance (OAM) traffic (such as ping, traceroute, lsp-ping, mac-trace, etc.) is considered to be network control traffic. These packets are forwarded to the BE forwarding class by default. However, configuration options allow you to map these packets to any of the eight forwarding classes (mapping OAM utilities to different forwarding classes is covered in Chapter 13).

VoIP Service Requirements

Voice over IP (VoIP) application traffic consists of two different traffic streams: a bearer stream and a call-signaling stream. In an ALSRP network, it is recommended that you forward both the streams to one forwarding class, either H1 or EF; correspondingly, these types of traffic can be marked with a DSCP marking of NC1 or EF. However, if a distinct DSCP marking is required for signaling packets, then CS3 is recommended.

Note: CS3 is not mapped to any forwarding class in the default Network policy. Therefore, if CS3 is used a new Network policy should be created and applied to accommodate the CS3 mapping.

According to the ITU standard G.114 for voice application, a one-way end-to-end latency (speaker to listener) of less than 150 ms is acceptable and greater than 400 ms is unacceptable. The standard also suggests that as the latency increases from 150 ms and approaches 400 ms, there will be performance degradation. However, in practice a one-way end-to-end latency of 200 ms is considered acceptable without having any significant impact on the voice quality.

Playout buffers of the end devices dictate the acceptable level of jitter. Recently, adaptive playout buffers have become more common. An adaptive playout buffer makes the jitter requirement for voice traffic a bit more lenient. Typically a jitter of 20 ms is considered acceptable.

The number of packets lost, loss pattern, and location of packet loss all have an impact on the perceived speech quality of VoIP. (For more information on this, see *Perceived Speech Quality Prediction for Voice Over IP-Based Networks* by L. F. Sun, and E. C. Ifeachor; *IEEE International Conference on Communications*, Volume 4, 2002.) Internal packet loss concealment algorithms in codecs such as G.711, G.729, and G.723.1 can minimize the impact of a few widespread and non-consecutive packet losses. In practice, a widespread packet loss of less than one percent is deemed acceptable.

The factors impacting the required bandwidth of a VoIP call are the sampling rate, the codec algorithm used, and the packet overhead. Based on these factors, bandwidth required for a VoIP call can range anywhere between 17 Kbps (kilobits/sec) and 192 Kbps.

Interactive Video and Gaming Service Requirements

Traffic from applications such as video conferencing, interactive TV, and interactive video gaming falls into this category. These applications' traffic mostly includes the audio codec. Moreover, the user interaction with these applications is in real time. These applications are gaining popularity. If a network specializes in supporting interactive TV and interactive video gaming applications, a separate forwarding class is suggested for this class of traffic within that network. Otherwise, these applications' traffic can be mapped to the same forwarding class as that of broadcast TV (BTV) channel traffic.

Because of the inclusion of the audio codec for voice within these applications' traffic, the service requirements for aspects, such as latency, jitter, and loss, are the same as for VoIP. However, bandwidth requirements for this traffic varies widely, and the traffic is also bursty. The committed bandwidth for the corresponding forwarding class queue should accommodate the full burst.

Streaming Video Service Requirements

Streaming video traffic can be classified into two categories: BTV and Video on Demand (VoD). These two types of application traffic can differ significantly from a network service requirement point of view. Typically, only one stream of traffic for each BTV channel is transmitted through a network core, and this stream may be subscribed to by any number of end users. For each VoD subscriber, a separate traffic stream is transmitted.

Almost all the end applications use the User Datagram Protocol (UDP) or Real-time Transport Protocol (RTP) for transporting the BTV traffic stream. However, some of the end applications use the Transmission Control Protocol (TCP) for transporting VoD traffic stream. Playout buffers meant for a BTV channel typically accommodate 4 to 5 seconds of traffic, while a playout buffer meant for VoD can accommodate anywhere from 10 seconds to a few hours.

The suggested forwarding classes for the streaming video traffic are EF or H2. If different forwarding classes are required for BTV and VoD traffic, then EF is suggested for BTV and H2 for VoD. Depending on the mapping of the forwarding class, a DSCP marking of EF or AF41 is recommended.

The worst-case targeted latency for these applications' traffic is usually dependent on the playout buffer capacity of the end application devices. However, some end applications (either explicitly or implicitly by virtue of using TCP) request any missing packets; in such cases, the packet request timer threshold should be taken into consideration. Typically, the targeted latency including worst-case jitter should not exceed 4 to 5 seconds.

The worst-case packet loss for streaming video traffic again depends on whether the end application requests the retransmission of any missing packets. If the end application ignores any missing packets, then a widespread (not a burst of loss) loss of less than 1 percent is acceptable.

The bandwidth requirement for streaming video varies widely depending on a number of factors, including the sampling rate of the video stream, encoding format used, underlying protocols (UDP or RTP), packet and Layer 2 overhead, standard or high-definition content, and packet sizes. Typically for standard-definition BTV channel content, 3–4 Mbps (megabits/sec) is allocated, and for high-definition content 8–12 Mbps is allocated. The committed bandwidth for the corresponding forwarding class queue should accommodate the full burst.

Data Service Requirements

Generally, summarizing QoS requirements for data traffic is difficult. There are thousands of data applications, and their QoS requirements vary widely. Some are extremely sensitive to packet loss, some to latency, some to jitter, and some to all three. Some applications put heavy demand on bandwidth. The packet sizes and traffic characteristics also vary widely. Some applications use TCP, and others use UDP. Thus, the differences are many.

Typically, the data traffic is broadly categorized into the following four different categories for QoS requirement consideration: mission-critical data, transactional data, assured data, and best-effort data.

Why Recommend More Than One Forwarding Class for Each Application Category?

All the application categories may not necessarily be supported in a network. Therefore, depending on the application categories, the service provider may prefer one forwarding class over another. The options provide increased flexibility.

Mission-Critical Data

The data application that has high strategic or commercial importance for a network service provider falls into this category. Supervisory Control and Data Acquisition (SCADA) or real-time automated control system traffic, and database application query traffic supporting real-time transaction applications are considered mission-critical data. These applications tend to have smaller packet size and usually are packet loss and time sensitive.

The H2 or L1 forwarding class is recommended for mission-critical data. If the H2 forwarding class is used, then DSCP markings of AF4x (AF41 for high-queuing priority, AF42 for implicitly choosing the packet profile through a profile mode access queue, and AF43 for low-queuing priority) are recommended. If the L1 forwarding class is used, then DSCP markings of AF3x or AF2x are recommended.

Adequate bandwidth should be guaranteed, and in particular there should be sufficient committed bandwidth for high-queuing priority packets. If the applications are time sensitive and the L1 forwarding class is used, configuring the associated queue's arbitrator type selector parameter as **expedite** is recommended.

Transactional Data

Any application traffic that has a high level of importance to the service provider but is not considered mission-critical data falls into this category.

The L1 or AF forwarding classes are recommended. If the L1 forwarding class is used, DSCP markings of AF3x or AF2x are recommended. If the AF forwarding class is used, DSCP markings of AF1x are recommended. Adequate bandwidth should be guaranteed, and in particular there should be sufficient committed bandwidth for high-queuing priority packets.

Assured Data

Essential applications' traffic such as database synchronization, network-based backups, email, and FTP traffic falls into this category. For assured data traffic the L2 forwarding class and DSCP marking of CS1 are recommended. If a secondary DSCP marking is required to separate high- and low-queuing priority packets, then CS1 is suggested for high-queuing priority packets and CP6 is recommended for low-queuing priority packets.

> **Note:** CP6 is not mapped to any forwarding class in the default Network policy. Therefore, if CP6 is used, a new Network policy should be created and applied to accommodate the CP6 mapping.

For this class of traffic reasonable bandwidth should be committed at least for high-queuing priority packets. As discussed in Chapter 12, the peak information rate (PIR) of associated network queues should be configured close to 100 percent to maximize the network utilization in the absence of any higher-priority traffic.

Best-Effort Data

All miscellaneous traffic falls into this category. There are no service commitments associated with the class. The BE forwarding class and DSCP marking of BE are recommended. All the datagrams are to be marked as low-queuing priority.

If required, best-effort data can coexist along with assured-type data within the same forwarding class. In such cases, all BE data traffic should be marked as low-queuing priority and assured-type data traffic markings can be either high- or low-queuing priority, depending on the access ingress policing function. Reasonable bandwidth should be guaranteed for high-queuing priority assured-type data datagrams. If the two classes are forwarded to the L2 forwarding class, CS1 and CP6 DSCP markings are recommended. However, if the two classes are forwarded to the BE forwarding class, CS1 and BE DSCP markings are suggested.

14.3 QoS Design Approach: A Case Study

This section uses a case study to show you a step-by-step approach for designing QoS in an ALSRP network. BankNet is an imaginary service provider, specializing in providing VPN services to banks for interconnecting their branch offices to their headquarters and bank machines (automated teller machines) to their operations center. Figure 14.1 shows BankNet's network.

Figure 14.1 An Example of a Service Provider Network Interconnecting Banks and Bank-Machine Terminals

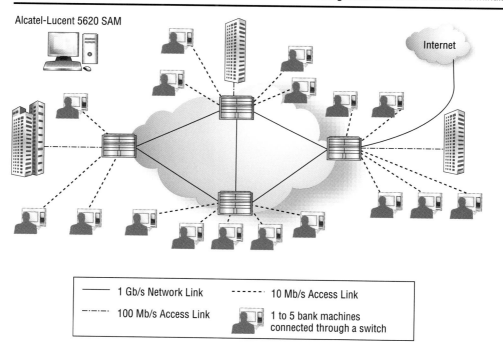

As a service differentiation, BankNet also offers video telephony services at bank machine locations. Using the video telephones, bank customers can seek limited assistance from a bank officer from any bank machine location.

Step 1: Identify the Services and Applications to be Supported

The first step in the QoS design is to determine which services and applications your network will need to support. For a new commercial network, the services and applications to be supported can be identified from the business objectives for the network. Our example service provider, BankNet, wants to offer video conferencing, VoIP and data services to its customers.

For noncommercial networks (such as those belonging to institutions and organizations) similar information can be obtained through network application analysis.

For existing networks, this information can be obtained through the combination of analysis of the existing network traffic, projected growth plans, and analysis of new targeted applications for the network.

Step 2: Categorize All the Applications into Different Classes of Services

In this step, you assign the applications into different classes of services based on a combination of the strategic and commercial importance of each application, and its service requirements.

You may ask why the strategic or commercial importance of an application should be considered when categorizing the application traffic into a class of service. Depending on its relative importance, you could map video traffic, for example, to either a high-priority- or best-effort-type forwarding class.

If it is a requirement for your network to support the video traffic, you should map the application traffic to either the EF or H2 forwarding class, as recommended in the previous section. On the other hand, suppose that this is a specialized network giving high importance to mission-critical data, and video traffic is meant for the entertainment of the employees at remote locations. In that case, there is no harm in mapping the application traffic to one of the low-priority forwarding classes or even to the BE forwarding class. Thus, the class mapping should reflect the relative priority of the application.

Table 14.1 summarizes the classes of service categorization of the identified applications in the BankNet example.

Table 14.1 Categorizing Applications into Classes of Service for the BankNet Example

Classes of Service	Application
Network control	All network control protocol traffic
Real-time communication	VoIP, video telephones, video conferencing
Transaction data	ATM and branch transaction data, network management traffic
Assured-type data	DB sync and backup, email
Best-effort data	Internet applications

Step 3: Based on Functional Groups of Nodes, Create One or More Network Policies

Before creating the network QoS configuration, you must identify the different functional groups of nodes in the network. A *functional group of nodes* is a collection of nodes within a network that has the same network function or service behavior.

In most common types of network you would have only one functional group of nodes, whose function is to transport the aggregated traffic between SAPs across the network.

In some sophisticated networks, for example triple-play networks, there can be more than one functional group of nodes. In a triple-play architecture, as suggested in the *Triple-Play Guide*, which is a part of the ALSRP product manuals, there are the following three functional groups of ALSRP nodes: Broadband Service Aggregator (BSA), Broadband Service Router (BSR), and Application Head-end routers. BSAs perform subscriber-specific functions, BSRs do the core routing, and Head-end routers perform application-specific functions. The suggested triple-play architecture is illustrated in Figure 14.2.

In networks that have only one core functional group of nodes, only one set of network QoS mappings (classes of service to forwarding class and forwarding class to network queues) is required for the entire network. In networks that have multiple functional groups of nodes, more than one set of QoS mappings may be required.

For the rest of this discussion, it is assumed that the network has only one core functional group, and therefore only one set of QoS mappings is required.

Figure 14.2 Different Functional Groups of Nodes in a Triple-Play Architecture

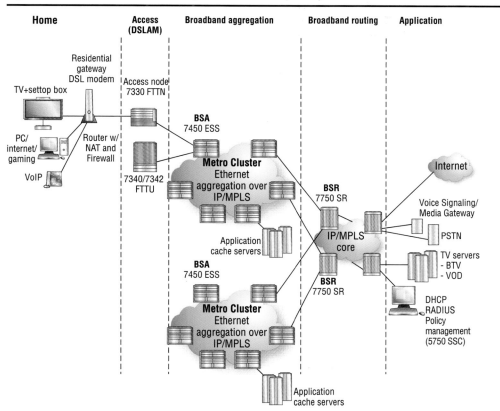

In this step, you map the classes of services determined in the previous step to different forwarding classes. Determine the classes of service for which high- and low-queuing priority packets have to be distinguished. Assign a DSCP marking for different queuing priorities within each forwarding class. If the network core is going to be based on MPLS switching, then assign an EXP marking for different queuing priorities within each forwarding class. Using the mapping and QoS markings that you have determined, create a Network QoS policy.

Table 14.2 summarizes the forwarding class mapping and QoS markings for different classes of service identified for the BankNet example.

Table 14.2 BankNet Example Mapping of Classes of Traffic to Forwarding Classes and QoS Markings

CoS	FC	Queuing Priority	DSCP	EXP
Network control	H1	High	NC1	6
Real-time communication	EF	High	EF	5
Transaction data	H2	High	AF41	4
		Low	AF42	4
Assured data	AF	High	AF11	3
		Low	AF13	2
Best-effort data	BE	Low	BE	0

For the BankNet example, the default network QoS policy is sufficient. However, to follow the best practice, the default policy is copied into a new policy with a description to identify that this is the Network policy applied to BankNet. Listing 14.1 shows the BankNet example Network QoS policy. Unused mappings and markings copied from the default policy are not shown in the code.

Listing 14.1 Network QoS policy for the BankNet example

```
network 7 create
    description "BankNet network QoS policy"
    scope template
    ingress
        default-action fc be profile out
        no ler-use-dscp
        dscp be fc be profile out
        dscp ef fc ef profile in
        dscp nc1 fc h1 profile in
        dscp nc2 fc nc profile in
        dscp af11 fc af profile in
        dscp af13 fc af profile out
        dscp af41 fc h2 profile in
        dscp af42 fc h2 profile out
        lsp-exp 0 fc be profile out
        lsp-exp 2 fc af profile out
        lsp-exp 3 fc af profile in
        lsp-exp 4 fc h2 profile in
        lsp-exp 5 fc ef profile in
```

(continued)

```
                lsp-exp 6 fc h1 profile in
                lsp-exp 7 fc nc profile in
        exit
        egress
            no remarking
            fc af
                dscp-in-profile af11
                dscp-out-profile af12
                lsp-exp-in-profile 3
                lsp-exp-out-profile 2
            exit
            fc be
                dscp-in-profile be
                dscp-out-profile be
                lsp-exp-in-profile 0
                lsp-exp-out-profile 0
            exit
            fc ef
                dscp-in-profile ef
                dscp-out-profile ef
                lsp-exp-in-profile 5
                lsp-exp-out-profile 5
            exit
            fc h2
                dscp-in-profile af41
                dscp-out-profile af42
                lsp-exp-in-profile 4
                lsp-exp-out-profile 4
            exit
            fc h1
                dscp-in-profile nc1
                dscp-out-profile nc1
                lsp-exp-in-profile 6
                lsp-exp-out-profile 6
            exit
        exit
    exit
exit
```

This Network QoS policy is to be provisioned on all the ALSRP nodes within the network regardless of their speed or media, in order to ensure that the traffic is treated in the same manner across the entire network.

Step 4: Determine Queue Parameters and Configure Network-Queue Policies

As in the case of Step 3, depending on the number of functional groups of nodes in the network, one or more Network-Queue policies may be required. Also if there are drastic differences between different network interface transmission rates, different Network-Queue policies may be required to adapt queue parameter configurations according to the interface speeds. For the remainder of this section, it is assumed that only one Network-Queue policy is sufficient for the network. To configure a Network-Queue policy, you need to map the different forwarding classes shortlisted in Step 3 to queues. For each queue, appropriate queue parameters have to be determined depending on the service requirement of the traffic mapped to them. As discussed in Chapter 12, the parameter values of a queue in relationship to each other dictates the type of rate-limiting approach enforced over the traffic flowing through the queue. Table 14.3 (shown earlier as Table 12.1) summarizes the rate-limiting approaches recommended for different types of application traffic at different network points.

The values for queue parameters can be determined in the following order: rate (CIR and PIR) parameters, buffer size (CBS and MBS) parameters, HPO threshold. Change the default arbitrator selection rule and adaptation rule of a queue only if it is essential for the service requirements of a given network scenario.

Map Forwarding Class to Unicast and Multicast Queue

For each forwarding class, you need to allocate a forwarding queue. If multicast traffic is supported in the network, then for each forwarding class allocate a multicast queue as well. For most scenarios, the default Network-Queue policy's queue mapping for forwarding classes would be suitable, because in the default Network-Queue policy each forwarding class has its own unicast queue and multicast queue.

If the default Network-Queue QoS policy is suitable for the network under consideration, follow the best practice of making a copy of the default Network-Queue QoS policy and customize it as needed.

Table 14.3 Rate-Limiting Approaches Suitable for Different Types of Traffic and for Different Network Points

Rate-Limiting Approach	Parameter Relationship	Effect on Datagrams	Traffic Type Suitable to Regulate	Network Point to Apply	Comments
Policing by discarding	$PIR = CIR = SpR$ $CBS = 0$ and $MBS = 1$	Traffic is strictly policed at the specified rate (SpR). All the excess datagrams are dropped.	Real time	Access ingress	For T1/E1 rates or for rates less than that, use the `police` keyword option.
Policing by tagging	$PIR > CIR = SpR$ $MBS > CBS \propto CIR$ $0 < HPO < 100\%$	Excessive datagrams are tagged as out-of-profile, and conforming datagrams are tagged as in-profile.	Assured-type and best-effort-type forwarding classes	Access ingress	For adopting the approach for best-effort traffic, configure $CIR = 0$ so that all the datagrams of the traffic type will be tagged as out-of-profile.
Soft policing	$PIR > CIR = SpR$ $MBS > CBS \propto CIR$ $0 < HPO < 100\%$	Drops out-of-profile datagrams before dropping in-profile datagrams under congestion.	Assured-type and best-effort-type forwarding classes	Network egress Network ingress Access egress	Although the queue parameters' relationship is the same as that of the policing by tagging approach, recall only access ingress queues have the ability to tag datagrams, and queues at other network points rely on tagging done by access ingress queues.
Shaping	$PIR = CIR = SpR$ $MBS \geq CBS \propto CIR$	Shapes traffic to the specified rate.	Assured-type forwarding class	Network egress Network ingress Access egress	Suggested only if the flow will be subjected to a downstream policer.
Shapeless policing	$PIR = LR^* > CIR = SpR$ $MBS = CBS \propto CIR^{**}$ $HPO = 100\%$ * PIR need not be LR, but should be sufficiently larger than SpR. ** Keep the buffer sizes to the minimum required.	Expedites datagrams' delivery without shaping.	Real-time	Network egress Network ingress Access egress	Provided that the traffic will not be subjected to a downstream policer.

For the rest of the discussion, it is assumed that each forwarding class in the Network-Queue policy is mapped to its own unicast and multicast queues, which would be the case normally. Therefore, parameters of a queue are referred to as that of the forwarding class to which it is mapped. If multicast traffic is supported in the network, queue parameters for unicast and multicast queues for each of the forwarding classes has to be determined separately.

Determine the Committed Information Rate and the Peak Information Rate

Determine the percentage share of specified rate (SpR) to be allocated in the network core for each forwarding class by taking the following into consideration:

- Traffic and capacity analysis (for an existing network)
- Projected growth plan
- Network failure analysis

Based on the specified rates and the guidelines provided in Table 14.3, determine the CIR and PIR for each of the network queues. As mentioned in Chapter 12, the summary entries in the table are only recommendations, and the configuration may have to be tailored according to the specific needs of different application traffic.

Determine the Committed Buffer Size and the Maximum Buffer Size

Once the CIR and PIR for each forwarding class has been determined, the CBS and MBS can be determined based on the Table 14.3 guidelines. Wherever the buffer parameters are suggested to be in correlation to rate parameters, use Equations 8.1 and 8.2 to determine the values for the buffer parameters. The two equations can be generalized as in Equation 14.1.

Equation 14.1 Generalized Correlation between a Buffer Size and a Traffic Rate

$$BufferSize(KB) = \frac{ServiceRate(kbps) * MaxDelay(sec)}{8}$$

To determine an appropriate value of MaxDelay for a given traffic type, consider its latency and delay tolerance, as discussed in the section titled "Service Requirements of Common Application Traffic," earlier in the chapter.

Determine High Priority Only Threshold

According to the best practices addressed in Chapter 8 and recommendations made in Table 14.3, for forwarding classes in which only high-queuing priority packets are permitted, the high priority only (HPO) can be configured as high as 100 percent. For forwarding classes in which only low-queuing priority packets are expected, the HPO can be configured to be 0 percent.

Therefore, HPO has to be determined only for forwarding classes in which both high- and low-queuing priority packets are expected. By default, HPO is configured to be 10 percent of MBS. For dropping low-queuing priority packets more aggressively under congestion, increase the HPO value, and vice versa.

For the BankNet example, Table 14.4 summarizes the queues mapped to different forwarding classes, and the parameter (CIR, PIR, CBS, MBS, and HPO) values determined for each of the queues.

Table 14.4 Summary of Determined Rates and Buffer Spaces for Unicast Network Queues of the BankNet Example

FC	Q. Id	CIR	PIR	CBS	MBS	HPO
H1	7	5%	15%	0.60%	0.60%	100%
EF	6	30%	40%	1.65%	1.65%	100%
H2	5	25%	40%	5.87%	9%	50%
AF	3	25%	100%	20.00%	100.00%	30%
BE	1	5%	100%	10.00%	100.00%	0%

For H1 and EF forwarding class traffic, shapeless policing has been sought. For H2, AF, and BE forwarding class traffic, soft policing has been implemented. The CBS values are determined taking into consideration the corresponding CIR values, buffer pool size at the network ingress and network egress, and maximum delay tolerated by each class of service. For the BankNet network architecture in Figure 14.1, the per hop maximum delay taken into consideration for the real-time services are summarized in Table 14.5.

Table 14.5 Per-Hop Maximum Delay Considered for Real-Time Services in the BankNet Example

CoS	Max Delay/Hop
Network control	50 ms
Real-time communication	10 ms
Transaction data	100 ms

Because most applications in the BankNet example that contribute traffic to high-priority forwarding classes would be using UDP, it is not desirable to let these traffic types overflow into shared buffer space, which would be managed using Random Early Detection (RED). Therefore, the MBS of these forwarding classes are configured to be equal to their corresponding CBS. However, the MBS of the AF and BE forwarding classes are configured to be 100 percent to let the traffic flowing through these classes maximize the network resource utilization.

Listing 14.2 shows the customized Network-Queue QoS policy configured for BankNet. Configurations not listed in Table 14.4 are stripped from Listing 14.2. The policy is created by copying the default Network-Queue QoS policy and modifying the queue parameters. The queue mappings to forwarding classes of the default policy are kept intact. The parameters of the queues, which are not listed in Table 14.4, are configured as follows:

```
rate 25 cir 0
mbs 10
cbs 0
```

This configuration would ensure that any unexpected traffic flowing through these queues would not be blocked and that these unexpected flows would not significantly impact the performance of the offered services.

Listing 14.2 Network-Queue QoS policy for 1 Gbps interfaces of the BankNet example

```
network-queue "BankNet" create
    description "BankNet network queue QoS policy for 1 Gbps interfaces"
    queue 1 create
        rate 100 cir 5
        cbs 10
        high-prio-only 0
    exit
    ...
    queue 3 create
        rate 100 cir 25
        cbs 20
        high-prio-only 30
    exit
    ...
```

(continued)

```
        queue 5 create
            rate 40 cir 25
            mbs 5.87
            cbs 9
            high-prio-only 50
        exit
        queue 6 create
            rate 40 cir 30
            mbs 1.65
            cbs 1.65
            high-prio-only 100
        exit
        queue 7 create
            rate 15 cir 5
            mbs 0.60
            cbs 0.60
            high-prio-only 100
        exit
        ...
        fc af create
            multicast-queue 11
            queue 3
        exit
        fc be create
            multicast-queue 9
            queue 1
        exit
        fc ef create
            multicast-queue 14
            queue 6
        exit
        fc h1 create
            multicast-queue 15
            queue 7
        exit
        fc h2 create
            multicast-queue 13
            queue 5
        exit
    exit
```

Step 5: Optionally Configure the Reserved Portion Size for Network Ingress and Network Egress Buffer Pools

As discussed in Chapter 8, the size of the reserved portion of buffer pools can be configured either explicitly or implicitly. Table 8-1 summarizes the differences between the explicit and implicit configuration.

The default configuration of a buffer pool allows implicit configuration of the reserved portion size of the buffer pool. Under the implicit configuration, the size of the reserved portion of a buffer pool is automatically determined as the sum of the CBS of the queues configured within the buffer pool.

For the BankNet example, the default implicit configuration of the reserved portion size is sufficient for network ingress and network egress buffer pools.

Step 6: Optionally Enable RED-Based Buffer Management for the Shared Portion of Network Ingress and Network Egress Buffer Pools

RED-based buffer management is available for the shared portion of a buffer pool. RED-based buffer management is discussed in detail in Chapter 8. By default, RED-based buffer management is not enabled. In order to enable RED-based buffer management, a custom Slope policy has to be configured and applied under the appropriate entity. For a network ingress buffer pool, the Slope policy has to be applied under the corresponding media-dependent adapter (MDA) configuration. For a network egress buffer pool, the Slope policy has to be applied under the corresponding port configuration.

When RED is enabled to manage the shared portion of a buffer pool, TCP sources sending traffic through the portion would regulate their transmission rate in response to RED dropping packets belonging to them; however, UDP streams will not be responsive for dropping packets. As a result, TCP streams could be left to starve. Therefore, it is recommended that packets belonging to the non-real-time UDP streams be marked as low-queuing priority.

In the BankNet example, the Network-Queue QoS policy is configured so that only assured-type data and best-effort data traffic use the shared portion of the network buffer pools. Therefore, enabling RED for the network buffer pools would be beneficial. A custom Slope policy is required to enable RED, because RED slopes are disabled in the default Slope policy. Listing 14.3 shows the Slope policy customized for the BankNet example.

Listing 14.3 Slope policy for the BankNet example

```
slope-policy "BankNet" create
    description "BankNet slope policy."
    high-slope
        start-avg 70
        max-avg 90
        max-prob 80
        no shutdown
    exit
    low-slope
        start-avg 50
        max-avg 75
        max-prob 80
        no shutdown
    exit
    time-average-factor 7
exit
```

Figure 14.3 graphically shows how the RED slopes are configured according to the customized (copied from default) Slope policy. The low-slope is for managing low-queuing priority packets, and the high-slope is for managing high-queuing priority packets within the shared portion of a buffer pool.

Figure 14.3 RED Slopes According to the Default Slope Policy Configuration

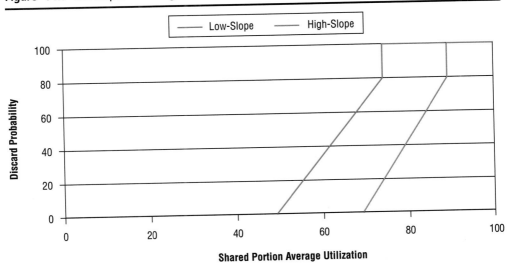

Step 7: Based on Scheduling Needs, Configure Scheduler Policies

You must analyze the traffic to determine if basic scheduling is sufficient for all SAPs/multi-customer-sites in both ingress and egress traffic direction. If the need for hierarchical scheduling is justifiable, then configure Scheduler policies as required. Different SAPs/multi-customer-sites may need different hierarchical scheduling designs, and as a result different Scheduling policies may be required. Also, for a given SAP/multi-customer-site, different Scheduler policies may be required for ingress and egress traffic direction.

In the BankNet example, the basic scheduling is adequate. For an example of the analysis and configuration of a Scheduler policy see Chapter 15.

Step 8: Analyze Service Needs of Application Traffic and Configure SAP-Ingress QoS policies

Unlike Network QoS policies, SAP-ingress (or SAP-egress) policies may not be restricted to one or a few template policies. Different customers may have different service agreements, or even a single customer may have a different service agreement for different sites. Different service level agreements may have conflicts with each other and may not be tackled using one template SAP-ingress policy. Therefore, the first step in configuring access QoS policies (SAP-ingress and SAP-egress policies) is to determine the minimum number of different template policies required.

Best Practices: Having fewer QoS polices makes maintenance and troubleshooting of a node configuration easier.

Remember, if the configuration to accommodate the service requirements of a few SAP instances needs only minor modifications to a template access policy (SAP-ingress, SAP-egress or a Scheduler policy), as discussed in Chapter 13, QoS policy overrides can be used to do the customization.

Once the number of template policies required has been determined, a SAP-ingress policy can be created by analyzing the following factors:

- Criteria to classify different application traffic to forwarding classes.
- Forwarding class to queue mappings.
- Service requirements of each application stream.

- Appropriate rate-limiting technique for each application, including whether the technique should be color-aware.
- The need for ingress marking.
- Is a Scheduler policy used?

In the BankNet example, there are two different types of customer premises equipment (CPEs): bank machines and branch office gateways. The service requirements of different application traffic arriving from the two types of CPEs are substantially different. Therefore, two different template SAP-ingress and SAP-egress policies are required for the SAPs connected to the two different types of CPEs. Furthermore, a separate set of SAP-ingress and SAP-egress policies is required to handle traffic arriving at the SAP, which is acting as the Internet gateway within the network. Similarly, a separate set of SAP-ingress and SAP-egress policies is required for the SAPs connected to the system manager (Alcatel-Lucent 5620 SAM) of the network.

Table 14.6 lists all the application traffic expected at different access ingresses, along with the traffic classification criteria appropriate for classifying the traffic at the access ingress.

Table 14.6: Access Ingress Traffic Classification Criteria for the BankNet Example

Applications	Traffic Classification Criteria
VoIP, video telephone, video conferencing	DSCP marking EF
Bank transaction	DSCP markings AF41 and AF42
Network management SSH Telnet SNMP SNMP Trap	Destination port 22 23 161 162
Assured data POP3 IMAP/IMAP3 FTP IDAP DB Sync	Destination port 110 143/220 21 389 156
Internet applications	Default

To understand the approach for analyzing the service needs of applications and configuring a SAP-ingress policy, consider the example of configuring the template policy required to handle the traffic arriving from the bank machines. For configuring the other SAP-ingress policies, the approach is the same.

From a bank machine, only video telephone and bank transaction traffic are expected. BankNet's service level agreement with its customers suggests that a 1.2 Mbps of bandwidth is sufficient for each video telephone traffic stream in both directions. Similarly, 200 Kbps of bandwidth is required for bank transaction traffic destined to or originating from one bank machine.

The other service requirement for the video telephone application is the same as the VoIP, because of the presence of the voice component. As indicated earlier in this chapter, for VoIP a one way end-to-end delay of 200 ms is tolerable, and a one-way end-to-end jitter of 20 ms is tolerable. Packet loss should be infrequent and should be less than 1 percent. If adequate bandwidth is allocated for the application and if high-priority is given in scheduling the traffic, then the service requirement can be exceeded. Because adequate bandwidth is allocated for the application, the likelihood of congestion occurring is minimal. Therefore, the video telephone application does not require much buffer space.

The video telephone service is a real-time application using RTP. As recommended in Table 14.3, the real-time application traffic will be subjected to a shapeless policing rate-limiting approach at all the network queuing points and will be subjected to policing by discarding at the access ingress. Therefore, let us configure PIR = CIR = specified rate, MBS = 1, CBS = 0, and HPO = 100% for the application.

For bank transaction traffic, a maximum end-to-end one-way delay of 1 second is acceptable and a maximum end-to-end one way jitter of 200 ms is acceptable. Packet loss should be infrequent.

The CBS for the bank transaction traffic can be calculated using a CIR of 200 Kbps and a max delay of 50 ms per hop. The calculated CBS is 1.25 KB, and it can be approximated to 1 KB. Per Table 14.3, bank transaction traffic will be subjected to soft policing at all network queuing points and subjected to policing by tagging at the access ingress. Therefore, we can configure PIR > CIR = specified rate, MBS > CBS $\propto$ CIR, and 0 < HPO < 100% for the application.

Table 14.7 summarizes the queue parameter value for the SAP-ingress QoS policy.

Table 14.7 SAP-Ingress Policy Queue Configuration Summary for the BankNet Example

Application	FC	Q. Type	Q. Id	CIR (Kbps)	PIR (Kbps)	CBS (KB)	MBS (KB)	HPO
Video telephone	EF	U/C	6	1200	1200	0	1	100%
Bank transaction	H2	U/C	5	200	300	1	3	10%

Because the bank machines are properly marking the ToS field of IP packet headers, there is no need for any ingress re-marking. However, for bank transactions traffic color-aware profiling is required. Therefore, we need to use subclasses for the H2 forwarding class for specifying packet profiles, and forward the traffic to a queue created in **profile-mode**. Listing 14.4 shows the SAP-ingress QoS policy.

Listing 14.4 SAP-ingress QoS policy for SAPs connecting bank machines in the BankNet example

```
sap-ingress 7 create
    description "for SAPs facing bank machines"
    queue 1 create
        rate 1
        mbs 1
        cbs 0
    exit
    queue 5 profile-mode create
        rate 300 cir 200
        mbs 3
        cbs 1
    exit
    queue 6 create
        rate 1200 cir 1200
        mbs 1
        cbs 0
        high-prio-only 100
    exit
    queue 11 multipoint create
```

(continued)

```
                    rate 1
                    mbs 1
                    cbs 0
            exit
            fc "ef" create
                    queue 6
            exit
            fc "h2" create
                    queue 5
            exit
            fc "h2.out_profile" create
                    profile out
            exit
            dscp ef fc "ef" priority high
            dscp af41 fc "h2" priority high
            dscp af42 fc "h2.out_profile" priority low
        exit
```

In the SAPs connecting bank machines in the BankNet examples, no traffic other than video telephone and bank transaction traffic is expected. Therefore, as a security measure, in the SAP-ingress policy shown in Listing 14.4, the parameters of the default queues are configured such that only negligible traffic would flow through them.

Step 9: Based on the Service Needs of Application Traffic, Configure SAP-Egress QoS Policies

A SAP-egress policy can be created by analyzing the following factors:

- Forwarding class to queue mappings.
- The service requirement of each application stream.
- The appropriate rate-limiting technique for each application.
- The need for access egress marking.
- Is a Scheduler policy used?

In the BankNet example, the characteristics of video telephone and bank transaction traffic destined to or originating from bank machines are symmetrical. Therefore, the bandwidth requirement of the traffic will be the same in both directions. As suggested in Table 14.3, a shapeless policing rate-limiting approach will be suitable for video telephone traffic and soft policing for transaction traffic. Listing 14.5 shows the template SAP-egress QoS policy. In the policy 802.1p marking is not necessary, but it is shown as an example.

Listing 14.5 SAP-egress QoS policy for SAPs connecting bank machines in the BankNet example

```
sap-egress 7 create
    description "for SAPs facing bank machines "
    queue 1 create
    exit
    queue 5 create
        rate 300 cir 200
        cbs 1
        mbs 3
        high-prio-only 100
    exit
    queue 6 create
        adaptation-rule pir min cir min
        rate 1500 cir 1200
        cbs 1
        mbs 1
        high-prio-only 100
    exit
    fc ef create
        queue 6
        dot1p 5
    exit
    fc h2 create
        queue 5
        dot1p 4
    exit
exit
```

Step 10: Optionally Configure the Reserved Portion Size for Access Ingress and Access Egress Buffer Pools

For Step 10, you will need to conduct an analysis similar to the one that was done in Step 5, and if required, configure the reserved portion size for access ingress and access egress buffer pools.

For the BankNet example, the default implicit configuration of the reserved portion size is sufficient for access ingress and access egress buffer pools.

Step 11: Optionally Enable RED-Based Buffer Management for the Shared Portion of Access Ingress and Access Egress Buffer Pools

The analysis for Step 11 would be similar to the one carried out in Step 6.

In the BankNet example, enabling RED in the access buffer pools would be beneficial for the assured-type and best-effort data traffic belonging to the branch offices. The same Slope policy used for the network buffer pools, shown in Listing 14.3, can be reused here.

Step 12: Additional QoS Design Considerations

Depending on the service requirements of the network under consideration, additional QoS features such as time-based QoS, link fragmentation and interleaving, adapting SLAs over access Link Aggregation Groups (LAGs), hierarchical scheduling, and QoS policy overrides may be required.

As part of the design validation process Service Assurance Agent (SAA) tests can be configured and executed. To help constantly monitor the QoS offered by the network for different application traffic, these SAA tests can be automatically triggered at certain time intervals and alarms can be raised if the test results exceed certain thresholds.

Summary

This chapter laid out the basic principles of a good network design and the related QoS design. You saw best practices for successful QoS design in a commercial network and in a noncommercial network. You also learned about best practices that make a QoS configuration easy to maintain and troubleshoot.

You learned about the service requirements of some of the common application traffic that you will need to address in your QoS design. The chapter presented the bandwidth requirement, latency, loss, and jitter constraints of network control, VoIP, online gaming, and video application traffic. You acquired the knowledge on how to best serve data traffic by categorizing them into mission-critical, transaction, assured, and best-effort data.

Finally, the chapter walked you through the steps involved in a QoS design. You saw how to analyze the traffic and configure a design to address the specific needs of an example network.

Hierarchical Scheduling Design—A Case Study

15

For a given network scheduling scenario, a number of hierarchical scheduling designs are possible. However, the design with the minimum complexity and the one that satisfies all the scheduling requirements should be chosen.

Chapter Objective
- To walk through a case study of HQoS design

In the previous chapter, you learned about the basics of designing QoS in an IP/MPLS network, including QoS design principles, service requirements of common application traffic, and a step-by-step approach for designing QoS in an ALSRP network. In this chapter, we carry forward the QoS design discussion with a case study on hierarchical scheduling design.

For many network scenarios, basic scheduling offered by ALSRP is sufficient. However, as discussed in Chapter 11, ALSRP offers flexibility to service providers to customize scheduling with the help of hierarchical quality of service (HQoS) to satisfy the scheduling needs of a wide variety of network application scenarios. This chapter considers a hierarchical scheduling design for access egress scheduling at the ports of a triple-play network that are connected to subscribers through a Digital Subscriber Line Access Multiplexer (DSLAM). The design options demonstrate how including one or a few virtual schedulers can substantially change the way that the queues are scheduled in a given scenario. This example should be a good starting point as you develop QoS designs to meet your own triple-play scenarios.

The chapter begins by outlining the details of the case study. It then describes the design requirements. The chapter explains the basic configuration details of the design that are common among all the design options considered, and then presents three different design options and explains how each succeeding option improves the design and thus comes closer to realizing the design requirements.

15.1 Case Study Details

A triple-play service provider wants to offer Voice over IP (VoIP), broadcast TV channels (BTV), Video on Demand (VoD), and High Speed Internet (HSI) Data services. The service provider uses the Microsoft Internet Protocol Television (IPTV) middleware solution. Figure 15.1 shows the triple-play architecture used by the service provider.

In this case study, the focus is on the access egress scheduling of Broadband Service Aggregator (BSA) nodes. In other words, the focus is on scheduling the traffic flowing toward a DSLAM (and from the DSLAM to end subscriber) at the port of a BSA. A BSA (Alcatel-Lucent 7450 ESS) performs the user aggregation and subscriber management. Among the different service models proposed for a BSA in the *Triple-Play Guide* of the ALSRP product manuals, the service provider has chosen the *one SAP per subscriber* (also referred to as *one VLAN per subscriber*) model. Figure 15.2 illustrates the one SAP per subscriber service model, customized for the service provider's network.

Figure 15.1 Triple-Play Service Network Architecture

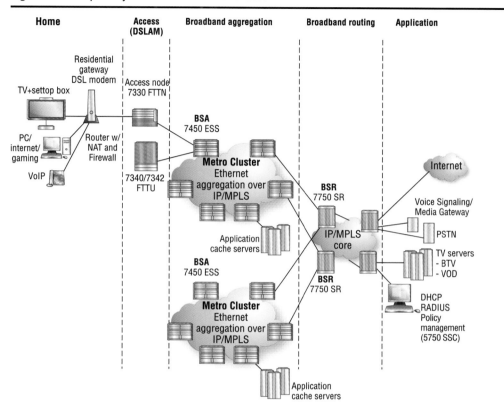

As shown in Figure 15.2, among the types of service traffic, VoIP, VoD, and HSI traffic flows through the BSA as unicast streams, while the BTV traffic flows through the BSA as a multicast stream. Besides the service traffic, DSLAM and residential gateway management traffic also flows through the port.

The BTV multicast traffic has a separate service configuration at the BSA and flows through its own SAP toward a DSLAM. All the traffic from the BTV channels flow as multicast streams up to the DSLAMs. When a subscriber requests a BTV channel, a temporary unicast stream—Microsoft Instant Chanel Change (ICC)—is sent to the requesting set-top box and in the meantime an Internet Group Management Protocol (IGMP) join request is made. On receiving the IGMP request, the multicast traffic stream belonging to the channel is merged at the DSLAM to the rest of the traffic stream flowing toward the residential gateway of the customer. On successful completion of the IGMP request handling, the temporary ICC stream is stopped.

Figure 15.2 One SAP per Subscriber Service Model for BSA

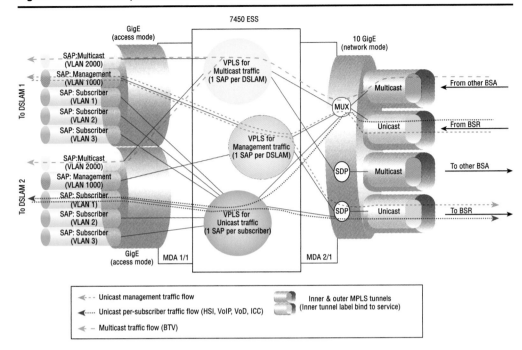

Similar to BTV traffic, the management traffic also has a separate service configuration at the BSA and it flows through its own SAP toward DSLAM.

The unicast subscriber traffic—VoIP, VoD, ICC, HSI and retransmitted lost packets of BTV streams—belonging to each customer shares a separate service configuration at the BSA. All the traffic streams belonging to a subscriber flow through a SAP configured exclusively for that customer.

Each DSLAM used in the network can handle close to 200 subscribers. The Gigabit Ethernet (GigE) port between a BSA and a DSLAM is overbooked by a few hundred percent.

15.2 Design Requirements

The following list summarizes the QoS requirement for servicing the access egress traffic of a BSA:

- The service level agreement in place for each of the offered services has to be guaranteed.

- The priority for different traffic going from highest to lowest priority is:
    - VoIP
    - BTV
    - Management
    - VoD
    - ICC
    - HSI
- ICC should be given enough bandwidth and treated better than HSI.
- All customers subscribing to a given service should be treated fairly equally in terms of bandwidth allocation.
- Low-priority service classes should not be starved even when there is severe congestion. For example, a minimum bandwidth should be allocated to HSI to keep Transmission Control Protocol (TCP) connections alive even under severe congestion.

15.3 Basic Configuration

Table 15.1 summarizes the forwarding classes to which the different types of application traffic are mapped at the BSA. Although both the management and VoD traffic are mapped to the H2 forwarding class, they are held in separate queues at the access egress because they belong to two different virtual private LAN service (VPLS) instances, as shown in Figure 15.2. Similarly, unicast traffic belonging to different subscribers is held in a different set of queues at the access egress because they belong to different SAPs.

Table 15.1 Forwarding Class Mapping for the Example Triple-Play Service Scenario

Application Traffic	Forwarding Class
VoIP	H1
BTV	EF
Management	H2
VoD	H2
ICC	AF
BE	L2

Each forwarding class is mapped to a separate queue. All queues are configured with the default (`auto-expedite`) arbitrator type selector value.

The bandwidth requirement for the different application traffic is as follows:

- Multiple VoIP service connections are reserved for each subscriber, and a bandwidth of approximately 700 Kbps (kilobits/sec) is reserved for each customer.
- For all the BTV channels approximately 300 Mbps (megabits/sec) is reserved. This is the amount of bandwidth required for transmitting all the BTV channels from a BSA to a DSLAM.
- For the DSLAM and residential gateway management traffic, approximately 5 Mbps is reserved. Again, this is the bandwidth required for the management traffic over the link between a BSA and a DSLAM.
- Each subscriber VoD/ICC stream can consume anywhere between 2 and 8 Mbps.
- Depending on the service package, from 3 to 6 Mbps is required for HSI for each subscriber.

By taking into consideration that a DSLAM can support close to 200 subscribers and the capacity of the link between the BSA and the DSLAM is 1 Gbps (gigabits/sec), you can determine that the link is heavily overbooked. Because of the excessive overbooking, scheduling at the access egress of the BSA is the key to guaranteeing the SLA for each of the offered customer services.

15.4 Design Option 1: Basic Scheduling

In this first design option, consider how the default basic scheduling, without any overriding virtual hierarchical schedulers, schedules packets in the given scenario. The underlying mode of the basic scheduling at the egress of the GigE ports of the BSA is the dual arbitrator scheduling mode. The dual arbitrator scheduling mode behavior is explained in Chapter 10.

Figure 15.3 shows how the basic scheduling functions in the given scenario at an access egress port of a BSA. In the figure, queues are isolated based on the SAPs to which they belong. Only one queue per port is mapped to carry BTV traffic toward a DSLAM. Similarly, one queue per port is mapped to carry the management traffic. However, as specified in Table 15.1, unicast traffic belonging to a subscriber is mapped to four different forwarding classes, and each forwarding class is mapped to its own queue. In Figure 15.3, the bottom left panel enclosing the four queues represent a subscriber SAP. The multiple shadows of the panel indicate that multiple instances of per-subscriber SAP exists and each one is assigned with four queues. All the queues configured at the egress of the port are serviced by a pair of arbitrators. As discussed in Chapter 10, dual arbitrators schedule traffic in three different loops.

Figure 15.3 The Functional View of the Default Basic Scheduling for the Example Triple-Play Service Scenario

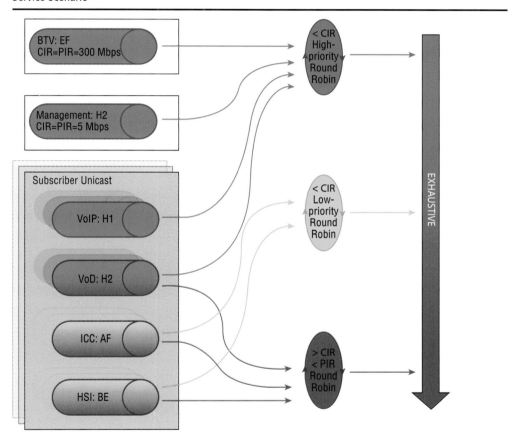

BTV, management traffic, and VoIP are mapped to high-priority forwarding classes and their corresponding queues are configured such that PIR = CIR. VoD traffic is also mapped to a high-priority forwarding class; however, the corresponding queue is configured such that PIR > CIR. The ICC and HSI traffic is mapped to low-priority forwarding classes and their corresponding queues are configured such that PIR > CIR.

As a result of the above configuration, all queues carrying BTV, management, VoIP, and VoD traffic are serviced in round robin fashion in the first scheduling loop. The queues carrying VoD traffic are serviced in the first scheduling loop only up to their CIR.

The queues mapped to ICC and HSI are scheduled up to their CIR in round robin fashion in the second scheduling loop. In the third loop any excess bandwidth is distributed among the queues whose PIR is greater than their CIR and that have excess traffic.

The configuration is very simple; it will work if there is no port congestion, and the CIR of high-priority queues is not overbooked. Individual subscriber services are rate-limited at the queue level.

However, there is no specific order of service priorities, particularly among high-priority services. In other words, the strict services priority between different types of traffic, which is a crucial design requirement, cannot be honored. Also, under congestion the lower-priority services could starve.

In short, this design option does not satisfy all the design requirements.

15.5 Design Option 2: Single-Tier Virtual Hierarchical Scheduling

Under Design Option 1, we noted that there are no specific service priorities among different types of application traffic, and lower-priority services could starve. Therefore, Design Option 2 introduces a strict service priority among unicast application traffic belonging to a subscriber by using a virtual scheduler. In other words, Design Option 2 provides an aggregate rate-limit for all the unicast traffic belonging to a subscriber. In the process, this design option improves the prospects for lower-priority services to get some bandwidth while under congestion.

The Scheduler policy with one virtual scheduler is applied under each SAP, corresponding to a subscriber, within the VPLS service configuration that handles unicast subscriber traffic. As a result of applying the Scheduler policy under each subscriber SAP, an instance of the virtual scheduler is created for each subscriber. Figure 15.4 shows the proposed functional aspect of the single-tier virtual hierarchical design.

Figure 15.4 Functional View of a Single-Tier Virtual Hierarchical Scheduling Design for the Example Triple-Play Service Scenario

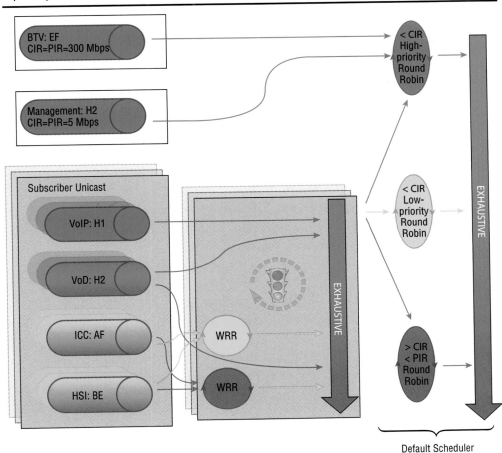

As shown in Figure 15.4, the flow of BTV and management traffic is not affected by the introduction of the virtual scheduler. Only queues belonging to the VoIP, VoD, ICC, and HSI services form child-parent relationships with the virtual scheduler. The virtual scheduler PIR is configured to be equal to the line rate (LR). The CIR of the scheduler is configured according to the following equation:

$$CIR = \frac{LR - [CIR(BTV) + CIR(Mgmt)]}{No.\, of\,\_Subscriber\_per\_DSLAM}$$

According to the configuration, VoIP is serviced exhaustively over the rest of the unicast subscriber services. VoD gets the next priority. Any excess bandwidth (more than CIR and less than PIR) requested by the queue carrying the VoD traffic of a subscriber is provided only after the committed bandwidth for the lower-priority services is provided.

ICC and HSI get the third level of priority. However, within the same level, ICC gets more weight for receiving scheduling bandwidth compared to HSI. Once these queues are serviced up to their CIR, any excess bandwidth is allocated first to the VoD queue and then to the ICC and HSI queues.

As with Design Option 1, individual subscriber services are rate-limited at the queue level.

As mentioned earlier, as an improvement over Design Option 1, this design option provides a certain service priority among the unicast service traffic of a subscriber. As a result, a fair share of bandwidth is guaranteed among customers. The service priorities of BTV, management, and VoIP traffic are equal to one another but greater than VoD, ICC, and HSI. VoD has a higher service priority than ICC and HSI. ICC, has a higher weight to receive more bandwidth than HSI. Design Option 2 also improves the prospects for lower-priority services to get some bandwidth while under congestion.

This design option fulfills almost all the design requirements, with one exception. Although a fair share of bandwidth is guaranteed among subscribers, service priorities are not upheld among customers under severe congestion as specified in the design requirement. For example, under congestion a customer watching a VoD may not get a better service guarantee compared to a customer using the HSI service.

Had the design requirement been billing the subscribers according to their bandwidth usage and prioritizing services within the allocated bandwidth, this option would have been appropriate.

15.6 Design Option 3: Two-Tier Virtual Hierarchical Scheduling

Design Option 2 does not provide the scheduling priority among the different types of traffic according to the design requirements. To fix this issue, Design Option 3 introduces a two-tier virtual hierarchical scheduling structure. Figure 15.5 illustrates the proposed hierarchical scheduling structure.

Figure 15.5 Structural View of a Two- Tier Virtual Hierarchical Scheduling Design for the Example Triple-Play Service Scenario

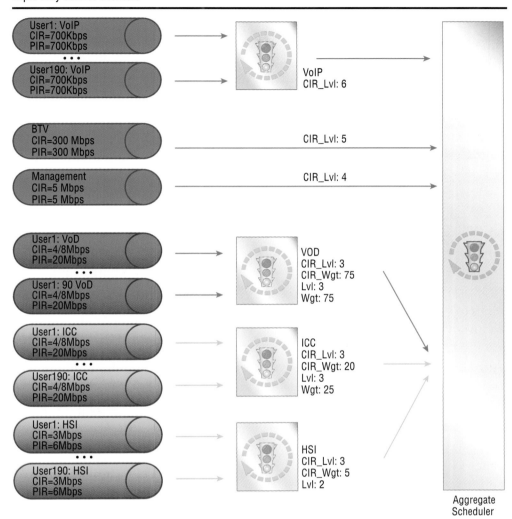

Aggregate
Scheduler

Because queues belonging to multiple SAPs seek a parent-child relationship with the same instance of virtual schedulers, the Scheduler policy has to be applied under a `multi-service-site` to which all those SAPs are assigned.

As shown in Figure 15.5, there are two tiers of virtual schedulers. At tier 1, there is the aggregate scheduler with its PIR configured to be the line rate. At tier 2, there are four virtual schedulers to aggregate each of the following unicast services independently: VoIP, VoD, ICC, and HSI.

Design Option 2 provided an aggregate limit per subscriber traffic, whereas design Option 3 provides aggregate rate-limits for each type of traffic flowing through a port and thereby to all the subscriber traffic belonging to an application. In addition, by using the tier 1 virtual scheduler, Design Option 3 provides the scheduling priority to all the traffic flowing through an access egress port of a BSA as specified by the design service requirement.

Figure 15.6 shows how the design schedules different types of traffic flowing through the GigE port of a BSA. The priority of different services is as follows: VoIP > BTV > Management > VoD > ICC >= HSI. The ICC and HSI are configured to be in the same levels, but their weights are configured such that ICC gets better service treatment compared to HSI. Any bandwidth in excess of the committed bandwidth requested by the VoD queues is allocated only after providing the committed bandwidth for ICC and HSI queues. However, any excess bandwidth requested by the ICC and HSI queues is provided only after allocating the requested excess bandwidth for the VoD queues.

Similar to the previous designs, individual subscriber services are rate-limited at the queue level, but the aggregate rates of each service are also rate-limited by the tier 2 virtual schedulers.

Although this design option is more complex than the previous two design options, the advantages of this design option include:

- The SLAs in place for each of the offered services is guaranteed.
- The suggested priority of different services is maintained.
- ICC is given enough bandwidth and treated better than HSI.
- All customers subscribing to a given service are treated fairly equal in terms of bandwidth allocation.
- Lower-priority service classes will not be allowed to starve even under severe congestion.

Thus, this option satisfies all the design requirements.

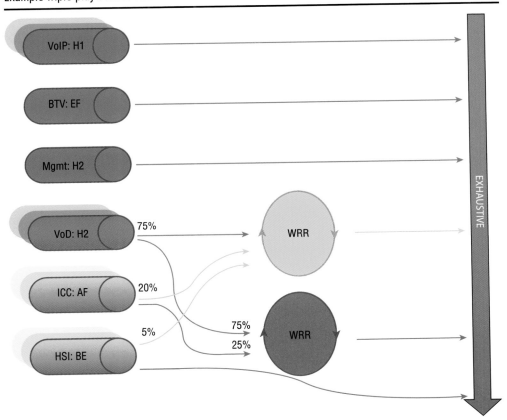

Summary

The chapter presented a case study for designing hierarchical scheduling at the access egress of a triple-play network. Three different design options are presented. In Design Option 1, default basic scheduling without any Scheduler policy is presented. In Design Option 2, a Scheduler policy with only one virtual scheduler is considered; the Scheduler policy is applied under each SAP, corresponding to each subscriber, to provide an aggregate rate limit for all the unicast application traffic belonging to a customer. In Design Option 3, a two-tier hierarchical virtual scheduler design is considered to provide priority in scheduling different types of traffic as specified in the design requirements. In addition, Design Option 3 provides an aggregate rate-limit for each type of traffic flowing through the access egress. In the case of Design Option 3, the Scheduler policy is applied under `multi-service-site` configurations.

The design options considered in this chapter demonstrate how including one or a few virtual schedulers can substantially change the way the queues are scheduled in a given scenario. Although Design Option 3 is slightly more complex than the first two design options, it satisfies all the design requirements listed for the case study.

Glossary

Access egress The data path (more specifically the fast-path complex) in the egress direction of an access port. Also referred to as *service egress*.

Access ingress The data path (more specifically the fast-path complex) in the ingress direction of an access port. Also referred to as *service ingress*.

ALSRP *Alcatel-Lucent Service Router Portfolio* A collective term used to refer to the Alcatel-Lucent 7750 Service Router, the Alcatel-Lucent 7450 Ethernet Service Switch, and the Alcatel-Lucent 7710 Service Router platforms.

Apipe *ATM Pipe* ATM VLL service.

APS *Automatic Protection Switching* APS reserves a protection channel (1:1 or n:1) with the same capacity as the channel to be protected.

ASIC *Application-Specific Integrated Circuit* An integrated circuit custom designed for a particular use.

ATM *Asynchronous Transfer Mode* ATM is the international standard for cell switching. It employs 53-byte cells as a basic unit of transfer. ATM networks can carry traffic for multiple service types (e.g., voice, video, and data).

BA *Behavior Aggregate* DiffServ term for class of service.

BSA *Broadband Service Aggregator* BSA is a high-capacity Ethernet-centric aggregation device that supports hundreds of Gigabit Ethernet ports. In a triple-play type of network, BSA performs wire-speed security, per-subscriber service queuing, scheduling, accounting, and filtering.

BSR *Broadband Service Router* In a triple-play type of network, BSR terminates the Layer 2 access and routes both unicast and multicast traffic over an IP/MPLS core. BSR supports hundreds of ports and provides QoS differentiation between services.

CBS *Committed Buffer Size* One of the parameters associated with queue configuration in ALSRP. This is the guaranteed buffer space available for the traffic flows associated with the queue.

CE *Customer Edge* CEs are the routers in a customer's network that connect to provider edges (PEs).

CIR *Committed Information Rate* A configurable ALSRP queue parameter. This is the guaranteed scheduling rate reserved for the traffic that flows through the queue.

CLI *Command Line Interface* A text-based user interface to configure an ALSRP node (in contrast to a graphical user interface, or GUI).

CoS *Class of Service* A category into which datagrams are classified. The classification helps to provide differentiated service to each class within the network.

CPE *Customer Premises Equipment* Equipment that is installed in customer premises to connect to a specific network service.

Datagram A collective term used to refer packets, frames, and cells.

DiffServ *Differentiated Services* A simple, scalable, and coarse-grained QoS model standardized by IETF. DiffServ maintains per-customer states and performs QoS functions on microflows from customers only at the edges of a DiffServ domain. In the core of a network, DiffServ aggregates microflows with similar service requirements into a limited number of forwarding classes and provides QoS guarantees for the aggregated forwarding classes.

Dot1p *IEEE 802.1p bits* The IEEE 802.1p is an extension of the IEEE 802.1Q (VLANs tagging) standard. IEEE 802.1p establishes eight levels of priority (0 to 7). Highest priority is 7 and the lowest one is 0.

DSCP *Differentiated Service Code Point* In the DiffServ QoS model, the ToS field of each IP packet is marked with a 6-bit value to indicate the behavior aggregate that the packet belongs to. Based on the marking, the network routers apply differentiated grades of service to various packet streams.

DS Domain *DiffServ Domain* A contiguous set of DiffServ nodes that operates with a common service-provisioning policy and set of PHB groups implemented on each node. In practice, an IP network that supports DiffServ.

DSLAM *Digital Subscriber Line Access Multiplexer* A network device that is connected to the network core of a service provider and helps aggregate connections from customer Digital Subscriber Lines (DSLs).

Epipe *Etherent Pipe* Ethernet VLL service.

EXP *EXPerimental bits* Experimental bits are the three ToS bits in an MPLS shim header. EXP bits are similar to the 3 precedence bits in the IP header.

FC *Forwarding Class* In ALSRP, traffic that belongs to different classes of service can be classified in up to eight forwarding classes. The service commitments to different traffic services are achieved by providing a differential treatment for each forwarding class. The eight forwarding classes of ALSRP are: Network Control (NC), High 1 (H1), Expedite Forwarding (EF), High 2 (H2), Low 1 (L1), Assured Forwarding (AF), Low 2 (L2), and Best Effort (BE).

Fpipe *Frame-Relay Pipe* Frame-relay VLL service.

FR *Frame-Relay* A data transmission technique that combines high-speed and low-delay circuit switching with the port sharing and dynamic bandwidth allocation capabilities of X.25 packet switching. Like X.25, Frame-Relay divides transmission bandwidth into numerous virtual circuits and supports bursts of data. But unlike X.25, Frame-Relay does not require a lot of processing at each node, delegating error correction and flow control to the attached user devices.

GRE *Generic Routing Encapsulation* GRE is a tunneling protocol. Using GRE, packets belonging to a wide variety of protocol types can be encapsulated inside IP tunnels. Each IP tunnel creates a point-to-point link over an IP network.

HPO *High Priority Only* A watermark threshold on ALSRP queues. Once the queue occupancy reaches this threshold, only high-queuing priority datagrams are admitted into the queue, and low-queuing priority datagrams are dropped.

HQoS *Hierarchical Quality of Service* Another term for virtual hierarchical scheduling of ALSRP.

HSI *High Speed Internet* An Internet access service. The service is considered to be high speed if the throughput achieved between the CPE and PE is significantly higher than that of narrow-band (128 kbps).

IES *Internet-Enhanced Service* IES provides direct Internet access for the customers. From a customer perspective, it seems as though there is a direct connection to the Internet.

IGMP *Internet Group Management Protocol* IGMP is used to manage the membership of IP multicast groups.

IMA *Inverse Multiplexing for ATM* With IMA, two or more T1 circuits can be bundled together to gain 3 Mbps or more link bandwidth. The bundled group of T1s are referred to as *IMA bundle* or group. IMA bundle carries ATM traffic.

IntServ *Integrated Services* A fine-grained QoS model standardized by IETF. Often contrasted with the DiffServ QoS model. IntServ keep track of state information of individual flows to provide per-flow QoS guarantees.

IOM *Input/Output Module* ALSRP module that interconnects two MDAs with a fabric core. The module also performs Layer 3 traffic management.

IP *Internet Protocol* A network layer protocol underlying the Internet, which provides an unreliable, connectionless, packet delivery service to users. IP allows large, geographically diverse networks of computers to communicate with each other quickly and economically over a variety of physical links.

Ipipe *IP Pipe* IP interworking VLL service

ISP *Internet Service Provider* A business or an organization that provides external transit connectivity to access the Internet for consumers or businesses.

LAG *Link Aggregation Group* According to the IEEE 802.3ad standard, multiple Ethernet ports between two network nodes can be aggregated and used in parallel to form a Link Aggregation Group. LAGs can be configured to increase the bandwidth available between two network devices. All physical links in a given LAG combine to form one logical interface.

LAN *Local Area Network* A system designed to interconnect computing devices over a restricted geographical area (usually a couple of kilometers).

LFI *Link Fragmentation and Interleaving* A QoS feature that provides the ability to interleave high-priority traffic within a stream of fragmented lower-priority traffic over low-speed PPP links.

LSP *Label Switched Path* A sequence of hops in which a packet travels by label switching within an MPLS network.

LSR *Label Switch Router* An MPLS node capable of forwarding datagrams based on a label.

MAC *Media Access Control* A media-specific access control protocol within IEEE802 specifications. The protocol is for medium sharing, packet formatting, addressing, and error detection.

MAN *Metropolitan Area Network* A network usually spanning an area the size of a city, designed to interconnect computing devices.

MBS *Maximum Buffer Size* One of the parameters associated with queue configuration in ALSRP. This is the maximum buffer space available for the traffic flows associated with the queue.

MDA *Media-Dependent Adapter* MDAs are ALSRP modules that are housed in IOMs and in which a physical interface terminates.

MPLS *Multi Protocol Label Switching* MPLS technology supports the delivery of highly scalable, differentiated, end-to-end IP and VPN services. The

technology allows core network routers to operate at higher speeds without examining each packet in detail, and allows differentiated services.

Network egress The data path (more specifically the fast-path complex) in the egress direction of a network port.

Network ingress The data path (more specifically the fast-path complex) in the ingress direction of a network port.

OSI *Open Systems Interconnection* The OSI reference model is a seven-layer model for network architecture. The model was developed by ISO and CCIT (now ITU-T). Each layer consists of an abstract description of protocols related to particular network functions such as addressing, flow control, error control, and reliable data transfer. From top to bottom the seven layers are Application, Presentation, Session, Transport, Network, Data Link, and Physical layers.

PDB *Per-Domain Behavior* Externally observable behavior experienced by packets belonging to a class of service as they transit through a DS domain.

PE *Provider Edge* PEs are the routers in a service provider's network which connect to customer edges (CEs).

PHB *Per-Hop Behavior* Defined in RFC2475 as "the externally observable forwarding behavior applied at a DS-compliant node to a DS behavior aggregate". Some of the externally observable forwarding behaviors are latency, jitter, packet loss, and throughput.

PIR *Peak Information Rate* A configurable ALSRP queue parameter, which defines the maximum rate at which datagrams are allowed to exit a queue.

P-node *Provider Node* A node that is part of the network core and has all its ports connected to other nodes in the network core.

PoP *Point of Presence* A PoP is the location of an access point to the Internet.

PPP *Point-to-Point Protocol* A data link protocol used to establish a direct connection between two network nodes over a telephone line, serial cable, specialized radio links, or fiber optic links.

QinQ *IEEE 802.1Q-in-Q VLAN Tag* A QinQ tag permits expansion of the VLAN space by tagging the tagged packets, thus producing a "double-tagged" frame.

QoS *Quality of Service* The ability of a network to recognize different service requirements of different application traffic flowing through it and to comply with SLAs negotiated for each application service, while attempting to maximize network resource utilization.

RED *Random Early Detection* A buffer management algorithm that randomly discards packets when buffer occupancy rises beyond a certain threshold.

RSVP *Resource ReSerVation Setup Protocol* A signaling protocol used to reserve resources across a network. RSVP was developed to support IntServ, but can be used independently.

RTP *Real-time Transport Protocol* RTP provides end-to-end delivery services for real-time traffic, such as VoIP and video, over multicast or unicast network services.

SAP *Service Access Point* A SAP identifies the customer interface point for a service in an ALSRP.

SDH *Synchronous Digital Hierarchy* Optical fiber communication standard developed by the International Telecommunication Union (ITU), documented in G.707 and its extenstion G.708 standards, used around the globe except in the U.S. and Canada. Also, see SONET.

SDP *Service Distribution Point* An SDP acts as a logical way to direct traffic from one ALSRP node to another through a unidirectional service tunnel.

SLA *Service Level Agreement* A contractual agreement between a service provider and a customer stipulating the minimum standards of service.

SNMP *Simple Network Management Protocol* A standard operation and maintenance protocol defined by IETF. It is used to exchange information between a network management system and network devices regarding conditions that warrant administrative attention.

SONET *Synchronous Optical NETworking* Optical fiber communication standard developed by Telcordia, documented in GR-253-CORE, used in the U.S and Canada. Also, see SDH.

STP *Spanning Tree Protocol* STP is used between bridges to detect and logically remove any redundant paths generated during the bridge database creation process.

TAF *Time-Average Factor* In ALSRP, TAF is a parameter associated with RED buffer management. The TAF is the relative weight given to previous shared buffer average utilization and the new shared buffer utilization in determining the new shared buffer average utilization.

TCP *Transmission Control Protocol* TCP enables two hosts to establish a connection and exchange streams of data. TCP guarantees delivery of data and also guarantees that packets will be delivered in the same order in which they were sent.

ToS *Type of Service* Specifically, an IPv4 header field, used to specify the required service priority for the packet. However, generally used to refer to the header field of all Layer 2 frames or Layer 3 datagrams that specifies the priority of the datagrams.

UDP *User Datagram Protocol* A connectionless transport layer protocol belonging to Internet protocol suite. In contrast to TCP, UDP does not guarantee reliability or ordering of the packets.

VBR *Variable Bit Rate* Variable bit rate traffic is bursty in nature. In ATM networks VBR virtual connections are configured with two different cell rates: Peak Cell Rate (PCR) and Sustained Cell Rate (SCR).

VCCV *Virtual Circuit Connectivity Verification* An OAM procedure for verifying VLL connections

VLAN *Virtual Local Area Network* A logical group of network devices that appear to be on the same LAN, regardless of their physical location.

VLL *Virtual Leased Line* A Layer 2 point-to-point service also referred to as Virtual Private Wire Service (VPWS). A VLL service is a pseudo-wire-service used to carry traffic belonging to different network technologies over an IP/MPLS core.

VoD *Video on Demand* A streaming video service offered by service providers, whereby a user can select video content over the network and play it on a television (or on a monitor) almost instantaneously.

VoIP *Voice over IP* VoIP, also referred to as IP Telephony, is a term used to refer transmitting voice traffic over an IP network.

VPLS *Virtual Private LAN Service* VPLS is a class of VPN that allows the connection of multiple sites in a single *bridged* domain over a provider IP/MPLS network. VPLS is a multi-protocol solution and with it customers retain routing control.

VPN *Virtual Private Network* A way to provide secure and dedicated communications between a group of private servers over a common provider network.

VPRN *Virtual Private Routed Network* VPRN is a class of VPN that allows the connection of multiple sites in a routed domain over a provider managed MPLS network. VPRN is an IP solution, and with it a service provider retains routing control.

VPWS *Virtual Private Wire Service* Another term for VLL.

WAN *Wide Area Network* A network spanning a broad area (crossing metropolitan, regional, or national boundaries), designed to interconnect computing devices.

Index

Note to the Reader: Throughout this index **boldfaced** page numbers indicate primary discussions of a topic. *Italicized* page numbers indicate illustrations.